At Home in the City

Becoming Modern: New Nineteenth-Century Studies

SERIES EDITORS

Sarah Way Sherman, Department of English, University of New Hampshire
Janet Aikins, Department of English, University of New Hampshire
Rohan McWilliam, Anglia Polytechnic University, Cambridge, England
Janet Polasky, Department of History, University of New Hampshire

This book series maps the complexity of historical change and assesses the formation of ideas, movements, and institutions crucial to our own time by publishing books that examine the emergence of modernity in North America and Europe. Set primarily but not exclusively in the nineteenth century, the series shifts attention from modernity's twentieth-century forms to its earlier moments of uncertain and often disputed construction. Seeking books of interest to scholars on both sides of the Atlantic, it thereby encourages the expansion of nineteenth-century studies and the exploration of more global patterns of development.

Stephen Carl Arch, *After Franklin: The Emergence of Autobiography in Post-Revolutionary America, 1780–1830* (2001)

Justin D. Edwards, *Exotic Journeys: Exploring the Erotics of U.S. Travel Literature, 1840–1930* (2001)

Edward S. Cutler, *Recovering the New: Transatlantic Roots of Modernism* (2002)

Margaret M. Mulroney, *Black Powder, White Lace: The du Pont Irish and Cultural Identity in Nineteenth-Century America* (2002)

William M. Morgan, *Philanthropists in Disguise: Gender, Humanitarianism, and Complicity in U.S. Literary Realism* (2004)

Piya Pal-Lapinski, *The Exotic Woman in Nineteenth-Century British Fiction and Culture: A Reconsideration* (2004)

Patrick H. Vincent, *The Romantic Poetess: European Culture, Politics and Gender, 1820–1840* (2004)

Betsy Klimasmith, *At Home in the City: Urban Domesticity in American Literature and Culture, 1850–1930* (2005)

David L. Richards, *Poland Spring: A Tale of the Gilded Age, 1860–1900* (2005)

Angela Sorby, *Schoolroom Poets: Childhood, Performance, and the Place of American Poetry, 1865–1917* (2005)

AT HOME IN THE CITY

Urban Domesticity in American Literature and Culture, 1850–1930

Betsy Klimasmith

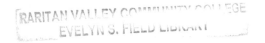
University of New Hampshire Press
Durham, New Hampshire

PUBLISHED BY UNIVERSITY PRESS OF NEW ENGLAND
HANOVER AND LONDON

University of New Hampshire Press
Published by University Press of New England,
One Court Street, Lebanon, NH 03766
www.upne.com
© 2005 by University of New Hampshire Press
Printed in the United States of America

5   4   3   2   1

Library of Congress Cataloging-in-Publication Data

Klimasmith, Elizabeth, 1969–
  At home in the city : urban domesticity in American literature and culture, 1850–1930 / Betsy Klimasmith.
    p.   cm. — (Becoming modern)
  Includes bibliographical references and index.
  ISBN–13: 978–1–58465–496–4 (alk. paper)
  ISBN–10: 1–58465–496–1 (alk. paper)
  ISBN–13: 978–1–58465–497–1 (pbk. : alk. paper)
  ISBN–10: 1–58465–497–x (pbk. : alk. paper)
    1. American fiction—19th century—History and criticism. 2. Domestic fiction, American—History and criticism. 3. American fiction—20th century—History and criticism. 4. Architecture, Domestic—United States. 5. Architecture, Domestic, in literature. 6. City and town life—United States. 7. City and town life in literature. 8. Dwellings in literature. 9. Family in literature. 10. Home in literature.
  I. Title. II. Series.
PS374.D57K57   2005
813'.409357—dc22   2005019248

The author gratefully acknowledges permission to reproduce sections of "The 'Hotel Spirit': Modernity and the Urban Home in Wharton's *The Custom of the Country* and Gilman's Short Fiction," *Edith Wharton Review* (Fall 2002): 25–35. With permission of The Edith Wharton Review.

For Sophie

With love

Contents

Illustrations

Acknowledgments

At Home in the City is dedicated to my daughter Sophie, who was born as I began my dissertation and is now old enough to read the book it has become. I have many people to thank for their help in bringing this project to fruition.

Profound thanks go to two powerfully intelligent, creative teachers whose intellectual generosity and collegial spirit have fostered my scholarship. When I began my M.A. program at the University of New Hampshire, I was certain that I would never continue on for a Ph.D. Melody Graulich taught me otherwise. Melody set high standards, read my writing with a careful eye, and encouraged me to see myself as a scholar. She also encouraged me to leave New Hampshire for the University of Washington. There, I had the incredible good fortune to meet Priscilla Wald, whose curiosity, questions, challenges, and support propelled me to think and write in new ways. Her direction on my dissertation was invaluable; her continuing presence in my career and life incomparable. I hope that my work with my own students will begin in a small way to pass on the intellectual gifts that Melody and Priscilla have given to me.

Perhaps the best gift from Melody and Priscilla has been the introduction to academic communities that are humane, challenging, creative, and fulfilling. In New Hampshire, Lisa MacFarlane, Nancy LeCourt, Meg Kerr, and Nancy Von Rosk; at Washington, Susan Glenn, Richard White, Gail Stygall, Gretchen Murphy, Rich Heyman, and Janis Caldwell all have lent their companionship and support at different stages of the project.

I make my current academic home at the University of Massachusetts, Boston, an urban campus full of vibrant faculty and students. Above all, Lois Rudnick and Bob Crossley have offered me unfailing support in navigating the demands of teaching and scholarship. I am also very grateful to Louise Penner, Cheryl Nixon, Rajini Srikanth, Michael LeBlanc, Bettie Oliver, and Adam Beresford, as well as Kathy Crowley, Victoria Harris, Chris Doyle, and Cindy Kaplan—colleagues, students, and friends, for all of their interest. They have commiserated with me, cheered for me, and finally are celebrating the finished project.

I am grateful to the National Endowment for the Humanities for funding a year-long grant to support this project. Eileen K. Morales, the Manager of

Collections Access at the Museum of the City of New York, and Harvard University librarian Helene Williams have helped immensely with needed resources. For their comments on the manuscript I thank Renée Bergland, Sarah Luria, Anne Raine, Lawrence Buell, and Elissa New and her graduate seminar at Harvard. I am thankful to my UPNE readers, Adam Sweeting, and an anonymous reader, for their generous comments and useful suggestions. I thank Sarah Way Sherman for her input on chapter 6, as well as for teaching the seminar on sentimentalism at the University of New Hampshire that taught me to take domestic literature seriously.

Finally, and most importantly, I thank my family. My father, Jerry Klima, and my stepmother, Bobbi Sroka Klima, hosted my family and me for six months when we moved to Boston and have continued their unflagging support. I thank my sisters for their contributions as this book took shape: Abigail Klima developed the concept and several prototype designs for the book's cover, and Kate Wilson gave her enthusiastic support at every step. My mother, Melinda Ponder, understands better than anyone the challenges of combining scholarship and parenting. I am immensely grateful for all of the ways, large and small, in which she has helped me throughout this endeavor.

But my deepest gratitude goes to my husband, Bayard. Without his humor, energy, dedication, and love, this project would not have been possible.

At Home in the City

Introduction

*It is an immense joy to set up house in the heart of the multitude, amid the
ebb and flow of movement, in the midst of the fugitive and infinite.*
—Charles Baudelaire[1]

*. . . he is beguiled by remembering how many of the things said in America
are said for the house.* —Henry James[2]

In 1904, expatriate novelist Henry James returned from Europe to his childhood home in New York City. It was a profoundly dislocating experience.
Where houses and churches had stood, tall anonymous buildings had risen,
transforming the appearance and scale of the city James once had known intimately. But "nowhere," James writes in *The American Scene,* is his shock
at the changes in the landscape "quite so sharp as in presence, so to speak,
of the rudely, the ruthlessly-suppressed birth-house on the other side of the
Square." His birthplace has "vanished" leaving "a high, square, impersonal
structure" in its place. In the process, and without being aware of it, James
has been "amputated of half [his] history."[3] Place shapes Henry James's sense
of self; the salient place of his self-construction is, significantly, his urban
home. His house "destroyed to make room for a skyscraper," James's own
history seems to have disappeared.[4] In twentieth-century New York, the impersonal has replaced the personal, and with the passing of the home has
come the loss of a past written in space.

   At Home in the City traces the architectural and literary evolution of the
urban home as the United States increasingly became industrialized in the late
nineteenth and early twentieth centuries. With the development of the industrial city, notions of private and public space shifted as the commonly held
belief that individual homes would nurture a moral American citizenry confronted an increasingly complex and unstable landscape.[5] Tensions between
home and city were central to works by, among many others, Nathaniel Hawthorne, Theodore Dreiser, Edith Wharton, and Nella Larsen, authors whose
novels explore relationships between modern settings and modern subjects.

Characters in these urban texts interact with and are integrated into cities through the domestic spaces they inhabit. In various and significant ways, such novels reflected and participated in a national struggle to understand the individuals—and the society—that would emerge from urban landscapes and homes increasingly characterized by mutability and connection. Through a variety of novels and architectural structures, *At Home in the City* analyzes the changing forms and functions of the American urban home as it was represented from the mid-nineteenth through the early twentieth century in order both to explore the process of modernity as it unfolded and to uncover the modern subjects—mobile and mutable—who emerged in the industrial city.

As Americans built, inhabited, and altered their cities, a simultaneous embrace and rejection of architectural determinism—the "belief that spatial environments determine the social arrangements, daily behaviors, and political status of those who inhabit them"—structured and complicated their experiences in the physical and cultural urban landscape.[6] The nation itself had been constructed in part on foundations of architectural, or at least environmental determinism; the idea that built space could shape its inhabitants has marked the American landscape and shaped our notions of citizenship from the seventeenth century on. In its earliest incarnations, "America," whether configured as Eden or wilderness, simultaneously seemed to be empty, eminently shapeable, and capable of molding a distinctly American identity. At the same time, the salient feature of citizenship in the republic was land ownership, a condition that was not restricted by birth, rank, or familial connections, but which carried with it the spoken or tacit assumption that the owner would "improve" the property, and in so doing, integrate it—and himself—into the republic. Theoretically, through primeval confrontation or through legal possession, or both, the land could Americanize its inhabitants, for even as they confronted untamed wilderness, settlers had both the right and the responsibility to participate in creating a new nation by building "cities on a hill" in the new world. Houses, commons, public buildings, parks, model tenements, and utopian plans for cities all drew on the idea that particular building designs could produce particular types of people.[7]

The bluntest architectural determinist would argue that landscapes can be regenerative or degenerative, that they can either help or harm their inhabitants, and therefore the culture, of which they are a part. In the early nineteenth century, architectural determinists and reformers such as Andrew Jackson Downing and Catharine Beecher believed that the American home could nurture a national moral regeneration. They precisely instructed homebuilders and homemakers on how to develop the physical surroundings that would produce a medically and morally healthy American citizenry. According to Beecher, nothing "more seriously involved the health and daily comfort of American women," and of course the men who lived there, too, "than the proper construction of homes."[8] Reformers and other middle-class Americans conceived of the home as an inviolable yet surprisingly mobile space where the family could develop under the mother's watchful eye and then go forth as emissaries to transform the world beyond. As domestic space became "an identity, rather than simply . . . a fixed location for women's lives," Lora Romero argues, "domesticity could—and did—travel."[9] "Home" operates best as an ideological space when defined in opposition to its surroundings, and in the early years of the republic that other world frequently was figured as wilderness: space either dangerously savage or empty, implicitly waiting to be transformed by productive landowners à la Jefferson and Crèvecoeur. But by the mid-nineteenth century, the burgeoning American city presented a different and more complex specter of wilderness. Urban space became a new anti-home—a repository for fears of chaos, mingling, and all of the dark and lurid enterprises that could not bear scrutiny in the order and intimacy of idealized domesticity.[10]

The anxieties about anonymity, disorder, and vice in the urban landscape that become pronounced in the nineteenth-century literature and culture with which I open this study were neither new nor uniquely American. But urban historians and theorists tend to agree that the nineteenth century saw a significant shift: In this era the city became "modern." Janet Wolff argues that "the critics (and defenders) of modernity believed that urban existence took on an entirely different character around the middle of the nineteenth century."[11] Wolff's focus is the modern European city of Baudelaire's flâneur. Yet the revolutionary changes in European cities had parallels in the United States, and these shifts provoked a range of strong reactions in observers. Walt Whitman, for instance, was an urban enthusiast who celebrated New York's human and architectural energy in poems such as "Crossing Brooklyn Ferry" and "Leaves of Grass." In *Invented Cities,* her study of Boston and New York, geographer Mona Domosh notes, "Whitman identified characteristics of New York's landscape that were to become symbols of the modern city—the sheer mass of urban growth, vertical as well as horizontal, and the new building materials that made such growth possible. Already by mid-century, New York's Wall Street, Broadway and Fifth Avenue were beginning to take on the characteristics that would make them symbols of the modern capitalist city. By mid-century, Boston, too, was being shaped into a physical form that would identify the city as modern."[12] In the urban spaces of the United States, modernity was increasingly transatlantic.

Nationally, both home and city changed significantly in the 1850s as new physical, technological, economic, and cultural networks increasingly bound American cities to their hinterlands and redefined the spaces and meanings of "home" in developing urban centers. And home always has had multiple meanings. The tension surrounding urban homes may derive not just from anxieties about urban space, but from the tensions inherent in the word home itself. A brief look at home's changing definitions shows how loaded the term is, and how slippery it can be. The oldest definition of home in the *Oxford English Dictionary,* from old English and cited as obsolete, is "a village or town, a collection of dwellings." This notion of home as a collective, a place of interdependence and connection, operates in opposition to the definition derived from the German. Here, home is "a dwelling-place, house, abode; the fixed residence of a family or household; the seat of domestic life and interests; one's own house; the dwelling in which one habitually lives, or which one regards as one's proper abode. Sometimes including the members of a family collectively; the home-circle or household." This definition associates the home with private (or at most familial) ownership; home is bounded property, "one's *own* house." The conflict between home as a collective and home as private property is complicated further by a third definition. Also from Old English comes what we might call the affective meaning of home: "The place of one's dwelling or nurturing, with the conditions, circumstances, and feelings which naturally and properly attach to it, and are associated with it."[13] Together, these three definitions make home the nexus of the concrete and the fleeting; of place and "conditions, circumstances and feelings"; of circumscribed and indefinite spaces.

This accretion of meaning in a space, the city, that at times seemed to militate against all of the meanings of home, is precisely what is at stake in the novels I discuss. For many observers, the urban home is an oxymoron; cities are not frequently understood as particularly "fixed" or especially nurturing places. But architecturally and in literary representations, urban homes bring the oldest definition of home as collective back into play, destabilizing the reassuring boundedness of home as "one's proper abode." Thus, I will argue, urban homes have the potential to integrate these three definitions of home, bringing the notion of home as a place of connection back into the word's meaning.

For the majority of those who were living in or moving to U.S. cities in the nineteenth century, as well as for their fictional counterparts, urban housing did not resemble the detached, unique, single-family cottage that reform-minded domestic architects idealized as "home." Most middle-class urban Americans did not own their own homes, but rented rooms in row houses, boarding houses, tenements, and hotels, buildings where public and private, interior and exterior, and familial and shared spaces mingled. Neither unique nor self-contained, these spaces threatened to foster an urban subjectivity that compromised the distinct family unit theoretically produced by contained homes that were occupied by their owners. Observers versed in notions of architectural determinism worried that the uncontrolled spaces of an urban landscape characterized by indeterminate ownership would reproduce themselves in their inhabitants. Chaotic streetscapes would produce an uncontrollable populace; a lack of the recognizable order enforced by the home would produce a disorderly citizenry; crowding and dirt would produce mentally and physically stunted people who were morally unclean.

An architectural determinism that assumed the presence of bounded, coherent spaces was destabilized by the ever-changing urban landscape. As opposed to the stability and order associated with the sentimentalized rural home, urban spaces were characterized by motion, randomness, change, connection, and repetition. Detached homes might present a variety of designs; in contrast, row houses sharing roofs, walls, and fences had a uniform, even monotonous appearance. In urban boarding houses, apartment buildings, and hotels, the halls, stairways (or later, elevators), lobbies, entryways, and dining rooms facilitated extra-familial connections within the walls of the place called home. Sound, heat, and smells traveled between residences. Urban dwellings thus exemplified permeable architecture; once inside a building, inhabitants could pass from place to place, entering and sharing interior spaces that would have been shared only by family members in the cottage home.[14]

The buildings' porosity echoed and was reinforced by their urban surroundings, where streets, stores, restaurants, parks, and taverns increased and extended the possibilities for contact among strangers and for the mixing of classes and genders. In the modern urban landscape, theatricality, voyeurism, and proximity simultaneously fragmented the broad notion of public space into individual stages, performances, and stories, and transformed private spaces into shared spaces. And critically, urban spaces that confounded physical, linguistic, and imaginary boundaries—including city homes—necessitated new understandings of the relationships between space and subjectivity. The formative power ascribed to environment, and specifically to architecture, would only become more complex with the rise of cities whose landscapes concretized a continual process of drastic and radical transformation. Relationships between city dwellers and their changing surroundings became correspondingly multifaceted.

As Americans attempted to understand what such changes in the urban landscape would mean to their conceptions of individuality and community, the novel emerged as the textual form that could creatively and critically explore the complexities that arose as city, home, and self converged. During the nineteenth century, the novel became a testing ground for examining relationships between urban spaces and the development of an unsettled and unsettling modern subjectivity. By the early twentieth century, the social sciences, particularly geography and sociology, would contend for primacy in analyzing urban landscapes. Nineteenth-century novelists had several things that these social scientists did not: a long tradition, an established language,

and a range of prior narratives to draw on as they attempted to articulate
what inhabiting city landscapes would mean to individuals and communities, as well as how urban settings would shape notions of individualism and
community.

Highlighting the operations of urban domestic spaces considerably blurs,
expands, and enriches traditional conceptions of the urban (and domestic)
novel. As Sharon Marcus notes of British and French texts: "Novels that
have been described as urban because they represent panoramas, streets, and
crowds . . . can also be understood as urban because . . . they situate the
city's flow and multiplicity *inside* the home."[15] Through narrative, authors
could explore new spatial relations more quickly and on a wider scale than
was possible even in the rapidly transforming landscape.

Marcus's expansive definition of urban literature may be applied usefully
to a range of nineteenth- and early twentieth-century American novels. Writers from Horatio Alger, George Lippard, and Herman Melville to Theodore
Dreiser, Edith Wharton, and F. Scott Fitzgerald textually constructed urban
architectures that allowed for the development—and tested the limits—of a
mobile, permeable, and mutable modern subject. While authors imaginatively experimented with the possibilities and dangers of the fictive city,
transformative experiments on the city's physical landscape were carried out
by reformers, planners, and engineers. In order to explore relationships between the fictive and the physical, I examine literary treatments of urban domesticity alongside architectural, urban planning, and domestic advice texts
of the period. My readings show that the distinctively urban domestic spaces
of the modern landscape, such as apartments, tenements, and hotels, disrupted and forced revisions of the notions of public and private space foundational to early nation-building in the United States.

Significantly, as the industrial landscape increasingly dominated the cultural horizon, it emerged in nineteenth- and early twentieth-century American literature as a place of connection, not containment. Yet if these literary
representations of urban space anticipate Michel Foucault's assessment that
"our experience of the world is less that of a long life developing through
time than that of a network that connects points and intersects with its own
skein," critical readings of urban novels have generally emphasized quite the
opposite.[16] We tend to represent the cultural landscape of the nineteenth and
early twentieth century as structured not by networks but by spheres. This
is unsurprising given the tenacity with which, as Foucault saw it, we cling to
spatial "oppositions that we regard as simple givens: For example between
private space and public space, between family space and social space, between cultural space and useful space, between the space of leisure and the
space of work. All these are still nurtured by the hidden presence of the sacred."[17] Foucault argues that we reinforce these divisions through lived experience today, even in the face of their obvious breakdown; we have only

begun to question the ways in which such spatial oppositions have structured our conceptions of the past.

Literary and historical analyses of gender in the nineteenth-century United States have upheld these divisions by relying, at least in part, on separate spheres as an organizing metaphor.[18] "According to this metaphor, nineteenth-century America was neatly divided up according to an occupational, social, and affective geography of gender."[19] Stemming from such varied sources as de Tocqueville and Engels, the logic of separate spheres asserts that in contrast to the public (male) sphere, women's sphere was private, the realm of the domestic and the sentimental. Considered spatially, women's sphere was the home. Many treatments of urban space, even those focused on gender, reinforce this binary opposition. Wolff, for instance, argues that "the literature of modernity ignores the private sphere and to that extent is silent on the subject of women's primary domain. This silence is not only detrimental to any understanding of the lives of the female sex; it obscures a crucial part of the lives of men, too, by abstracting one part of their experience and failing to explore the interrelation of public and private spheres. For men inhabited both of these."[20] Attending to the operations of domesticity in urban landscapes helps to illuminate the interrelation of public and private spaces—and spheres. Urban homes, it turns out, are surprisingly and very satisfyingly unsilent.

Close examinations of the spatial operations of the urban home, even in the mid-nineteenth century, reveal that the "spheres" were far from separate. Sharon Marcus, one of the few scholars to analyze the cultural operations of the urban home (in London and Paris) describes "houses that were not enclosed cells, sealed off from urban streets, markets, and labor, but fluid spaces perceived to be happily or dangerously communicating with more overtly public terrain."[21] Yet in the United States, the notion of home usually was deployed to construct the city as anti-domestic space, even as increasing numbers of Americans made the city their home. Similarly, domestic literature has been considered anti-modern and anti-urban, when in fact domestic novels often speak quite radically about the possibilities for social change in urban space. When the categories of domestic and urban are brought into spatial and literary dialogue, the logic of separate spheres comes to resemble an ideology constructed to separate public from private precisely at the moment in which the city's new organization of space was bringing private and public spaces together, changing the social landscape along with the physical. As historian Linda K. Kerber suggests, the persistent "noise we hear about separate spheres" in nineteenth-century life and texts may signal "its breakdown . . . the shattering of an old order and the realignment of its fragments."[22] Exploring the spatial and literary dimensions of urban domesticity shows why and how the notion of home was deployed rhetorically, linguistically, and physically to help order the potential chaos—and to subvert the developing order—of the growing industrial city.

With few exceptions, urban domesticity has not been explored widely by academics and has been neglected by literary scholars. While social historians like Elizabeth Blackmar and Gwendolyn Wright, along with urban geographers such as Paul Groth and Dolores Hayden, provide powerful and evocative analyses of urban homes, critical attention to the juncture between urban space and domestic space in American literature is surprisingly sparse, especially considering what such an analysis yields. Marcus, for instance, derives from her study of the spatial operations of European apartment houses "an urban geography of gender that challenges current preconceptions about where women and men were to be found in the nineteenth-century city, allowing us to see, for example, that the home was often a masculine domain, and that heterosexual imperatives demanded the presence of women in streets as well as homes."[23] Similarly, in the United States the urban homes of the industrial era—both physical and fictional—put on display the changing gender, class, and spatial relations that characterize this moment in literary and cultural history.

In order to understand how, in theorist Henri Lefebvre's terms, "social relations are achieved from the sensible," I draw my approach to urban novels in part from historians of housing such as Wright and Hayden.[24] I stress the "interplay between the metaphorical and the literal" in order to examine the ways in which notions of home and city, of containment and dissolution, helped to structure both the industrial city and a modern subjectivity.[25] Far from operating as conservative spaces of containment, stasis, and safety, "havens in a heartless world," the urban homes of nineteenth- and early twentieth-century fiction were important connective and connecting spaces.[26] Indeed, as urban homes became increasingly integrated into networks of transportation, communication, and consumption, these nominally separate social and geographic spaces were mutually constituted and inseparably linked through the physical and imaginative networks that made up the modern American city. Mobility, agency, and mutability were central to urban homes in ways that the literary historical narrative of separate spheres has obscured. Urban dwellings and their inhabitants changed social relations and helped to shape inherently porous, transformable, and public subjectivities.

The approach to urban space taken by David Harvey and other urban geographers, particularly Doreen Massey, provides a useful theoretical framework for reading the novels. Harvey's understanding of urbanization as a *process* gives weight to the concrete, the daily, and the lived as the foundations for the construction of theory. Exploring these forces in contemporary urban landscapes, Doreen Massey aims to "counter those views of [domestic] space which understood it as static, as the dimension precisely where

nothing 'happened,' and as a dimension devoid of effect or implications."[27] But if, as Massey does, we see space itself as "inherently dynamic," an "ever-shifting social geometry of power and signification," we can recognize "the existence in the lived world of a simultaneous multiplicity of spaces: cross-cutting, intersecting, aligning with one another, or existing in relations of paradox or antagonism."[28]

The urban novels at the heart of *At Home in the City* fictively anticipate and animate Massey's notion of dynamic space. Settings shift, conflict, alternate, kaleidoscope, collage, accrete, become palimpsests. Characters are identified with settings, represent and echo settings, but also disrupt, disturb, and become disoriented by the settings they inhabit. As we read these interactions, narrative allows us to be within and outside of the text. Readers render novels' spaces associative, simultaneous, blended, bounded—and the experience of reading reveals an unboundedness of setting, narrative, and self that is particularly useful for readers of cities. As Harvey notes, "The closure that we often seem compelled to search for in a piece of cultural or political economic research can more easily remain perpetually open for reflection in novel form."[29] Urban novels resemble the cities of which they are a part; as cities are built and rebuilt, and changed landscapes are encountered anew, so do novels give readers multiple points of entry and, as we read and re-read a text, innumerable opportunities for interpretation.

And in these novels, urban homes act as microcosms of the changing city, revealing and magnifying the networks of spatial, technological, and personal connection that helped to construct American urban landscapes in the industrial era. My approach to the subject of urban domesticity in *At Home in the City* reflects the architectural qualities of the domestic spaces that are my focus in that it echoes and emphasizes the degree of connection that characterized urban living spaces. Although my work draws upon the extensive literature on domesticity, as well as on literary, historical, and geographical approaches to urban America, I attempt to do more here than bring historical contexts to bear on fictional urban homes. Rather, I analyze literary and non-textual representations of urban domestic spaces in order to make visible the conceptions of subject formation in relation to environment that are at work in the period and that are less accessible through other approaches. As did many of my authors, I see in these connections the potential for unlocking new and powerful ways of understanding relationships between self and setting.

Unlike older European cities, American cities of the industrial era were characterized by an impressive rate and scale of architectural change that became visible in varied streetscapes and remarkably un-standardized housing forms; the structure of my study reflects the landscape it examines. In the chapters that follow, I explore how five totemic forms of urban housing—the boarding house, the row house, the tenement, the apartment building, and the luxury hotel—impacted the ways in which Americans understood urban space, whether they lived in such homes or merely absorbed the cultural commentary about them. Like the cities they were part of, urban homes were characterized both by variety and repetition. Boarding houses, row houses, tenements, apartment buildings, and hotels all operated within the industrial city, but dominated conceptions and offered choices for city dwellers at different yet overlapping moments in time. Accordingly, while each chapter focuses primarily on one housing type, I also emphasize the connections among them that tend to blur distinctions. This blurring of categories reflects the connectivity and permeability that structured urban homes and helped to distinguish them from their contained counterparts. I track the relationships among changing urban structures and different literary and cultural manifestations of "home" in a roughly chronological order to show the uneven, halting, yet marked evolution of the urban landscape—and urban subjects—through the industrial era.

Finally, significant structural parallels between subject and argument mark this study. For example, just as apartment dwellers might hear their neighbors through the walls, each of the following chapters is marked by reverberations from the others. While this approach unsettles a more linear argumentative structure, it also allows for exciting insights to develop. For instance, architect Calvert Vaux, generally overlooked as a major figure in nineteenth-century culture, appears in several of my chapters: in chapter 1 as the architect for a showplace villa home in the Hudson River Valley, in chapter 2 as one of Central Park's two landscape architects, in chapter 3 as an important theorist and architect of "improved" tenements, and in chapter 4 as an early designer and inhabitant of New York's first middle-class "French Flats," the architectural form that brought to the American city apartment living as we still know it. Far from being an ineffectual dabbler, Vaux had an impact on almost every form of urban housing through New York's rapid changes. He thus embodies the possibilities for creative adaptation and flexibility inherent in the urban landscape and in urban texts, and deserves to be assessed in this light.

Vaux's career demonstrates a degree of versatility and adaptability shared by many of the urbanites in the novels I study. I embrace the sense of creative possibility exemplified by a career like Vaux's by highlighting the sometimes surprising moments of insight that arise when unexpected meetings and interactions occur. As these interactions help to create the network of encounters that structures an individual's urban experience, intertextual connections open new possibilities not simply for reading urban novels, but for reading urban culture itself. The networks of connection that structure urban space work to transform the ways in which we understand ourselves in relation to the people and structures that comprise our settings.

At Home in the City moves geographically and chronologically, historicizing textual and visual representations of changing manifestations of "home" within the developing urban infrastructure. In each chapter, I place literary texts in the context of a particular cultural moment, exploring resonances and dissonances among cultural constructions of the city and literary visions of modern subjectivity. Chapter 1, "Architectural Determinism and the Industrial City in *The Blithedale Romance* and *Ruth Hall*," argues that the prototypical modern urban subject first becomes visible in texts that dislocate sentimental and pastoral plots and reset them in urban landscapes. Such novels chronicle the development of a new kind of individual—adaptable, mobile, and transformable—within the permeable spaces of the networked city. This modern subject troubles Hawthorne's text but invigorates Fern's. What theorist Michel de Certeau defines as the "migrational, metaphorical city" emerges in these novels, engendering powerfully new conceptions of the modern individual.

In chapter 2, "The City's Drawing Room: Spatial Practice in *The Bostonians* and Central Park," I read Henry James's novel in tandem with the development of New York's Central Park. Landscape architects Frederick Law Olmsted and Calvert Vaux turned sentimental notions about the private home inside out by putting domestic relations on public display in Central Park, an act James anxiously echoes in his analysis of public womanhood in *The Bostonians*. Whether attractive or alarming, the urban subjects produced in the novel and the park embody an early version of Doreen Massey's notion of space as "inherently dynamic."

My third chapter, "The Tenement Home: Pushing the City's Limits," focuses on the extreme version of architectural determinism associated with New York City's tenements, which both attracted and threatened Progressive Era projects of urban improvement. Jacob Riis's *How the Other Half Lives* recorded and dramatized tenement life for a mass audience. An unruly and highly networked city surfaces through Riis's deterministic efforts to define and contain it. In response, Riis pathologizes the tenement by invoking notions of the contained home's moral and affective influence, an effort that such novels as Stephen Crane's *Maggie, A Girl of the Streets* and Abraham Cahan's *Yekl* recognize and revise.

In chapter 4, "The Apartment as Utopia: Reimagining the City, Reconstructing the Home," I look at apartment buildings as representations of the utopian spaces that Michel Foucault terms heterotopias: "effectively enacted utopia[s] in which the real sites, all the other real sites that can be found within the culture"—the home, the street, the railroad car and the stage in Theodore Dreiser's *Sister Carrie*, for instance—"are simultaneously represented contested, and inverted."[30] I read *Sister Carrie* in the context of the promise in cooperative apartment living that Charlotte Perkins Gilman and popular periodicals celebrated for the era's new urban citizen: the bachelor girl. Gilman's portrayals of women remaking social relations by restructuring their domestic spaces are powerful, yet they seem surprisingly conservative when compared to the radical vision of apartment-derived social justice embedded in *Sister Carrie*.

The fifth chapter, "From Artifact to Investment: Hotel Homes, the Economics of Luxury, and *The Custom of the Country*" puts the early twentieth-century American fascination with luxury hotels in the context of the anxiety about the loss of a spatial past that these structures evoked, an anxiety Henry James articulates in *The American Scene* and Edith Wharton enlarges in *The Custom of the Country*. The bourgeois fear that "home" was becoming a temporary investment transformed a fascination with a new form of domestic space into a debate about the fate of history itself in modern culture. This chapter—and the next—take issue with Edward Soja's contention that questions of space were subsumed to questions of time in the early twentieth century.

My final chapter, "The Paradox of Intimacy: Mobility, Sociology, and the Function of Home in *Quicksand*," examines the preoccupations with marginality, home, and homelessness in Nella Larsen's *Quicksand*. I read the novel's concerns through the frame of the developing discipline of sociology, particularly Robert Park's 1928 essay "Human Migration and the Marginal Man." While Park's "disinterested" social science celebrates an idealized urban rootlessness, Larsen asks how urban women, ambivalent about racial identity and the traditional family home, might practically tap into the creative and personal freedom that Park ascribes to the condition of marginality. As the automobile and rapid transatlantic crossings were opening American cities to new conceptions of mobility, *Quicksand* and other Harlem Renaissance novels revised spatial constructions of the urban home, animating old and new concerns about mobility, modernity, and the destabilized self.

My overlapping chronology follows the development of modern subjects, the "curious persons," as Henry James terms them, who inhabit the urban landscape. Considering the importance James attributes to his own home in the formation of his sense of self, it is not surprising that he pays particular attention in *The American Scene* to the new types of housing that have come to characterize American cities during the decades he has spent in Europe. In what are now called apartments, public and private spaces merge in ways that disconcert James. Like Harvey and Lefebvre, James is particularly attuned to the ways in which this architecture will shape its inhabitants. As he muses on the distinctly American style of domestic architecture that dominates New York in the early twentieth century, James begins to theorize how its networked spaces operate in relation to modernity:

the universal custom of the house with almost no one of its indoor parts distinguishable from any other is an affliction against which he has to learn betimes to brace himself. This diffused vagueness of separation between apartments, between hall and room, between one room and another, between the one you are in and the one you are not in, between place of passage and place of privacy, is a provocation to despair which the public institution shares impartially with the luxurious "home."[31]

The degree of connection and diffusion among the apartment's indistinguishable spaces forces James to refrain from calling even the most luxurious spaces homes without qualifying quotation marks. The home has become public, institutional. Accustomed to privacy and differentiation among spaces, James is afflicted by the vagueness and lack of definition he encounters. But what should be separated in order for a structure to claim the powerful title of "home"? Different dwellings should be separate; unrelated individuals should have their own spaces within which to define themselves as unique. Different functions should be clearly linked to specific rooms. In sum, the architecture should speak about itself and help the inhabitant understand how to experience it. Such specificity would help to ground James, who otherwise becomes so dissociated from the spaces he occupies that he cannot tell where—or who—he is. Fundamentally, James's architectural unease stems from his inability to distinguish places of passage from places of privacy. Following his earlier assertion that his home has shaped at least half of who he is, the replacement of private space by spaces for passage is equivalent to a threatening substitution of containment by mobility, of enclosure by connection. Architectural vagueness threatens the integrity of the self.

Not limited to New York, this degree of connection characterizes architecture "throughout the country": to James, there is something distinctly American about the connectedness that has become "the very law of the structural fact." He continues:

Thus we have the law fulfilled that every part of the house shall be, as nearly as may be, visible, visitable, penetrable, not only from every other part, but from as many parts of as many other houses as possible, if only they be near enough. Thus we see systematized the indefinite extension of all spaces and the definite merging of all functions; the enlargement of every opening, the exaggeration of every passage, the substitution of gaping arches and far perspectives and resounding voids for enclosing walls, for practicable doors, for controllable windows, for all the rest of the essence of the room-character, the room-suggestion which is so indispensable not only to occupation and concentration, but to conversation itself, to the play of the social relation at any other pitch than the pitch of a shriek or a shout.[32]

The openness, visibility, and public-ness of supposedly interior spaces clearly alarm James. The architecture enlarges, exaggerates, and gapes, distending and amplifying the individuals within, straining social relations. Confronted with a dizzying array of openings, such as passages, arches, and voids, James longs for containment. He wants walls, windows, and doors—anything representing enclosure. In these public interiors, both solitude and sociability as James understands them are eroded by "the complete proscription of privacy."

Most upsetting for James is the impact these spaces have on his self-conception. As he looks around the modern home, he sees no protective structures, but only "doorless apertures, vainly festooned, which decline to tell him where he is, which make him still a homeless wanderer, which show him other apertures, corridors, staircases, yawning, expanding, ascending, descending, and all as for the purpose of giving his presence 'away,' of reminding him that what he says must be said for the house."[33] Decidedly modern in their arrangement, the rooms with their "yawning and expanding" connecting features do not simply render the house penetrable, they render James penetrable as well. He echoes the architecture in two ways. First, he becomes transparent and empty in that both his presence and his thoughts are given away. Second, he begins to exhibit the decentered mobility, significantly conceived here as homelessness, associated with modernity. He becomes a "homeless wanderer," mobile, public, and permeable.

If people are formed by their environments, as James claims, what are the implications of these gaping structures for the American subject? That the architecture has such a disturbing effect on James during his short visit does not bode well, he argues, for the people who inhabit it for the long term. He writes:

> The instinct is throughout, as we catch it at play, that of minimizing, for any "interior," the guilt or odium or responsibility, what ever these may appear, of its *being* an interior. The custom rages like a conspiracy for nipping the interior in the bud, for denying its right to exist, for ignoring and defeating it in every possible way, for wiping out successively each sign by which it may be known from an exterior.[34]

The notion of the interior, a contained self nurtured in a contained domestic space, is exploded by the penetrable space of the modern dwelling. The home has been exonerated from the "responsibility" of producing an individual with an interior of his or her own. Interiors, both architectural and psychic, are nipped, ignored, defeated, and wiped out by the almost violent penchant for openness and connectedness James attributes to modern American urban domestic architecture. This process, James fears, will bring about the decay of society.

The fluid subject James describes (and constructs in many of his novels), while unsettling to many, was liberating to other observers who believed, as James did, that a new type of subject would be shaped by domestic spaces structured by architectural connection. The texts I explore here, including James's *The Bostonians,* trace the development of modern urban subjects, figures who, in many guises, both anticipate and complicate the alienated, fractured subjectivity associated with the literary modernism of the twentieth century. I present the novels that anchor the following chapters less as typical than as suggestive, in the hope that readers will see in my approach new possibilities for considering the urban attributes of other spaces both fictive and concrete.

Through a variety of modes and narratives, these novels construct a model of selfhood that is highly attuned to the changing and interconnected spaces of the city. The novel's modern subject emerges in *At Home in the City* as a malleable yet active agent who is simultaneously shaped by and actively building the urban landscape. My readings reveal that urbanites did not typically see themselves as helpless in the face of a burgeoning modernity. Rather, by embracing the challenges posed by a rapidly changing landscape, characters, authors, and readers could learn to navigate a complex environment that nevertheless opened new possibilities for growth, change, and progress. I hope that my approach will be similarly liberating as my readers turn to other texts—and to the landscapes that surround them—and ask how to understand, to navigate, and perhaps even to improve a world in which subjectivity and boundaries are ever more diffuse.

Chapter 1

Architectural Determinism and the Industrial City in *The Blithedale Romance* and *Ruth Hall*

I try to take an interest in all the nooks and crannies and every develop-
ment of cities.   —Nathaniel Hawthorne[1]

In Herman Melville's "Bartleby the Scrivener," the narrator, a successful if uninspired lawyer, watches, perplexed, as his new employee makes himself very much at home in the office, "where privacy and society were conjoined."[2]

> Upon more closely examining the place, I surmised that for an indefinite pe-
> riod Bartleby must have ate, dressed, and slept in my office, and that, too,
> without plate, mirror, or bed. The cushioned seat of a rickety old sofa in one
> corner bore that faint impress of a lean, reclining form. Rolled away under his
> desk I found a blanket; under the empty grate, a blacking box and brush; on a
> chair, a tin basin, with soap and a ragged towel; in a newspaper a few crumbs
> of gingernuts and a morsel of cheese. Yes, thought I, it is evident enough that
> Bartleby has been making his home here, keeping bachelor's hall all by him-
> self. Immediately then the thought came sweeping across me, what miserable
> friendlessness and loneliness are here revealed. His poverty is great, but his
> solitude, how horrible![3]

Yet however horrible Bartleby's solitude, it also dawns on the narrator that by setting up housekeeping in the office Bartleby has "unmanned" him. In effect, Bartleby has trumped conventional notions of property rights by claiming the office as his home.

Many of Melville's fictional characters attempt to make sense of alien spaces by making themselves at home in them, as is clear in *Moby Dick* and *Typee*. In claiming the office as his home, and in refusing to leave until he is forcibly evicted, Bartleby heralds a concern central to American novels of the industrial era: What will it mean to make one's home in the city? Melville had begun to explore this question in his 1852 novel *Pierre*. *Pierre* opens with a view of a country cottage where, "upon the sill of the casement, a snow-white glossy pillow reposes, and a trailing shrub has softly rested a rich, crimson flower upon it."[4] But eventually, residence in a broken-down tenement transforms its characters; the novel ends with murder and suicide in a prison cell. Although *Pierre*'s nightmare of incest begins in the country, the city is where efforts to normalize incestuous relations through domesticity turn deadly.[5] For Melville, urban domesticity is fraught with threats of insanity, destruction, and death.

As "Bartleby" and *Pierre* reveal, by the mid-nineteenth century, domesticity in the United States was produced in relation to an increasingly urban landscape. Even in the domestic novels that dominated the literary marketplace in the 1850s, such as *The Lamplighter* and *Ruth Hall,* industrial cities exert a powerful force on character and plots. Despite his famous antipathy toward "scribbling women," Nathaniel Hawthorne "had a considerable stake in domestic ideology himself," as is clear in his two novels that deal specifically with nineteenth-century urban homes, *The House of the Seven Gables* (1851) and *The Blithedale Romance* (1852).[6] *Blithedale* concludes with a scene that might pass for the happy ending of a sentimental novel. Priscilla, redeemed from a life of poverty, a questionable stage career as the Veiled Lady, and possibly a second career as a prostitute, has married Hollingsworth, the rugged reformer she formerly worshipped; a model wife, she dotes on her husband in their secluded cottage. But, in a far gentler version of *Pierre*'s denouement, Hawthorne twists this ending so that the cozy scene becomes disturbing. Hollingsworth is broken and bitter, living with crushed ambitions and the knowledge that he is at least partially responsible for the death of Priscilla's half-sister Zenobia. Seclusion becomes isolation and Priscilla's devotion mere denial.

Yet for all of the anxiety over urban domesticity expressed in Hawthorne and Melville's texts, other mid-nineteenth century novels saw the city more positively: as a space where a new brand of connective individualism could emerge. Fanny Fern's 1854 novel *Ruth Hall,* for instance, rewrites the familiar tale of moral decay in the city. *Ruth Hall*'s beginning echoes Hawthorne's "happy ending," but Fern follows her eponymous heroine beyond the conventional finale. Fern removes Ruth from her secluded cottage home to the city, where she is forced to develop the skills that allow her to succeed and eventually prosper there as a single mother. Ruth ends up with no husband, two daughters, a brotherly manager, and a good deal of bank stock; not coincidentally, she has traded her cottage for a hotel. Ruth's engagement with the artistic and commercial world of the city nets her personal, artistic, and financial profit.

In disrupting their readers' expectations for the narrative inevitability of marriage, home, and family, and in positing alternative settings and definitions for success, the endings of *Blithedale* and *Ruth Hall* call attention to an important and overlooked thematic concern about the fate of the home in an urban nation, a concern common both to these texts and to American culture generally in the mid- to late nineteenth century. In exploring what it means to make the city one's home, these novels analyze the relationships between setting and psyche in the transition of the United States from a rural to an urban nation. *Blithedale* and *Ruth Hall* undermine the redemptive power attributed to the rural cottage and imagine what kind of subject might emerge from an urban landscape dominated by hotels, boarding houses, and tenements. In each novel, the networked spaces of the industrial city—spaces traversed by new conduits of transportation and communication—help to shape a subject that registers both hope and anxiety about urban culture in the United States. Together, the novels narrate the birth of an urban subjectivity that reflects the permeable, transformable architecture of the industrial landscape.

The *Blithedale Romance* and *Ruth Hall* examine the onset of the historical and imaginary transition between the bounded spaces labeled as "rural" and "home" and the interconnected spaces of the American city. Through narrative, Hawthorne and Fern tease out the development of a new urban subjectivity as they explore the limits of architectural determinism in the urban landscape, specifically in urban domestic spaces. Both novels depict the city as a landscape increasingly organized by networks of transportation and communication; both present views of urban domesticity that complicate commonly held notions of the nineteenth-century middle-class home as a "separate sphere" where the "angel of the house" presided.[7] In so doing, like other domestic novels of the period, they "problematize the relationship between interior and exterior," exploring a "breakdown between internal and external spaces."[8] And as Melville uses the space of the office to emphasize that Bartleby is carving his domesticity from the city's economic structure, Hawthorne and Fern let urban domestic architecture signal that the industrial city's new spatial realities will produce new structures within and among the people who live there.[9]

In redefining "home" as a permeable structure whose spaces mirror and help constitute the city's networks, Hawthorne and Fern explore the promise and expose the threats posed by the unfamiliar subject who develops in the city's domestic spaces. Hawthorne's vision of the city culminates in a paralysis that anticipates modernist ideas about the fragmented individual the modern landscape will produce. *Ruth Hall* shares with *Blithedale* the notion that the urban landscape shapes and rewards a consumable persona. But for Fern, commodifying the psyche leads not to paralysis but to profit; the novel's economic logic situates *Ruth Hall* as a precursor to the realism of later decades.[10] Although *Ruth Hall* questions the notion that urban space shapes its inhabitants in predictable ways, like *Blithedale* it positions the city as a fundamentally transformative place. The power of urban architecture to shape its inhabitants can be seen most clearly in the relationships Hawthorne and Fern analyze between urban subjects and the domestic spaces of the boarding houses, tenements, and hotels that they inhabit.

As they explore the development of urban subjects and analyze how these subjects are shaped by urban homes, *Ruth Hall* and *Blithedale* develop paradigms for literary conceptions of modern subjectivity that help to structure American urban fiction well into the twentieth century. The hopes and anxieties reflected in Hawthorne and Fern's cities are exacerbated as urban transportation and communication networks increasingly dominate the national landscape. The future Hawthorne and Fern imagine for modern men and women, as well as the types of modern settings within which they will thrive, culminates in the fractured, rootless, anonymous subject we associate with literary modernism. That mobile figure has a history in nineteenth-century literature.

Undermining Pastoral Domesticity: Leaving the Cottage

In revising notions of character and setting to fit a new landscape, *Ruth Hall* and *The Blithedale Romance* break down ideas about separate spheres, fictively reconfiguring "private" and "public" spaces. In so doing, they enact a modern version of architectural determinism. *Blithedale* shows how an urban setting characterized by connection and open to Coverdale's gaze shapes an urban subjectivity inherently porous and transformable. Like *Blithedale*, *Ruth Hall*'s plot develops through descriptions of different nineteenth-century urban housing arrangements whose multiplicity and permeability argue for complex formulations of domestic and public space. *Ruth Hall*, however, claims that while the networks connecting the city's spaces fragment familial relations, they also offer alternative sites for connection, resistance, and self-commodification through story and memory.

Ruth Hall and *The Blithedale Romance* both begin in the settings commonly considered regenerative by American architectural determinists: the cottage and the farm. As I have noted, nineteenth-century reformers saw both "home" and "rural" as spaces that could produce moral and physical improvement; by inhabiting these settings, individuals (and by extension, the republic) could be transformed for the better. As Gillian Brown argues, "utopian projects shared domesticity's ideal of creating a sphere apart from the marketplace" where individual morals could temper the market's force.[11] Like "Bartleby," Fern's exposé of rural domesticity's ultimate impotence in a market economy and Hawthorne's ironic treatment of the Blithedalers' rural experience raise questions about whether and how this separation between home and city could be maintained. If it cannot, these texts ask, what will become of home?

In parodying Brook Farm's utopian project, *Blithedale* critiques romantic and pastoral formulations of rural landscapes. For romantic poets, natural settings offered the transformative experience necessary to remake the self and the world. The natural environment served as a space for regeneration— a place to which the artist could escape from society and be shocked, inspired, calmed, or reassured. To narrate this potential, romantic writers drew in part on the form of the pastoral, in which "the story of reunion with nature and a more natural past is the essential drama. . . . By resorting to nature and the past, the hero seeks to rejoin the self fragmented by experience."[12] Hawthorne ironizes this potential in *Blithedale;* reintegration of self becomes impossible because the "natural" spaces are so closely connected to the urban. Here, the urban setting rewards transformation, reinvention, and the fragmented self's flexibility.

While the city plays a significant role in all pastorals, and not just as a place from which to escape, in *Blithedale* the meaning of movement between city and country changes as the connections between rural landscapes and urban modes of production become increasingly obvious. According to Leo Marx, the trajectory of the complex pastoral leads from city to country and back again, bringing a "world which is more real into juxtaposition with an idyllic vision."[13] Critic Judy Anhorn concurs, noting that "the cycle of recovery remains incomplete until the traveler returns to the city, where the complementary phase of his adventure begins," and the traveler gains the means to transform his journey into literature.[14] By the 1850s in the United States, this timeless motion from city to country and back took on new valences because urban networks made "escaping" to untouched rural places increasingly difficult. The regenerative power Thoreau felt at Walden Pond and Mount Katahdin would be tapped by tourists heading north by train to the White Mountains and to coastal Maine; the nine-mile trip from Blithedale to Boston would become a commute; the pastoral would be integrated into mass-produced plans for suburban cottages.[15] In order for environmental determinists to vaunt the transformative power of rural locations, their urban connections had to be elided. Yet while utopians may have wanted to escape the marketplace, they embraced other elements of city life. While rarely urban, nineteenth-century American utopian designs wove elements of urbanity, particularly opportunities for human connection, into their public and domestic architecture. Dolores Hayden writes, "even the most isolated communes created centers of community life which were far more urbane in character than the isolated homesteads that surrounded them."[16] This tension between isolation and connection is integral to *Blithedale*. As Dana Brand notes, "while conceiving itself as a cure for them, Blithedale, if successful, would intensify the conditions of cosmopolitanism."[17]

In *Blithedale,* rural space, like nature, is "thoroughly mediate"; it is a space both enmeshed in urban economics and overdetermined by artistic and literary representations of the pastoral.[18] The farm is located near Boston, and many Blithedalers regularly commute between farm and city. The presence of these urbanites renders rural escape less authentic. Coverdale remarks, "the presence of Zenobia caused our heroic enterprise to show like an illusion, a masquerade, a pastoral, a counterfeit Arcadia, in which we grown-up men and women were making a play-day of the years that were given to us to live in. I tried to analyze this impression, but not with much success."[19] Coverdale's pairing of terms like masquerade, illusion, and counterfeit with pastoral and Arcadia is worth analyzing. Juxtaposing gestures toward the rural with nineteenth-century anxieties about the urban—namely, that identities could be concealed, appearances transformed, and histories falsified in a setting removed from rural intimacy—further links the two settings. Encapsulated in the force of Zenobia's public persona, the power of the urban to disrupt and reconfigure the rural shows that the rural experience, like the urban, is artificial and obviously produced. Both farm and city are environments where shifting conceptions of identity involve illusion and masquerade; both are places of modern deception.[20]

The pastoral Arcadia at Blithedale, then, must be read as a particular kind of urban illusion; it is, in the chapter's title, "A *Modern* Arcadia" (my emphasis). It is a place for performing the rural. Though Coverdale notes, "our costume bore no resemblance to the beribboned doublets, silk breeches and stockings, and slippers fastened with artificial roses, that distinguish the pastoral people of poetry and the stage," to describe Blithedale and its inhabitants he evokes characters and quotations from notable pastoralists (*BR,* 58–59). For instance, Hawthorne alludes to Virgil, in whose *Eclogues* were created Arcadia, "the symbolic landscape, a delicate blend of myth and reality, that was to be particularly relevant to the American experience."[21] His other references, to Milton, Spenser, and Shakespeare, show that Coverdale can only imagine his surroundings through a literary lens.[22] Traditionally, the pastoral serves to mediate between nature and art, rural and urban, garden and machine.[23] Here, however, the landscape is simply a set, a stage upon which "pastoral" may be played out, albeit in costumes of "honest homespun and linsey-woolsey" instead of silk and ribbon. The setting and costumes, however, do not transform the urbanites into rustic, honest farmers. Indeed, the land's potential for regeneration and inspiration becomes ironic, even comic.

Because Coverdale, Zenobia, and the other Blithedalers can perceive their environment only as art, the rural landscape in general and the utopian project at Blithedale in particular lose their potential as sites for personal and cultural regeneration. All of the novel's characters come to Blithedale for escape or for rejuvenation. Yet the city-born desires binding half-sisters Zenobia and Priscilla to Hollingsworth only grow at Blithedale, eventually causing Zenobia's death, Hollingsworth's suffering, and Priscilla's marriage. Blithedale's impotence either to hide or to heal crystallizes in the moments following

Zenobia's suicide in the river that traverses the settlement. Though her body is frozen in an attitude of prayer, Coverdale can see this posture only as the last of Zenobia's performances. "Zenobia, I have often thought, was not quite simple in her death. She had seen pictures, I suppose, of drowned persons, in lithe and graceful attitudes. . . . But in Zenobia's case, there was some tint of the Arcadian affectation that had been visible enough in all our lives, for a few months past" (*BR*, 218). Instead of gaining the beauty of pathos or sacrifice, Zenobia's body decays into an object of horrifying fascination. The farm has failed to improve her and nature fails to redeem her.

Examples of Blithedale's failure to transform its residents abound in the text; from the beginning of the novel, Hawthorne makes clear that working the soil will not elevate Blithedale's residents to the intellectual and spiritual heights toward which they strive. Coverdale notes, "the peril of our new life was not lest we should fail in becoming practical agriculturists, but that we should probably cease to be anything else. . . . The clods of earth, which we so constantly belabored and turned over and over, were never etherealized into thought. Our thoughts, on the other hand, were fast becoming cloddish" (*BR*, 61). Here, Coverdale directly equates environment to mentality, but this determinism is fleeting. Coverdale, of course, is a confirmed bachelor who revels in an urban existence consisting of writing poetry, reading diverting books, attending "wonderful exhibitions," basking in warm fires, and sipping fine sherry (*BR*, 5).[24] Luckily for Coverdale's sybaritic tendencies, his exposure to farm life does not distort his body or mind in any lasting way. Though farming makes him "quite another man," when he returns to Boston he notes, not at all dispiritedly, that, "all the effeminacy of past days had returned upon me at once" (*BR*, 57, 135). Close physical connection to the land proves to have limited power to transform the body and even less potential to ennoble the mind. This impotence reinforces the dominance of urban forms and spaces in the networked culture that *Blithedale* constructs.

Like Hawthorne, Fanny Fern both ironizes the regenerative potential of the rural and exposes the economic and physical networks linking rural settings to the city. *Ruth Hall* begins with a happy marriage and blissful motherhood, but after her husband dies, Ruth is left alone and destitute to raise her two young daughters. Unskilled and friendless, Ruth tries a variety of occupations including seamstress, washerwoman, and teacher, before eventually achieving financial success and fame as a writer.

Ruth's early happiness as the wife of "handsome Harry" is predicated in part on the setting they share. Their cottage, with its "nice old-fashioned beams," sports "honeysuckle, red and white, wreathed around the porches."[25] The cottage follows nineteenth-century pattern-book and advice manual descriptions of the ideal structure in which to practice, in Catharine Beecher's terms, "domestic economy." Yet, located at the end of a "lovely winding lane . . . about five miles from the city," and linked to the city by Harry's daily commute to his job as an investment banker, the cottage's suburban setting positions rural domesticity within the networked space of the urban landscape (*RH*, 28). As urban theorist Henri Lefebvre explains, "a de-urbanized yet dependent periphery is established around the city. Effectively, these new suburban dwellers are still urban even though they are unaware of it and believe themselves to be close to nature, to the sun, and to green-ery."[26] Indeed, Ruth performs a rural lifestyle that befits the idealized views of cottage life propounded in fiction and advice manuals in this era, and in so doing elides the city's undesirable presence.

Novels like *Ruth Hall* and *Blithedale* make clear that while specific narratives help to construct our conceptions and experiences of space, individuals may retain the agency to transform the spaces they inhabit. For instance, while nineteenth-century architectural determinists glorified the single-family home's promise to reform the nation's morals in texts that emphasized cottages' rural aspects, *Ruth Hall* initially highlights but eventually negates the cultural assumption that perfect homes like Ruth's would create an ideal citizenry.[27] In location and appearance, Ruth's house epitomizes the Gothic cottage made popular in the designs and writing of Andrew Jackson Downing, who, like other pattern-book publishers, hoped to shore up American virtue by designing virtuous American homes. Downing wanted "the country homes of a whole people [to] embody such ideas of beauty and truth as shall elevate and purify its feelings."[28] The 1840s witnessed the publication of popular architecture books that included details ranging from floor plans to personal testimonials, effectively advice manuals on how to, as Gwendolyn Wright puts it, "create perfect homes."[29] Periodical publications participated in this trend as well; *Godey's Lady's Book* published roughly five hundred house designs in the second half of the nineteenth century, the models, Wright notes, for more than four thousand homes.[30] Ironically, the modern print media responsible for *Ruth Hall*'s eventual national success— and the success of the book's eponymous heroine—reinforced the very notions of rural domesticity that the novel challenges.

Although Ruth's house is not new, it features many architectural elements that to Downing symbolized domestic virtue and which, he claimed, would elicit order and virtue from its inhabitants. Ruth's little house indeed might have been one of Downing's, "whose humble roof, whose shady porch, whose verdant lawn and smiling flowers; all breathe forth to us in true, earnest tones, a domestic feeling that at once purifies the heart, and binds us more closely to our fellow-beings!"[31] (see figure 1). In cottages like Ruth's, un-painted wood, local materials, and exterior colors chosen to blend with the immediate surroundings were desirable on two levels: first because they emphasized the home's picturesque qualities, and more importantly because these "honest" materials and colors marked the cottages as distinctly rural dwellings.[32] The age of the structure, emphasized by the "patches of moss

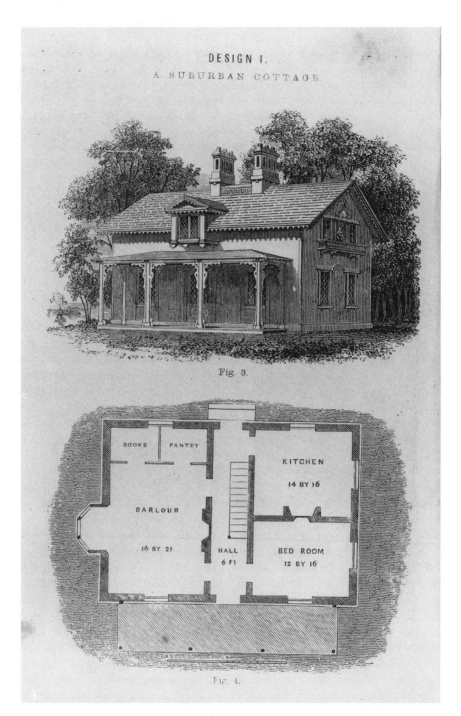

FIGURE 1. Figures 3 and 4 from Andrew Jackson Downing, "A Suburban Cottage," *Victorian Cottage Residences* (1842; New York: Dover, 1981), 27. Library of Congress, Prints and Photographs Division, LC-USZ62-056059.

[that] tuft the sloping roof" and the "tumble-down old summer house" in the backyard, both reinforces the setting's picturesque quality and links it closely to nature and thus to virtue (*RH*, 28). According to Downing and the pattern-books, the more "natural" the house, the better, morally speaking.

Like its exterior, the cottage's interior emphasizes the young Ruth's adherence to the values upheld by nineteenth-century domestic reformers. Though we never see Ruth reading advice books or periodicals, she quickly undergoes a complete transformation from a girl "just home from boarding-school" to a paragon of virtuous homemaking (*RH*, 20). Her house is spotless from the parlor to the bedroom, where "a snow-white quilt and a pair of plump, tempting pillows" grace the bed; "the furniture and carpet are of a light cream color; and there is a vase of honeysuckle on the little light-stand.[33] Nothing could be more faultless, you see" (*RH*, 35). If Ruth's environment is faultless, so will she be. Susan Harris notes, "By associating Ruth with flowers and piety, Fern creates a protagonist her readers will recognize as deeply feminine, a woman who feels as a woman should feel, and who therefore qualifies as a heroine the general culture can accept."[34] Ruth imparts a virtuous beauty even to "the long, white curtains, looped up so prettily from the open windows, [of] plain, cheap muslin . . . no artist could have disposed their folds more gracefully" (*RH*, 34).

Significantly, Ruth does not simply absorb this environment, she creates it; her "tastes and morals naturally enhance the environment around her."[35] Ruth covers her own furniture, makes beautiful and delicious preserves, and decorates her home with the woodland flowers she collects, efforts that all correspond to advice she might have gleaned from domestic manuals.[36] The symbolic, architectural and material language of "home" evoked by Ruth's house would have been easily read and understood by Fern's readers. This spatial vocabulary reinforces the sacred happiness Ruth experiences during her early marriage and adds to the affective quality of later scenes when Ruth, living in far different material surroundings, recalls images and experiences of her cottage home.

Ruth's house, then, operates as a setting that demonstrates and solidifies her status as happy, productive mother and wife; it performs all of the functions that an architectural determinist like Downing or Beecher could hope for. In this setting, Ruth clearly fulfills the prerequisites to become an idealized wife and mother—the proud heroine of her separate sphere. As her husband Harry remarks, "You will be happy here, dear Ruth. . . . You will be your own mistress" (*RH*, 28). Harry, after all, has "chosen a separate home, that he might be master of it" (*RH*, 38). Individualism begins with a link to property; Ruth can be mistress of herself in a place where distance and ownership separate her from others, particularly from members of her extended family. The promise of this enclosure is signaled inside and out. The porch that dominates Downing's prototypical cottage façade adds a layer of privacy by throwing the public face of the house into obscurity. Similarly, the floor plan emphasizes seclusion with the parlor offering the interior's sole "public" space. And as we see in Beecher and Stowe's only images of people inside their model American home, domestic interiors are for the family's use, and they are divided by gender (see figure 2). In the masculine library, the extended family gathers, while in the maternal corner, the family extends to pets but excludes adult men. If, Gillian Brown points out, nineteenth-century "self-definition was secured in and nearly synonymous with domesticity," it was also synonymous with the enclosed space of the home, and with its "removal from the marketplace."[37] However, in *Ruth Hall,* any equation between a contained home and a unified subjectivity dissolves because "home" is in fact neither contained nor divorced from the marketplace.

If Ruth's cottage home "visually and emotionally suggested a life outside the dominant economic ethos," Ruth's experience of the space demonstrates that for the American woman, no solid boundary divides private space from public, domestic space from the world outside.[38] Economic and social realities quickly erode the order and containment advocated by domestic reformers. If women were the "mistresses" of their "separate sphere," they enjoyed little privacy there. Privacy did not even become part of the common law until well after the novel's publication.[39] That is to say, home historically was neither a place of containment nor of privacy. Ruth's little cottage, for instance, ceases to be private soon after Harry and Ruth move in, for Harry's invasive parents quickly take up residence only "a small piece of woods" away from Ruth and Harry (*RH,* 32). Her prying mother-in-law gains access to Ruth's house by the cook's permission. That the boundary lines of private property may be crossed easily by family members is a pattern that has precedents in Ruth's earlier life. Both Ruth's boarding school experience, "where she shared a room with four girls," and the early days of her marriage, when she and Harry live in "their own set of apartments, while the old people [Harry's parents] keep house," take place in settings where Ruth enjoys little privacy (*RH,* 14, 22). While Ruth is living in his house, Ruth's father-in-law takes up the Coverdalean occupation of voyeur, "speculating on what Ruth was about, peeping over the balustrade, to see who called when the bell rang" (*RH,* 23). Historically, it was quite common for young married couples to live with their parents; hotels and boarding houses drew a substantial percentage of their clientele from the ranks of the newly married, who saw boarding house life as an alternative preferable to living with their families.[40] By exploring alternatives to the contained home both before and after vaunting Ruth's early marriage and her homemaking skills as the middle-class ideal, Fern undermines the notion that Ruth and Harry's detached home is particularly contained. In so doing, Fern simultaneously erodes the transformative power of the cottage linked to its detachment from economic and social realities and makes acceptable, even inevitable, Ruth and Harry's move

FIGURE 2. Family group from cover and frontispiece of Catharine E. Beecher and Harriet
Beecher Stowe, *The American Woman's Home* (1869; reprint, New York: Arno Press, 1971).
Harriet Beecher Stowe Center, Hartford, CT.

from their cottage to a modern hotel. Thus Fern's apparent narrative endorsement of architectural determinist tenets is replaced with a skepticism toward the notion that domestic space is particularly beneficent.

Interior Networks in Upper-Class Lodgings

Different pressures compel Miles Coverdale and Ruth Hall to leave their rural settings for urban spaces; their reasons for leaving and their respective fates reveal much about the gendering of urban space in the mid-nineteenth century. The boarding houses and hotels to which Ruth and Coverdale resort complicate notions of home based on containment. Their new homes are places of connection where private space mixes with public and domestic space mingles with the realm of the market. But these categories mix in different measures depending on the gender of the lodger and the class of the lodgings in question.

Hawthorne and Fern's urban lodgings, like their historical counterparts, disrupt the ideas about the power of home promulgated by architectural reformers. Beecher and Downing, for instance, each stressed that single-family homes could be designed toward particular social and cultural ends; they argued that families who inhabited these contained homes eventually would send their children forth as emissaries who would improve the wide, wide world. Yet at this time, owning a home was not economically feasible for most young families, particularly in the nation's growing cities. As Anthony Trollope remarked in his 1861 travelogue *North America*: "Housekeeping is not popular with young married people in America," an assertion that echoes Walt Whitman's 1856 claim that "almost three-fourths of middle and upper-class New Yorkers were either boarders or permanent hotel guests."[41] In addition to lodging in formal boarding houses and hotels, approximately twenty percent of American families in the 1850s took in paying lodgers; boarding "represented a normal stage in the transitional period between the departure of individuals from their parents' family to the setting up of their own family."[42] At the mid-nineteenth century, urban boarding houses and hotels served the population across the class spectrum, attracting long-term as well as transient residents, sometimes simultaneously. They offered quick turnover and required no permanent commitment on the resident's part.[43]

The nineteenth-century urban hotel and boarding house each helped to shift the operations of public and private space, and as such, notes Gwendolyn Wright, they raised "complaints that they were improper, that they encouraged transience and discouraged domesticity."[44] More private than many homes, boarding houses and hotels offered their residents the freedom to live outside of the gaze of family members and allowed guests to mingle within the walls they shared, as we see in this circa 1840 "Scene in a Fashionable Boarding House," where at least one woman chats with the men gathered around the fireplace (figure 3). This image stands in stark contrast to Beecher's interior (see figure 2), where contact between genders happens only under the mother's benign but watchful eye. In reconfiguring the spaces of the home and devoting whole rooms of prime real estate to facilitating connections between mobile strangers, boarding houses and hotels threatened to redefine gender, class, and family relations.

The hotel to which Ruth and her family retreat after the death of her eldest child is a seaside resort located far from the city yet inhabited mainly by vacationing urbanites; the presence of these tourists signals that the hotel is connected to the city. A "large hotel in one of those seaport towns," the Halls' lodgings offer ample opportunity for interaction through innovative activities and architecture (*RH*, 49). "There were 'hops' in the hall, and sails upon the lake; there were nine-pin alleys, and a gymnasium; there were bathing parties, and horse-back parties; there were billiard rooms and smoking rooms; reading rooms, flirtation rooms,—room for everything but— thought" (*RH*, 50). The various public spaces encourage gregarious inter-

FIGURE 3. Scene in a Fashionable Boarding House, ca 1840, colored lithograph. Museum of the City of New York, Gift of James M. Holzman, 51.299.

action and militate against privacy; connections among guests, as well as between guests and servants, are actively promoted by hotel architecture. And while other authors make a strong distinction between the hotel as a "public house" and the boarding house as "private lodgings," Fern does not differentiate between the two categories.[45] Thus in *Ruth Hall*, we begin to see in the middle-class hotel the emergence of a model of home founded on sociability, a gregarious alternative to the detached cottage. Here, the quality of Ruth's interactions with others, and not the transparency of her jewel-like jellies, will measure her worth.

Though distinct from the boarding house, the hotel in *Ruth Hall* foreshadows the potential for new architectural forms to enable positive interpersonal connections. While potentially intrusive, relationships with fellow boarders also could hold the promise of community. The power of these connections is emphasized when Harry contracts a fatal case of typhus. His illness evokes the threat of urban contagion, but also elicits a degree of support from the Halls' fellow guests that works to neutralize this anxiety.[46] As Ruth tends Harry alone, refusing any relief, "regardless of the lapse of time—regardless of hunger thirst or weariness," she enacts the role of the devoted wife that readers of nineteenth-century domestic novels usually would associate with the closed circle of the family and home (*RH, 53*).[47] Yet in *Ruth Hall*, "many a friendly voice whisper[s] at the door" as Harry is dying (*RH, 53*). The shared spaces of the hotel offer numerous opportunities for people to exchange information; thus, the family circle widens to include the waiters, porters, and "gentlemen friends" who express concern for and gain knowledge about the dying man through the hotel's architectural design. Along with the specialized rooms and activities that draw individuals into a network of interaction, the hotel's servants and services reflect and promote interpersonal connection.

The potential for these connections to stand in for family ties is made clear when a fellow lodger offers to take up a collection for Ruth and her two daughters. As he tells Ruth's brother Hyacinth, "I have had the pleasure of living under the same roof, this summer, with your afflicted sister and her noble husband, and have become warmly attached to both" (*RH, 59*). This attachment holds promise as a desirable alternative to the actual ties of family, especially as the novel's denouement is punctuated by Ruth's family members' schemes to pay as little as possible to support Ruth and her daughters. As I will discuss in more detail later, the reconstruction of family in urban space is a significant element of *Ruth Hall*; many quasi-familial connections are made possible by the shared spaces of the architecture Ruth inhabits.

If the hotel seems like a surprising choice of domestic setting for the middle-class Hall family, it would have been a logical destination for Miles Coverdale, who as a wealthy single man could enjoy the amenities of luxury service and accommodation more economically at a hotel than in a home of his own. On his return to Boston, Coverdale notes parenthetically that his "bachelor rooms, long before this time, had received some other occupant," establishing the mobility and impermanence of city living (*BR,* 134). Mobility and transience are equally characteristic of boarding house and hotel guests, who in *Blithedale* come both to embody the buildings' porous architecture and to exemplify transience in their economic status as renters. Yet Hawthorne's juxtaposition of the two housing types in chapters named respectively "The Hotel" and "The Boarding House" indicates a subtle distinction between the two. For instance, as a hotel resident, Coverdale dines out, often in the Albion restaurant, where he can choose from the "hundred dishes at command," while Zenobia and Priscilla have the option of eating in their boarding house on the "soup, fish, and flesh" their "respectable mistress" serves (*BR,* 37, 141). The hotel lets rooms on the basis of availability—Coverdale occupies the rooms that are open when he checks in. In contrast, the "rather stylish boarding house" visible through Coverdale's window keeps rooms vacant for their long-term residents; as he looks from his window he notes that the housemaids are busily preparing for the return of "its most expensive and profitable guests" (*BR,* 139, 140). Guests are both expensive and profitable because they require extra servants, luxurious food and drink, and other amenities provided by the boarding house. These particular guests, who of course turn out to be Zenobia and Priscilla, apparently keep the rooms rented even in their absence; Coverdale recalls that Zenobia "had retained an establishment in town, and had not unfrequently withdrawn herself from Blithedale" (*BR,* 145). The boarding house, it appears, is more homelike than the hotel. Other boarding-house fiction underscores this distinction; one character chooses "private lodgings" in a boarding house instead of a hotel because his "mother's solemn injunction was to avoid a public house."[48] Further, a boarding house would have been the only respectable housing option for a single woman in mid-nineteenth-century Boston. As Norman Hayner notes, "Before the Civil War . . . respectable hostelries would not give shelter at night to unaccompanied ladies," and even by 1885, "only 11 per cent of the guests at New York's four largest hotels were women."[49]

Although upper-class hotels and boarding houses differed slightly, they offered—for a price—both urban location and the opportunity to change settings at will, affording Coverdale and his contemporaries (both fictional and historical) the opportunity to avoid fixed identities and retain the fluidity the city required. Both Coverdale's hotel and Zenobia's boarding house occupy the upper echelons of available rental housing. The stylishness of Zenobia's boarding house is evident not only in the "exceedingly rich" furnishings, but also in its clients (*BR,* 151). Zenobia's fellow boarders include a young man who patronizes a tailor and primps for half an hour before dinner parties, along with a family headed by a man employed in a "counting room or office" (*BR,* 140). All of them are served by a shared "man-

servant in a white jacket" (*BR*, 141). In the 1857 *Physiology of New York
Boarding Houses,* Zenobia's lodgings would be classed among the "Tip-
Top" boarding houses, "huge, stylish mansions" catering to "families who
preferred this mode of residence on the score of fashion or—convenience."[50]
The hotel and boarding house share a city block; proximity reinforces their
shared upper-rank status. Though downtowns were far more economically
mixed in the nineteenth century than they are today, class distinctions separated neighborhoods from one another.[51] And like all tip-top boarding
houses, these lodgings confer status upon their dwellers.

As early as the 1830s, architectural designs helped to identify different
ranks of hotels—and clientele—even as they shaped public and private
facets of the client's experience. Luxury is visible in Coverdale's "pleasant
bachelor-parlor, sunny and shadowy, curtained and carpeted, with the bed-
table adjoining" (*BR*, 37). Featuring both a centre-table and a writing desk,
his room resembles those in Boston's Tremont House, generally considered
the nation's first modern hotel, which opened in 1829.

The exterior aesthetics of the Tremont were as arresting as its interior; the
hotel was a powerful classical presence in downtown Boston (figure 4). The
ground floor plan for the Tremont House shows the hotel's public rooms fac-
ing Tremont Street, with guest rooms filling the South Avenue wing (figure 5).
Guest rooms also fronted Tremont Street on the second and third floors. The
Tremont was an anomaly when it opened, not simply because it featured
suites, but because it "was also one of the first hotels with truly private
rooms: each room had a separate key, and strangers were not sent to share
rooms."[52] According to geographer Paul Groth, for wealthy patrons, "hotel
life allowed tenants—especially single people—to push . . . privacy and autonomy to a new limit."[53] The layout and design of the Tremont and its de-
scendants allowed customers a new way to inhabit domestic space in the city.

However, even within first-class hotels and boarding houses, private and
public spaces mixed, underlining the anxieties about privacy and urban connection that are highlighted in the novel by Coverdale's incessant peeping
into his neighbors' windows. The Tremont House exemplifies this blend.
While the hotel itself was private, with a lobby clerk (the first in an American hotel) to enforce this privacy, the hotel operated as a vibrant extension
of Boston's public life, a function signaled by the Tremont House's façade
(see fig. 4). Unlike Downing's suburban cottage, which occupies an indeterminate grassy space, the Tremont House is clearly situated in a particular location, and it is surrounded by human activity. While large, the columned
entry does not dominate the Tremont House's façade; rather, it has the effect
of simultaneously focusing the eye on the liminal space of the hotel while visually scaling down the entrance.

Its distinctive façade and innovative spatial arrangements made the Tremont one of Boston's most recognizable buildings. "Every *American* knows

FIGURE 4. Tremont House exterior. From W. H. Eliot, *A Description of the Tremont House* (Boston: Gray and Bowen, 1830), 32, by permission of Houghton Library, Harvard University.

the Tremont House," notes Costard Sly (a pseudonym) in his *Sayings and Doings at the Tremont House in the Year 1832.* This gossipy volume, comprised mainly of "Conversations Overheard," notes that all of Boston's most illustrious residents may be seen at the Tremont, particularly in the dining room, which was the large columned room fronting Beacon Street in the Tremont House plan (see fig. 5). This plan, which "was to become the standard reference work for hotel construction [and] marked the end of the casual era of innkeeping," reveals a careful attention to the operations of bounded and connected spaces within the hotel's walls.[54] The sitting rooms along Tremont Street, for instance, could be connected or separated from one another by sliding doors (see fig. 5). In *Sayings and Doings,* these rooms, like the dining room, are intermediate spaces where public and private interactions mesh. "Number Eighty-Seven," for instance, becomes the location where infidelities concealed within a marriage are revealed: "Spite of his pretended fondness for Harriet," one character announces gleefully, "Mr. Debangs is at this *very* moment in a room in this very house,—and that room is occupied by a WOMAN!"[55] This information, gained by glimpses through windows, is verified when Mrs. Debangs herself becomes a witness: "I saw the door of *that* room—(*you* know)—open, and my husband come out, accompanied by that vile woman. They were talking and laughing—and seemed in such *high* spirits!"[56] The situation is defused, predictably, when the

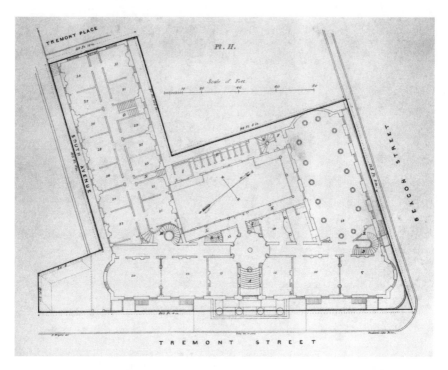

FIGURE 5. Tremont House plan. Also from Eliot, 32, by permission of Houghton Library, Harvard University.

vile woman is identified as Mr. Debangs' innocuous sister. While it offered its tenants a new type of anonymity, the hotel put private interactions on display to partially informed observers, a fact that brings us back to Hawthorne.

In *Blithedale,* private and public spaces mix audibly as well as visually; even the highest-class lodgings echo with the characteristic sounds of the urban dwelling's shared interior spaces. Like the city street, whose sounds bring to Coverdale's mind the "entangled life of many men together," the hotel's sounds identify it as a permeable space where classes and genders mingle (*BR,* 135). The hotel's life and pulse rush through its halls, entrances, and other internal spaces. From his rooms, Coverdale can hear "the stir of the hotel; the loud voices of guests, landlord or barkeeper; steps echoing on the staircase; the ringing of a bell, announcing arrivals or departures; the person lumbering past my door with baggage, which he thumped down upon the floors of neighboring chambers; the lighter feet of chamber-maids scudding along the passages;—it is ridiculous to think what an interest they had for me" (*BR,* 135, 136). Though Coverdale retrospectively terms his interest in the noise that surrounds him "ridiculous," he is highly attuned to the intramural connections that exist within the confines of the hotel. Though some-what anonymous, the sound makers can be classed as guests, landlords, and servants. As he listens, Coverdale's memories of Blithedale become "far-off and intangible . . . vague [and] shadowy," (*BR*, 134). The sounds of the city enmesh him in urban space, where lives are audibly entangled.

Like the hotel's interior sounds, the noise penetrating Coverdale's room from outside helps to build a particular urban consciousness—or so he thinks. As the external sounds enter Coverdale's mind, they emphasize the dissolu-tion of individual boundaries within repetitive urban patterns. The only specific sounds that Coverdale picks out from the general hum that perme-ates his room are all mechanized, machine-like, or military. "City-soldiery, with a full military band," clocks, and bells, for instance, reinforce his asso-ciation of urban space with mechanized time (*BR*, 135). But the most significant sound that Coverdale hears is that of the "mechanical diorama," whose thrice-daily "repetition of obstreperous music, winding up with the rattle of imitative cannon and musketry and a huge final explosion" trans-forms the audience into so many automatons whose "clap of hands, thump of sticks, and . . . energetic pounding of their heels" is just as predictably timed as the mechanized entertainment they view (*BR*, 136). These sounds have the potential, like the "general sameness" of the houses Coverdale can see from his window, to shape a society of "inhabitants . . . cut out on one identical pattern, like little-wooden toy-people of German manufacture" (*BR*, 139).[57] The mechanical city seems apt to produce a culture of ma-chines. In theorist Henri Lefebvre's view, the city's networks transform the rural in part by "mak[ing] simultaneous what in the countryside and ac-cording to nature passes and is distributed according to cycles and rhythms. It (the city) grasps and defends 'everything.'"[58]

The pattern that results from this transformation of rural rhythms be-comes one of the city's distinguishing characteristics, and potentially one of its great pleasures. On leaving Boston, Coverdale moves "far beyond the strike of city clocks," a phrase we might read as marking his eagerness to im-merse himself in nature (*BR*, 11). But in context, the phrase parallels other city pleasures Coverdale is somewhat loath to give up, such as his "warm fireside [and] freshly lighted cigar" (*BR*, 11). Thus, the individual sounds that make up the "tumult of the pavements," and melt into "a continual up-roar, . . . broad and deep," are inescapable, yet somehow pleasurable for urban dwellers (*BR*, 136). Sound becomes, in Michel de Certeau's words, "the mass that carries off and mixes up in itself any identity of authors and spectators."[59] But as de Certeau points out, this uniformity is only audible and enforceable when one looks at or listens to the city from a distance. Up close, it becomes "an innumerable collection of singularities . . . [whose] intertwined paths give their shape to spaces. They weave places together."[60]

To see these singularities clearly and explore how they might shape a distinctly urban subjectivity, Coverdale must look beyond the city's façades. Hawthorne comments in his *American Notebooks* on "the greater pic- turesqueness and reality of back-yards, and everything appertaining to the rear of a house; as compared with the front, which is fitted up for the pub- lic eye. There is much to be learnt, always, by getting a glimpse at rears."[61] This passage is directly echoed in *Blithedale,* when Coverdale asserts that the front of a building "is always artificial; it is meant for the world's eye, and is therefore a veil and a concealment. Realities keep in the rear, and put for- ward an advance-guard of show and humbug" (*BR,* 138). Coverdale hopes that with its public identifiers effaced, the back of a house will offer a glimpse into the true nature of that house (and therefore its inhabitants). As Lefebvre notes, "spaces made (produced) to be read are the most deceptive and tricked-up imaginable."[62] Like Priscilla, who performs as the Veiled Lady, Zenobia, who adopts a stage name to complement her public persona, or Westervelt, with his false teeth and costume-like glasses, houses in *Blithedale* fit themselves up to be seen in particular ways, from the front *and* the back. From the back, identities are delineated less clearly; a waiter must inform Coverdale that the house he is looking at is not a private home but "a rather stylish boarding house" (*BR,* 139). Yet, even in a novel featuring masques, concealed identities, false teeth, and a veiled lady, the backyards do more than merely reflect the novel's emphasis on concealment; rather, they emphasize a connectivity constructed in part by architecture and in part by the eye.

Urban buildings in *Blithedale* are permeable structures. The "brick- blocks" that Coverdale inhabits before and after his time in Blithedale are permeable to heat; buildings warm themselves and their neighbors, "each house partaking of the warmth of all the rest, besides the sultriness of its in- dividual furnace" (*BR,* 10). From his hotel perch, Coverdale sees "one long united roof, with its thousands of slates glistening in the rain, extended over the whole" (*BR,* 139). The individual dwellings share a roof, and the roof in turn emphasizes the repetition that characterizes the urban landscape. Other shared spaces include the "grass plots, and here and there an apology for a garden, pertaining severally to these dwellings" (*BR,* 137). And foreshadow- ing the city-produced permeability of self embodied by Priscilla, who makes an ideal psychic medium because other people's ideas can pass through her, urbanites even share the air they breathe. Upon leaving Boston, Coverdale gratefully inhales "air that had not been breathed, once and again! Air that had not been spoken into words of falsehood and error, like all the air of the dusky city!"(*BR,* 11).

In slate and dirt, in heat and breath, the city engenders connection and permeability. The architectural determinist in Coverdale assumes that this setting necessarily will shape inhabitants who echo these qualities. When he looks at the rowhouses, Coverdale concludes that:

It seemed hardly worth while for more than one of those families to be in existence; since they all had the same glimpse of sky, all looked into the same area, all received just their equal share of sunshine through the front windows, and all listened to precisely the same noises of the street on which they bordered. Men are so much alike, in their nature, that they grow intolerable unless varied by their circumstances. (*BR,* 139)

Coverdale believes that the uniform sights and sounds that percolate through the walls and windows of the city's residences will shape a group of uniform people. Just as these individuals are constituted by their settings, the settings register what the city produces; for urban architects "the repetition of simple forms in housing was taken as visible evidence of equality of station in society."[63] Yet Coverdale's "overreductive reading" of this scene is not, Brand notes, shared by Hawthorne: in *Blithedale,* if not in Coverdale's narration, city people do not simply reflect their environment; they internalize its characteristics in surprising ways.[64]

In *Blithedale,* the city both marks its inhabitants as urban and rewards them for taking on the architectural qualities—the permeability and mutability—of the built spaces they inhabit. Urban realities cannot be reduced to the mechanized patterns Coverdale's eye and ear construct. Close physical proximity disrupts both the city's repetition and its effect on urban subjects. The city does transform people, but far from rendering them uniform, it renders them transformable, a fact that becomes clear in Hawthorne's descriptions of lower-class boarding houses and their inhabitants.

Moodie's Lodgings: Architectural Determinism and the Lower Class

Because they cannot always choose where to live or whether to own property, lower class urbanites' relationships to their surroundings are both more tenuous and more fixed than those enjoyed by the more mobile upper classes. Though constantly threatened by displacement, poorer people lack the resources to choose their settings freely. Accordingly, Hawthorne's treatment of lower-class lodgings, especially his descriptions of the boarding house where Priscilla and Moodie live, involves an even more insistent version of architectural determinism than appears elsewhere in *The Blithedale Romance.* These chapters depict an urban environment that selects and shapes people who are mobile and changeable, creating and rewarding the unfixed persona of the modern urbanite.[65]

As Coverdale explores the shared spaces of Boston's lower classes, he narrates a direct relationship between built structures and the urban subjectivity that develops within them. Like its upper-class counterparts, Moodie's urban boarding house is characterized by permeable spaces. In addition, mutability visibly characterizes the poorer boarding houses, a quality that is passed on to its inhabitants. As cities develop, the tides of fashion mark different neighborhoods as desirable. When new construction goes up, poorer people like Moodie and Priscilla move into formerly fashionable quarters that have been transformed physically to meet new needs, a phenomenon that continues to mark the urban landscape, whether through neglect or through gentrification. After losing his fortune, Fauntleroy, father to Priscilla and Zenobia, changes his name and takes up residence as Moodie in a "squalid street" where he lives "among poverty-stricken wretches, sinners, and forlorn, good people, Irish, and whomsoever else [is] neediest" (BR, 169). There, he pays "weekly rent for a chamber and a closet," a lodging situation far removed from Coverdale's hotel room or Zenobia's boarding house, but not the worst of the lodging options even in this fictionalized city—in the same house "twenty Irish bedfellows" share one room (BR, 169).[66] Here, public and private spaces function differently as physical structures are transformed according to economic exigency.

Ever-changing physical environments like Priscilla's childhood home become collages of history, shaping inhabitants who are marked indelibly as urban even as they adapt to fit new surroundings. Moodie's room, which will eventually become the site of Priscilla's childhood, has been transformed into its current incarnation from prouder beginnings as a colonial governor's mansion, and the room serves as a palimpsest revealing the different eras and classes that have transformed it.

> Tattered hangings, a marble hearth, traversed with many cracks and fissures, a richly-carved oaken mantle-piece, partly hacked-away for kindling-stuff, a stuccoed ceiling, defaced with great, unsightly patches of the naked laths;— such was the chamber's aspect, as if, with its splinters and rags of dirty splendor, it were a kind of practical gibe at this poor, ruined man of show. (BR, 169)

While Coverdale announces a straightforward parallel between the room and the man, the room is more than Moodie's mirror. Not simply a stage set, the room becomes a good example of the ways in which past social and economic relationships reveal themselves through the structures they leave behind. Standing as a record of past activities and inhabitants, the house exhibits the ravages of time, neglect, and intentional destruction. In boarding-house fiction, reminders of these relationships often linger on either as rarely seen attic lodgers or as ghosts.[67] The Physiology of Boarding Houses describes a stately residence "humiliated to the condition of a Cheap Boarding House . . . [where] many a powdered beauty has [had], in ante-revolutionary days, a red-coated, cocked-hatted officer of King George as escort. If such a couple could, by the pale moonlight peering into the skylight above, and stealing down onto the shabby, cracked, dirty plastered wall, revisit the scene now!"[68] While memories of the past remain embedded in the building, changing economic demands force its (incomplete) transformation so that only a ghost can gain such an historically totalizing view of the landscape.

Although the colonial economy has given way to a budding mercantilism, its vestiges continue to exert a powerful force. As geographer David Harvey suggests, landscapes stand as monuments to the economic relationships that have produced them, and in turn they reinforce and help to maintain those relations. An urban landscape constructed under capitalism, then, becomes "the crowning glory of past capitalist development."[69] The governor's mansion testifies to the economic relations of the past. But it also bears witness to the struggle Harvey details between economic relationships and the landscapes they produce, in that "capital builds a physical landscape appropriate to its own condition at a particular moment in time, only to have to destroy it . . . at a subsequent point in time."[70] Reflecting his Marxist perspective, Harvey presents capitalism as a force that somewhat autonomously engages in building and remaking the urban landscape. But in *The Blithedale Romance,* individual actors, while bound by the relations that position them economically and geographically within the urban setting, act to shape their own environments, remaking their settings in order to extract the resources necessary for survival (such as kindling from the mantelpiece) in a changing economic landscape.

Yet *Blithedale* underscores Harvey's claim that urban consciousness is shaped by the city's physical environment by demonstrating the complexity of that consciousness. Harvey notes that "to dissect the urban process in all its fullness is to lay bare the roots of consciousness formation in the multi-layered material realities of daily life."[71] The "multi-layered material realities" of the palimpsest-like urban home presented in *Blithedale* point to complex formulations of urban consciousness. Moodie's room, for example, has exerted a profoundly transformative force on the man: "Into (his) brain each bare spot on the ceiling, every tatter of the paper-hangings, and all the splintered carvings of the mantel-piece, seen wearily through long years, had worn their several prints!" (*BR,* 176). Through a "familiarity with objects," his psyche is shaped by his immediate surroundings (*BR,* 176). Here, the physical environment exerts the power to shape individuals who exemplify the transformability and permeability of the city's structures.

In Hawthorne's novel, urban domestic spaces render the boundaries of property and self indistinct. The transformable, transparent Priscilla is completely a product of this urban environment, as is made clear from Moodie's story of her early upbringing. To describe Priscilla's initial appearance, Hawthorne draws on a Lamarckian conception of genetics, explaining that Priscilla embodies her parents as they have become. "The younger child, like his elder one [Zenobia], might be considered as the true offspring of both parents, and as the reflection of that state" (*BR,* 171). That is, Priscilla takes on the characteristics of both parents, at least one of whom, Moodie, has been completely transformed from a prior identity, in part by his actions and in part by the resulting environment. Priscilla inherits different characteristics from her father, the "unseen . . . grey and misty" Moodie, than Zenobia did in his previous incarnation as the flashy Fauntleroy. Thus, in contrast to the fully embodied Zenobia, the "tremulous" Priscilla "lack(s) human substance" (BR, 171). Dubbed "ghost-child," she is described as transparent: "the sun at midday would shine right through her; in the first gray of the twilight she lost all the distinctness of her outline; and if you followed the dim thing into a dark corner, behold! she was not there" (BR, 172). Born to a man transformed by his surroundings, Priscilla literally changes as the architecture transforms both her father and herself.

Like the structures she inhabits, Priscilla is mutable and permeable. Together, these qualities become more than a literary device to link her with the Veiled Lady or to render understandable her submission to more powerful personalities like Westervelt, Zenobia, and Hollingsworth; in fact, they mark her as produced by and particularly suited to urban spaces. Beyond being simply transparent, Priscilla becomes a medium through which the architectural features of her surroundings become visible. "[I]t seemed as if, were she to stand up in a sunbeam, it would pass right through her figure, and trace out the cracked and dusty window-panes upon the naked floor" (BR, 171). As de Certeau puts it, "In this place that is a palimpsest, subjectivity is already linked to the absence that structures it as existence."[72] That is, Priscilla embodies and utilizes the caesurae in the changing architecture that surrounds and shapes her. Emphatically a "personality," Zenobia is destroyed by a change in her economic status. Priscilla, in contrast, is mutable. She can adapt to new surroundings, transforming herself according to her environment's exigencies. This quality will make her the survivor she becomes.

As half-sisters raised in very different environments, Priscilla and Zenobia exemplify distinct subjectivities; Zenobia mirrors the stability associated with the past while Priscilla embodies the mutability of the modern. Throughout much of the novel, Priscilla is portrayed as weak, colorless, and cool in contrast to Zenobia's strong, vibrant warmth. Yet it is Priscilla, with "no free will," and none of the advantages of a wealthy upbringing (except eventually the inheritance) that Zenobia has, who survives and "triumphs" in her marriage to Hollingsworth while Zenobia drowns herself, her final appearance as a bloated, grey corpse effacing her once vivid beauty. Priscilla's ability to survive in the urban environment hinges on her transformability along with her ability to sell herself and her products on the modern market for luxury goods and entertainment. That she eventually ends up settling into a quiet, "retired" existence with Hollingsworth in the "Blithedale Pastures" chapter both highlights and makes ironic her ability to tear down and reconstruct herself according to the exigencies of the relations that define her (BR, 223).

Priscilla is, of course, the novel's most permeable character, a medium both by nature and by profession. Yet Priscilla's penetrability is shared by Coverdale and Moodie, and in Gillian Brown's reading, by most of the characters in the novel, all of whom are "impelled . . . to live in other lives" (*BR*, 179). As Coverdale remarks, "Hollingsworth, Zenobia, Priscilla! These three had absorbed my life into themselves" (*BR*, 179). Brown notes that, "In *The Blithedale Romance* . . . Hawthorne pictures individuality as always vulnerable to a self-interested mesmeric control," and that "the mesmerist makes commerce of individual penetrability."[73] Yet Priscilla is not simply vulnerable to others. Combined with her ability to transform herself, Priscilla's transparency gives her the mobility that the modern city requires for survival.

Attention to the relationship between Priscilla's identity and her surroundings adds a layer of complexity to critical formulations of Priscilla's role in the novel. Richard Brodhead convincingly argues that in her dual identity, Priscilla/the Veiled Lady is a "public-private" figure, a receptacle for anxieties and expectations fueling the rise of public figures who could fulfill the needs of domestic spectators. The term "public-private" usefully describes the novel's representations of space. For although Priscilla may have been "bred in a 'little room,'" her life has not "been circumscribed in such a way that extradomestic space has become terrifyingly alien to her."[74] The fact that "the sense of vast undefined space, pressing in from the outside against the black panes of our uncurtained windows, was fearful to the poor girl, heretofore accustomed to the narrowness of human limits," should not register simply as a "perfect description of the agoraphobia" of the era (*BR*, 36).[75] Though she may not relish her role as the Veiled Lady (quite the contrary), Priscilla embarks on several careers, not just on the stage but also as a maker of silk purses that traverse the networks of capital. Further, although her neighbors' "busy tongues spared Priscilla in one way" by not naming her as a prostitute, several critics have done so, illustrating that Priscilla's sphere is not as limited as her "little room" might imply (*BR*, 173).[76]

Priscilla is a product of the city—and in the urban frame her distinguishing transformability becomes visible. As Nina Baym points out, "In Boston, Priscilla comes to life. In the city she is in her element."[77] Costumed by Zenobia, Priscilla embodies a persona different from the Veiled Lady, the sickly slum girl, or the worshipful admirer. She transforms herself in response to changes in setting. For instance, when she imagines Zenobia, "it was as if, in her spiritual visits to her brilliant sister, a portion of the latter's brightness had permeated our dim Priscilla, and still lingered, shedding a faint illumination through the cheerless chamber, after she came back" (*BR*, 172). If her transparency makes her vulnerable to Westervelt, frightening the neighbors, who "averred that [Westervelt] had taken advantage of Priscilla's lack of earthly substance to subject her to himself, as his familiar spirit, through whose medium he gained cognizance of whatever happened, in regions near or remote," it becomes a decided advantage for the adolescent urbanite (*BR*, 173). Her facility for transformation, combined with her permeability, mark Priscilla as modern and connect her to other city people.

Chance, Connections, and Class in Ruth Hall's Lodgings

In *Ruth Hall,* Fanny Fern echoes Hawthorne's narrative claim that the industrial city produces a mobile, mutable urban subject, but Fern recasts the city as a place where networks and connections offer women the means to profit both personally and economically from their newfound mobility and flexibility. *Ruth Hall* shows how the melding of private and public spaces that happens in the city allows for women to develop public personalities, as well as the means to profit by them (almost) respectably. In this way, Ruth departs from Priscilla. It has been argued, of course, that Priscilla does profit from a public persona by prostituting herself. *Blithedale's* critics have not emphasized, however, the way in which Priscilla's real threat, her ability to move between classes, is elided in the novel. Though Coverdale may have been, as the novel's last line attests, "in love with—Priscilla!" the novel's class structure is maintained when the tenement girl marries Hollingsworth, the former laborer (*BR,* 228). *Ruth Hall,* in contrast, highlights and celebrates the class mobility made available to urban women who embrace mobility, mutability, and display of the self to the public gaze. Fern is far more graphic than Hawthorne in her descriptions of lower-class life in the city; even so, her narrative reveals that while residence in the slums transforms Ruth, it does not ruin her. Rather, the city elicits from the former boarding-school girl and sheltered wife the drive and market savvy that will bring her popularity and economic success as a writer. Like many of her counterparts in sentimental fiction, Ruth moves from prosperity to poverty and back again, but instead of enjoying her success only within the family circle, as Priscilla does, Ruth's residence in the city ultimately gives her a public voice—and cultural power—in a national network of homes.

Like the boarding houses that Hawthorne describes, boarding and lodging houses in *Ruth Hall* are settings where the boundaries maintaining a discrete subjectivity break down. However, *Ruth Hall* more thoroughly explores how the boarding house allows Ruth to make interpersonal connections that engender and sustain her agency. Ruth begins her urban life in a boarding house classed closer to Moodie's lodgings than Zenobia's; her boarding house becomes a site from which she can develop a career by selling her handiwork. Destitute and fairly desperate, Ruth and her two daughters take up residence "in a dark narrow street, in one of those heterogeneous boarding-houses abounding in the city" (*RH,* 73). Their neighbors are "clerks, market-boys, apprentices and sewing-girls"—though only "six miles" from their old cottage, Ruth's family has moved worlds away in terms of class distinction (*RH,*

73, 32). Ruth's urban home can support none of the cottage's aesthetics, spatial arrangements, or routines. Historically, for lodging-house tenants, "home
was scattered up and down the street. They slept in one building and ate in
another. The surrounding sidewalks and stores functioned as parts of each
resident's home."[78] The breakdown of boundaries separating home from
street becomes especially visible through Ruth's daughters, who spend much
of their time looking out of their attic windows at the street as Ruth writes.
The girls also go on errands for Ruth, and in these scenes Fern effectively conveys the overwhelming quality of the urban street by presenting it through a
child's perspective. Finally, the lodging house is where Ruth's own nuclear
family breaks down more completely: While she lives there Ruth is forced to
send her elder daughter Katie to live with her detested parents-in-law.[79]

Like other boarding-house fiction, *Ruth Hall* divests the boarding house
of the regenerative potential of "home" and presents urban domesticity as a
profitable venture. And not just for tenants. In fiction at least, if the boarding house projects a homelike appearance, this impression often serves as a
thin cover for a shrewd businesswoman's practice. The boarding-house proprietress is often described in periodical fiction as "an obliging, motherly kind
of a woman, who only [keeps] a few boarders just for company," the boarding house as a place where "'for a consideration' they will be received . . . 'into
the bosom of the family.'"[80] Historically, this distinction was probably gendered, for as hotels professionalized they were increasingly managed by men,
whereas women were the primary proprietors of boarding houses.[81] Yet the
"homelike" appearance of these fictional boarding houses fools only the most
naive boarders from the country, and the boarding house is quickly revealed
to be a place of business only distantly related to the idealized cottage home.

One distinctive feature of boarding-house business was the communal
dining room where tenants gathered for meals; *Ruth Hall* and other contemporary boarding-house stories satirize the potential of these rooms' contri-
bution to an elevating, homelike environment. Perhaps hoping to capitalize
on the potential of home life to improve its adherents, architectural determinist reformers who designed model boarding houses would often include
an "eating-room, where meals could be had or provisions purchased ready
for eating."[82] In fiction, however, the dining room rarely serves a noble purpose. The food always occasions gibes at inadequate portions and bad quality. For instance, in one story the narrator warns his readers that "if they
would rather have a time-honored carpet, and a table fuming with joints and
turkeys, than a bright new Brussels and a board whose platters are sparse
and delicately tenanted, let them avoid [the boarding house] as sailors would
an iceberg."[83] In "Mrs. Sad's Private Boarding House," breakfast consists
of a "tough beefsteak," and the proprietress has "succeeded in reducing her
boarders to excellent training" in taking "genteel" portions.[84] In Ruth's far
less genteel boarding house, "one plate suffices for fish, flesh, fowl, and

dessert; soiled tablecloths, sticky crockery, oily cookery and bad grammar predominate" (*RH,* 71). Along with marking Ruth's lodgings as lower-class, the mingling of fish, flesh, and fowl in this passage emphasizes the motif of mingling that is so prevalent in fiction about boarding houses.

For their reformers, denigrators, lampooners, and other commentators, the mingling among guests that characterized the urban boarding house was loaded with tension. The chance encounters made possible by boarding-house architecture—its dining rooms, parlors, hallways, and entrances—became a source of anxiety that reformers counteracted with measures such as prayer meetings and architectural reform.[85] Paul Groth notes that

> In rooming houses men's and women's lives crossed constantly. Gendered realms were scarcely circumscribed in the way that suburban or rural standards prescribed and the spatial arrangements of polite households reinforced. Single women in rooming houses shared hallways with single men, without familial or community supervision. Unlike the better hotels, there were not even servants or clerks to observe the activity.[86]

It was precisely because these lodgings were not "better" that they were seen as spatially disrupting the conventions from which the contained home gained its power.

In fiction, great narrative possibilities unfold in settings where men and women of different classes mix, as in the "fashionable boarding house" (fig. 3), where a flirtation clearly is developing between the seated woman and her standing admirer in the shadow of the snoring gentleman to her right. The surveillance that an older generation might have provided in a family home (recall the elder Mr. Hall's incessant "peeping" at Ruth) is asleep at the switch. In a later fictional example, *Little Women*'s Jo March meets her future husband, Professor Bhaer, in an urban boarding house where she is living and working out of Marmee's sight. Without chaperones, boarding-house dining rooms become places of courtship, both clandestine and open, where reading the countenance and clothing of the fellow traveler is crucial to success in the form of a financially advantageous marriage. Ruth, for instance, is eyed and her merits as a potential partner discussed by two of her fellow boarders, one of whom plans "to request 'the dragon' [the landlady] to let me sit next her at the table. I'll begin by helping the children, offering to cut up their victuals, and all that sort of thing—that will please the mother, you know; hey?" (*RH,* 74) Here, proximity, aided by the proprietress, will allow for courtship to take place. Interaction, surveillance, and elaborate plans to snare members of the opposite sex become commonplace features of boarding-house fiction, and in most cases these plans ultimately hinge on a desire to rise economically through marriage. When Ruth's poverty is revealed to her would-be suitors, their attentions evaporate.

The redemptive features of the homelike dining and sitting rooms lose their force in fiction, where they are revealed to be connected spaces that encourage sociability and reward it with class mobility. Ruth's middle-class sensibilities are offended by the layout of a boarding house that requires the landlady to ask her gentlemen boarders to smoke in their rooms because, as she says, "the parlor is the only place I have to dress in" (*RH,* 74). But even as they offend her, the physical and economic relations engendered by the boarding house elicit from Ruth a distinctly urban identity.

The breakdown of cottage domesticity forces Ruth to find alternative means of survival; in tracking Ruth's attempts to navigate urban networks Fern analyzes the development of a model of modern female subjectivity that is far more positive than those Hawthorne constructs for Zenobia or Priscilla. For as Ruth expands her conception of home to include the networks in which urban homes are enmeshed, the lodging house becomes the site from which she begins to make the connections that enable her to succeed as a writer. Karen Waldron notes: "Ruth's city life, her subjective exposure to 'a decrepit old woman' (*RH,* 90) or a 'wan and haggard face' at a tenement or brothel window, finally articulates what she has been experiencing all along, the voyeuristic invasion and language that prove that there is no protected private sphere. The result is authorship."[87] Importantly, Ruth makes her connections in networks and among individuals far removed from her immediate family. They happen among what Henri Lefebvre calls the "crevices" of the urban.[88] Ruth emerges from these crevices with rich material for storytelling; the stories she tells resist and disrupt the status quo. Her writing emblematizes and broadcasts the threat that Ruth's economically mobile body represents for an ideology of domestic containment. In *The Practice of Everyday Life,* Michel de Certeau explores the possibilities for resisting the totalizing urban networks through narrative, explaining that "beneath the discourses that idealogize the city, the uses and combinations of powers that have no readable identity proliferate."[89] One mode of resistance, though not necessarily readable, is the story. According to de Certeau, "stories diversify, rumors totalize . . . stories [become] private and sink into the secluded places in neighborhoods, families and individuals."[90] Privacy is emphasized in *Ruth Hall* by the attic location from which Ruth writes. Yet Ruth takes her stories into the public arena by commodifying them for the popular press, claiming the networks of the publishing industry as a means for both economic and personal gain. In the networked domestic spaces of the city, Ruth makes her private life into public property.

In *Ruth Hall,* the urban landscape dissolves the boundaries separating an interior self from a public, commodifiable subjectivity while disassembling the structure of the extended family. Fern's contemporaries and current critics alike note how stridently the novel condemns Ruth's family's behavior. In her introduction to the 1986 reprint of *Ruth Hall,* Joyce W. Warren cites an 1885 review: "As we wish no sister of ours, nor no female relative to show toward us, the ferocity she has displayed toward her nearest relatives we take occasion to censure this book that might initiate such a possibility."[91] In part, this condemnation arose from the fact that Fern's vitriol extended from her fiction into her own family; Fern particularly singled out her brother, influential editor Nathaniel P. Willis (fictionalized as Hyacinth Ellet) for attack. Similarly, Elizabeth Cady Stanton noted that *Ruth Hall* presented "tyrannical parents, husbands and brothers."[92] Fern's vituperative prose emphasizes Ruth's condemnation of her father, brother, in-laws, and other relatives, but even as Fern castigates unfeeling families, her heroine is reconstructing an alternative family through the city's networks. As Maria C. Sanchez points out, "*Ruth Hall* traverses the . . . home and marketplace to conjoin them in a fantastical rendition of that affective family [of sentimental literature]: it mourns and simultaneously reproduces it."[93]

In making use of the city networks required to further her career, Ruth demonstrates the market-oriented mentality of the modern individual. The virtues of home, hard work, faith, and family, which by the logic of the domestic plot should have brought financial and emotional support to a young widow, break down in *Ruth Hall*; chance, instinct, and interpersonal connections allow her to survive and eventually prosper. Chance operates to help Ruth on several occasions: once, a former friend recognizes daughter Katie on the street and upon learning Ruth's declassé address, gives her some money; later, Ruth is rescued from a fire by the very same Johnny Galt she employed as a farmhand in her cottage days. Instinct makes Ruth decide to retain the copyright to her book, a decision that earns her enough money to reclaim her daughter. And connections made in the streets, in the boarding house hallways, and through the modern popular press find her a devoted readership and an astute manager. In this way, she resembles a far better known urban subject of the nineteenth century: Horatio Alger's Ragged Dick.

If Priscilla's modern identity hinges on her ability to dissolve, Ruth's depends on her ability to connect. The networks of the publishing industry bring her into contact with Mr. Walter, the publisher who writes to Ruth out of a "brotherly interest" far more supportive than the interest demonstrated by Ruth's actual brother, who is also an editor and publisher. Ruth writes "a long letter—a sweet, sisterly letter—pouring out her long pent-up feelings, as though Mr. Walter had indeed been her brother" (*RH*, 143–44). The nominal relationship becomes more meaningful than the biological as Ruth and Mr. Walter maintain and develop their bond through the mail. Mr. Walter's connections and advice help Ruth to attain financial independence, and he continues to help her through the novel's end. Though there is no indication that they will marry, the novel shows that the connections forged through the networks of the popular press and the postal service afford Ruth economic mobility and self-sufficiency. Ruth does gain a family, but its form does not correspond to the cottage plans of most domestic fiction. Thus, although the shared spaces of the city work to erode the traditional family, at the same time they offer the potential to reconstitute an urban family more desirable, supportive, and profitable than Ruth's family of origin.

Importantly, the success of Ruth's writing career does not depend on familial connections or an "objective" examination process in the ways that her attempts at careers as seamstress, washerwoman, and teacher do; modern urban subjectivity revolves around creatively adapting to a changing environment rather than playing established roles. Ruth's successful authorship depends on two related networks: the network of the publishing industry that disseminates her material and the network of readers who integrate "Floy," as Ruth is known in the press, into their personal lives. Letters from Floy's fans comprise several complete chapters of *Ruth Hall*. Most of these are concerned with personal matters: marriage proposals, family troubles, even the deaths of pets. Here we see a meta-version of a phenomenon David Henkin sees at work in the typical epistolary novel of the day that "encouraged readers to imagine their own experiences while reading as similar to the emotionally charged (often written) encounters of the books' characters."[94] *Ruth Hall*'s readers might identify with Ruth's personal trials, or they might see themselves in the fictional readers included in the text. Either way, the novel incorporates readers as participants in its construction, developing readers whose subjectivity is located "not in the ability to internalize and resolve exchanges among self-possessed speakers, but rather in the ability to peruse, select, discard, and reassemble a range of messages and options."[95] We will see this ability embodied in many successful fictive urbanites, such as Verena Tarrant in *The Bostonians,* whose almost unconsciously assembled speeches meld ideas from a variety of sources, and *Sister Carrie*'s Carrie Meeber, who derives her urban affect by choosing which qualities to emulate in the women she sees around her. Along with this autonomy comes an opportunity to join a new type of community.

Just as Mr. Walter becomes Ruth's "brother" through the mail, Ruth's readers become part of her family through modern communication conduits. Among her readers, rampant gossip about Floy's real identity both increases newspaper circulation and emphasizes narrative's ability to connect its readers to one another, making *Ruth Hall* exemplary of what Karen Waldron terms the "private-public novel."[96] As Richard Brodhead notes, "Ruth's fan mail makes clear that a home audience consumes her work to help satisfy cravings domestic life has not allayed."[97] These connections become yet another network as readers imagine themselves to be part of Floy's "family" of readers. Thus, the novel helps to construct what Henkin refers to as the "new urban public" of the nineteenth century, in that it "collapse[s] the distinction between imagining a community and participating in it."[98] Ruth's phenomenal success, then, depends on her ability to emulate the networks that dominate her urban environment; even as the city annexes its hinterlands, so does Ruth.

Breaking Down Architectural Determinism through Narrative

Ruth Hall's urban identity evokes a great deal more optimism about the prospects of modernity than does Hawthorne's anxious representation of vulnerable, mutable, deceptive, artificial urbanites. Part of the difference resides in the structures of the two narratives. *Ruth Hall* is a narrative pastiche. Successive brief chapters feature different narrative voices including Ruth, her family members, her neighbors, her readers, and an omniscient narrator. Lefebvre sees "plurality, coexistence and simultaneity in the urban patterns, ways of living urban life."[99] This simultaneity derives from the actions of individuals within what Lefebvre terms the urban fabric. In *Ruth Hall,* simultaneity, expressed in part by Ruth's experiences, is reinforced by the simultaneity of the narrative and the multiplicity of voices that tell Ruth's story. Together, these voices register resistance to the unitary plot of the traditional romance, a narrative that embodies a more private, individual notion of reading and writing.[100] *Blithedale* is emphatically a romance, and as such emphasizes "Hawthorne's unwillingness to use modern fictional techniques to deal with modern issues."[101] At the same time, Hawthorne's novel is written through Coverdale's point of view, and this unreliable narrator both emphasizes the ways in which urban space undermines attempts at isolation or a unitary point of view and argues that vision is always partial and is itself frequently deceptive.[102] Coverdale's fragmented narration derives from his voyeurism; the narrative highlights the continual peeping and observing that is shaped by the architecture and other features of the urban landscape that surrounds him.

Coverdale may be a voyeur, but he hardly has the power de Certeau attributes to the urban voyeur of "'seeing the whole,' of looking down on, totalizing the most immoderate of human texts."[103] In this novel, sight, however unreliable, is Coverdale's major, if partial, source of information about his environment. In addition, vision operates as an important connector between spaces. Even if Coverdale's vision is partial, Hawthorne's use of this vision within the narrative anticipates cultural geographer Denis Cosgrove's formulation of "the tension between visual and textual truth . . . as a dialectic between representational modes, or metaphors, historically in a constant and intense struggle over meaning."[104] Just as Coverdale's pastoral vision reveals the extent to which the rural landscape of Blithedale serves the economic and aesthetic uses of the urban, Coverdale's urban vision, here exemplified by the view from his hotel window, serves to structure a penetrable, networked urban space.

The stylish boarding house and the hotel's shared backyards allow Coverdale simultaneously to continue the peeping that occupied much of his time at Blithedale and extract himself from the messy, complex urban. He wants to "linger on the brink, or to hover in the air above it" (*BR*, 136). Critics have read this hotel room as a "hermitage" where Coverdale enjoys "social isolation and physical separation," while in fact he remains highly engaged in his urban surroundings.[105] Unlike de Certeau's voyeur whose "text . . . lies before [his] eyes," Coverdale's view both asserts itself as an unreadable text and draws him back down to the street to tangle once again with the "bewitching world" of the urban.[106]

Coverdale's window offers him the opportunity to get around the barriers to vision enforced by streets and sidewalks and gain a more complete, if more removed, sense of his surroundings. Yet while his view simplifies what he sees, allowing him to streamline the objects of his gaze into something simultaneously theatrical and silent, Coverdale cannot avoid being drawn back into the very scenes that his detached perspective creates. For example, Coverdale can see Zenobia "like a full-length picture, in the space between the heavy festoons of the window-curtains" (*BR*, 143). She is objectified, an image open to his gaze. Viewed, her actions transform themselves into Coverdale's private drama until she looks back, recognizes him, and lets fall "a white linen curtain between the festoons of the damask ones. . . . like a drop-curtain of a theatre in the interval between the acts" (*BR*, 147). The object of his gaze can assert herself to disrupt his formulation of her by using the very props appropriate to the scene he has created.

Coverdale cannot confine his urban visions to the objectifying gaze; indeed, he is drawn, "in compliance with [a] sudden impulse, [to find himself] actually within the house, the rear of which, for two days past, [he] had been so sedulously watching" (*BR*, 149). Combining of voyeurism and participation yields a very different city for Coverdale. In short, he must confront the objects of his gaze, especially Priscilla and Zenobia, as acting subjects who can and do disrupt his reading. In de Certeau's terms, "a *migrational*, or metaphorical city thus slips into the clear text of the planned and readable city."[107] Through episodes of chance encounters, changing identities, and misreadings, all part of Coverdale's urban experience just as they are part of any urban dweller's, the novel constructs the urban as a space where architectural determinism is both built and broken down. In *The Blithedale Romance*, the migrational city's force is magnified through narrative. The novel's readers are denied a "planned and readable" text by a very unreliable narrator.

The "Happy Ending"

The modern city's networked spaces in *The Blithedale Romance* and *Ruth Hall* shape characters who are enmeshed and implicated in urban networks of communication and exchange. Though a nominally rural landscape is presented in the settlement at Blithedale, that rural landscape is firmly implicated in the urban economy and aesthetic. It is constructed by the hands and eyes of urbanites who are attempting to create an environment for their own uses. Yet in exploring the development of urban subjects in relation to their urban homes, *The Blithedale Romance* helps to develop a paradigm for conceptualizing a modern urban subjectivity through narrative. By fictively reconfiguring "private" and "public" spaces, via the boarding house, the hotel, and the backyards, the novel demonstrates how an urban setting characterized by connection and open to a reader's gaze marks its inhabitants as urban and rewards them for taking on the architectural qualities—the permeability and mutability—of the built spaces they inhabit.

Ruth Hall uses the model of porosity exemplified by the domestic spaces of Hawthorne's urban landscape to construct a model of authorship that resolves private concerns through the public narratives Ruth publishes. By publishing elements of her life, as well as gleaning material for her writing from the exigencies of her domestic situation, Ruth maintains the agency necessary to attain financial success and necessary also for her to build an alternative model of family after the dissolution of her own. At the same time, the novel's structure, particularly the inclusion of Ruth's readers in her narrative, argues for the development of participatory urban subjects. In short, *Ruth Hall* asserts that a powerful modern individuality is better enabled by the permeable urban spaces Ruth inhabits than by the realities of cottage life. And this assertion troubles the rhetoric of nineteenth-century domesticity just as powerfully as Fern's substitution of a stock certificate for a marriage certificate unsettles the end of a novel that begins so conventionally.

In emphasizing the agency that city dwellers exert as they move through their urban settings, *Ruth Hall* can be seen as a direct response to the "happy ending" Hawthorne proposes or satirizes for Priscilla with Coverdale. Though Hawthorne co-opts and questions the happy ending of the sentimental genre by turning it into a scene of subtle horror, Fern rewrites this ending by transforming it into the beginning of her own heroine's tale. *Ruth Hall* reverses Priscilla's trajectory from urban boarding house to Downingesque cottage and claims the city's potential as a location offering both peril and profit for the people who inhabit it by choice or from necessity. The futures Hawthorne and Fern imagine for modern men and women—and the types of urban settings within which they will thrive—would thread through novels set in U.S. cities for the half-century that followed. After the Civil War made clear that the nation's future was largely industrial, American writers and planners would grapple anew with how changing paradigms of publicity and privacy would shape the future of nature and the nature of home in the urban United States. Whether viewed with anxious irony, as by Henry James in *The Bostonians*, or with progressive conservatism, as we see in the designs for Central Park, new tensions over the fate of home in the city emerged to shape the nation's physical and fictive landscapes.

Chapter 2

The City's Drawing-Room

Spatial Practice in The Bostonians *and Central Park*

The number of persons in circulation was enormous—so great that the question of how they had got there, from their distances, and would get away again, in the so formidable public conveyances, loomed, in the background, like a skeleton at the feast; but the general note was thereby, intensely, the "popular," and the brilliancy of the show proportionately striking. —Henry James on Central Park[1]

While the shifting domestic roles and expectations for women in the mid-nineteenth century industrial city empowered a character like Ruth Hall, the opportunities that opened to Ruth in the changing city threatened her fictional brother, Hyacinth Ellet. One of *Ruth Hall*'s more ridiculous characters, Hyacinth is a well-connected, immoral fop of an editor who rejects his inconveniently impoverished sister and subsequently refuses to use his sizable influence to help her break into a career in publishing. However, a severe pen-lashing awaits him; as Ruth seizes publishing networks to further her own career, she takes her revenge upon her brother's reputation.

Hyacinth's historical counterpart, Nathaniel P. Willis, was the influential if "snobbish" tastemaker who edited nineteenth-century periodicals such as the *Home Journal*.[2] His published views on domestic ideology, and particularly on cottage domesticity, were directly opposed to those that his sister, Sara Payson Willis Parton, published under her pseudonym, Fanny Fern. Like his sister, Willis both witnessed and participated in the mid-nineteenth century evolution of the American urban landscape.

Nathaniel Willis cannily used nascent urban networks of publication and publicity to earn money and fame as the quintessential man about town, yet even he occasionally needed to escape from the pressures of the city.[3] Like many members of New York's social elite, Willis kept homes both in New York City and in the Hudson River Valley, where in 1853 he commissioned a country villa from Andrew Jackson Downing's protégé, British-born architect Calvert Vaux. The resulting villa, called Idlewild, was spectacular. "High up among the trees, and apparently on the very edge of a precipitous ascent, it seems to peer over the topmost branches of the dark pines and to command the whole valley below."[4] Overlooking Newburgh Bay, the Hudson River, and four of its tributaries, the house and setting combined the beautiful with the picturesque. The commission was an unquestionable coup for the young Vaux; of the thirty houses pictured in his 1857 book *Villas and Cottages,* Idlewild is the only one displayed with a testimonial letter from its owner. Yet as the city grew and the pace of urban life quickened, a country villa was no longer refuge enough. New Yorkers like Willis would desire an escape within the city—a place where they could experience rejuvenating encounters with nature without going out of town. At the time, however, New York lacked the appropriate facilities. As Willis put it in 1844, "as a metropolis of wealth and fashion, New York has one great deficiency—that of a driving park."[5] Again, Calvert Vaux designed a solution to Willis's problem, this time with his plans for Central Park.

In partnership with Frederick Law Olmsted, Vaux designed the Greensward Plan for Central Park in 1858. The park was intended to offer New Yorkers, and not just those of the growing carriage-driving class, a respite from the business of the city. Vaux and Olmsted believed that the park literally could cure urban ills: Trees would help to clean the smoky air, and city dwellers could purge their urban malaise simply by walking or driving the paths that wound among the park's meadows, ponds, and grottos. Central Park was the landscape architects' living testament to their belief that the environment was the salient force governing personal and social development. Together, Olmsted and Vaux transformed the landscape in order to carry out a social mission; they hoped that the park would produce urbanites embodying civilization's highest ideals.

Vaux and Olmsted understood that the physical landscape would change over time. But even these visionaries could not foresee that the development of transportation and communication networks in New York would transform the city and make Central Park the emblem of the profound cultural shift that had begun to reverberate through American cities in the 1850s and only accelerated after the Civil War. These urban networks would invert configurations of and ideas about public and private space, destabilizing relationships between environment and subject both in theory and in practice. To an observer like Henry James, the changes that transformed New York, and with it the nation, had profound implications for its citizens. In his novels, James returns again and again to the question of who would populate an increasingly urban America.[6] Characters whose lives are tied deeply to industrialism appear throughout James's œuvre, from Christopher Newman in *The American* to Maggie Verver in *The Golden Bowl*. Yet James's concerns

FIGURE 6. Currier and Ives, Central Park, The Drive, 1862. Library of Congress, Prints and Photographs Division, LC-USZ62-971.

about just how the modern American city would affect the home, as well as the ideologies of privacy, stability, and interiority it enforced, receive their fullest fictional treatment in *The Bostonians* (1886), where the very notions of privacy and domesticity must be reconfigured spatially in response to new urban realities.[7] In the novel, Basil Ransom's reaction to the modern American city is to retreat to a time in which the public and private spheres seem to be distinct. He withdraws from the industrial era to the "earlier" space of Mississippi, taking Verena Tarrant with him. Basil's cousin Olive Chancellor, in contrast, gradually seizes the opportunities that arise as spheres that she might prefer to keep separate inexorably begin to mingle. Following Verena's example, Olive opens herself to the city's networks and attempts to use them to further her political and social goals.

In *The Bostonians*, James conveys his uneasiness with the onset of modernity through his treatment of urban domestic spaces. In this chapter, I read *The Bostonians* in the context of the ideas about public and private space encoded in Central Park's design in order to trace the ways in which modern notions of publicity and privacy are spatialized in the novel. Like Vaux and Olmsted as well as, more recently, Mona Domosh, I draw a parallel between residential and park architecture, and consider the ways in which parks, like homes, operate as urban domestic spaces.[8] While Vaux and Olmsted saw in the urbanization of private spaces the promise for an increasingly civilized and democratized American society, James depicts the inversion of interiority far more ambivalently. *The Bostonians* examines the effects of late nineteenth-century shifts in public and private space, showing how the modern home, permeated by publicity, opens the contained self to urban networks.[9] James's nostalgia for the home as a site of containment reveals an anxiety that echoes Hawthorne and anticipates later writers such as Jacob Riis. In the process he narrates a widely shared response to the urban landscape that geographer Doreen Massey has explored: the "fear which is apparently felt by some, including many writers on the subject, when the boundaries dissolve (or are felt to do so), when the geography of social relations forces us to recognize our interconnectedness."[10] Yet seen as its designers saw it, as an urban domestic space, Central Park supports Massey's larger argument that domestic spaces never have been contained or fixed. Rather, as Olive's drawing-room comes to demonstrate, "just as personal identities are argued to be multiple, shifting, possibly unbounded, so also . . . are the identities of place."[11] Exploring the spatial relations at play in Central Park elucidates the new relation between an unstable environment and a shifting subject that emerges in James's text.

Central Park: Urban Space, Social Function

Like *The Bostonians*, Central Park put theories of environment on center stage in the changing urban landscape. Designed to improve New York and serve as a model for the nation, the park was to be part of "an ideal American city where landscape architecture, housing, and urban physical and social planning were intertwined."[12] To this end, the theories shaping Central Park's design ranged from the aesthetic to the physiological, blending an ineffable sense of physical beauty with hypotheses about the physical operations of sight. Embracing the ideas of Edmund Burke and his heirs, Olmsted and Vaux designed spaces with the understanding that the eye offered access to the outside world and opened a person's interior to the outside. By connecting interior to exterior, Burke claimed, the process of seeing allowed for transformative influence to occur.[13] This influence could inspire individual artistic production; Calvert Vaux believed that such internal transformation could have societal implications. Vaux argues in *Villas and Cottages* that sight is not merely the most important physical sense, but that it operates metaphysically as well. "[F]or the light of the body is the eye," Vaux writes, "and it is to the eye, with the infinite host of progressive ideas, to which it acts as the mysterious portal, that the design of every building has the opportunity of artistically ministering."[14] Here, the eye becomes a mechanism

by which shared visions can be internalized and individualized. At the same time, an individual who partakes in the ministry of beauty will necessarily produce it for others; Vaux's designs aim to tap this dual process of aesthetic influence. For Vaux, then, beauty had individual and social significance.

In his designs for buildings and carefully constructed landscapes, Vaux aimed to create transformative spaces. Vaux and Olmsted's plans for Central Park reveal how artistically these improving visions were built. Adopting Andrew Jackson Downing's professional designation as landscape architects, Vaux and Olmsted planned landforms, selected plantings, and designed architectural features that would coalesce into an aesthetically ennobling landscape. Like landscape painters, they hoped to recreate in Central Park the "civilizing and uplifting function of landscape" that middle-class Americans increasingly applauded.[15] In Central Park, urban transformation would begin with an individual's vision. "Adapted to please the eye," Olmsted notes in an 1870 address to the American Social Science Association on "Public Parks and the Enlargement of Towns," the park's "circumstances are all favorable to a pleasurable wakefulness of the mind without stimulating exertion."[16] Later in the lecture, Olmsted emphasizes that influence extends through the eye to the mind. He writes, "a great object of all that is done in a park, of all the art of a park, is to influence the minds of men through their imagination."[17] Carefully designed and controlled landscapes like Central Park or paintings, as art historian Angela Miller notes, "worked better than actual landscapes in inculcating values."[18] And these values, Olmsted asserted, could be made universal and widely accessible; whether bourgeois businessman or Bowery Boy, anyone who saw the landscape would experience a similar elevation. "No one," Olmsted argues, "can doubt that [Central Park] exercises a distinctly harmonizing and refining influence upon the most unfortunate and the most lawless classes of the city, an influence favorable to courtesy, self-control, and temperance."[19] Significantly, the influence that could unite harmoniously an increasing diversity of New Yorkers would come in part from subtle visual allusions to bourgeois domesticity.

Olmsted and Vaux incorporated visual and ideological references to the cottage home into their plans for Central Park in order to civilize the urban psyche. Even in the urbanizing nation, the home was still considered the single most powerful influence on individual development. As Oliver P. Smith noted in 1852, "Nothing has more to do with the morals, civilization, and the refinement of the nation, than its prevailing architecture. . . . Our minds and morals are subject to constant influence and modification, gradual yet lasting, by the inanimate walls with which we are surrounded."[20] Accordingly, Vaux and Olmsted use a language of domestic interiors to describe the largest outdoor space in Manhattan. Vaux "thought of the Terrace as the Park's drawing-room,"[21] while Olmsted hoped that the public park could take on the character of "a parlor" where city dwellers would (figuratively, of course) "spread carpets on the floor to gain in quiet, and hang drapery in their windows and papers on their walls to gain in seclusion and beauty."[22] Olmsted extends his metaphor of the park as the city's parlor so far as to call trees "the permanent furniture of the city."[23] Evoking cozy domestic scenes, Olmsted's descriptions are "a pictorial expression of social containment"; the homelike park is framed by the city yet impervious to it.[24] But in reality, neither the park nor the home it was designed to evoke was nearly so enclosed; the influence of the park, its designers hoped, would extend, like Beecher's idealized home, far beyond its physical bounds.

In promising to improve physical space, heal individuals, and shape society, Central Park echoed the improving and disciplining functions of the home so central to the sentimental fiction that remained popular even after its heyday in the 1850s. As a built landscape, the park blurs boundaries between nature and culture; in a similar blurring, the city's most open space becomes an intimate domestic space. The park begins to resemble:

> a familiar domestic gathering, where the prattle of the children mingles with the easy conversation of the more sedate, the bodily requirements satisfied with good cheer, fresh air, agreeable light, moderate temperature, and furniture and decorations adapted to please the eye. . . . The circumstances are all favorable to a pleasurable wakefulness of the mind without stimulating exertion; and the close relation of family life, the association of children, of mothers, of lovers, of those who may be lovers, stimulate and keep alive the more tender sympathies, and give play to faculties such as may be dormant in business or on the promenade; while at the same time the cares of providing in detail for all the wants of the family, guidance, instruction, reproof, and the dutiful reception of guidance, instruction, reproof, are, as matters of conscious exertion, as far as possible laid aside.[25]

A middle space resembling Leo Marx's pastoral, the park "naturally" evokes the best qualities of the domestic sphere, screening out the evident discipline necessary to make the family function.

This mode of discipline has powerful counterparts in domestic ideology, particularly as Catharine Beecher conceived of it. Both as a visual construct and as a homelike space, the park becomes profoundly transformative for the individual and for society. As in the home, in the park the mind can "unbend" and accept an improving influence. After this experience, transformed emissaries can be sent forth into the world as civilizing agents. Olmsted and Vaux believed that the paradigm of societal improvement via domestic discipline was not limited to the sphere where mother presided; Olmsted notes that the "mingling," "association," and "close relation" he connects with the domestic scene generally can be extended to the park. This extension is possible because Olmsted's conceptions of home and park are far more flexible

than his "parlor" images imply to an audience of literary critics trained to read domestic space as a "separate sphere."

Although the park-as-parlor might seem to signify containment, neither Olmsted nor Vaux understood the home as contained space per se. Rather, they believed that domestic spaces, particularly in urban homes, were organized by internal and external connections. The Central Park Terrace, which Vaux designed to be the park's drawing-room, with its fountain, wide stairways, and ample gathering space, encourages interaction (figure 7).[26]

Shortened from "withdrawing room," the term "drawing-room" originally signified a private sanctum within a home otherwise characterized by sociability.[27] Vaux, however, did not exactly embrace this notion of the drawing-room in his design for the Terrace; neither did he consider it a necessary component of his housing designs. In *Villas and Cottages*, for example, he advocates eliminating the private room "called either library or drawing-room," in order to cut costs, or at least combining it with the dining room.[28] He writes, "there is no necessity in any country house that such a room should be restricted to its use in one purpose."[29] Instead, Vaux architecturally combines the solitary, interior space of the library with the

FIGURE 7. Terrace and gondola, Central Park, New York, 1894. Library of Congress, Prints and Photographs Division, LC-USZ62-113569.

highly sociable space of the dining room. "Fitted up with books, and enlivened by engravings," the library also is enlivened by the family. Mixing
solitude and sociability, the library-cum-dining room becomes "one of the
most agreeable [rooms] in the house, so as to heighten the value of this constant and familiar reunion as much as possible, and to encourage in every
way, by external influences, a spirit of refinement and liberal hospitality."[30]
As in the Tremont House, whose sliding walls allowed for flexible use, Vaux
designed his cottage interiors for multiple purposes, architecturally blending
private and public spaces so that the positive qualities of one, in this case the
"refinement" of the library, might influence the dining room's potentially
more lively interactions.

In addition to changing the spatial arrangements of the cottage home,
Vaux designed urban dwellings that would reshape city living radically.
When he moved to Manhattan in 1857, Vaux "proposed the first design for
New York City apartment dwellings, or 'separate suites of rooms under the
same roof' on the 'European plan.'" His design, fittingly named the Parisian
Buildings, "was a novel idea for New York of the 1850s where hotels, boarding houses or room rentals, whether for families or individuals, were the
norm, except for crowded slum-like tenement buildings with hall or outside
toilets."[31] But Vaux did more than propose designs for apartments; when
New York's first apartment building, the Stuyvesant Apartments, opened in
1869, Vaux and his family moved in immediately.[32]

In arguing that a blend of private and communal spaces would best suit
and shape the growing city's inhabitants, Vaux dramatically revised notions
of urban domesticity, offering a middle ground between rural isolation and
the excessive urban connections that Hawthorne describes with alarm in
The Blithedale Romance. Vaux was particularly interested in designing a
middle ground for the urban family, for he, like Downing and Beecher, maintained a belief that domestic spaces did shape their inhabitants, even if their
homes happened to be in cities. He writes, "a family may live at a hotel or
in a boarding-house, but the ceaseless publicity that ensues, the constant
change, and the entire absence of all individuality in the everyday domestic
arrangements, will always render this method of living distasteful, as a permanent thing, to the heads of families who have any taste for genuine home
comforts."[33] He presents apartments as a desirable housing choice because the
space can be made more private, permanent, and personalized than a boarding house or hotel, blending "home comforts" with urban convenience. But
Vaux clearly understands the Hawthornean fear of excessive connection, and
designs accordingly. He anticipates that a dark public staircase in the building's center—a site where residents might mingle uncontrolled—could easily
cause "a prejudice . . . to be excited against the whole effect." Vaux counter-
acts this prejudice against shared internal spaces by designing attractive stairways that are "light, airy, and elegant; and, if possible, lighter, airier, and more

elegant than any other part of the house."[34] Like Central Park's Terrace, the Parisian Building's common spaces receive Vaux's special aesthetic attention. In addition to the stairway, Vaux included balconies and airshafts that allowed for light and air to enter exterior and interior rooms. His attempts to heighten the appeal of his novel design reveal a clear understanding of his middle-class clientele's anxieties about mingling, their desires for "home comforts," and their conceptions of how and when these comforts should be shared.

In all of his designs, including those for the Parisian Buildings, Vaux consistently advocates taking a building's particular location into consideration. In *Villas and Cottages,* he urges that "country houses . . . be adapted to the location, and not the location to the design, for it is undesirable, and generally impracticable, to make the natural landscape subservient to the architectural composition."[35] Vaux carries this environmental commitment into the city, where the cultural landscape continually remakes and obscures what is "natural." In New York, that means incorporating the peculiarities of an urban blend of public and private into the living spaces. In his descriptions of the Parisian Buildings, Vaux notes that he is working from European designs for apartments but is adapting them to suit the needs and preferences of the American urbanite. For instance, Vaux explains the lack of an open interior courtyard by noting that in New York: "Every family that owns or rents a house wishes to have the principal parlor command a view of the street; and American ladies, who are in the habit of spending the greater part of their time in their own apartments, think it far more lively and cheerful to look out on a busy thoroughfare than on a monotonous quadrangle, however elegantly it may be decorated."[36] Although the apartments are designed to accommodate American women's preference to remain at home and pursue a style of living reminiscent of that encouraged by the detached home, Vaux's design also incorporates these women's fascination with the outside and the "busy thoroughfares" of the urban scene. The exterior views both acknowledge and heighten the urban home's connection to its location, updating another feature of urban architecture recalled by Edith Wharton: "those little mirrors which her Dutch ancestors were accustomed to affix to their upper windows, so that from the depths of an impenetrable domesticity they might see what was happening in the street."[37] These thoroughfares, along with streetcars and later, subways, eventually would allow women's participation in the public sphere that they could only gaze upon in the mid-1850s. Central Park would help to speed this transition.

Domestic Influence in Urban Space

Though they evoked images of middle- and upper-class domestic arrangements in their designs for Central Park, Olmsted and Vaux emphasized that

the park was designed to be used by all of the city's social classes.[38] For both
men, the city was a place of crowds, energy, and economic activity where
people of different classes and nationalities mingled; in cities, they agreed,
civilization was at its best. Personally, Vaux reveled in the urban and spent
most of his seventy-one years living in Manhattan. Olmsted was more ambivalent. He saw the potential for the civilized city to turn dangerous, threatening the body, "the mind and moral strength." One possible danger resided
in the crowd, where, "to merely avoid collision with those we meet and pass
upon the sidewalks, we have constantly to watch, to foresee, and to guard
against their movements. . . . Every day of their lives," he writes, city dwellers "have seen thousands of their fellow-men, have met them face to face,
have brushed against them, and yet have had no experience of anything in
common with them."[39] One cure for the mental and physical strains urbanites endured could be found in the park, whose foliage could screen out both
the city's "confined and vitiated air" and the close physical presence of
other bodies.[40] The park, Olmsted hoped, could serve as a common experience, one that could transform the dangerous crowd into benevolent
"fellow-men."

Whether domesticated or "natural," the park was presented as the city's
opposite; it was constructed deliberately to allow the city dweller an opportunity to trade grey streets for green grass. To Olmsted, the park's green
space only made sense in the context of its urban surroundings: The antidote
it offered to the sights and sounds of the city ultimately fitted users to participate in urban life. He writes, "the park should, as far as possible, complement the town. . . . Let your buildings be as picturesque as your artists
can make them. This is the beauty of the town. Consequently, the beauty of
the park should be the other. It should be the beauty of the fields, the
meadow, the prairie, of the green pastures, and the still waters."[41] Into his
litany of images central to the canon of American landscape painting, Olmsted incorporates the language of the twenty-third psalm, situating the park
and its social function as a simultaneously secular and religious experience.
The park ministers aesthetically and economically to the growing city.

In order to be "efficiently attractive to the great body of citizens," Olmsted argues, the park must offer city dwellers a kind of human contact that
is diametrically opposed to the brush of bodies on the streets.[42] The park,
then, must be simultaneously close to and far away from the city.

> We want a ground to which people may easily go after their day's work is
> done, and where they may stroll for an hour, seeing, hearing, and feeling noth-
> ing of the bustle and jar of the streets, where they shall, in effect, find the city
> put far away from them. . . . We want, especially, the greatest possible contrast
> with the restraining and confining conditions of the town, those conditions
> which compel us to walk circumspectly, watchfully, jealously, which compel us
> to look closely upon others without sympathy.[43]

The park blurs the temporal and spatial differences between the city's rush and the soothing "greensward," allowing people who live near enough to the park to experience both bustling and calm landscapes on a daily basis. In creating, recuperating, and enforcing this visual organization, Central Park distills the disciplinary power of domesticity and broadcasts it on a carefully constructed screen of nature. As Henry James would later write, "To pass, in New York, from the discipline of the streets to this so different many-smiling presence is to be thrilled at every turn."[44] Thus, the park's influence extends to encompass the entire urban landscape.

While it was designed to attract the "great body of citizens," in practice Central Park initially served as a recreation ground for the middle and upper classes. Nathaniel Willis did indeed drive his carriage in the park, a pastime Olmsted considered to be psychologically beneficial. In promoting Central Park, he cites testimonials from doctors, one of whom notes, "Where I formerly ordered patients of a certain class to give up their business altogether and go out of town, I now . . . prescribe a ride in the park before going to their offices and again a drive with their families before dinner. By simply adopting this course as a habit, men who have been breaking down frequently recover tone rapidly."[45] In its early years, the park was enjoyed mainly by people "of a certain class," those, like this doctor's patients, with enough money and leisure time to pursue the types of recreation, especially carriage driving, that dominated the park in the 1850s and 1860s. Yet despite this initial association with the upper and middle classes, Central Park increasingly became accessible to the broader metropolis. Changes in the city would reshape patterns of park use dramatically, and significantly, its function in the national imagination. The social relations that developed as the park became increasingly public and urban had unforeseen—and very public— influences of their own.

The Networked Park

Although Central Park may have been designed to provide "the greatest possible contrast" to urban space, the success of its social mission depended on its links to the city. And as part of the city, the park necessarily would be affected by the developing transportation and communication networks that were transforming New York. Given his deep interest in the possibilities that new technologies could offer to the nation, Olmsted certainly must have wondered how these changes would affect Central Park.

By 1870, twelve years after the first ice skaters had informally opened the park in 1858, Olmsted could reflect on its status to his colleagues in the American Social Science Association, opening with a lengthy discussion of the connections between rural and urban spaces (figure 8).[46] Exploring the

FIGURE 8. Skating on the Lake, Central Park, New York, N.Y., ca 1902. Library of Congress, Prints and Photographs Division, LC-USZ62-099776.

national impact of new transportation technologies, he notes that, "if we stand, any day before noon, at the railway stations of these cities, we may notice women and girls arriving by the score, who, it will be apparent, have just run in to do a little shopping, intending to return by supper time to farms perhaps a hundred miles away."[47] Olmsted emphasizes the multiple connections binding city to country, claiming that

> the intimacy of [the farmer's] family with the town will constantly appear, in dress, furniture, viands, in all the conversation. If there is a piano, they will be expecting a man from town to tune it. If the baby has outgrown his shoes, the measure has been sent to town. If a tooth is troublesome, an appointment is to be arranged by telegraph with the dentist. The railway timetable hangs with the almanac.[48]

The rural family's connections to the city are visible throughout their home, even in the most mundane details of everyday life: the baby's shoes, the troublesome tooth. The folksy predictions about the seasons, crops, and weather contained in the almanac coexist easily with the standardization of trade and commerce represented by the railway timetable. Just as the park was connected intimately to the city, here the rural home is ensconced firmly in urban time and space. These intimacies between technology and the family elicit neither surprise nor alarm from Olmsted. Instead of evoking a nostalgic sigh for a simpler past, the urbanized rural home represents new possibilities for progress.

To Olmsted, urban networks do not simply represent civilization; they make civilization. "No nation," he points out, "has yet begun to give up schools or newspapers, railroads or telegraphs, to restore feudal rights or advance rates of postage."[49] To align transportation and communication networks—railroads, telegraphs, syndicated newspapers, a national postal system—with schools is to claim that such networks are foundational to the formation of an advanced citizenry, one far removed from the feudal system to which both institutions are opposed. Thus, according to Olmsted, every nation, and especially the United States, should acknowledge and plan for a trend "from, not toward, dispersion."[50] Instead of the expansionism ordinarily associated with the United States, Olmsted predicts a return to urban centers. Distant places and people will be brought together, unified by their connections to a common space. Olmsted goes on to imagine the powerful roles that the telegraph, pneumatic tubes, street railways, and communal heat and hot water systems might play in the development of the modern city and suburb. What he does not discuss, however, even in his longest and most detailed defense of public parks, is the effect technologies like these would have on the park itself.

As New York and the nation increasingly became crisscrossed by transportation and communication networks, Central Park became a more noticeably urban and public place, a setting where the modern metropolis displayed its evolution on a vast and highly publicized stage. By the 1870s, a major class and conveyance transition transformed the city to the extent that "ordinary New Yorkers, who made their way to the park in growing numbers, transform[ed] the social character of the crowds. In the process, they also introduced new modes of socializing that subverted the genteel decorum of the first decade, making the park more like the rest of the city."[51] In terms of gender and class, the park was bearing a closer resemblance to Vaux's democratic urban ideal. For upper-class women, mobility and display increasingly became acceptable within the bounded space of Central Park. For them, "Central Park offered contact with [an] intensely urban world, while controlling and limiting its terms."[52] As early as 1860, women could drive their own carriages, walk without chaperones, and see and be seen in a public, non-commercial space, a liminal zone that was neither home nor street. Previously, leisure-class women's "movement through the city [had been] tied to a regular series of duties and obligations—churchgoing, charitable work, visiting friends, and tending sick relatives. After 1859 the Central Park drive offered women a less confined space . . . for recreation, not duty."[53] It is easy to imagine women like Vaux's voyeuristic apartment dwellers or Olmsted's mobile matrons seizing the opportunity to alter their domestic routines and venture into the park, which, while still homelike, offered a new degree of freedom.

Because it offered space away from the home's intense scrutiny, the park became a place where families' domestic rituals and class standings were put on display. As Wharton describes in *The Age of Innocence*, carriages were readily recognizable and associated with their owners. Women of the elite class who frequented the park could identify easily the other people who were out driving and take stock of their financial situation by the coaches and teams of horses they displayed. Mobile and unchaperoned women thus became part of the park scenery as the enclosed space of Central Park unfolded to display them publicly.

The use of public space for personal pursuits was not limited to the upper classes. For New Yorkers who did not drive carriages, Central Park was made accessible by new transportation technologies: five different horse car lines and three elevated train lines reached the park by 1880. In addition, as the city's population increased and spread to the north, many more New Yorkers came to live within walking distance of the park. Finally, officials changed some of the rules governing Sundays at the park, allowing members of the working class to visit the park on their single day off.[54] As the park increasingly became accessible to families of all classes, a greater variety of domestic relationships were put on display. Equipped with a dairy and children's shelter, the park became a popular destination for New York's upper-class children and their caretakers. Central Park also offered working-class families a gathering place for the camaraderie of concerts and ballgames. Courting couples found the park to be a setting that, while public, offered substantially more privacy for romantic rendezvous than they could find elsewhere. The park became well known as a trysting site both in the popular press and in more highbrow novels by authors such as Wharton and James. As a contemporary pointed out in the *Herald*, those who "belong to the working classes . . . have no homes in which to make love, so they are compelled to make a public exhibition of themselves."[55] In a certain sense, then, the park came to stand in for domestic space, offering privacy and a distance from neighbors and extended family that were otherwise unavailable to members of the working classes. In *The Custom of the Country,* Wharton shows that members of the upper classes used the park for similar ends; a young Undine Spragg naively accepts her riding instructor's dubious marriage proposal in the park, and later relies on the Ramble's seclusion to obscure a clandestine meeting with Elmer Moffatt. For men and women of all social ranks, the park offered a place to establish relationships through a quasi-public intimacy operating outside of the kinship and community bonds that might have structured earlier courtships and marriages.[56]

While it provided a public setting for New Yorkers' most personal interactions, the park also became a tourist destination, a place where the city itself was put on display for the rest of the world. Newspapers took up numerous images of Central Park and disseminated them to a national audience, transforming a city park into a national landmark. "It is 'fast becoming the chief attraction not only of New-York, but of the whole country,' the *Tribune* boasted in 1860. Tourists became one of its most important con-

FIGURE 9. In Central Park, New York. Library of Congress, Prints and Photographs Division, LC-D4-13624.

stituencies, and those who did not visit 'viewed' the park in the stereographs, lithographs, and illustrated weeklies that advertised it to a national audience."[57] By 1890, approximately fifteen million people would visit Central Park each year.[58] Through the operations of transportation and publicity networks, the park became a stage of sorts, a setting where personal relations were put on public display, first within its boundaries, then to the city, and later, through the networks of the publishing industry, to the nation and beyond. Functioning as an ever-expanding urban stage, Central Park moved beyond its intended role as a respite from urban ills to become a symbol of the American urban landscape—a transformation for which Olmsted and Vaux could not have planned.

A basic tenet of landscape architecture is to design for change, and Olmsted and Vaux did their best to plan for an unpredictable future. They could anticipate, for instance, how plants would grow, which ones would die, what elements would be removed and what added as the living landscape changed over time. And while such change requires active maintenance; it is qualitatively different from the changes effected by the unseen hand of a bur-

FIGURE 10. Lover's Lane, Central Park, New York, ca 1896. Library of Congress, Prints and Photographs Division, LC-USZ62-133260.

geoning capitalist economy. Changes Olmsted and Vaux could not have foreseen meant that if the individual was transformed in the park of the 1870s and 80s, he or she was certainly not transformed by the "familiar domestic gathering" Olmsted had envisioned, but by a networked site implicated in and transformed by the mechanisms of modernity.

What Central Park Signaled to Henry James

Urban networks radically altered Central Park, destabilizing notions of privacy and publicity. For Henry James, the transformation of Central Park from elite playground to urban space registered a broader and more powerful cultural change in the industrial city. As the park became more public, it emblematized the ways in which the personal—property, relationships, social status—entered into public space and became performance in the modern city.

By 1905, when Henry James commented on Central Park in *The American Scene*, the park had been integrated fully into the urban fabric; to James it signified modernity. James describes the park with a series of analogies, and it is telling that all of his comparisons reference performance and commerce. James claims, for instance, that because the park is the city's lone aesthetic feature:

> To the Park, accordingly, and to the Park only, hitherto, the aesthetic appetite
> has had to address itself, . . . acting out year after year the character of the
> cheerful, capable, bustling, even if overworked, hostess of the one inn, some-

where, who has to take all the travel, who is often at her wits' end to know how to deal with it, but who, none the less, has, for the honour of the house, never once failed of hospitality.[59]

Though the park remains "cheerful," retaining the city's "honour," it is nevertheless portrayed as a commercial proprietress responding to the "clamour of its customers."[60] As we saw in chapter 1, the social status of boarding house keepers was a vexed issue. With the park personified as a lady of cheer but not of leisure, the city becomes this lady's inn, a place of transitory stays in temporary lodgings. James continues by comparing the park to an actress, another not-entirely-respectable occupation for women.[61] Through display, this theatrical figure transforms the "polyglot Hebraic crowd," a crowd from which James elsewhere distances himself, into his "fellow spectators at the theater" through her "vocalizing" and "capering."[62] Whether cavorting or hostessing, the park remakes the people it touches, changing New Yorkers into cosmopolitan travelers, effacing cultural and linguistic difference by becoming a consumable spectacle. The park, like urban boarding houses and hotels, becomes a site where the process of modernity unfolds and where James can witness modern subjectivity developing.

Considering the park together with the city, James has the singular impression that he is witnessing modernity taking shape through display. In a "walk across the Park," combined with a "consequent desultory stroll" through new neighborhoods, the urban landscape "define[s] itself as intensely rich and intensely modern."[63] What then, James wonders, is "locked up in that word 'modern'?"[64] What will modernity mean for the urban subject? Though sharply evoked by this New York experience, the question clearly had preoccupied James before; it is at the center of his 1886 novel *The Bostonians*, where Central Park plays a small but significant role. Basil Ransom's courtship of Verena Tarrant advances "on a sequestered bench, where, however, there was a pretty glimpse of the distance and an occasional stroller creaked by on the asphalt walk."[65] Here, as Olmsted and Vaux had planned, the park fulfills the desire shared by the novel's characters for "an actual and physically tangible site within which the reclusive private consciousness can emerge without fear of attack."[66] For James, the park's liminal location between private and public emblematized a new and modern experience of urban space that prefigures the changing function of Olive Chancellor's home.

Attempting Containment in The Bostonians

The Bostonians, which tracks the course of a love triangle comprised of a Boston bluestocking, Olive Chancellor; a chauvinistic Mississippi lawyer, Basil Ransom; and a striking but poor young public speaker, Verena Tarrant;

explores the modern subjects produced by an increasingly networked urban landscape. Urban domestic spaces play a central role in shaping the fates of James's characters. As Janet Wolf Bowen notes, to James, "a self-proclaimed analyst of the 'human history of places,' architecture is the perfect symbol for the fluidity of interior and exterior being, home and homelessness, and private and public life during the final decades of the nineteenth century in America."[67] Bowen sees this fluidity at work in most of the novel's buildings. I build on her discussion by discussing the novel's physical architecture in the context of the changing spatial practices at work in the cities where the novel is set. Like Central Park, Olive Chancellor's drawing-room unfolds; it is transformed from a place of respite to a node in the developing networks of transportation and communication. The process by which the contained space of Olive's home merges with urban space echoes domestic influence's transition to media influence in the industrial American city.

The novel opens onto the drawing-room of Olive Chancellor, a wealthy spinster (although she is actually quite young) dedicated to the "woman question." Olive owns a row house on Boston's Charles Street, which runs along the base of Beacon Hill. At the time, the northern portion of the street, where Olive's house is set, bordered Boston's West End and looked out on the working Charles River with its ropewalks and other industries. At the novel's opening, Olive's drawing-room exemplifies the feminized privacy originally associated with the word, for it protects her from uninvited contact with the world outside.

Only two of the row house's spaces are very public: the hall and the front parlor. Olive's more public drawing room corresponds to the front parlor. Karen Halttunen notes that "the Victorians distinguished between the parlor, where outside visitors were received; and the sitting room, where the family gathered in privacy, protected from the intrusions of outsiders by the vestibule, hall, and parlor."[68] With kitchen and dining room on the lower level and bedrooms above, the house's owner could control guests' access to the family's more intimate activities. As Calvert Vaux put it, "one style of best parlor found in America . . . becomes a sort of quarantine in which to put each plague of a visitor that calls; and one almost expects to see the lady of the house walk in with a bottle of camphor in her hand, to prevent infection, she seems to have such a fear that any one should step within the bounds of her real every-day home life."[69] Olive's drawing-room initially echoes Vaux's description; confined there on his initial visit, Basil Ransom, Olive's southern cousin and eventual romantic rival, muses that "he had never seen an interior that was so much an interior as this queer corridor-shaped drawing room of his new-found kinswoman; he had never felt himself in the presence of so much organized privacy" (*TB,* 45). The room reflects Olive directly; she owns the property and has filled it with objects that reflect her taste and personality. Like Olive herself, the room is narrow and linear. Further, as private property, Olive's house protects her from the vicissitudes of the housing market with which renters and boarders must continually contend. It is a haven that allows Olive self-possession.

This "interior that is so much an interior" both reflects and helps to maintain a containment of self that protects Olive from the traffic of the urban landscape. Her economic haven is also a psychic one. For at first, while Olive enters the urban networks by riding streetcars and attending lectures, she keeps her house separate from these ventures. The narrator notes:

> Olive had been active enough, for years, in the city-missions; she too had scoured dirty children, and, in squalid lodging houses, had gone into rooms where the domestic situation was strained and the noises made the neighbors turn pale. But she reflected that after such exertions she had the refreshment of a pretty house, a drawing-room full of flowers, a crackling hearth, where she threw in pine cones and made them snap, an imported tea-service, a Chickering piano, and the *Deutsche Rundschau;* whereas Miss Birdseye had only a bare, vulgar room, with a hideous flowered carpet (it looked like a dentist's), a cold furnace, the evening paper, and Doctor Prance. (*TB,* 190)

Here, the Jamesian obsession with the fate of the waning aristocracy in the face of the rising middle class is written in and through domestic space. Olive takes real pleasure in her particular possessions and what they say about her. Her imported tea set and Chickering piano mark her as a woman of taste and class; the *Deutsche Rundschau,* a German literary magazine, marks her as a cosmopolitan intellectual. These objects' origins and trademarks allow Olive to possess herself—or at least, to believe she does. Here, there is a correspondence among the enclosed space of Olive's drawing-room, the objects it contains, and the self-possession that Olive desires. Olive would no doubt subscribe to folklorist Henry Glassie's notion that one should "not change the arrangement of the rooms or their proportions. In these volumes—bounded by surfaces from which a person's senses rebound to him—his psyche develops; disrupt them, and you disrupt him."[70]

The passage equally underscores Olive's familiarity with the permeable living spaces of the city; while relaxing in the drawing-room she recalls the connections exemplified by the lodging house: the sounds passing from room to room, the presence of the ubiquitous (and communal) newspaper, and the proximity of other boarders. While Olive's gender and her class status almost require her to help those less fortunate than she, her class position allows her to enter and leave their world on her own terms.[71]

Like the Central Park of Olmsted and Vaux's initial vision, Olive's drawing-room operates as a contrast to the urban world outside. It is pretty; the tenements are squalid. She has a piano; they have noises. Even the lodging house shared by Olive's old friends, Miss Birdseye, an elderly reformer, and Doctor Prance, a radical physician, is bare and vulgar, while her own drawing-

room is warmly refreshing. For Olive, the drawing-room is a place of possession, a place for consumption, not production. The lodging house already
embodies an admixture of the physical and social worlds that Olive would
like to keep separate—it looks like a dentist's office (which in and of itself
evokes fears about violating bodily boundaries) and is home to a practicing
doctor. No withdrawal from the city is possible for lodging-house boarders
like Miss Birdseye and Doctor Prance.

As I discuss in chapter 1, in nineteenth-century fiction, urban domestic
spaces like those of the lodging house became settings where authors could
stage the development of a modern, mobile, transformable subjectivity that
reflected and was reinforced by the permeable buildings. Historically, most
tenants chose lodging houses out of economic necessity; in *The Bostonians,*
Basil Ransom resorts to a "decayed mansion" that he shares with "certain
curious persons of both sexes, for the most part not favorites of fortune,
who had found asylum there" (*TB,* 196). With an ever-changing clientele,
the eroding building serves as an unstable setting where James's "curious
persons," his modern subjects, can develop. Dr. Prance, for instance, can
practice her personal politics, see patients, and perform experimental research under the obscurity of her lodging house roof. Dr. Prance's lodging
house is also the site of Verena Tarrant's first bewitching performance, a
stream of consciousness talk she can only give after her mesmerist father
"starts her up" with a laying on of hands. Verena's performance stirs desires
in both Basil Ransom and Olive Chancellor that blur divisions of class, re-
gion, and gender. Their modern desires fittingly are born in the lodging house
hall, a space that produces "the similitude of an enormous streetcar"(*TB,*
59). In contrast to this liberating anonymity, a certain publicity of the individual emanates from Olive's personal space, a publicity that only increases
as the novel unfolds.

Although her drawing-room offers privacy and protection, Olive's home,
after all, is urban. Like the houses Miles Coverdale views through his hotel
window in *Blithedale,* Olive's row house is connected to the city on all sides:
by the street and sidewalk that front it, by the view of the Charles River visible through the windows, and by the walls and roof it shares with the neighboring buildings on either side.[72] The street is clearly public territory. It is
where Olive catches the streetcars she rides in order to associate herself with
"the people," and it is where Basil Ransom can gain access to Verena without
Olive's knowledge. Even the sidewalk is a space outside of social obligations
and entanglements; for instance, here Ransom can learn of Verena's where-
abouts while avoiding contact with the servants or the ladies of Olive's house.

Olive's river view further cements her home's connection to the modern
city. From her rear windows, she sees a working harbor, smokestacks, "the
chimneys of dirty 'works,'" and an illuminated "row of houses, impressive to
Ransom in their extreme modernness" (*TB,* 45). That the row houses im-
press the reactionary Ransom as extremely modern and *not* homelike is

significant. From the 1820s onward, Boston had operated "not as a site of revenue producing—although that idea was never absent—but as a domestic space to live and play, to attend the theater and stroll through parks and gardens, and to make social calls."[73] By the late nineteenth century, this function had begun to change; new urban networks were making Boston a more insistently modern city, and in this context, existing residential structures took on new valences. Olive's row house, designed as a space of stable containment, becomes exemplary of "extreme modernness." And indeed, with the arrival of Verena Tarrant, Olive's withdrawing-room begins to fulfill its modern function as drawing-room—a magnetic space that attracts people and creates a public setting within the home. It begins to resemble the "city's drawing-room" as conceived by Calvert Vaux and developed through the spatial practices of Central Park's visitors. Not merely corridor-shaped, the drawing-room begins to function as a connective corridor. The text's most intensely private space becomes a hub for developing networks of information and publicity. As Olive's drawing-room changes from a highly personalized inner sanctum of privilege into the "headquarters" for Verena Tarrant's publicity machine, James marks the loss of privacy and interiority that accompany the rise of urban networks.

Just as Central Park evolved gradually from a contained space to a networked public space, the drawing-room's private spaces slowly open to the city. The process begins when Olive invites Verena to live with her, transforming Olive's solitary retreat into what Caroline Levander identifies as an "intimate, homosocial world."[74] Olive believes that "home-culture," her own version of Catharine Beecher's world-changing domestic ideology, can both bind Verena to her and transform the younger woman into an effective public voice for the cause of women's rights. And in Verena, Olive seems to have an ideal subject for transformation. From childhood, Verena has been in public: the narrator notes, "she had been nursed in darkened rooms, and suckled in the midst of manifestations; she had begun to 'attend lectures,' as she said, when she was quite an infant, because her mother had no one to leave her with at home" (*TB*, 105). This public upbringing, combined with her father's overwhelming fascination with the press, hotels, streets, and other manifestations of modernity, predisposes Verena toward a selfhood marked by permeability and performance, a subjectivity much like that which Priscilla exhibits in *The Blithedale Romance*. Both women's inheritance and environment destine them to become mediums.

James's modern subject is at once susceptible to influence and capable of widely transmitting the influences he or she absorbs. The narrator of *The Bostonians* notes:

> Olive had always rated high the native refinement of her country-women, their latent "adaptability," their talent for accommodating themselves at a glance to changed conditions; but the way her companion rose with the level of the civ-

ilization that surrounded her, the way she assimilated all delicacies and absorbed all traditions, left this friendly theory halting behind. (*TB*, 184)

Verena inherits Priscilla's capacity to assimilate, to absorb, and as a medium
to channel. Just as Priscilla embodies her surroundings, Verena becomes the
embodiment of the row house's "extreme modernness." Infinitely transformable, she can accommodate to any "changed conditions." Her multiva-
lent and adaptable subjectivity makes Verena a natural for performing in
public and transmitting her messages to a receptive audience. In this way, she
echoes Priscilla and foreshadows later figures like Theodore Dreiser's Carrie
Meeber. When Carrie performs on stage for the first time, she electrifies her
audience. *Sister Carrie*'s narrator notes, "All the gentlemen yearned toward
her. She was capital."[75] Figures like Verena, Priscilla, and Carrie all reflect
and channel the influences of the modern world they inhabit. The modern
city, in turn, rewards their skills with survival, and in some cases, with tremendous success. The very qualities that mark Verena as modern mean that
she will be transformed by any space she enters, whether it is Olive's drawing-
room or the city beyond.

But one salient historical development separates Verena and Carrie from
Priscilla: the rise of modern media networks that transmit messages nationally instead of restricting them to the audience in a single lyceum. By Verena's
day, as Lynn Wardley notes, "to enter urban speech is to find speech recon-
stituted within the city's expanding parameters and under such novel forms
of production as the advertisements and the daily news."[76] Most of *The
Bostonian*'s characters, even Miss Birdseye and Dr. Prance, interact with the
networks of publicity in one way or another.[77] But the intensity and—in
James's view—the absurdity of these networks is embodied especially in several of the men who are closest to Verena. Her father, Selah Tarrant, is a mesmeric healer turned media hound, while her first suitor, Matthias Pardon, is
a journalist whose stories go national via the syndicated press. Both men
reflect that a powerful, if not palatable, change is in the air.

Publicity Networks: Transforming Domestic Influence

That novelists and architects share the language of influence is no coincidence; they are drawing on a strong tradition in American letters, beginning
with the "city on a hill," that imbues the environment with the power to
influence the development of individuals, and therefore, of society. In the
United States, the notion of influence is an idea with a national past, and the
evolution of its operation is also firmly tied to the networks of modernity.
An expansive concept, influence affects spaces and persons far beyond its
point of origin.

James introduces Verena Tarrant as a character decidedly under the influence. Like *Blithedale*'s Priscilla, she is a performer whose routine revolves around mesmeric influence. In her first appearance, after Verena's father "starts her up" with a laying on of hands, she proceeds to deliver a stream-of-consciousness speech on women's rights, a performance that exerts its own mesmeric force on Basil Ransom and Olive Chancellor. Afterward, Basil and Verena banter on the topic of women's power. Ransom remarks, "Do you really take the ground that your sex is without influence? Influence? Why, you have led us all by the nose to where we are now! Wherever we are, it's all you. You are at the bottom of everything" (*TB*, 110). His remark highlights the centrality of influence to the text. Here, Verena's conservative southern suitor smilingly gives women's power its chivalrous due while consigning Verena herself to the very sphere her public performances seem designed to avoid. Ransom's use of the word "influence" borders on accusing "forward-thinking" women like Olive and Verena of using political methods no more revolutionary than those used by the republican mothers—or sentimental novelists—of an earlier generation. But influence is remade in the novel; it becomes the force that spans public and private, operating equally well within isolated domestic circles and along the urban networks that increasingly penetrate these homes. In *The Bostonians*, influence makes things happen, even though the novel's ending is ambiguous about the possibilities for exerting feminine influence in the public sphere.[78]

If the mind could be transformed by a laying-on of hands, it equally could be influenced by its physical surroundings. As I have noted, the ideology of domesticity both solidified women's influence within the home and emphasized the transformative potential of domestic environments. As American women increasingly became politicized in the early nineteenth century, first around the issue of women's suffrage and then around abolition, the rhetoric of republican motherhood both tightened the domestic circle and offered a means by which women could affect the world beyond the walls of their homes. These influential domestic environments were described, and in a sense, codiiied, in popular nineteenth-century fiction, particularly works by women who aimed to use their texts to broadcast the home's religious influence. Jane Tompkins argues in *Sensational Designs* that sentimental novels "were written . . . in order to win the belief and to influence the behavior of the widest possible audience."[79] In this context, influence is emotional, conveyed through the heart and perpetuated by mothers and/or in novels. Catharine Beecher and Harriet Beecher Stowe, for instance, express the hope that the family (developed, of course, within the home) will "go forth to shine as 'lights of the world' in all the now darkened nations. Thus the 'Christian family' and 'Christian neighborhood' would become the grand ministry, as they were designed to be, in training our great race for heaven."[80] Though it seems to be located firmly and innocuously within the home,

Gillian Brown points out that "maternal influence travels with every individual, and in America, where individuals moved often and extensively, socially and geographically, maternal power held sway over a limitless domain."[81] Tompkins and Brown both are commenting on Stowe's *Uncle Tom's
Cabin*, where domestic influence is highly politicized, but environmental
influence is central to less overtly political texts as well. In *The Lamplighter*,
for instance, the rebellious Gertie must learn to produce an ordered coziness
in her tenement home before she can begin the religious transformation that
eventually allows her to marry Willie, her predestined love. Only the proper
domestic environment can ensure that the children that Willie and Gertie
produce and send out into the world will be shaped appropriately as American citizens. In Olive Chancellor's mind as well, home-culture has the potential to reconfigure society as "the happiness women create in their domestic isolation finally reaches to the ends of the earth."[82]

The Bostonians investigates the transformation of influence from a domestic to a national tactic inseparable from the rise of modern urban culture
in the United States. Verena's highly publicized movement from Miss Birdseye's boarding house to Boston's Music Hall is one notable trajectory made
possible by this change, as is Olive's gradual acceptance—and eventual
embrace—of new publicity technologies. Basil Ransom's effort to contain Verena's influence by relegating her to the domestic sphere of his rural Mississippi
home even as his own influence spreads by way of the national press counters these impulses. The conflict between Basil and Olive becomes a battle
over influence, but while they each attempt to mobilize influence toward their
respective social aims, only one of them will gain influence over Verena.

Spatializing Influence: Syndication and the Sitting Room

In *The Bostonians*, a society where "domestic culture is understood to be re-
generated by women in the home" must come to terms with the powerful
influence made possible by the modern media.[83] Matthias Pardon, one of
Verena's more persistent suitors, sums up the possible conflicts between the
two. When he considers Olive's power over Verena, he hopes "that she
wasn't going to exercise any influence that would prevent Miss Tarrant from
taking the front rank that belonged to her. He thought there was too much
hanging back; he wanted to see her in a front seat; he wanted to see her name
in the biggest kind of bills and her portrait in the windows of the stores"
(*TB*, 142). But the tension Pardon feels between Olive's influence and the
media does not materialize as he fears it will. Instead, Olive modernizes the
tactics of domestic influence, aligning them with the media's aims.

If, as Chris Walsh argues, publicity becomes a religion in *The Bostonians*,
offering "a world of transcendence and . . . a unifier of a decidedly non-
transcendent, fragmented society," then this spirituality begins in the body,

just as Vaux and Olmsted believed that aesthetic influence was generated through the eye.[84] An early form of media influence, for instance, is practiced by Verena's maternal grandparents, the abolitionist Greenstreets, who "had never set much store by manual activity; they believed in the influence of the lips" (*TB*, 96). Her father, Selah Tarrant, exerts a different kind of influence upon his wife, his daughter, and his patients. Mrs. Tarrant is especially susceptible: "She knew that he was very magnetic (that, in fact, was his genius), and she felt that it was his magnetism that held her to him. . . . She hated her husband for having magnetized her so that she consented to certain things, and even did them, the thought of which today would suddenly make her face burn" (*TB*, 94–95). But by Verena's heyday, forms of communications such as daily papers, the penny press, and advertisements emanating from the city have redefined speech.[85] Verena's early public speaking begins with the physical touch of her father's hands; by the novel's end, this physical element is erased as Verena's speech becomes just one part of Olive's publicity machine. Through this evolution, we see urban speech leave the realm of the body and begin to be disseminated amorphously through new and invisible networks.

Certain of *The Bostonian*'s characters have especially strong ties to these modern modes of influence: Selah Tarrant, Matthias Pardon, and Basil Ransom all are involved with and fascinated by the networks of publicity and journalism that construct personalities and make palpable the forces of modernity.[86] Tarrant fantasizes about the mechanisms of publicity, while journalist Matthias Pardon parlays a youth spent haunting hotel lobbies into a career as a society reporter. For Basil Ransom, who attempts to distinguish the message from its mode of transmission, media networks are more elusive. For all three men, however, the print media's influence proves irresistible. Tarrant, Pardon, and Ransom share an overwhelming desire to be processed by the machinery of journalism, a desire that, while slightly ridiculous, signifies one way of reckoning with the modern changes that will reorganize perceptions and experiences of public and private spaces, especially as those spaces are gendered. While James's medium is female, those interested in crafting and disseminating the message are male. Except one.

Selah Tarrant fantasizes about dissolving his personal boundaries and embodying mobility, traveling spiritually and bodily through journalistic networks:

Nothing less than this would really have satisfied Selah Tarrant; his ideal of bliss was to be as regularly and indispensably a component part of the newspaper as the title and the date, or the list of fires, or the column of Western jokes. His vision of that publicity haunted his dreams, and he would gladly have sacrificed it to the innermost sanctities of home. Human existence to him, indeed, was a huge publicity, in which the only fault was that it was sometimes not effective. (*TB*, 121)

Newspapers offer Tarrant the intriguing possibility of replacing space with information. An alternative to the "innermost sanctities of home," the regular newspaper features promise to construct and broadcast a new reality in which not content, but repetition matters.[87] Tarrant imagines appearing regularly in a predictable space on the newspaper page, simultaneously bounded and mobile, part of the paper and as such, renewed with each day's issue. Though Tarrant's fascination is exaggerated, it is not heightened simply for comic effect. Rather, Tarrant's newspaper fantasy is a version of the ramifications of modernity that both fascinate and repel James in *The Bostonians* and elsewhere.[88]

Tarrant yearns to become transmittable material, an essence to be taken up and consumed by a broad public. He dreams of dissolving himself in the streams of media that structure his existence: "He was always trying to find out what was 'going in'; he would have liked to go in himself, bodily, and, failing in this, he hoped to get advertisements inserted gratis" (*TB*, 123). His desire to circulate is almost a holy mission. "The newspapers were his world, the richest expression, in his eyes, of human life; and, for him, if a diviner day was to come upon earth, it would be brought about by copious advertisements in the daily prints" (*TB*, 120). Physically, Tarrant is already in circulation. He spends his days in "multifarious wanderings through the streets and suburbs of the New England capital" (*TB*, 122). While this wandering allows him to enter his patients' houses and transmit his influence through the laying on of hands, it pales in comparison to the possibilities for multiple and simultaneous connections made possible by newspapers.

The link that James proposes between the body and publicity emphasizes transmission over dissolution. Tarrant's attempts to transmit himself through the medium of the newspaper echo the transmissions he sends to Verena (and that she pretends to absorb) at the beginning of her career. When he physically enters the newsrooms, he pervades the atmosphere with his conversation and penetrates the text as well: He "edged into the printing rooms when he had been eliminated from the office, talked with the compositors till they set up his remarks by mistake, and to the newsboy when the compositors had turned their backs" (*TB*, 123). Selah's actions do not simply betray a disinterest in the hierarchical differences between editor, printer, and newsboy. Rather, they reveal his awareness that the newspaper itself is a threefold production: creative, mechanical, and circulating—and that all of these elements are necessary for the newspaper to perform its function in the city's communication networks.

The novel's narrator draws a clear parallel between Tarrant's physical mobility and his fascination with all kinds of modern transmissions.

> This effort with him had many forms; it involved, among other things, a perpetual perambulation of the streets, a haunting of horse-cars, railway stations, shops that were "selling off." But the places that knew him best were the of-

fices of the newspapers and the vestibules of the hotels—the big marble-paved chambers of informal reunion which offer to the streets, through high glass plates, the sight of the American citizen suspended by his heels. . . . He could not have told you, at any particular moment, what he was doing; he only had a general sense that such places were national nerve centers, and that the more one looked in, the more one was "on the spot." (*TB*, 123)

Tarrant wants to be where modernity's action is. All of his haunts are places where public and private mingle, where the street touches the hotel, where the railway trains converge. If Tarrant went to New York, no doubt he would have haunted the borders of Central Park, where "the street-cars rattled in the foreground. . . and the beer-saloons, with exposed shoulders and sides . . . announced themselves in signs of large lettering to the sky"(*TB*, 332). James frames these border spaces as "national nerve centers," offering a bodily image to contain the incorporeal impulses that travel along the city's imaginary ganglia.

Syndication offers Tarrant another way to imagine himself and his influence multiplying and traveling effortlessly around the nation. "Success was not success so long as his daughter's physique, the rumour of her engagement, were not included in the 'Jottings', with the certainty of being copied" (*TB*, 123). And in this way, Tarrant's publicity fantasies clearly are bound to other modern technologies such as the telegraph that make syndication possible. Syndication removes writing from its original context and transmits it worldwide. Unconcerned with the economics of this transaction, Tarrant is fascinated with the possibility of traveling the airwaves. He yearns to transform a bodily influence into a media influence that penetrates and reshapes conceptions of time and space.

Although journalist Matthias Pardon shares "the faith of Selah Tarrant— that being in the newspapers is a condition of bliss," he is a younger man who represents a transition both to journalism as a profession and to a more completely modern view of public relations (*TB*, 121). A society reporter, Pardon understands that the newspaper plays only one part in an orchestrated publicity campaign. Like Tarrant, Matthias Pardon has risen to a position (if a dubious one) in Boston society from lowly beginnings. Tarrant began "life as an itinerant vendor of lead-pencils," a career that does nothing to ameliorate the fact that "his birth, in some unheard-of place in Pennsylvania, was quite inexpressibly low" (*TB*, 93, 129). Likewise, Pardon has "sprung from the 'people', [has] an acquaintance with poverty, a hand-to-mouth development, and an experience with the seamy side of life" (*TB*, 157). But while Tarrant, with his marriage to the daughter of a Boston abolitionist, his associations with free love and Cayuga, and his reliance on mesmerism through touch evokes an earlier era, Matthias Pardon embodies the future. "He was only twenty-eight years old, and, with his hoary head, was a thoroughly modern young man; he had no idea of not taking advantage of all the modern conveniences. He regarded the mission of mankind upon earth as a perpetual evolution of telegrams . . . the newest thing was what came nearest to exciting in his mind the sentiment of respect" (TB, 140). The fascination with newness that makes Pardon "thoroughly modern" clearly governs his journalistic production of novelty.

Pardon shares Tarrant's utter fascination with the newspapers, but instead of attempting to penetrate the papers' mechanical production, Pardon aims to mold content by publicizing private affairs.

> For this ingenuous son of his age all distinction between the person and the artist had ceased to exist; the writer was personal, the person food for newsboys, and everything and everyone were everyone's business. All things, with him, referred themselves to print, and print meant simply infinite reporting, a promptitude of announcement, abusive when necessary, or even when not, of his fellow-citizens. He poured contumely on their private life, on their personal appearance, with the best conscience in the world. (TB, 139)

To Pardon, who has "condensed into shorthand many of the most celebrated women of his time," personal affairs are the raw material for production; bodies, both his own and those of his subjects, must cross the eroding boundaries between public and private spheres in order for him to produce journalism (TB, 139). As David Kramer points out, Pardon is a highly feminized character; perhaps his flexible gendering allows him access to all kinds of spaces.[89] Thus Pardon's methods, his material, and his body all become conduits for connection within the city and beyond its borders.

The admixture of private and public exemplified in Pardon's journalistic production extends to his personal life. Tarrant thinks hopefully that "if Matthias Pardon should seek Verena in marriage, it would be with a view to producing her in public; and the advantage for the girl of having a husband who was at the same time reporter, interviewer, manager, agent, who had the command of the principal 'dailies', would write her up and work her, as it were, scientifically—the attraction of all this was too obvious to be insisted on" (TB, 140). To Verena's parents, Pardon's approach makes perfect sense. Pardon represents the possibility for a virtual vertical monopoly over Verena. He is a one-man publicity machine. Here, the institution of marriage is not simply a business proposition; almost "scientific" in its efficiency, this modern marriage would integrate the machinery of publicity with the private and intimate relations associated with domesticity. Tarrant and Pardon foreshadow how Olive's "home-culture" will be transformed into popular culture.

Pardon's fantasies for Verena are very similar to Selah's. Indeed, Matthias Pardon has "a remarkable disposition to share the object of his affection with the American people" (TB, 140). As Verena explains, "He does place things in a very seductive light. . . . he says that if I become his wife I shall be carried straight along by a force of excitement of which at present I have no idea. I shall wake up famous, if I marry him; I have only to give out my feelings, and he will take care of the rest" (*TB*, 159). Marriage here becomes not simply a relationship between performer and manager; Pardon's writing becomes a conduit to carry Verena's energy and emotion and transform it into a profitable spectacle. The seductive thrill Verena links with giving out her feelings imparts a sexual charge to what otherwise seems purely a business proposition. Indeed, Pardon and Verena's marriage would reconfigure reproduction, channeling that force into reproducing and disseminating Verena's personality. In their imagined marriage, Pardon embodies communication networks and Verena becomes the message. Together, he hopes, they can become a modern marvel of syndication.

This model of marriage is founded on spectacle; fame seduces. The effect of these modern networks of communication and publicity is not so much, as Anthony Scott argues, that, "the expansion and retrenchment of the consumer economy—hypostasized by James as 'publicity' . . . threatens to overwhelm an older world of privacy and artistic sensibility," but rather that privacy and domesticity themselves must be reconfigured in order to account for publicity's power.[90] Brook Thomas notes that the rise of the modern media and the construction of a legal definition of privacy were powerfully connected in the United States. As Supreme Court Justice Louis Brandeis argued in 1890:

> The intensity and complexity of life, attendant upon advancing civilization, have rendered necessary some retreat from the world, and man, under the refining influence of literature and culture, has become more sensitive to publicity, so that solitude and privacy have become more essential to the individual; but modern enterprise and invention have, through invasions upon his privacy, subjected him to mental pain and distress, far greater than could be inflicted by mere bodily injury.[91]

Here, Brandeis opposes the positive and refining influence of literature and culture to the media industry's alarming mechanics. But more significantly, he sees influence as a force that must be resisted. An invasive influence necessitates a reinforcement of privacy; the effect of "literature and culture" has been to open peoples' minds, ironically rendering them all the more vulnerable to the "mental pain and distress" inflicted by the "enterprise and invention" of the publicity networks. Two reactions to this phenomenon are delineated in *The Bostonians*. Justice Brandeis's reaction, personified in the novel by Basil Ransom, is to withdraw to Mississippi and take Verena with him, while Olive Chancellor's strategy is to open herself further to the media and then harness it to further Verena's public career. In order to accomplish their aims, both Olive and Basil must enter into the networks of publicity as authors of public speech. In this novel, complete withdrawal from the modern networks of publicity is impossible without essentially going back in time.

Private Spaces Turned Public Stages: Verena's Influence

Central Park's users integrated the park into public space in part through the cultural desire lines they imprinted on the landscape.[92] Transformed by the park, they transformed the space as well. In *The Bostonians,* if Olive's drawing-room resembles the park, Verena plays the people's role, changing the settings she inhabits. Verena has a penchant for making private spaces and relationships public. James establishes this pattern in Verena's relationship with Olive; by thoroughly recounting all of her exploits to the older woman, Verena lessens their potential impact. By divesting herself of these events, Verena transforms them into public property, and when they become public they are defused. This pattern of publicity extends to the spaces Verena inhabits.

Through both her speech and the very public quality of her private relationships, Verena modernizes the spaces she inhabits. This is particularly visible in her relationship with Basil Ransom. Ransom only meets Verena in public during the first third of the novel, and by the time he goes to see her at her home in Monadnoc Place, the character of their relationship is set. He notes that, "If at Mrs. Birdseye's, and afterwards in Charles Street, she might have been a rope dancer, today she made a 'scene' of the little room in Monadnoc Place, such a scene as a prima donna makes of daubed canvas and dusty boards" (*TB,* 230). Verena neutralizes Ransom's potential threat by playing the role of performer to his audience, a relationship with which she is familiar and which, of course, she is pursuing professionally under Olive's tutelage. As he listens, Basil is amused by Verena's predilection for making her conversations into theatrical display: "There was indeed a sweet comicality on seeing this pretty girl sit there and, in answer to a casual, civil inquiry, drop into oratory as a natural thing. Had she forgotten where she was, and did she take him for a full house? She had the same turns and cadences, almost the same gestures, as if she had been on the platform; and the great queerness of it was that, with such a manner, she should escape from being odious" (*TB,* 232). If Verena herself is not transformed, her presence blurs the workings of private space, making it seem more public to Ransom and allowing Verena the freedom to spend time alone with him. Their subsequent walk around Cambridge foreshadows their later trip to Central Park; lacking privacy in their domestic spaces, Verena and Basil must find it in public. Significantly, Verena hesitates to reveal these particular interactions with Basil to Olive. Although she and Basil meet in public, Verena retains their encounters as her private property.

Similarly, Mrs. Burrage's New York mansion, under other circumstances a place where "perfect privacy" can "be best assured" is transformed into semi-public space when Verena speaks there (*TB,* 295). Of Verena's performance at Mrs. Burrage's, Basil notes, "The platform it evidently was to be—private if not public—since one was to be admitted by a ticket given away if not sold" (*TB*, 250–51). The platform's private or public status hinges on whether or not money changes hands. The singular form of publicity for Verena's engagement, hand-addressed cards, further muddies the house's status; it is neither fully public nor completely private. In this way, as Lynn Wardley notes, the Burrage house begins to resemble Boston's Gardner Museum, in that both "enable traffic between private and public space."[93] For Mrs. Luna, Olive's widowed sister (who has her own designs on Basil), Verena's performance creates public space within a domestic interior. In Mrs. Luna's eyes, the arrival of Verena, "who looks like a walking advertisement," completely alters Mrs. Burrage's home (*TB*, 261). In this transformed space, Mrs. Luna chastises Ransom for neglecting his public duties as a gentleman: "You won't speak to me in my own house—that I have almost grown used to; but if you are going to pass me over in public I think you might give me warning first" (*TB*, 257). Later, when Basil attempts to leave Mrs. Luna in order to go watch Verena's performance, "she only remarked, with light impertinence, that he surely wouldn't be so wanting in gallantry as to leave a lady absolutely alone in a public place—it was so Mrs. Luna was pleased to qualify Mrs. Burrage's drawing-room" (*TB*, 261). Mrs. Luna's emphasis on how public Mrs. Burrage's home has become clearly denigrates Verena's influence; for a proponent of such a conservative view of domesticity, the transformation of private space into public moves beyond alarming to become laughable, offering the "pleased" Mrs. Luna a smug self-satisfaction.

In this private setting turned public stage, Basil famously formulates his feelings for Verena in terms that allow him simultaneously to acknowledge and undermine her public role: "her apostleship was all nonsense, the most passing of fashions, the veriest of delusions . . . she was meant for something divinely different—for privacy, for him, for love" (*TB*, 269). The privacy to which Basil refers is contained domestic space, perhaps his home in Mississippi, a secluded setting inhabited only by his mother and sister. Ransom's native Mississippi, not yet embedded in urban networks, represents both a contained space and an earlier time in which containment is possible.[94] In his conception of a future with Verena, she will have "no place in public. My plan is to keep you at home, and have a better time with you there than ever" (*TB*, 328).[95] Basil must rescue Verena from public space in order for her to inhabit the private space where he believes she belongs. He engages with public spaces in order eventually to escape the commercial and ensure that Verena's "influence becomes really social" (*TB*, 380). In so doing, he reanimates the interpersonal model of influence that has been otherwise overwhelmed by publicity networks.

For Basil Ransom, the answer to the problem of Verena's public influence is to contain her in his own home. Marriage is not, as Pardon would have had it, a conduit to publicity; rather it is a transaction of ownership that removes the commodity from the marketplace, much as the collector Elmer Moffatt removes his objets d'art (and later his wife Undine) from the market in Wharton's *The Custom of the Country*. Verena is "an object of desire intended for display rather than consumption."[96] The path Ransom takes to achieve Verena's containment, however, leads him to enter and negotiate the uncontained spaces of the networked city.

The majority of Basil's meetings with Verena happen in settings that contain elements of both public and private space: Memorial Hall in Cambridge, Central Park, Mrs. Burrage's home-turned-lecture-hall, and the "big, hot, faded parlor of the boarding house in Tenth Street, where there was a rug before the chimney representing a Newfoundland dog saving a child from drowning, and a row of chromolithographs on the walls" (*TB*, 279).[97] All of these places serve as alternatives to the "intensely personal" space of Olive's still-contained drawing-room and the containment Basil proposes for Verena. Though Ransom may seem to "maintain the schisms of male and female, work and home, personal (private) and public," the modern world he inhabits does not allow for such clear dichotomies.[98] Ransom may attempt to remove Verena from the public sphere, but removal is impossible in urban spaces that are no longer structured by separate spheres. He can succeed only by removing her bodily from the city.

James encapsulates and registers this blurring between private and public spaces in his depictions of Central Park. Whereas in *The American Scene* James describes the park as the city's most important public space, in *The Bostonians* the park operates as a space for privacy. When Verena Tarrant goes to New York, she makes two separate visits to the park. The first, an excursion with the wealthy Henry Burrage, is marked by "the swiftness of his horses, the softness of his English cart, the pleasure of rolling at that pace over roads as firm as marble" (*TB*, 284). Here Verena experiences the Olmstedian version of the park; the carriage ride evokes the upper-class world of Nathaniel Willis to which the park initially catered.

Encapsulating a new mode of use for Central Park, her second visit is much more momentous both for Verena and the text. During an afternoon in the park with Basil Ransom, Verena's "submissive" nature surfaces, eliciting "the deepest feeling in Ransom's bosom . . . that she was made for love" (*TB*, 324). Love inevitably is associated with domesticity and motherhood; when a nursery maid passes, Verena is caught "looking with a quickened eye at the children (she adored children)" (*TB*, 325). Basil, in turn, develops a "plan. . .to keep [her] at home," making arguments about women's roles that resound "privately, personally" (*TB*, 328, 332). And yet these "personal" affections develop in distinctly urban space; James emphasizes the park's connections to the city, highlighting that for urban dwellers without money, public space is the place to pursue interactions that evoke the "private." Verena listens to Basil's "warm, sweet, distinct voice" through the "warm, still air touched with the far-away hum of the immense city" (*TB*, 322). The city reveals itself even more explicitly in the streetcars, advertisements, and the "groups of the unemployed, the children of disappointment from beyond the seas, [who] propped themselves against the low, sunny wall of the Park; [while] on the other side the commercial vista of Sixth Avenue stretched away" (*TB*, 332). Decidedly urban, the public park nevertheless stirs deep personal emotions, countering the narrative transition that will occur in the urban home.

The turning point in Basil and Verena's relationship occurs in Central Park, when Basil announces that one of his reactionary essays will be published in the *Rational Review*. Basil, Verena assumes, has succeeded in attaching himself to the press; he will "go in" in a way that her father has only dreamed about. And through the press, she imagines, his influence will travel farther even than her own. The publishing and postal networks of the nineteenth century reached beyond those established by telegraphs and trains, eventually incorporating rural residents like Basil's mother and sister into urban networks. Having established this authorial foothold, Basil proposes marriage. He aims to extract Verena from the multiple networks of publicity and promotion in which she participates as a public personality—a celebrity in the newly coined modern lingo—and to restrict her performances to his home.[99] Marrying Basil would return Verena to the corporeal realm: Brook Thomas notes that in her marriage Verena cannot "'assert the full possession of an individual self,' because the sphere she is about to enter, while decidedly private, does not allow her the space for a self to exist. Indeed, the marriage contract incorporates her into the body of her husband."[100]

Contrasted to the terms of marriage offered either by Pardon or Henry Burrage, each of whom would help build Verena's career, marriage to Basil represents a step back in time toward a vision of containment to which Ruth Hall, for one, would never agree. Yet such an incorporation also shows that Verena's modern self is fundamentally permeable; she represents woman as essentially transformable, equally fitted for the stage and the home. Ransom may claim Verena, but James's unhappy ending and his general sense of subjectivity as decentered argue against seeing this as the only or primary possibility for the modern self.[101] Indeed, in transporting Verena back to the South, Basil carries her back in time and space to a place where a unitary self may be imaginable, even though when women marry, that self legally dissolves. As James makes clear, however, the world of this novel is not one where private lives are contained; indeed, "the city of Boston itself is . . . alarmingly permeable."[102] It is a setting where privacy erodes under the stream of media and publicity generated by and constructing the city, a force that transforms all who experience it.

Even Olive Chancellor is changed by urban spaces where public and private blend. Fittingly, the reticent Olive's entrance into the networks of the modern media happens in New York, a metropolitan environment that will launch her into the world of production and performance. A transition between the private space of a boudoir and the public domesticity of a park sets Olive's new life in motion. While Verena is in Central Park with Basil, Olive decides to launch Verena publicly, instead of attempting to contain her. Her decision grows from a discussion she has about Verena's future in the wealthy Mrs. Burrage's boudoir, ostensibly the most private room in this quasi-public home. Yet even the boudoir may take on a public role; as tastemaker Elsie de Wolfe later would point out: "The boudoir has a certain suggestion of intimacy because it is a personal and not a general room, but while it may be used as a lounging-place occasionally, it is also a thoroughly dignified room where a woman may receive her chosen friends when she pleases."[103] When Mrs. Burrage offers to publicize Verena in New York, Olive becomes "deeply agitated . . . excited and dismayed." Her possession has been eroded. Blindly, she makes her way to Washington Square. "Open to the encircling street," the square is a public place where domestic rituals are enacted, where "the infant population fill[s] the vernal air with small sounds that ha[ve] a crude, tender quality, like the leaves and the thin herbage" (TB, 310). And here, where domestic activity blends into the urban landscape, Olive realizes that she is "face to face with her destiny" (TB, 311). Olive's destiny pushes her into the networked world and modern subjectivity. The public park offers her the anonymity and privacy she needs to make a most difficult personal decision. Here, Olive realizes that she, too, may find a personal profit in integrating her domestic space into the urban world and taking Verena public. Neither she nor her drawing-room will ever be the same.

The novel takes a hiatus from the urban at this point. Olive, Verena, and eventually Basil Ransom go to Cape Cod, where the women craft Verena's victorious Music Hall debut. But instead of withdrawing from the urban in this pastoral setting, Olive lays the groundwork for a modern advertising campaign—a campaign that will emanate from her drawing-room. As Mona Domosh notes, in this period, "The domestic sphere of home and family was meant to be untainted by commercial concerns; the home was to be a haven from the economic world. But again, the very circumstances of bourgeois life undermined this separation."[104] Domosh links this phenomenon to a new focus on consumerism within the home; in the following chapter, I will explore this effect at work in tenement homes. In The Bostonians, the home's entanglement in modernity is demonstrated differently.

When the ladies return from Cape Cod, the increasingly public function of Olive's drawing-room becomes apparent through the number and type of unsolicited callers she receives and the trajectories their visits take. For in-

stance, there are Matthias Pardon's unexpected visits, which begin long before Olive decides to take Verena public and show just how ineffectual Victorian proscriptions against unwanted intrusions will be in the modern era.
When Pardon first enters Olive's house, the narrator notes that "she had
never invited him to call upon her. . . . She thought Mr. Pardon's visit a liberty; but, if she expected to convey this idea to him by withholding any suggestion that he should sit down, she was greatly mistaken, inasmuch as he
cut the ground from under her feet by offering her a chair" (*TB*, 54). Ever a
representative of the journalistic mechanisms that are busily publicizing private relations, Pardon makes an entrance that inverts the power relations inherent in the traditional interactions between hosts and guests. Pardon does
not simply disrupt the containment of Olive's home; like Verena he turns it
into the site of public exchanges. As the scene continues and Pardon conveys
his proposals for "running" Verena, the interaction becomes more than a
simple clash of classed ideas of public and private. Rather, it represents an
early erosion of the separation between Olive's drawing-room and the world
beyond, a development over which Olive eventually takes control.

Pardon's initial visit begins a series of surprise appearances that puncture
the containment of Olive's home; it also foreshadows the role that he will
play later in Verena's Music Hall debut. Pardon's second unbidden visit to
Olive's drawing-room comes at the novel's end. His entrance resembles a
melodramatic actor's: "the curtain in the doorway was pushed aside and a
visitor crossed the threshold" (*TB*, 408). The transformation of Olive's
house from enclosed space to public stage that was initiated with Basil's arrival and punctuated with Pardon's visits is complete. Olive's home has become a staging ground for information that Pardon can transmit through the
papers to a national public. He probes for information, badgering Mrs.
Luna: "I'm not going to let you off! We want the last news, and it must come
from this house" (*TB*, 409). As he exits, he "drop[s] the portière of the
drawing-room," signaling the end of his dramatic scene and ostensibly returning Olive's home to its "contained" state.

But by this point Olive's home has unfolded fully to become a node on the
information network, so much so that Pardon's visit seems less an intrusion
than a strand of Olive's exhaustive publicity campaign. "With her portrait
in half the shopfronts, her advertisement on all the fences," Verena is professionally produced (*TB*, 406). Her Music Hall performance is "immensely
advertised," and in the hall "itinerant boys [hawk] 'Photographs of Miss
Tarrant—sketch of her life!' or 'Portraits of the Speaker—story of her career!'" (*TB*, 413, 415). These efforts to reproduce Verena for public consumption, the reader must assume, are Olive's doing. As part of Olive's "new
system of advertising," she has hired a professional agent to "run the pair,
as you might say. He's in the lecture business" (*TB*, 417, 421). The model of
marriage that Pardon and then Burrage proposed to Verena—a relationship

predicated upon publicity—while initially odious to Olive, is also accessible to her thanks to her wealth. She, after all, is not married. Olive may never have been as attractive to Verena as Basil is, but she can offer the powerful seductions of excitement and fame. Thus, Olive herself sets the machinery of publicity in motion, organizing the print media, photography, and mass plastering of posters and photographs in order to sell Verena, to broaden her influence, and to protect her from marrying Basil.

The extent to which Olive embraces the networks of publicity is most noticeable in her home. Mrs. Luna compares Olive's efforts to a military campaign, remarking, "She can't sit still for three minutes, she goes out fifteen times a day, and there has been enough arranging and interviewing, and discussing and telegraphing and advertising, enough wire-pulling and rushing about, to put an army in the field. What is it they are always doing to the armies in Europe?—mobilizing them? Well, Verena has been mobilized, and this has been headquarters" (*TB*, 407). If Verena has been made mobile in one sense, it is Olive who has mobilized militarily to defend Verena from Basil Ransom's offensive campaign. But more important is Mrs. Luna's image of Olive's parlor as a nerve center for numerous modern modes of communication. Olive's drawing-room, like Central Park, has been turned inside out. As Joyce A. Rowe argues, Olive's home gives only "the illusion or suggestion of a sheltering privacy"; in fact, "privacy is precisely what Olive's domestic order denies."[105] Instead of serving as a refuge, the drawing-room has become a transmitter of influence, emitting its vibrations to the world outside through the media. The novel's most interior space assumes a new position in the urban networks of communication. And in James's architectural dialectic, as a newly modern Olive transforms her home, her home demands additional changes.

The fate of Olive's drawing-room raises the question of how modern influence will be transmitted and asks whether a change in the mode of transmission—in this case a transition from domestic influence to a commercial influence—will alter the message itself. In *The Bostonians*, the effect is to transform Verena's message from something to nothing, and thus to silence the feminist speech and victorious debut that Olive has been crafting. Instead of gaining the biggest and most influential audience of her career, Verena leaves the Music Hall shrouded in a hood, destined not to perform but to shed tears. Verena's silence and her decision to marry Ransom have parallels with the feminist movement's decline in the 1920s as chronicled by Nancy Cott, when "feminist intents and rhetoric were not ignored but appropriated" by the industries of advertising, mass-marketing, and the glorification of consumption.[106] The end of Olive Chancellor's women's movement was inevitable in the face of a renewed drive toward marriage and consumption. Perhaps Verena's modern adaptability empties her of the will to resist Ransom. But the message is not completely silenced. It is Olive, whose home has become fully networked, who begins to embody an alternative version of the modern subject. In the novel's final moments, the heretofore timid Olive decides to speak on the Music Hall stage that Verena has abandoned. Olive, finally, will "go in" to public discourse more thoroughly than Tarrant, Pardon, or Ransom. Her speech takes place outside of the text—the possibility that a woman might be the most influential embodiment of modernity was unwriteable for James.[107] In fact, when seen in the context of what is happening in her home, Olive's act both echoes *Ruth Hall*'s move to bring domesticity into the public sphere and anticipates a current argument forwarded by geographer Doreen Massey. "In brief, the argument is that the need for the security of boundaries, the requirement for such a defensive and counterpositional definition of identity, is culturally masculine. . . . [M]any feminists have argued against such ways of thinking, such definitions of identity. . . . [W]e need to have the courage to abandon such defensive—yet designed for dominance—means of definition."[108] Clearly, inhabiting networked space has transformed Olive from silent would-be mastermind into, potentially, a public advocate for feminist concerns.

James's narrative of Olive's changing drawing-room emphasizes the profound power that domestic space—especially as it is increasingly integrated into the urban landscape—exerts in relation to modern subjectivity. In an era that would see the beginnings of social scientific inquiry about the environment in the new disciplines of sociology, ecology, and human geography, *The Bostonians* anticipates and incisively explores questions that these disciplines would raise about the development of a modern subjectivity and its relation to urban space. The urban home and the urban park are spaces whose role in the development of modernity has been overlooked. Yet they are spaces where individuals exert agency within urban space, transforming themselves as they transform the physical spaces around them. In *The Bostonians*, James's anxiety over the mingling of private and public in the urban home encapsulates a deeper fear for the future of the middle-class home, a fear that soon would be directed against the tenement. Yet the tenement is closer to Olive's burgeois home than current readers of *The Bostonians* may recognize.

Most discussions of Olive Chancellor's Charles Street home, including much of mine in this chapter, focus on the house's interior and implicitly extend Olive's class status to the neighborhood that surrounds her.[109] But while placing Olive's rowhouse in the Back Bay or Beacon Hill neighborhoods offers coherence to Olive's bluestocking spinsterhood, it obscures the reality of Charles Street in the 1880s. As I have noted, one end of Charles Street runs along the base of Beacon Hill with its old-guard wealth. But given its river view, Olive's section of the street would have been considered part of the West End, the working-class tenement neighborhood bordering Beacon Hill that was razed in 1959. Less radical (and far better received) im-

FIGURE 11. Charlesbank Park. Frederick Law Olmsted Architectural Drawings and Plans, #462. Courtesy of the Division of Rare and Manuscript Collections, Cornell University Library.

provement projects had been attempted in the West End for almost a century before it was obliterated. For example, in Boston's Park Plan for 1879, the area between Charles Street and the Charles River (which Olive sees from her back windows) was slated to be developed as a neighborhood park designed by Frederick Law Olmsted himself.

For Olmsted, Charlesbank Park represented a departure from his previous urban work (see figure 11). Neither an independent landscape park nor a part of Boston's famed Emerald Necklace, Charlesbank was "the first open-air gymnasium in a public park," featuring running tracks for men and women, sand courts, and a variety of gymnastic equipment.[110] Where his designs for Central Park had assumed that the carriage-driving class would be the park's primary clientele, by 1887, when construction of Charlesbank had finally begun, Olmsted clearly had "those who pass most of their time in monotonous occupations and amid sombre surroundings" in mind.[111] Like much of the reform architecture that his former partner Calvert Vaux designed, Olmsted planned Charlesbank "as an isolated feature for the enjoyment and health of the crowded working-class population nearby": Olive Chancellor's neighbors.[112] That James sets Olive's house in such close proximity to the West End emphasizes its multiple connections to, indeed, its inseparability from the diverse and vibrant city that surrounds and permeates it. And as was true in Central Park, these connections come spatially to define Olive's urban home. As Doreen Massey notes, "the particularity of any place is . . . constructed not by placing boundaries around it and defining its identity through counterposition to the other which lies beyond, but precisely (in part) through the specificity of the mix of links and interconnections *to* that 'beyond.' Places viewed in this way are open and porous."[113] Just as the increasingly porous, open, public character of Olive's private home is a potent source of tension for James in *The Bostonians*, the operations of public and private in the tenement house became a powerful touchpoint for Progressive Era urban reformers.

Like Vaux and Olmsted's designs for Central Park, Olive's tactic of blending private and public in order to further a social agenda would have powerful historical parallels as the Progressive Era unfolded. Photographer Jacob Riis would do just this in his efforts to ameliorate housing conditions in the burgeoning tenements of New York City. Riis's methods and message relied on his sense of the powerful influence of domestic space; his photographs and lantern-slide shows (many of which took place, like Verena's speech, in private homes) reveal the home's permeability even as they express his alarm about urban connection and contagion. As the urban landscape became increasingly networked, Riis and other authors saw in the tenement—as James had in the park-like drawing-room—both a source of anxiety and a site ripe for social transformation.

Chapter 3

The Tenement Home

Pushing the City's Limits

> *That is the one thing that is the matter with the slum—it makes its own heredity. The sum of the bad environment of to-day and of yesterday becomes the heredity of to-morrow, becomes the citizenship of tomorrow.*
> —Jacob Riis[1]

As we saw in chapter 2, the narrator of Henry James's *The Bostonians* is condscendingly indulgent of Olive Chancellor's work in the tenements near her home. A decade later such philanthropy by a bourgeois woman would be viewed with greater alarm. In Edward Townsend's 1895 novel *A Daughter of the Tenements,* a wealthy young teacher ventures into New York's Lower East Side tenement district to visit one of her immigrant pupils. While she is in the child's home, the teacher is exposed to typhus fever and is ordered into quarantine. But before leaving the dangerous building for the safety of her home, she glimpses "a tenant from another floor, who was soon staggering toward a clothing factory, bent beneath the mound of garments which had made the typhus-fever patient's bed; each garment to be offered for sale over some counter the next day; a bargain, verily, for a death warrant would be included free with every garment!"[2] The infected clothing, we imagine, is destined to enter a bourgeois home, its origins and its threat undetected. Townsend's language is lifted almost verbatim from *How the Other Half Lives,* in which Riis describes a typhus patient "discovered in a room whence perhaps a hundred coats had been sent home that week, each one with the wearer's death-warrant, unseen and unsuspected, basted in the lining."[3] Cindy Weinstein points out that "the economic and hygienic crossing of lines is paradoxically accomplished through the lining itself; an apt metaphor for the continual construction of lines, or 'barriers' [*OH,* 140, 147] as he [Riis] sometimes calls them, and their inevitable deconstruction."[4] Disease, contagion, quarantine, and invisible death warrants accompany interpersonal connection across ethnic and class lines. Even the "quarantine" of home is no protection from the contagious urban slum.

While alarmist, such depictions of tenements as sites of overwhelming and dangerous connection placed them at the center of Progressive Era architectural and public health reforms, especially in New York City, where reformers grappled with the task of improving how the "other half" lived. Years earlier, when Americans' homes in boarding houses and row houses blurred old definitions of domestic space, urban novels such as *Ruth Hall* and *The Bostonians* animated and revised the idea of the contained home in relation to the urban landscape. But at the turn into the twentieth century, an increased focus on tenement housing, particularly as framed by naturalistic fiction and the verisimilitude of journalism and photographs, forced middle-class Americans into an uneasy proximity with tenement life that threatened their own homes and identities. As the shifting spatial realities of home came into sharp focus in the tenement, reformers labored to enforce ideas about citizenship, health, morality, and subjectivity that remained persistently linked to the contained single-family home. Aiming to improve conditions in the slums, they animated an architectural determinism that both accounted for the moral degradation that they associated with tenement life and offered the possibility to ameliorate conditions and save lives in the city's poorest neighborhoods. Many reformers claimed that urban dwellings modeled on the contained home could offer "a seamless coherence of character, . . . an apparently comforting bounded enclosure," yet their work in actual tenements reveals, as geographer Doreen Massey has shown in the late twentieth century, that this "apparently reassuring boundedness" is in fact quite tenuous.[5] Tenement fiction and photography explore the limits of home; attention to setting and space in attempts to represent and reform the tenements demonstrates the instability of "home" and shows why reformers were committed to protecting it.

The best known interpreter of tenement life for the American middle class was immigrant journalist Jacob Riis. As he exposed sites where urban connection threatened to contaminate and erode the social order, Riis valorized the home as a source of control and containment. The idea that a home should be *separate* guided Riis's arguments for housing reform and anchors his theory that without the decency engendered by contained homes, the urban environment will produce a culture of deviance.[6] Defining separateness alternately as a separation between houses and as privacy within them, Riis implies that isolation (imagined by Townsend as quarantine; defined by Massey as boundedness) could protect the home environment from dangerous outside influences.

Riis's emphasis on separation and a concurrent demonizing of contact is especially evident in his best-known work, *How the Other Half Lives*, which opens by defining the home subjectively and spatially. Arguing that crowded cities are "nurseries of crime," Riis quotes a claim that eighty percent of criminal acts are "perpetrated by individuals who have either lost connection with home life, or never had any, or whose *homes had ceased to be sufficiently separate, decent, and desirable to afford what are regarded as ordinary wholesome influences of home and family*" (*OH,* 1, emphasis in original). Like many Progressive Era reformers, Riis attempted to use "the principal symbols of the Victorian age to his purposes, including . . . the home, privacy, and separation of the sexes."[7] Yet in most of his work, he focused on precisely the living spaces that confound this requirement for separateness.

Through journalism, photography, fiction, and autobiography, Riis engaged almost obsessively with the city, confronting an environment that demanded rational control but resisted his efforts to define, map, or label it. For reformers like Riis, as well as for the fiction writers such as Townsend, Stephen Crane, and Abraham Cahan, who focused on the New York slums in this era, the tenement landscape continually challenged efforts at definition, constraint, or control. The city disrupted attempts to impose boundaries, restrictions, or change upon it. Separations that reformers considered necessary to the development of a moral American citizenry, such as those dividing the home from work and the street, eroded as private and public spaces merged. Exploring the connections between public and private spaces, tenement fiction and journalism emphasize the visceral links among individuals and classes within the city landscape. Though these connections spur impulses for reform, their inherent ambiguities simultaneously disrupt reformist measures to order and contain them. The fundamental reaction for reformers like Riis is to demonize connection itself.

The extreme degree of connection exhibited in crowded tenement buildings elicited conflicting impulses in those who dramatized and narrated conditions there, as writers both transformed the tenement home into an open spectacle and reinforced middle-class notions of privacy and enclosure. This tension finds generic expression in the blend of a neosentimental focus on the moral values of domesticity and a gritty urban naturalism. A common concern with the tenement home links immigrant texts like Abraham Cahan's *Yekl* to Stephen Crane's *Maggie, A Girl of the Streets,* and ties them both to novels ranging from the sentimental *A Daughter of the Tenements* to the sensationalism of Edgar Fawcett's *The Evil That Men Do.* Through various genres and plots, writers dramatize the fictional and cultural conflicts and connections between the tenement and the middle-class home. In these texts, the shared living spaces of urban dwellings, where the home's nominally separate space is threatened by urban connection, stage a narrative conflict between spectacle and sentiment.

In fiction and documentary texts, tenement culture is not a contained threat. Rather, it is contagious. Because the tenements' permeability extends beyond the slums to touch upper- and middle-class homes via consumable products and entertainment, tenements come to embody the seamy side of the modern city, the dirty double to the uplifting public space of Central Park. The textual conflict between the idealized bounded home and its networked reality reflects the historical realities of domestic life at the turn into the twentieth century. At the same time, this conflict highlights the bourgeois anxieties that arose as the fate of the middle-class home increasingly became enmeshed in urban webs of communication, consumption, and display.

Physical Networks: Streets, Alleys, Passageways

Tenements had been a part of the New York landscape since the early 1830s, and because the city government was only beginning to inspect and regulate the structures, by the late nineteenth century overcrowding and squalid conditions had become synonymous with the word "tenement."[8] As Peter Hall notes of newcomers to New York's Lower East Side:

> they crowded into tenements that . . . perversely resulted from a so-called improved housing design: developed in a competition in 1879, the notorious dumb-bell tenement allowed twenty-four families to be crowded on to a lot 25 feet wide and 100 feet deep, with ten out of fourteen rooms on each floor having access only to an almost lightless (and airless) lightwell. Not infrequently, two families crowded into these wretched apartments; in 1908 a census of East Side families suggested that half slept at three to four people to a room, nearly a quarter at five or more to a room; they depended on a few communal taps, and fixed baths were nonexistent.[9]

Such substandard living conditions became the focus of great cultural concern.

Displayed in newspapers, tenement fiction, exposé texts, and photographs like Jacob Riis's, the crowded, dark tenement became unsettlingly familiar to the middle class. In New York, the El's third-story height added voyeuristic possibilities that Boston transplants Basil and Isabel March eagerly embraced in William Dean Howells's 1890 novel *A Hazard of New Fortunes*: "He said it was better than the theater, of which it reminded him, to see those people through their windows: a family party of work-folk at a late tea, some of the men in their shirt sleeves; a woman sewing by a lamp; a mother laying her child in its cradle; a man with his head fallen on his hands upon a table; a girl and her lover leaning over the window-sill together. What suggestion! What drama! What infinite interest!"[10] The elevated train, like Riis's photographs, opens the tenement to the urban gaze, allowing Basil March access to the drama and suggestion of the domestic scenes. Rendered as a series of connected tableaux, their interest is infinite, as is their influence.

Enmeshed in New York City's burgeoning transportation and communication networks, the tenement became a repository for fears about the dangerous power of urban connection; its threat heightened efforts to sanctify and protect the detached home and the family within. Even today, the home can be seen as a site protected from threatening surroundings; David Harvey notes that, "The family . . . exists as an island of relative autonomy within a sea of objective bondage, perpetually adapting to the shifting currents of capitalist urbanization through its relations to individualism, community, class and the state. It provides a haven to which individuals can withdraw from the complexities and dangers of urban life or from which they can selectively sample its pleasures and opportunities."[11] But far from operating as protected havens, tenement buildings were penetrable by all of the senses, negating the possibility, it would seem, for residents to exert agency either to withdraw from or to sample the pleasures of their urban surroundings. Constructed physically and textually as sites that mixed and inverted the public and private qualities of spaces such as the home, the street, and the workplace, tenements threatened to subvert bourgeois cultural values. Tenement narratives and photographs describe a human landscape that cannot offer the containment that signifies a regenerative environment. Jacob Riis's reaction, one common to many tenement narratives, is to pathologize urban connections. As Keith Gandal summarizes, Riis believed that "without domestic boundaries, without further separations within the family space, no family life is possible, and without family life moral character is impossible as well."[12]

In *How the Other Half Lives,* Riis examines and condemns two types of physical connections within and among tenements: structural connections including streets, hallways, alleys, and even sewers; and bodily connections, which he describes with contagion imagery and sensory language emphasizing vision, smell, and hearing. This pattern is refracted in other tenement texts. Reform writers invoke the language of contagion to emphasize the tenements' threat to order and prosperity, while fiction writers like Crane and Cahan glean from the tenements' sensory permeability differently nuanced representations of the networked city.

While the alley and the street symbolize connection and mobility in numerous urban narratives, for Riis these conduits do more than allow physical and visual passage; they enable people to connect to one another both in passing and through economic and social transactions that erode spatial distinctions. For instance, in *How the Other Half Lives,* Riis describes an Italian neighborhood where the street offers a living space far more appealing than the crowded tenements. "When the sun shines the entire population seeks the street, carrying on its household work, its bargaining, its love-making on street or sidewalk, or idling there when it has nothing better to do" (*OH,* 50). If they were unable to access the public domestic space of Central Park, tenement dwellers could use the street as a space for personal interaction. Activities ordinarily consigned to either home or marketplace merge on the street, transforming the space into a landscape that "might better be the market-place in some town in Southern Italy than a street in New York" (*OH*, 50).

Bringing marketplace activity to the street alters its physical structures as well. Purveyors of vegetables, fish, and tobacco claim the street's public space and moveable furnishings for impromptu shops. Riis describes curb women, for whom "ash-barrels serve . . . as counters," and bread-sellers, "camp-ing on the pavement," selling "exaggerated crullers, out of bags of dirty bed-tick . . . they probably are old mattresses mustered into service under the pressure of a rush of trade" (*OH*, 50). Materials from home and street together produce a temporary open-air market that transforms official maps drawn by municipal and corporate cartographers. "Trucks and ash-barrels have provided four distinct lines of shops that are not down on the insur-ance maps, to accommodate the crowds. Here have the very hallways been made into shops" (*OH*, 50). If private ownership remained beyond the means of most tenement dwellers, they could appropriate the street as a site for individual enterprise, rewriting official spatial narratives in the process.

Summer brings a more pronounced flouting of the boundaries between public and private spaces. Riis writes, "It is in hot weather, when life indoors is well-nigh unbearable with cooking, sleeping, and working, all crowded into the small rooms together, that the tenement expands, reckless of all restraint. . . . Then every truck in the street, every crowded fire-escape, be-comes a bedroom infinitely preferable to any the house affords" (*OH*, 126). Riis presents these spatial revisions as almost understandable within the context of the crowding and heat of a New York summer. However, moving one's bed into the street, an act made inevitable by tenement architecture, vi-olates one of the boundaries critical to middle-class spatial divisions within the home.[13] As Weinstein notes, "Tenements destabilize critical distinctions between persons, creating confusion where there should be difference, by es-tablishing themselves as a particular kind of space completely at odds with the moral, hygienic, economic, and sexual order of middle-class ideology."[14] Blurring the all important line between the private activities of the bedroom and the public realm of the street is just one way in which Riis sees the city's permeability and connectivity causing dangerous erosions of morality.

Although his prose emphasizes the dangers of mixing home and street, this arrangement's appeal surfaces in several of Riis's street images. In a photo-graph of "The Barracks, Mott Street between Bleecker and Houston Streets," for instance, links between home and street are visible both in the bodies of the women who sit on the tenement stoops and in the window boxes deco-rating the homes above (see figure 12). Embodying the home-street connec-tion, the women converse on the tenement steps with their feet on the side-walk and their babies on their laps. Older children, their images blurred as a result of the camera's long exposure time, examine the refuse that covers the sidewalk and spills into the gutter. This scene of family recreation seems

FIGURE 12. The Barracks, Mott Street between Bleecker and Houston, ca 1890. Museum of the City of New York, The Jacob A. Riis Collection (#116).

to have little connection to the green grass, playgrounds, and parks (such as Charlesbank in Boston) that reformers built to offer appropriately wholesome recreation to urban dwellers. The street, whose nickname, "The Barracks," emphasizes a different kind of containment than that linked to the bourgeois home, erodes the roles and relations that middle-class reformers believed were encoded within and enforced by the contained home and family.

Riis does not emphasize it, but city streets can also be sites where familial relations are extended, enlarging the home. Jane Jacobs points out that "instruction [in city living] must come from society itself, and in cities, if it comes, it comes almost entirely during the time children spend at incidental play on the sidewalks."[15] Belying Riis's analysis, the window boxes in "The Barracks" mark this positive extension of family and home, an extension Riis ignores in his text in order to discuss more alarming minglings between home and street. Flowers, plants, and bird cages decorate the building's sills, evidence of the overflowing quality of the tenements, but also public signs of a recognizable homemaking aesthetic that recalls Ruth Hall's treatment of her suburban cottage. The public face of the tenement both subverts and conforms to the precepts of domestic ideology. By way of aesthetics, the home enters the street.

The possibility that such connections might heighten the city's appeal occasionally penetrates Riis's anxiety. He notes that, "The metropolis is to lots of people like the flame to the moth. It attracts them in swarms that come year after year. . . . They come in search of crowds, of 'life'. . ." (*OH*, 69). Some of Riis's subjects simply desire urban excitement; for instance, in *The Children of the Poor*, Riis recounts the story of hosting a city "girl once at our house in the country who left us suddenly after a brief stay and went back to her old tenement life, because 'all the green hurt her eyes so.' . . . It was the slum that had its fatal grip upon her. She longed for its noise, its bustle and its crowds."[16] Although Riis's negative assessment of the city girl's desire is evident as he recalls the slum's "fatal grip," he also notes her pain and longing, rendering her physical and emotional attachment to the tenement comprehensible. Another of Riis's alarmist anecdotes reports that for the typical tenement boy, "All the freedom is in the street; all the brightness in the saloon to which he early finds his way."[17]

For other writers, the city-street-as-home presents different lures and dangers. The lack of separation between home and street is alarming at *Maggie*'s opening. "A dozen gruesome doorways [give] up loads of babies to the street and gutter," where "infants [play] or [fight] with other infants or [sit] stupidly in the way of vehicles," but the street is also where Maggie's initially thrilling romance begins.[18] Maggie loves the urban excitement—the theater, fashion, and sociability—that the street makes available. Similarly, in *The Evil That Men Do*, while urban entertainments like balls and parties serve as notable signposts on the beautiful Cora Strang's fall from virtue to prostitution to death, the narrator nevertheless acknowledges that the balls offer Cora her one source of pleasure.[19] And Abraham Cahan affectionately describes the Jewish ghetto's "'stoops,' sidewalks, and pavements . . . thronged with panting, chattering, or frisking multitudes."[20] In *Yekl*, Cahan offers a glimpse of a local ballroom, where "floating by through the dazzling light within were young women . . . with masculine arms round their waists. As the spectacle caught Jake's eye his heart gave a leap."[21] Though critics have termed this world a "sleazy" place of mere "glitter," to Jake it represents glamour, excitement, and romance.[22]

Some of Riis's images do make visible the street's allure; his photograph of the Feast of Saint Rocco gives a glimpse of the street's potential for freedom and beauty (figure 13). The shrine to Saint Rocco transforms the alley into a scene of celebration. Lanterns hang from fire escapes above the alley, while candles, ribbons, white linens, and miniature artificial trees decorate the shrine itself. The cobblestones are swept so thoroughly that a single, unidentifiable piece of debris at the center of the frame becomes quite noticeable. Children seem to be the shrine's primary devotees, their presence reinforcing not only the frightening erosion of the boundaries between street and home but also the potentially rejuvenating attraction that the street of-

FIGURE 13. Celebrating the Feast of Saint Rocco in Bandit's Roost, Mulberry St.— May 23, 1895. Museum of the City of New York, The Jacob A. Riis Collection (#266).

fers as a space to create and display art. If the Italians are considered to be picturesque subjects, "the delight of the artist," the street offers them a place to exhibit their own artistry publicly (*OH*, 33). Elsewhere in the text, Riis claims that the "tenement-houses have no aesthetic resources," so the shrine constructed for the Feast has a larger meaning in that it represents an aesthetic achievement that Riis's prose cannot acknowledge (*OH*, 124).

While streets have multiple meanings in Riis's text, sometimes assuming the valance of home, alleys invariably become threatening conduits. Narrow and twisting, the unmarked alleys operate as an alternative urban network for those who intimately know the landscape; they are sites where connections and mobility happen away from the gaze of outsiders and the law. Preoccupied with their extra-legal possibilities, Riis devotes an entire chapter of *How the Other Half Lives* to a discussion of alleys. He writes, "The sway of the excise law is not extended to these back alleys. It would matter little if it were. There are secret by-ways and some it is not held worth while to keep secret, along which the 'growler' wanders at all hours and all seasons unmolested" (*OH*, 34). Riis's image of "Gotham Court" shows an alley crowded with children, their faces focused intently on Riis and his camera, members, perhaps, of the army of children that travels through Riis's alleyways. He notes, "There is not an open door, a hidden turn or runway which they do not know, with lots of secret passageways and short cuts no one else ever found" (*OH,* 154). Like their older counterparts, children use the alleys to gain a mobility framed as inappropriate, especially for people their age. Children, Riis is certain, should be kept safe and immobile in the impenetrable family home.

Passageways are even more outside the pale for Riis; they comprise more secret, more hidden, and more fascinating networks that are further beyond rational control. One particular block on the East Side has a uniquely confusing effect on the ordinarily unflappable Riis. It has "thirty or forty rear houses in the heart of it, three or four on every lot, set at all sorts of angles, with odd, winding passages, or no passage at all, only 'runways' for the thieves and toughs of the neighborhood" (*OH,* 124). Here, the tour guide admits, "I actually lost my way once" (*OH,* 124). Passageways become all the more disorienting for Riis thanks to the ease with which local residents use them. For police (or reporters) on the trail of a young criminal, "pursuit through the winding ways and passages is impossible. The young thieves know them all by heart. They have their own runways over roofs and fences which no one else could find" (*OH,* 176). Because they facilitate illicit mobility, the passageways form an inaccessible and threatening network that emblematizes the threat of modern connectivity (see figure 16).

In *How the Other Half Lives,* "the Bend," as Riis calls his former newspaper beat, the Mulberry Bend neighborhood, epitomizes a space deformed by the passageway's connective power. To Riis, the Bend is the "foul core of New York's slums," "a vast human pig-sty," a place where even "incessant raids cannot keep down the crowds that make [the tenements] their home" (*OH,* 49). Riis blames the Bend's architecture for the problems that continually erupt there, claiming that "nothing short of entire demolition will ever prove of radical benefit" (*OH,* 49).[23] The buildings stand at random angles to one another, creating winding passageways between them that come in for particular scrutiny. "The whole district is a maze of narrow, often unsuspected passage-ways—necessarily, for there is scarce a lot that has not two, three, or four tenements upon it, swarming with unwholesome crowds. What a bird's-eye view of 'the Bend' would be like is a matter of bewildering conjecture" (*OH,* 49). Here, individuals are connected to one another by unmarked, unnamed, and unmappable networks whose patterns confound the rationalizing and reforming eye of Riis's camera. The haphazard spatial organization, Riis believes, engenders a particularly unmanageable population.

Urban dwellers' unpredictable use of alley networks emphasizes the risk that any network might be appropriated and transformed by a mobile urban population. To move more easily, tenement dwellers creatively adapt municipal networks of transportation and communication to their own needs; Riis is fascinated and frightened by the ways in which structures like sewers and telegraph poles become multiply useful conduits. A major modern improvement in sanitation, "big vaulted sewers" become "a runway for thieves," as well as for workers including one man who "used to go to his work along down Cherry Street that way every morning and come back at night. . . . Probably 'Jimmy' himself fitted into the landscape" (*OH,* 82). Telegraph poles, another emblem of modernity, have their communication potential expanded by Chinese New Yorkers. Riis notes derisively that Chinese immigrants have "enlisted the telegraph pole for the dissemination of public intelligence, but [have] got hold of the contrivance by the wrong end," posting notices on telegraph poles that become "the real official organ of Chinatown" (*OH,* 82). This form of communication, like almost everything about Chinatown, becomes threatening to Riis: "yellow and red notices are posted upon it by unseen hands . . .[in] a constant stream of plotting and counterplotting. . . . [T]he Chinese consider themselves subject to the laws of the land only when submission is unavoidable . . . they are governed by a code of their own" (*OH,* 82). Like the people who claim the sewers as their personal passageways, the Chinese who use telegraph poles as miniature kiosks undermine the control of official networks by making connections that Riis can only code as pathological. Thus transformed, monuments to progress and technological innovation invite new forms of illicit behavior.

Internal Passages: Tenement Hallways

As alleys do outside, for Riis the hallways inside tenement buildings signal a pathological degree of urban connection. Hallways erode the privacy that Riis considers fundamental to human development; privacy's "absence . . . is the chief curse of the tenement"(*OH,* 120). Constitutive architectural features within tenement buildings, hallways render the structures internally porous. Riis writes, "the hall that is a highway for all the world is the tenement's proper badge" (*OH,* 120). Within individual apartments, halls that might have helped to separate different spaces from one another largely had been eliminated in the 1850s with the rise of the railroad tenement. In this new configuration, "there were no hallways, so people had to walk through every room to cross an apartment, and privacy proved difficult."[24] As these railroad apartments were further subdivided, more tenants came to share the public hallways that Riis so abhorred. Reform reportage and fiction explicitly link tenement hallways to the development of a permeable and deviant urban subjectivity.

As conduits for sights, sounds, and smells, hallways become sites where spatial and sensory networks merge. Riis emphasizes this conflation's threat through the motif of physical and metaphorical contagion. He fears that hallways and other interior connections will render the tenements susceptible to "the dread of advancing cholera" or other contagious diseases such as smallpox, measles, or typhus (*OH*, 13). Other reformers emphasize the hallways' links to disease outbreaks with "scientific" data. However, not germs but connectivity itself is the prime culprit for at least one epidemic that Riis describes. To him, "the track of the epidemic through these teeming barracks was as clearly defined as the track of a tornado through a forest district," and leads to an outbreak of disease that Riis ascribes primarily "to the inability to check the contagion in those crowds" (*OH*, 129).

Beyond physical contagion, Riis claims, the buildings "touch the family life with deadly moral contagion," for their hallways lay tenement dwellers' lives bare to all the senses (*OH*, 2). The "common hall with doors opening softly on every landing as the strange step is heard on the stairs" exposes a tenant's every activity to his or her neighbors (*OH*, 124). Some more recent observers have argued that such scrutiny offers protection to urban dwellers, but for Riis it becomes the tenement's greatest evil.[25] The extent of the anxiety produced by hallways becomes clear when Riis plays tour guide, leading his readers through "No. _____ Cherry Street." Bathed in "utter darkness," the hall "turns and dives" uncontrollably and irrationally (*OH*, 38). Riis guides his followers, instructing them to listen "as we grope our way up the stairs and down from floor to floor . . .to the sounds behind the closed doors—some of quarreling, some of coarse songs, more of profanity" (*OH*, 38). Sound connects Riis's armchair tourists to the people who share the tenement, implying that such boundary erosion is incompatible with the morally uplifting home. "Close? Yes!" Riis exclaims to his imaginary followers, "All the fresh air that ever enters these stairs comes from the halldoor that is forever slamming," as shared air travels with the sounds to each crowded apartment (*OH*, 38). Hallways spread disease from floor to floor: "the sinks are in the hallway, that all the tenants may be poisoned alike by their summer stenches" (*OH*, 38). Further, "the saloon, whose open door you passed in the hall, is always there. The smell has followed you up" (*OH*, 38). Here, the hallway carries disease, deviance, and immorality; as it binds the building and its residents together, it exemplifies an unbounded environment incompatible with the detached home's goals.

For writers with a less fervent reform agenda, however, the hallway is a more ambiguous connector. For instance, hallways allow for information gathering and community surveillance in Crane's *Maggie, A Girl of the Streets* and *George's Mother*. In *Maggie,* hallway scenes function not simply as "an occasion for spectatorship" by voyeuristic readers, but as important opportunities for connection among the inhabitants of Maggie's tenement building, although the impact of these connections ranges widely.[26] Information gleaned from the hallway orders social relations within and outside of the tenement walls. For example, when Maggie's younger brother Jimmie escapes a beating in his apartment, he runs to a downstairs neighbor who has heard the ruckus. She opens the door and greets Jimmie with, "Eh Gawd,

child, what is it this time? Is yer fadder beatin' yer mudder, or yer mudder
beatin' yer fadder?" (*MG*, 11). As the evening progresses, Jimmie and the
old woman try to make out the battle's progress over the building's varied
nocturnal sounds. "Above the muffled roar of conversation, the dismal wail-
ings of babies at night, the thumping of feet in unseen corridors and rooms,
mingled with the sound of varied shouting in the street and the rattling of
wheels over cobbles, they heard the screams of the child and the roars of
the mother die away to a feeble moaning and a subdued bass muttering"
(*MG*, 11–12). Interior and exterior sounds penetrate the building, linking
neighbor to neighbor and private to public.[27]

Sensory messages make the hallways parallel the theaters and music halls
where the urban spectacle is performed publicly. Shared smells disrupt the
differentiation between home and street; Crane opens *Maggie* with an image
of a neighborhood where "a thousand odors of cooking food [come] forth to
the street" (*MG*, 7). Certain sounds inspire tenement dwellers to look out of
their doors; the hallway then allows them to share their impressions of what
they see. Jimmie's parents' fights, with their attendant "howls and curses,
groans and shrieks," invite the neighbors to watch: "Curious faces appeared
in doorways, and whispered comments passed to and fro. 'Ol' Johnson's
raisin' hell agin.' Jimmie stood until the noises ceased and the other inhabitants of the tenement had all yawned and shut their doors" (*MG*, 14). The
neighbors observe all of Mrs. Johnson's drunken comings and goings. On one
occasion, as she stumbles inside, "on an upper hall a door was opened and a
collection of heads peered curiously out, watching her." When she challenges
them to fight, "her cursing trebles [bring] heads from all doors" (*MG*, 36).
As the street becomes home, home comes to resemble the street.

According to the moral standards of bourgeois domesticity, Mrs. Johnson's disruptive drunken brawls, not to mention her frequent arrests and
trips to prison on Blackwell's Island, constitute behavior that should lead to
ostracism or at least condemnation from her neighbors. But in the tenement's networked space, an alternative set of criteria emerges for behavior
and community support, criteria that are codified in the tenement neighbors'
analysis of Maggie's behavior. Maggie's liaison with Pete introduces her to
the lures of urban entertainment and sex, a combination that transforms her
from an innocent to a prostitute. While this progression is not uncommon
in tenement fiction, neither does it conform to a certain code of tenement
morality. A much older Jimmie has "an idea that it wasn't common courtesy
for a friend to come to one's home and ruin one's sister," precisely because
of the object lessons taught by other neighbors, such as "dat Sadie Mac-
Mallister next door to us [who] was sent teh deh devil by dat feller what
worked in deh soap-factory, didn't I tell our Mag dat if she—" (*MG*, 39, 41).
Maggie's fall for Pete is a fall from grace within her neighborhood primarily
because her home is so highly networked that none of Maggie's actions can
escape her neighbors' notice. Thanks to the building's architecture, the neigh-

bors are familiar with Maggie's "jude fellow" and are privy to her conversations: "An' right out here by me door she asked him did he love her, did he. An' she was a-cryin' as if her heart would break, poor t'ing" (*MG*, 40).

The layout of the tenement does not simply broadcast Maggie's speech and actions; it makes her behavior the occasion for communal enforcement of morality through a narrative reconstruction of her past. Though the narrator explains that Maggie has not been tainted by her environment—"The girl, Maggie, blossomed in a mud-puddle. . . . None of the dirt of Rum Alley seemed to be in her veins"—her relationship with Pete leads to a transformation of her history in the community's memory, thus altering her destiny (*MG*, 20). This change occurs in the hallway, where women describe and condemn Maggie's behavior to the building's other inhabitants: "'She allus was a bold thing,' he heard one of them cry in an eager voice. 'Dere wasn't a feller come teh deh house but she'd teh mash him.' . . . 'Anybody what had eyes could see dat dere was somethin' wrong wid dat girl. I didn't like her actions'" (*MG*, 42). And when Maggie, abandoned, comes home via the tenement hallway, the neighbors' conjectures are confirmed.

Maggie's return to the tenement transforms her home into a stage and Maggie into a spectacle, emphasizing that "home" in the tenement is essentially a public space. As she stands in her mother's apartment, she becomes an object of fascination and horror for her neighbors, her life an equivalent to the moralistic melodramas she has seen with Pete. "Through the open doors curious eyes stared in at Maggie. Children ventured into the room and ogled her, as if they formed the front row at a theater. Women, without, bended their heads toward one another and whispered, nodding their heads with airs of profound philosophy" (*MG*, 61). Maggie's mother acts as mistress of ceremonies, binding the community to her by publicly displaying and rejecting her daughter's fallen status. She paces "to and fro, addressing the doorful of eyes, expounding like a glib showman at a museum. Her voice rang through the building. 'Dere she stands,' she crie[s]" (*MG*, 61). As the collective gaze shifts from Mrs. Johnson to Maggie, the neighbors assert their connection to the mother. Maggie's fate is determined by her community.

In rejecting Maggie's behavior and offering support to a mother who by most standards would qualify as unfit, the tenement community writes its own moral code that recapitulates "mother" as infallible even in a landscape where motherhood proves ineffectual and the home becomes a spectacle. At Maggie's death, her mother is supported by her wailing female neighbors, who use the "vocabulary . . . derived from mission churches" to comfort their friend (*MG*, 73). Reinventing the experience of mothering, Mrs. Johnson brings forth a sentimental token of Maggie's infancy: "In a moment she emerged with a pair of faded baby shoes held in the hollow of her hand. 'I kin remember when she used to wear dem,' cried she. The women burst anew into cries as if they had all been stabbed" (*MG*, 74). The shoes act as a talisman binding the women together in shared suffering.

Maggie's mother receives the same kind of unqualified support as the pious, thrifty, decent, and doting mother in another of Crane's stories, *George's Mother*. When George "goes to the bad" despite his mother's efforts, "the women of the tenement. . . came to condole with her. They sat in the kitchen for hours. She told them of his wit, his cleverness, his tender heart."[28] Similarly, Maggie's mother laments, "Wid a home like dis an' a mudder like me, she went teh deh bad" (*MG*, 50). Because the built space has the force to overcome individual efforts to fight it, in the tenement even Mrs. Johnson can claim the otherwise sacred title of mother. Significantly, as the networked space inside the fictional tenement becomes the site for alternative conceptions of home, motherhood, and morality that threaten middle-class ideals, connection itself comes to seem increasingly dangerous to the middle-class home.

Labor in the Home

Although physically distant from many middle-class homes, representations of the tenement home render it a spectacle so porous that it threatens the reassuring boundaries protecting individuals and classes. Journalistic and fictional networks running through tenement narratives identify and pathologize tenement dwellings as the antithesis of the detached home. Yet the contained home's role in consumer culture renders it permeable and therefore vulnerable to the city's influence. Through the marketplace, the detached home opens itself to the threatening connections associated with tenement homes. But to pathologize such marketplace connections is in a sense to condemn modern capitalism, a move that reformers guided by an ideology of progress cannot make easily.

Although the connections associated with tenement homes seemed dangerous to reformers like Jacob Riis, their threat paled in comparison to the eroded boundary between home and work, which clearly revealed that the modern home was not the "separate sphere" that Riis imagined it to be. As Mona Domosh notes, "In addition to the male-female, culture-commerce divide, production and consumption were ideologically kept separated. In reality, of course, these two different aspects of industrialization were completely interrelated."[29] Progressive Era reformers represent the anxiety produced by the home-work interrelation in two ways. First, they argue that work threatens the home by transforming it into a site of production rather than primarily a place of consumption. Second, because tenement products are sold to bourgeois consumers for use in their homes, consumer goods create a physical pathway between middle-class homes and tenements. Metaphors of contagion and disease animate these analyses, emphasizing the threat that tenement products such as clothes and food pose to middle-class consumers. By opening detached homes to the city's networks, these often unrecognized transactions between tenements and bourgeois homes demonstrate that, in this era, the home is enmeshed thoroughly in the modern city.

In *How the Other Half Lives*, Riis asserts that work and home should not mix because at-home work hinders tenement dwellers' attempts to approximate middle-class domesticity. Even though working at home might allow parents to be present with their children instead of leaving them in order to work elsewhere,[30] Riis claims that such an arrangement speeds the breakdown of family traditions: "In [the tenement] the child works unchallenged from the day he is old enough to pull a thread. There is no such thing as a dinner-hour; men and women eat while they work, and the 'day' is lengthened at both ends far into the night" (*OH*, 98). The presence of work in the home disrupts all of the routines, roles, and even the demarcations of time that Riis considers critical to maintaining a home. Without a dinner hour, without adequate time for leisure or sleep, without a sense of day or night, the tenement simply cannot reproduce the conditions necessary for the home to function as a regenerative space. This is not to say that Riis is trying to impose a middle-class use of time and space on resistant tenants; certainly it is difficult to imagine a home laborer rejecting a shorter workday or a paid lunch hour on the grounds that such reforms would represent bourgeois oppression. Riis supports his argument that using the private space of the home for market activities erodes social and familial relationships with pictures emphasizing the horror of the home turned workplace, raising the pitch of his claims that the tenement itself is everything the middle-class home rejects (figure 14). Domestic influence becomes domestic contagion.

To reinforce this analogy, Riis and other reformers identified the most intimate markers of middle-class conspicuous consumption as disease carriers. Clothes and food were particular targets, for they allowed intimate contact between the bodies of middle-class consumers and tenement dwellers. Contagion was associated directly with the architectural layout of tenement living quarters, where spaces for living mingled with those designated for work. As products and bodies mingled, each would contaminate the other. For instance, reformers argued that macaroni, manufactured by "Italians [who] not only have large families, but keep lodgers, [and whose] front shop then becomes a sleeping and living apartment," incorporated "the disease germ . . . in the paste of the macaroni."[31] The tenement's products, like its children, would take on and spread the polluting qualities of the environment. In the production of macaroni, one reformer recounted a physician's story of

> a child [who] lay sick of diphtheria in the back room where the physician visited her. The father manufactured macaroni in the front adjoining room, and would go directly from holding the child in his arms to the macaroni machine, pulling the macaroni with his hands and hanging it over racks to dry. The macaroni was then sold up and down Elizabeth Street.[32]

FIGURE 14. Bohemian Cigar Makers at Work, Their Tenement, ca 1890. Museum of the City of New York, The Jacob A. Riis Collection, 90.13.4.150.

A carrier of germs, the macaroni follows the child from sickroom to store-front on the body of the father, crossing boundaries between public and private space and connecting city dwellers' bodies to one another. Macaroni, in this era, did not cross class or ethnic lines; middle-class reformers could be "thankful that we did not have to eat the macaroni on our own tables."[33] Other foods traveled farther.

The most dangerous products issuing from the tenements were those that could pass as clean, safe, and hygienic, and thus could cross class lines, promising "the danger of the spread of a contagious disease [not only] among the people who are forced to buy cheap food in small neighborhood stores but to anyone buying in the best and most expensive stores in the city."[34] While "those who can afford to buy their food in cleaner and better stores feel safe when buying their nuts in glass jars, their peanut butter from a health food bureau, their cakes on Fifth Avenue and their candies wrapped in paper and apparently spotless," reformers point out that these foods, like the alien macaroni, carry hazards directly to middle-class consumers from the bodies of the immigrants who manufacture the products in their homes.[35] Nuts are packed into clean glass jars in homes where workers have "four rooms for nine people, indescribably filthy and crowded," or "in a rear tenement on Oliver Street . . . [where] the rooms are small, and one of [the] young boys is tubercular."[36] As middle-class consumers—even children (!)—wrest candies from transparent cellophane wrappers, they ingest the conditions surrounding the candy's production, for "candy sometimes leaks into the sleeping room," a "dilapidated and dirty" space where "the mother, father, and two small babies live, sleep and cook."[37] The candies threaten consumers not simply because they spread germs, but because they masquerade as "safe" food. Further, the manufacturers appropriate the power of advertising to speed their products' journey into "contained" homes. The nut producers "advertise the purity and cleanliness of their goods," to their consumers, who buy nuts at "all the best retail stores and health-food depots," while the candy company's products "are sold at retail stores in the city."[38] The products enter the middle-class home through the kitchen, bringing with them all of the conditions surrounding their manufacture.

Clothes, too, are seen as threatening carriers, especially when the clothing is produced in spaces where boundaries between home and work are blurred. "Every garment," wrote one reformer, "is found being manufactured in rooms whose legitimate use is for living purposes," an assertion borne out in Riis's photographs and text as well as in tenement fiction.[39] Like food, clothing could pass; everything from "the coarsest home-wrappers to the daintiest evening lace gown for a fine evening function are manufactured in these rooms."[40] And like food, clothing was thought to carry diseases directly from the mingled spaces of the tenement to the private life of the unsuspecting middle-class consumer. Middle-class women and children could be touched easily by the city's slums through intimate contact with clothing. As one reformer reported:

> The adornments of woman's dress, the flowers and feathers for her hats, the hats themselves—these I have seen being made in the presence of small-pox, on the lounge with the patient. In this case the hats belonged to a Broadway firm. All clothing worn by infants and small children—dainty little dresses—I have seen on the same bed with children sick of contagious diseases, and into these little garments is sewed some of the contagion.[41]

Women and children, ostensibly protected by the walls of the middle-class home, are seen here to be the primary consumers in the network of products binding the urban populace together. Even in a licensed tenement house, "when the sanitary conditions presumably were satisfactory to the Department of Health, the Tenement House Department, and the Department of Labor . . . it was found that for weeks a family . . . had been finishing clothing in the room where the oldest daughter . . . lay dying of tuberculosis."[42]

Even modern agencies of reform are powerless to stop either the contagion of the tenement or the spreading realization that no home is separate from the city.

The Limits of Architectural Determinism

In the face of such contagion scares, Riis's texts can be seen as a series of attempts to impose a notion of home as a separate space upon the tenements in order to contain their threat. Through "domestication," Riis hopes to "erect borders between the civilized and the savage . . . regulat[ing] traces of the savage within."[43] Yet these attempts are not always successful, even within Riis's texts. The city itself resisted Riis. Peter Hales argues in his photographic history *Silver Cities* that Riis constructed a "bumbling persona" precisely to cover the control he exerted over the images he produced, yet Riis's texts clearly display the city's refusal to submit to his hidden hand.[44] The tenements and their inhabitants confound Riis even when he is at his least bumbling, asserting their unknowability by refusing to conform to his structures of knowledge. This very unknowability shores up Riis's architectural determinist argument that the tenement, networked to a pathological degree, will produce pathological subjects.

Legal language and data gathered in the nascent field of sociology offer Riis official sanction for his strategy of textual and architectural containment. To bolster his argument that the environment makes the person, Riis quotes numerous reformers and government officials. After opening with the testimony given "before a legislative committee" by the Secretary of the Prison Association of New York claiming that the tenements "are to-day nurseries of crime and of the vices and disorderly courses which lead to crime," Riis goes on to buttress his own views with other "expert" commentary on the relationship between the environment and its inhabitants (*OH*, 1).[45] "Official reports, read in the churches in 1879, characterized the younger criminals as victims of low social conditions of life and unhealthy, crowded lodgings, brought up in an 'atmosphere of actual darkness, moral and physical'" (*OH*, 13). Throughout the text, Riis highlights the status of these experts and the documents they create. In the Progressive Era, theories of architectural determinism were becoming public policy.

Although *How the Other Half Lives* appeared at a moment when architectural determinism was in vogue among the reform-minded middle and upper classes of the cities, much of Riis's work, especially read in the light of tenement fiction, positions tenements at the limit of architectural determinism. Like his fellow reformers, Riis attempts to deploy the language of home to understand and solve the problems of the tenements, but his model of home as a contained and separate space cannot account for the physical and social realities that he confronts in the networked city. While reformers such as Riis attempt to explain and shape the tenements, they paradoxically describe the environment as singularly resistant to the reform practices that grow from their theory. The tenement is slippery, difficult to grasp. The buildings and their inhabitants elude expectations, boundary lines, and categories. Indeed, the very connections that endanger tenement dwellers connect the members of the "first half" of the city to the "other half." By pathologizing the interconnectedness of his subjects and ignoring middle-class and suburban participation in urban networks, Riis sets up a strategy for home-based reform that is spatially incompatible with the modern home's urban connections.

Riis's inability to contain his subject reinforces his desire to contain it. For instance, he notes with alarm that in a typical tenement yard

> every blade of grass, every stray weed, every speck of green, has been trodden out, as must inevitably be every gentle thought and aspiration above the mere wants of the body in those whose moral natures such home surroundings are to nourish. In self-defence, you know, all life eventually accommodates itself to its environment, and human life is no exception. (*OH*, 124)

In this case, the tenement environment is presented as the anti-pastoral. Riis's readers who imagined "natural" environments, whether Olmstedian parks or wilderness, to offer healing potential would have found resonance in the comparison between the grass and the individuals growing in the tenements. But at the end of the passage, Riis begins to move away from using environment as metaphor and begins to emphasize the environment's shaping force, the view that dominates his writing and political activity. In Riis's model, the environment is the primary influence on the development of "all life." Riis's description of the tenements' paupers is typical: "They are shiftless, destructive, and stupid; in a word, *they are what the tenements have made them*" (*OH*, 214, emphasis mine). Ultimately, *How the Other Half Lives* constructs a causal relationship between people's surroundings and their development: positive or negative changes to the environment will influence inhabitants accordingly; the slum will create a culture of inhabitants who personify its physical conditions. And they do. But not in the pathological ways that Riis leads his readers to expect.

Echoing the permeable, transformable architecture, tenement dwellers change the structures they inhabit by taking in boarders, subdividing rooms, turning living spaces into workspaces, and pursuing private activities outside. Along with his many disturbing images of homeless adults and children sleeping in alleys and under bridges, Riis includes a photograph of a smiling, parka-clad woman tenting atop her tenement, a cot clearly visible under the peaked canvas pitched on the snowy roof (figure 15). Although the caption, "Fighting Tuberculosis on the Roof," indicates that tenement dwellers risked more than symbolic contagion, the woman's expression hints that revising

FIGURE 15. Organized Charity, Fighting Tuberculosis on the Roof, ca 1890. Museum of the City of New York, The Jacob A. Riis Collection, 90.13.4.41.

architectural boundaries might be fun. Although Riis attempts to understand the relationship between this landscape and its inhabitants both ob-
jectively and subjectively, the slums and their residents continually position
themselves at the borders of knowability and control.

    The difficulty of controlling the networked city becomes evident when
Riis attempts to narrate a map of New York, "colored to designate nation-

alities" (*OH,* 20).[46] Though Riis begins by assigning colors to different races and separating the city into two easily defined halves, green for the Irish and blue for the Germans, the map's boundaries quickly become "intermingled [with] . . . an odd variety of tints that . . . give the whole the appearance of a crazy quilt" (*OH,* 20). Lines and colors, introduced to simplify the reader's encounter with unfamiliar territory, become living entities. For instance, the "red of the Italian . . . forc[es] its way northward . . . to lose itself and reappear" in another section of the city, while the "black mark . . . over-shadow[s] to-day many blocks on the East Side" (*OH,* 20). As Riis draws the map, the colors become animated, acting as substitutes for races and na-tionalities and challenging Riis's attempt to contain people by assigning them a fixed signifier. The "black of the Negro" becomes the "colored tide" that "engulf[s] uptown Manhattan," and the "Arab tribe," personified by a "dirty stain, spread[s] rapidly like a splash of ink on a sheet of blotting paper"(*OH,* 22). The motion of these races is uncontrolled. As each nation-ality or ethnicity asserts itself, it moves beyond the map's ability to contain and define, rendering the map useless as an instrument of boundary draw-ing. Riis's map is narrated but is never drawn; the decision not to accompany the unruly text with a more apparently objective image emphasizes the diffi-culty of rationalizing the tenement with the tools of cartography.

A useful comparison to Riis's narrative map may be found in *Hull-House Maps and Papers* (1895), a testament to the complex and intimate work re-quired to understand the urban neighborhoods that sociologist Robert Park would retrospectively term *terra incognita.* Together with her colleagues at Hull-House, Jane Addams produced the text, a groundbreaking statistical, geographical, and narrative map of the Halsted Street neighborhood sur-rounding the settlement house. In Park's words, the volume is "in the nature of an exploration and recognizance, laying the ground for the more system-atic and detailed studies which followed."[47] But the multicolored maps in-cluded with the text, coded to represent categories such as ethnicity and in-come level, convey a level of specificity that belie Park's assessment. Unlike Jacob Riis's narrative maps of New York, with their horrified descriptions of colors and races surging, uncontrolled, to take over whole sections of the city, the maps in *Hull-House Maps and Papers* construct the neighborhood as a variegated mixture in which ethnicity, family size, and income vary from household to household.[48] The detail and specificity achieved in the maps conveys the level of intimacy with the neighborhood achieved by the resi-dents of Hull-House. If Park reads this text as a factual recognizance, its au-thors use narrative to emphasize that their own intimacy with the neighbor-hood has taught them that reducing an urban neighborhood marked by mobility to static spatial or statistical representations is virtually impossible. In her comments, Agnes Sinclair Holbrook notes that any feature's "perma-nence seems less inevitable in a rapidly changing and growing municipality

than in a more immovable and tradition-bound civilization."[49] Like attempts to define spaces by their functions, attempts to classify people by race
ultimately become futile in the modern networked city. Riis's rebellious map
does not serve to contain populations even narratively; rather, it emphasizes
that containment is impossible in cities increasingly characterized by a mobile and interconnected population.

Even if people resist boundaries and elude census takers, refusing to be
incorporated into modern mechanisms for scientifically knowing the city,
buildings might seem to be more stable. Riis notes that "of its vast homeless crowds the census takes no account. It is their instinct to shun the light,
and they cannot be corralled in one place long enough to be counted. But
the houses can . . ." (OH, 22). Holbrook calls even this assumption into
question, noting that the buildings themselves are on the move in her
neighborhood: "almost any day in walking through a half-dozen blocks
one will see a frame building, perhaps two or three, being carried away on
rollers. . . . Suburban cottages, of remote date, with neither foundations
nor plumbing, travel from place to place, and even three-story tenements
make voyages toward the setting sun."[50] As they do in *Hull-House Maps
and Papers,* in *How the Other Half Lives,* the buildings themselves resist all
efforts to set boundaries, becoming unknowable, even uncountable. For instance, in the chapter titled "The Common Herd," Riis reprints a "Bird's-
eye View of an East Side Tenement Block," which shows a solid front of
buildings lining the sidewalk of the city block (figure 16). Though these
buildings are of varying heights and styles, they are still comprehensible as
a block of buildings, a fundamental component of the grid system organizing New York's streets. But within the block, buildings seem to have sprung
up randomly. At odd and surprising angles to one another, their locations
disrupt the order of the block formation. Further, there is no apparent way
to enter or leave the interior of the block. As Peter Hales points out in *Silver Cities,* bird's-eye views were a popular mode of urban photography in
the mid-nineteenth century, a way for lithographers and later photographers to elicit rational, governable patterns from the confusion the city
often displayed on the street level. Hales notes that "the virtue of the lith-
ographic bird's-eye view lay in its capacities to enclose and to order."[51] In
this way, bird's-eyes were similar to the photographic panoramas that "represented one of the most successful mechanisms photographers used to civilize the city and make it comprehensible. . . . To an urban culture characterized by vague, constantly shifting boundaries and a tenuous unity
threatening always to break down, . . . closure and identity were precious
commodities."[52] In Riis's image, the passageways so fully dominate the
area that even a bird's-eye view cannot assign a rational pattern to the
neighborhood. Hidden from plain sight, visible only through a bird's-eye
view, and accessible only to people with intimate, experiential knowledge

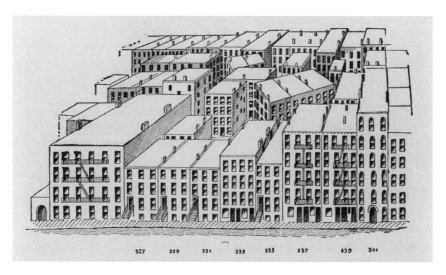

FIGURE 16. Bird's-Eye View of an East Side Tenement Block, Published in "How the Other Half Lives," from a drawing by Charles F. Wingate, Esq. Museum of the City of New York.

of the site, this group of interior tenements clearly presents a threat and a challenge to the rational forces of modernity and reform.

Like maps and diagrams, building plans seem to be under rational control because they are laid out by designers whose structures embody reform principles of rationality and improvement, if only on the level of the blueprint. Architects of model tenements such as Calvert Vaux, Frederick Law Olmsted's partner in the design of Central Park, put into spatial practice a proactive version of architectural determinism, arguing that design could solve problems at the root of urban decay.[53] Benevolent citizens willing to forego a slumlord's exorbitant income could instead charge modest rents for model tenements and expect an income of "philanthropy and five percent" profit per year.[54] Riis and other reformers cite examples of citizens whose commitment to such a plan has yielded economic and moral gain. In *How the Other Half Lives,* Riis accompanies this narrative with architect William Fields's floor plans and drawings for one of A. T. White's model tenements, the Riverside Buildings in Brooklyn (figure 17). Like most urban tenements, the Riverside Buildings fill a whole city block, but the block's interior, visible to every tenant through the back windows of each apartment, looks like Central Park in miniature. Winding paths meander through trees, leading promenaders to a fountain, a playground, and a music pavilion. A driveway and walkway surround the whole, unifying the space and offering opportunities for healthful recreation within the exterior walls of the complex. Even if there is chaos outside, there is order within. A resident wishing to go outside would never need to encounter the street. And in fact, the surrounding

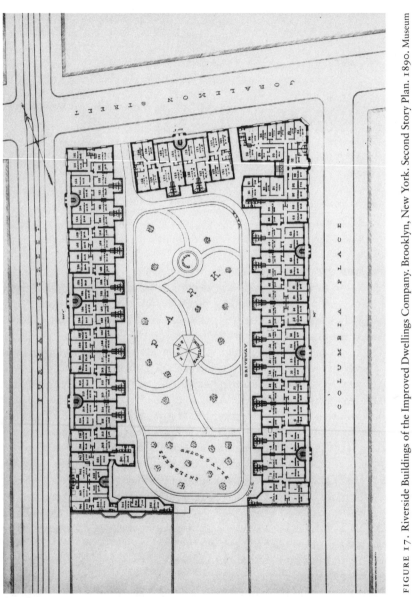

FIGURE 17. Riverside Buildings of the Improved Dwellings Company. Brooklyn, New York. Second Story Plan. 1890. Museum of the City of New York, The Jacob A. Riis Collection (LS 57).

streets are not even labeled; the blueprints essentially remove the Riverside Buildings from their specific and potentially chaotic locale. Plans like these reinvent tenements as places of order, light, rationality, and calm, oases in the midst of the city. The Riverside Buildings were built, but the drawings were far more attractive than the reality. In photographs, they appear blocky and stolid, offering little of the inspiration the drawings portend (figure 18). Further, even here residents do not conform to the performers' plans; in this photograph, tenement-style clotheslines dominate the would-be park.

Riis strikes an uneasy balance between the threat of connection and the promise of progress that is visible in his treatment of model tenement buildings like the Riverside. Given that the cost of Manhattan real estate made the construction of single-family homes close to city workplaces impossible, Riis and other reformers conceded that "home" would have to exist in cities, but only if "separate, decent and desirable" modern apartments could stem the tide of increasing connection that accompanied the spread of densely packed housing units. A model tenement could contain "three hundred real homes, not simply three hundred families," but only if the architecture was designed to keep them from making contact with one another. Thus, Riis's description of the Riverside Buildings reads like a checklist of remedies for the architectural features that, he believed, broke down the boundaries between public and private spaces in tenement homes. "Three tenants, it will be seen, use each entrance hall. Of the rest of the three hundred they may never know, rarely see, one. Each has his private front-door. The common hall, with all that it stands for, has disappeared. The fireproof stairs are outside the house. . . . Each tenant has his own scullery and ash-flue. There are no air shafts, for none are needed" (*OH*, 228–29). Though Riis notes features designed to bring tenants together in the Olmstedian mannner of a "familiar domestic gathering," such as a park, a playground, and weekly concerts, he is more interested in the architectural structures that will keep them apart.[55] He emphasizes the importance of separation by alluding to the dangers of the "common hall, with all that it stands for" (*OH*, 228). Urban dwellers' desires to connect to the street, incorporated into Calvert Vaux's designs and documented in Riis's own photographs and texts, are given little weight here. For Riis, the anxieties and social evils evoked by the tenement's characteristic permeability could be stemmed only by structures that would contain tenement dwellers and reduce the number of connections they would make in the networked city. Yet these modern technologies could not reliably contain the tenement.

Model tenement plans simultaneously organized space and attempted to order the lives of those who lived there according to a modified version of the contained home's moral and cultural principles. The symmetry, layout, and scale of model tenements were meant to inspire not just architectural but societal improvement. Architects encouraged particular lifestyles with

FIGURE 18. Riverside Buildings, Brooklyn; interior court, winter ca 1900. Museum of the City of New York, The Jacob A. Riis Collection (LS 59).

the spaces they designed, but they situated these designs in an urban land-scape that encouraged mobility and connection rather than stasis and con-tainment. Thus, the idealized version of tenement homes was attainable only in reformers' minds and in architects' blueprints. The contrast between this rationalized, carefully planned version of tenement life and the realities of extant tenements became a contest over the values that the spaces conveyed. The home was at the nexus of this conflict, serving as the source for both moral values and physical containment even as the unruly city revealed how tenuous the home's boundaries were.

Social Science and Sentiment: Defining the Home

It is not surprising that Riis places the "separate, decent, and desirable" home at the center of his architectural campaign against the tenement's influence. As the presumed primary environment of the child, the home was the site most likely to shape not only children but the adults they would become. In tenement fiction, as critic David Fine notes, "The slum child was both the most pathetic victim and, if he could be reached through schools, settlements and the church, the best hope for an end to the recurring cycle of urban crime, immorality, and disease."[56] As went the home, so went the nation. This was relevant especially for Americanized children of immigrants. "For the corruption of children," Riis writes, "there is no restitution. None is possible. It saps the very vitals of society; undermines its strongest defences, and delivers them over to the enemy" (*OH*, 169). Though Riis does not specifically mention national concerns here, his military language conjures up ideas of a nation under siege, a site that can only be protected by properly arming its inhabitants.[57] As Amy Kaplan notes, "the cultural work of domesticity" creates a "national domain and . . . generate[s] notions of the foreign against which the nation can be imagined as home."[58] Thus homes are not simply linked to a generic set of morals or ethics but to the development of a citizenry with specifically American values.

But what would this national home look like? In his autobiography, *The Making of an American,* Riis offers his own home as a starting point for imagining what kind of architecture could produce a nation-making influence. First, Riis's home is isolated geographically: "With a ridge of wooded hills, the 'backbone of Long Island,' between New York and us [,] the very lights of the city were shut out. So was the slum, and I could sleep."[59] Riis, of course, still commuted to the city to take photographs and write articles; he could ride "the trains that carry a hundred thousand people to New York's stores and offices from their homes in the country," daily maintaining his connection to the city.[60] But the house itself is "in the country," and its rural surroundings make it separate not just from other houses but from the urban landscape as well. Riis's house is decent and desirable, too; "white and peaceful under the trees," it is filled with children and presided over by an idealized mother: "the boys are all in love with their mother; the girls tyrannize and worship her together."[61] Finally, the house enacts Riis's national identity; the American "flag flies from it on Sundays," a symbol of nation as religion.[62] Riis's house is thus a site for and demonstration of personal and national acculturation. The ideal home is clearly "separate, decent, desirable"—and American.

Some immigrant groups, those Riis portrays as more easily assimilated into the culture of the United States, seem to share his spatial conception of the moral home. For example, he applauds the German immigrant who "makes himself a home independent of the surroundings, giving the lie to the sayings, unhappily become a maxim of social truth, that pauperism and drunkenness naturally grow in the tenements. He makes the most of his tenement" (*OH*, 25). Here, a transcendent notion of home helps to acculturate an immigrant group. Although the interesting notion that a home might operate "independent of the surroundings" never appears again in the text, it echoes nineteenth-century claims by Andrew Jackson Downing and Catharine

Beecher that the physical structures of an individual home could engender as well as enforce moral values.

Yet the physical attributes of home are far from permanent. Many tenement buildings at the turn of the century were constructed originally as the detached homes that Riis idealized but had been transformed into slums. Echoing the decline visible in Moodie's lodgings in *The Blithedale Romance* or Basil Ransom's boarding house in *The Bostonians,* in "the domain of the tenement" Riis notes, "the old Knickerbocker houses linger like ghosts of a departed day." Some of the buildings' physical structures remain, but they have been transformed by time and economic exigencies:

> This one, with its shabby front and poorly-patched roof, what glowing firesides, what happy children may it once have owned? . . . the broken columns at the door have rotted away at the base. Of the handsome cornice barely a trace is left. Dirt and desolation reign in the wide hallway, and danger lurks on the stairs. Rough pine boards fence off the roomy fireplaces—where coal is bought by the pail at the rate of twelve dollars a ton these have no place. The arched gateway no longer leads to a shady bower on the banks of the rushing stream, inviting to day-dreams with its gentle repose, but to a dark and nameless alley, shut in by high brick walls, cheerless as the lives of those they shelter. (*OH,* 27–28)

All of the architectural features that once marked this home as separate, decent, and desirable—a space that could have produced happy children and gentle repose—have been transformed. The vestiges of the past mock current realities. The fireplace, columns, cornices, and archways all have decayed, creating a new environment that will shape an entirely different inhabitant. Like other unfashionable lodging houses, these buildings have suffered from the elite class's desire for mobility. And as might be expected, Riis links these physical changes to a concomitant change in the home's potential for moral influence among tenement dwellers.

Tenements did not result simply from slow decay; as I have indicated, tenement dwellers actively altered the physical spaces they inhabited, making changes that challenged bourgeois expectations for domestic space. In the version of architectural determinism espoused by Riis and his contemporaries, "home" had to conform to specific architectural guidelines as well as a sentimental or affective description in order to effect a morally acceptable acculturation of its inhabitants. Accordingly, plans for middle-class homes designated rooms as kitchens, parlors, or bedrooms. Using rooms for improper or multiple purposes threatened the home's moral and physical impact.[63]

Like apartments, hotels, and boarding houses, tenements confound these architectural expectations, creating a confusion that stymies writers' attempts to understand tenement life. One reformer writes: "In one room, that which opens on the street or yard, is carried on all the domestic life. This room serves for parlor, dining-room, and kitchen; and in this room is in addition carried on the manufacturing. It is quite obvious that the word *home* was never intended to apply to such an apartment; neither does it give a description of an ideal place in which manufacturing should be done."[64] The tenement home crowds multiple uses into one space; in the reformer's mind the parlor should be distinct from the kitchen and both should be separate from the work room. Even more worrisome, the public functions of work and the more private ones of cooking (kitchen) and eating (dining room) happen in a room that "opens on the street or yard," a public space that is incompatible with "domestic life" as envisioned by the reformer. The permeability and mingled uses that characterize the rooms of the tenement dwelling disrupt the affective definition of home.

In order to prevent rooms from being used incorrectly, Progressive Era reformers targeted the long-standing practice of taking in boarders. Tamara Hareven points out that urban dwellers generally took in family members in order to help acculturate new arrivals to the city. *Sister Carrie*'s protagonist Carrie Meeber, who moves in with her sister when she arrives in Chicago, is an excellent fictional example of this practice. Sometimes, "where relatives were not available, strangers residing with the family as boarders fulfilled similar functions," often functioning as "surrogate kin."[65] We see this in *Yekl,* when Bernstein, Jake's co-worker, moves in with Jake and his family, eventually marrying Jake's wife Gitl after Jake departs. An informal version of the boarding or lodging house, the practice of taking in boarders historically had been seen as a "safety valve" offering cheap housing to those on the urban economy's periphery. Yet in the Progressive Era, reformers began to see in the practice "a manifestation of social breakdown."[66]

The emotional and rhetorical foundation on which Riis, tenement novelists, and official policymakers all rely derives from a tacit definition of home that is not necessarily shared by those who occupy the space. The uses to which inhabitants put a tenement home often disqualified it from its sentimental definition:

> Some twenty-five years ago the New York Court of Appeals handed down the following—known as the Jacobs decision: "It cannot be perceived how the cigarmaker is to be improved in his health or his morals by forcing him from the home with its hallowed associations and beneficent influences to ply his trade elsewhere . . ." How these miserable homework factories with their inmates working from daylight to six, eight, ten o'clock and even later in the night, can be defined as "homes" is beyond one's comprehension, and one must look through very rosy spectacles indeed to find the "hallowed" and "beneficent influences of a home" in which fur garments are stored in every conceivable corner and cranny of the living and cooking rooms, while all the members of the family toil from early morn to late night to earn enough to keep body and soul together.[67]

To this reformer, tenements cannot be defined as "homes" because their interior spaces are available for multiple uses; a space that operates as a site of economic production loses its potential to propagate a home's more elusive moral influence. While she rails against the court's decision to license certain tenements as workshops, the author does not dispute the dominant idea behind the court's decision, namely, that the home operates as a "beneficent influence." As Riis notes, "To the child of the tenements, home, the greatest factor of all in the training of the young, means nothing . . . but a pigeon-hole in a coop along with so many other human animals. Its influence is scarcely of the elevating kind, if it have any" (*OH, 138*). In 1912, James Quayle Dealey's "*Family in Its Sociological Aspects* likened even the modern urban family (biologically defined) to 'a temporary meeting place for boarding and lodging,' where strangers entered while family members passed large portions of their time on the streets or in other company."[68] Because they have succumbed to the city's increasingly powerful networks, tenements are impotent as "home." The resulting slums mark the city's inability to affect positive change and threaten the reformers' rationality.

For Riis, fully abandoning the rational would have meant alienating himself from those who could enact legal reform, yet the city forces a breakdown of the rational systems that he attempts to impose. As it is by his unruly maps, an erosion of rationalism is exposed by his attempts to balance scientific and sentimental approaches to his subject. Like many of Riis's other texts, including *Children of the Poor* and *The Making of an American*, *How the Other Half Lives* begins with a disclaimer in the form of an acknowledgment. Thanking those who have made the text possible, Riis cites "the patient friendship of Dr. Roger S. Tracy, the Registrar of Vital Statistics," saying he "has done for me what I could never have done for myself; for I know nothing of tables, statistics and percentages" (*OH, xv*). Even as Riis claims allegiance to "official" approaches to the tenements, he attempts to dissociate himself from the world of statistical rationality and to situate his project as an affective one. Riis's final acknowledgment, addressed to "the womanly sympathy and the loving companionship of my dear wife," likewise aligns him with feeling, sentiment, and the home, implying that his wife's influence—her sympathy—is foundational to his text (*OH, xv*).

Tenement literature echoes Riis's dual invocations of science and sentiment, constructing encounters with the tenement that are simultaneously emotional and physical. In *Daughter of the Tenements*, the wealthy young teacher must venture into the slums, exposing herself both to typhus and to the personal connection to tenement daughters that the disease represents in order to establish her missionary credentials. Riis's books, like tenement fiction, evoke emotion in various sentimental appeals for their readers to "feel right" and shockingly naturalistic dramatizations that force readers to recoil.[69] Both methods are dramatic, but the sentimental posits a personal relationship between reader and text, while the drama of naturalism relies on a distance between reader and subject that is ultimately containing.

In tenement fiction, interiors operate in a similar fashion, marking "a desire for beauty and tradition" that evokes the sympathy of a bourgeois reader's identification and simultaneously emphasizes the distance between reader and subject.[70] In *The Evil That Men Do*, for instance, the act of decorating brings classes together, while specific decorations separate them. One of the novel's characters, Mrs. Slattery, decorates her kitchen bedroom "with colored prints of the crucifixion and the martyred Virgin that might, in their red-and-yellow crudity, have made the bones of Rubens or Raphael rattle oversea."[71] Her misguided decorating choices portend that Mrs. Slattery will be powerless to stop the beautiful Cora's decline; the son she offers to Cora as a husband has been degraded by the slums outside.

Nowhere are both the aspirations and the failure of a middle-class aesthetic to improve the tenement more visible than in *Maggie, A Girl of the Streets*. Maggie's efforts to transform "the broken furniture, grimy walls, and general disorder and dirt of her home" into a scene that will meet her beau Pete's approval must be read as attempts, however futile, to connect herself to the consumption and display habits of the cottage home (*MG*, 23). To this end, she cleans the rooms and ties back the curtains with new blue ribbon. She even makes a lambrequin that differs from those pictured in Catharine Beecher and Harriet Beecher Stowe's advice manual *The American Woman's Home* only in its bold pattern (figure 19). (Beecher and Stowe recommend a subtle chintz.) But the lambrequin Maggie makes "with infinite care" and displays on "the slightly careening mantel, over the stove, in the kitchen" in the hopes that it would "look well on Sunday night when, perhaps, Jimmie's friend might come," becomes a symbol that prefigures Maggie's crushed hopes and ultimate destruction when, in a drunken frenzy, Maggie's mother destroys it. "She had vented some phase of drunken fury upon the lambrequin. It lay in a bedraggled heap upon the floor. . . . The curtain at the window had been pulled by a heavy hand and hung by one tack, dangling to and fro in the draft through the cracks at the sash. The knots of blue ribbons appeared like violated flowers" (*MG*, 26). Maggie's effort to create a setting that will appeal to the dapper Pete's taste mingles the pathos of identification with the naturalistic shock of distance. Maggie can never decorate tastefully enough to transform the tenement.

In *George's Mother*, Crane reiterates this futility by demonstrating that even the closest approximation to Beecher and Stowe's homemaking aesthetic is ineffective in the tenements. George's mother's kitchen echoes both immigrant and Americanizing aesthetics, producing a space that resembles Beecher and Stowe's rendition of a model tenement apartment (figure 20). "Three blue plates were leaning in a row on the shelf back of the stove. The little old woman had seen it done somewhere. In front of them swaggered

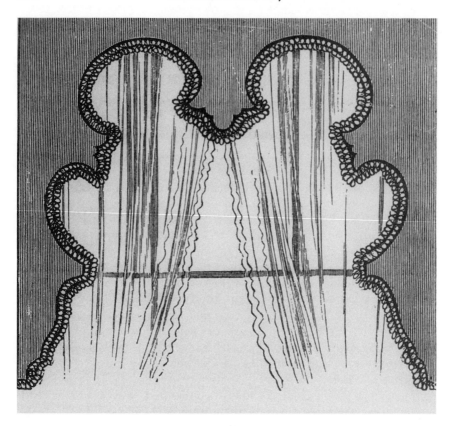

FIGURE 19. Lambrequins, from Catherine E. Beecher and Harriet Beecher Stowe, *The American Woman's Home* (1869; reprint, New York: Arno Press, 1971), 89. Harriet Beecher Stowe Center, Hartford, CT.

the round nickel-plated clock . . . Occasional chromos were tacked upon the yellow walls of the room. There was one in a gilt frame. It was quite an affair, in reds and greens. They all seemed like trophies."[72] This Beecherian space orders the mother's time just as a reformer might hope. Her days are spent appropriately performing the bourgeois rituals of cleaning, polishing, attending church, cooking nutritious meals, and worrying about her son. Yet while she decorates and maintains her tenement home according to familiar middle-class guidelines, her son George succumbs to the corrupting power of the broader environment. Here, even the model home is powerless against the slum.

Though Riis and Crane's narratives argue otherwise, historically the power of the tenement was not always overwhelming. While the authors and family groups presented in Riis's photographs would have appeared foreign to many of his readers, a number of the domestic interiors they produced—like

FIGURE 20. Tenement decorations, from Catharine E. Beecher and Harriet Beecher Stowe, *The American Woman's Home*, (1869; reprint, New York: Arno Press, 1971), 444. Harriet Beecher Stowe Center, Hartford, CT.

George's mother's kitchen—share the contained home's domestic aesthetic. For instance, in Jessie Tarbox Beals's "Room in a Tenement Flat, 1910," a family group gathers in a crowded tenement room with the attendant bare floor and single window (figure 21). But a closer look reveals the particulars of the family's housekeeping efforts. The glass cabinet on the wall holds a

FIGURE 21. Jessie Tarbox Beals, Room in a Tenement Flat, ca 1910. Museum of the City of New York, The Jacob A. Riis Collection (#502).

display of dishes. Carefully arranged corners of spotless napkins drape over the shelves. These decorations are echoed on the shelf over the stove where the points of a crocheted border peek out from above the teakettle. Other photographs reveal similar decorating touches: framed chromos (*OH,* 96, 185, 217), fringed shades (*OH,* 18, 96, 187), mantelpiece clocks (*OH,* 18), and large decorated seashells (*OH,* 185), all of which are recommended specifically as tasteful yet affordable decorations by Beecher and Stowe in *The American Woman's Home.*[73] These decorations are not just physically identical to the decorations described by Beecher and Stowe; they perform the same function of inexpensively transforming temporary living quarters into a home. These similarities simultaneously bring readers closer to the subject and impel them to make aesthetic and geographic moves to protect themselves from such proximity.

Technically, Riis's photographs also evoke both identification and distance. Though individual rooms generally appear dingy, Peter Hales points out that this appearance resulted in part from Riis's photographic techniques. In interior shots, Hales notes, "grease and dirt reveal themselves with incredible force, the result of his harsh light source. . . . His photographs make

everything seem, if possible, dirtier, more crowded, more chaotic than the reality."[74] Like Maggie's tenement home or Cora's final resting place in *The
Evil That Men Do,* the homes that Riis photographed were transformed into
spectacles, becoming settings for physical reactions of shock and revulsion
rather than identification and empathy. Yet, glimpses of the "other half's"
decorations, furnishings, and housekeeping efforts, many of which approximate a late nineteenth century middle-class domestic aesthetic, might have
allowed for an affective identification with tenement dwellers that Riis's sen-
sationalistic techniques otherwise would preclude. The bond of identification through setting blends the sentimental and sensational, producing fear
and reinforcing efforts to protect the middle-class home that some tenement
dwellers imitated.

Visually, especially in Riis's photographs, the similarities between the tenement aesthetic and Beecher's advice could have been obscured. Gwendolyn
Wright emphasizes that "what (reformers) disparaged as debris were often
family portraits, religious mementos, and objects the residents had brought
with them from their former homes. . . . tenement interiors often displayed
a carefully conceived aesthetic."[75] And indeed, the abundance of objects contained in the tenement marked it as anti-modern—the very opposite of the
straight lines and smooth walls that were coming into vogue at the time.[76]
Just as the modern aesthetic changed to reject what tenement dwellers imitated, so too did modern building practices change as many middle- and
upper-class families rejected the density of urban dwellings for the relative
isolation of suburban living.

The City as Home

In text and photographs, turn-of-the-century tenements figure as dangerous
physical residue that perpetuates eroded domestic boundaries. One of Riis's
photographs in *How the Other Half Lives* makes this very clear (figure 22).
Here, a group of children gather around a family table, calmly working on
what might pass for a wholesome craft project in a middle-class home-
maker's manual. Paper stars litter the floor, while a growing pile of paper
and fabric flowers occupies the center of the table. A young mother holds a
baby on her knee while directing the action, the ornate combs in her complicated hairstyle echoed in the children's proper dress, tidy hair, and clean
faces. Above a calendar on the wall hangs an image of a courting couple, the
woman complete with tiny feet, dainty slippers and numerous crinolines.
The success of this household's attempts to emulate a middle-class aesthetic
makes the photograph initially seem to be an odd companion to the text's
more lurid images. However, the children are not creating decorative craft
projects but are "making artificial flowers." The caption transforms the chil-

FIGURE 22. Family Making Artificial Flowers, 1910. Museum of the City of New York, The Jacob
A. Riis Collection (?15).

dren into slaves, the mother into a virtual Simon Legree. Opened to trade,
the home has become a space simultaneously public and private that will
send its emissaries forth into the world not as representatives of moral integrity, as Catharine Beecher promised, but as carriers of moral and physical
contagion. For Riis, the tenement home has come to symbolize a dangerous
connection, not a benevolent and reassuring containment. Exemplifying numerous threats to the middle-class home's boundaries, Riis's most gentle
photograph becomes most menacing.

Within the turn-of-the-century city, tenement spaces represent such a high
degree of connection and lack of separation that they are coded in texts and
photographs as pathologically networked. On the one hand, the tenement is
so highly networked both within and outside of it that its spaces become incompatible with the contained ideal of home and thus, according to the
tenets of architectural determinism, produce a threatening population untouched by the acculturating morality of domesticity. More importantly, the
tenements are linked so closely, if invisibly, to the spaces of the city occupied
by the middle class that they actively threaten the boundaries of the middle-

class home—a threat imagined in terms of contagion and disease. But condemning the tenement's connectivity is uncomfortably like condemning the very modernity that allows for separation.

Thus, a deep ambivalence accompanies fictional and journalistic explorations of urban networks in tenement homes. The incompatibility between the notions of tenement and home decried by Riis and his peers casts doubts on the compatibility between home and city or between home and modernity. This conceptual problem helped to cause a split in the next phase of urbanization. The move to the suburbs that accompanied the rise of urban networks was complemented by the reclamation of city homes as modern with the proliferation of apartment buildings in New York and other industrial urban centers. Like tenements, purpose-built apartments seemed threatening precisely because they might contaminate more traditional neighborhoods; as a Cleveland observer noted, "a city of private homes, grass plots, trees and open spaces, with the civic pride and quality of citizenship which is usually found in such circumstances, is powerless to protect itself against the obliteration of its private residence districts, by apartments, which shut out the sun and the sky from its streets, and one another."[77]

More optimistic was the idea that a well-designed apartment could produce a more positive contagion, subtly offering all who entered an infectious set of progressive values. In New York, "model flats" were domestic science stations set up in tenement buildings. "The flat, being in a tenement house, is directly in touch with the daily life of the people; she who lives there bids the mothers good morning as they empty the ashes together, and chats with them at the corner grocery."[78] Through proximity to a clean, well-ordered apartment, new habits would be adopted "almost unconsciously." As one observer noted, "the influence of such a center of good in every tenement-house in New York would be incalculable."[79] Running counter to Riis's fears of contagion in the uncontrolled city, the masterminds of the model flats and the designers of new apartment buildings saw in the permeable structures utopian possibilites for improving city life. Imagining homes that embraced urban connections, they aligned apartment homes with their hopes for a brighter urban and national future.

Chapter 4

The Apartment as Utopia

Reimagining the City, Reconstructing the Home

> *We have just so much time, so much money, and so much strength, and it behooves us to make the best of it. Why should we give our time and strength and enthusiasm to drudgery, when our housework were better and more economically done by machinery and cooperation? Why should we stultify our minds with doing the same things a thousand times over, when we might help ourselves and our friends to happiness by intelligent occupations and amusements? The apartment is the solution of the living problems of the city.* —Elsie DeWolfe[1]

While Stephen Crane and Jacob Riis's tenement texts emphasize the grimmest aspects of urban life, Abraham Cahan's short novel *Yekl* offers a more hopeful perspective on the relationships between tenement dwellers and their surroundings. The end of *Yekl* sees Jake leaving the New York he loves while his former wife Gitl stays in the city. Gitl plans to marry Bernstein the scholar and use her divorce settlement to open a shop.

New York initially intimidates and confuses Gitl. However, as *Yekl* unfolds, Gitl's fellow tenement dwellers help her to navigate the scene, introducing her to new behaviors that will allow her to prosper in urban America. Her neighbor Mrs. Kavarsky, for instance, offers Gitl fashion advice, replaces her Orthodox hair covering with a new uncovered hairstyle, and reassures her that divorcing Jake is in her best interest. More significant than a specific mentor, however, is the role that urban space itself plays in Gitl's transformation. The topsy-turvy world of the tenement puts the poor, uneducated Gitl in contact with the well-born, erudite Bernstein, eventually enabling a marriage—and constituting a new family—that would have been unthinkable in class bound Russia. As Mrs. Kavarsky points out, "It is only here that it is possible for a blacksmith's wife to marry a learned man, who is a blessing both for God and people."[2] For Gitl, the tenement is the site of bitter disappointment and

sadness, yet through luck, chance, and connections, it also operates as a micro-
cosm of a city where anything is possible, and where women often benefit
from the opportunities at play. Thus, even while Gitl mourns the divorce,
"at the bottom of her heart she felt herself far from desolate, being conscious
of the existence of a man who was going to take care of her and her child,
and even relishing the prospect of the new life in store for her."[3] In New
York, Gitl can adapt and exert her old-world values in a new environment.

While Cahan does not go so far as to construct the tenement as a utopia,
the prospects that open to Gitl in the city anticipate the utopian possibilities,
particularly for women, visible in the apartment architecture and fiction that
would appear in the years to follow. Aiming to demonstrate the liberatory
possibilities of urban architecture for women—and the world—the Progressive Era's best known author of feminist utopian fiction, Charlotte Perkins
Gilman, set several of her utopian stories and a novel, *Moving the Mountain*, in cities. Though *Sister Carrie*'s origin and intent were very different
from Gilman's utopian fiction, Theodore Dreiser's novel shares Gilman's vision of the city as a site of possibility. Critics of *Sister Carrie* have made much
of Hurstwood's passivity against the downward pull of the urban environment, especially in the context of Dreiser's fascination with and amendment
of Herbert Spencer's principles of environmental force. As for Yekl/Jake (and
for many of Gilman's unredeemed male characters), Hurstwood's expulsion
from his family and eventual downfall are hastened by the opportunities for
pleasure, excitement, and betrayal—his affair with Carrie, his theft from his
employers—that the city offers. Carrie, while hardly more morally upright,
seizes the city's possibilities for connection, enjoys personal fulfillment and
gains economic success. As this chapter will show, by positing an ending for
Carrie that opens up far beyond Gitl's happy marriage, Dreiser, like Gilman,
presents the city as a place that offers possibilities beyond domestic satis-
faction, especially for women. In *Sister Carrie,* as in other utopian urban
fiction, the city operates as the locus for powerful social change, and that
change, significantly, emanates from and emulates the relationships that constitute urban domestic space.

Because it is labeled most frequently a realist or naturalist novel, it may
seem a bit odd to consider *Sister Carrie*'s vision of urban spatial relations
utopian, and stranger still to compare it to Gilman's strenuously didactic
(and less self-consciously artistic) utopian fiction.[4] Yet when these works are
read spatially, useful parallels emerge. Realism, as Dreiser and Gilman both
understood, was a powerful form that could "narratize ideology into the
lives of readers."[5] Amy Kaplan points out that "realistic novels have utopian
moments that imagine resolutions to contemporary social conflicts by reconstructing society as it might be."[6] Although utopia is literally a "no
place," when people imagine utopias (and this includes the earliest editions
of Thomas More's *Utopia*), they are thinking spatially, imagining and de-

signing spaces that will help to demonstrate and exert a community's values.[7] Actual and fictive utopias necessarily have different particular aims. In constructing their texts, Dreiser and Gilman both emphasized the force of environment; both also saw in fiction a vehicle for effecting social change. Gilman, for instance, claimed that "the makers of books are the makers of thoughts and feelings for people in general."[8] Dreiser famously scoffed at the do-gooderism of his reformist contemporaries like Gilman. Yet Dreiser's "deep vein of romanticism," which derives "spiritual truth" from the "common realities of life," guiding us to see the possibilities and promise at work in alien and alienating spaces, reveals realism's utopian strain.[9] Reading with a spatial focus on homes that emphasize connection and flexibility, not enclosure, clarifies how Dreiser's and Gilman's texts promote social change.

Beyond revealing the connections between *Sister Carrie* and Gilman's utopian texts, a spatial focus shows how Dreiser overturns Gilman's essential moral conservatism to posit a radical realignment of social values. As Alan Trachtenberg suggests, *Sister Carrie* "fails as social reassurance, and in this lies much of its negative, subversive power. It alters the perspective in which Carrie, a representative character, only gets worse, and would have us believe at the end that she may yet better herself in a transvalued moral order."[10] *Sister Carrie* presents a vision of social possibility, however subversive to the traditional domestic order, that offers even poor, unmarried, sexually active women with checkered pasts the power to change society. The urban landscape emphasizes that change is inevitable; as long as Carrie continues to evolve, we can read the city and its metonym, the apartment, as the locus for continual, progressive social change.

In their urban fiction, neither Gilman nor Dreiser construct a new world per se; rather, they demonstrate how the possibility for profound social change can emanate from the familiar built structures of the industrial city. As David Harvey notes, "urban politics" and, I would add, urban spaces both physical and fictional, are "fraught with deeply held though often subterranean emotions and political passions in which utopian dreams have a particular place."[11] If not overtly political, *Sister Carrie* revolves around such "subterranean emotions"—unspoken feelings, undeniable passions, untapped dreams and, most significantly, Carrie's desire. In Donald Pizer's terms, "Carrie's essential nature—her capacity to dream and hope for the future and her emotional strength"—augur and argue for a vision of the urban as a place of possibility both personal and societal; further, the novel itself operates as a utopian space where "seduction by the city [is] an inevitable but morally elevating rather than degrading event."[12] As Gilman does in much of her fiction, Dreiser undermines idealized notions of traditional domesticity in order to initiate his protagonist's personal and social transformation. For both authors, as well as in the popular culture of their day, the apartment building emerges as a utopian design possibility, especially for single women in the modern city.

A City of Apartments — A City of Homes?

Especially in New York City, the two decades spanning the turn into the twentieth century saw major changes in domestic architecture as apartments became the dominant form of middle-class housing. While Jacob Riis was campaigning for the abolition—or at least, the improvement—of tenement conditions on the Lower East Side, the Manhattan landowners in his audiences were profiting from a tremendous rise in real estate values as buildings rose to new heights. From moderate walk-up flats to high-rise luxury "apartment hotels," as they were then called, apartments became the trademark urban dwellings in New York, lining the streets, altering the skyline, and introducing a mode of domesticity that radically transformed the ways in which New Yorkers, and eventually the nation, conceived of the urban home.[13] Manhattan actually had seen construction of its first apartment building, the Stuyvesant, in 1869 (where, according to an 1870 article in *Putnam's Monthly Magazine,* each apartment "contain[ed] exactly 1,788 superficial feet").[14] The years that followed witnessed a few other successful experiments in apartment dwellings for the middle class.[15] These dwellings mirror the qualities that Sharon Marcus observes in European apartments of the same era: "As a then uniquely urban form of housing that combined the relatively private spaces of individual apartment units with the common spaces of shared entrances, staircases, and party walls, the apartment house embodied the continuity between domestic and urban, private and public spaces."[16] By 1901, when the *Architectural Record* claimed that "To-day New York is a city of apartments," responses ranged from elation to despair.[17]

Some of the alarm over apartments stemmed from the fact that most nineteenth-century New Yorkers associated multi-family dwellings with the dreaded tenement—a spatial arrangement considered unsuitable for the middle class. Indeed, any New York building housing three or more families was defined legally as a tenement, but if apartments were to become culturally acceptable, they needed a distinct spatial and class-inflected identity. Given the looseness of the nomenclature, enthusiasts used the print media to define apartments as distinct from other urban housing forms and to promote them as a new and appealing bourgeois housing option. One commentator, for instance, derived social distinctions from etymological difference:

> "Tenement" is derived from the Latin verb "tenere" (to hold), and is . . . a
> building that is designed to hold or to give shelter to the greatest number of

persons, at the least possible cost to each tenant.[18] "Apartment," however, is an Anglicized derivation of another Latin verb, "parterre" (to divide), and with equal propriety is applied to a dwelling-house, of which the structural and social intent is to separate family from family, and to gratify the desire for privacy that every household naturally feels. . . . Economy, therefore, is the purpose of the tenement—comfort, that of the apartment.[19]

Just as the Anglicized derivation of "parterre" is seen as superior to the Latin verb "tenere," apartments here are clearly superior to tenements. The desire for privacy, here constructed as an ahistorical, almost instinctual desire, helps to distinguish the "natural" upper- or middle-class apartment from the "unnatural" tenement habitations of the lower classes, a distinction the author emphasizes when he rhetorically contrasts economy to comfort. Eventually, the average New Yorker drew clear distinctions: Most suites in tenement houses, intended as housing for the working class, lacked separate baths; flats, largely inhabited by middle-class tenants, had private baths but were in "walk-up" buildings; apartments were found in elevator buildings, had private baths, and were geared architecturally and culturally for an upper-middle- and upper-class clientele.[20] The features that made apartments desirable to bourgeois renters were architectural, aesthetic, cultural, and technological.

To attract middle-class tenants who needed reassurance that apartments were *not* tenements, developers cited the cleanliness, convenience, and classiness that characterized the gleaming towers. The buildings were given names; they were individual, unique. The opulent Ansonia, for instance, featured "pneumatic tubes, dumb-waiters, push buttons, long-distance telephones, and means of refrigeration as well as heating, so that winter or summer an equable temperature may be maintained."[21] All of these features helped to connect tenants to one another and to the centralized facilities while simultaneously producing the illusion of separateness. In Howells's *A Hazard of New Fortunes,* Isabel March is certainly quite susceptible to the appeal of such amenities; during the couple's house hunt she reads

> the new advertisements aloud with ardor and with faith to believe that the apartments described in them were every one truthfully represented, and that any one of them was richly responsive to their needs. "Elegant, light, large, single and outside flats" were offered with "All improvements—bath, ice box, etc."—for twenty-five to thirty dollars a month. The cheapness was amazing.[22]

While the narrator's tone foreshadows the Marches' shock and disappointment when they see the actual apartments, new technologies did improve the quotidian existence of apartment dwellers. They also allowed owners to exact premium rents. New York, of course, exemplified this trend, yet nationally, in articles about urban domestic life in publications ranging from the widely circulated, solidly middle-class *Ladies' Home Journal* to more up-

FIGURE 23. Ansonia Apartments, New York. Library of Congress, Prints and Photographs Division, LC-D4-17421.

scale shelter magazines such as *The House Beautiful*, commentators agreed that in urban settings, apartments had come to stay, largely because of the labor-saving advantages they offered to their residents. Apartment buildings offered services and spaces that made communal and thus affordable new technologies and services that, even if they were only intended to raise the level of tenants' comfort, were also compatible with notions of public good.

Technology and economics thus conspired to position new apartment buildings "in accord with the spirit of the age. . . . The modern and up-to-date
apartment offers to its tenants a measure of luxury and convenience totally
beyond the reach of the man of average income living under his own, 'vine
and fig tree.'"[23] As luxury and convenience mingled, they redefined home in
the city.

Apartment living offered a freedom from traditional notions of domestic
space and relations that both exhilarated and dismayed onlookers. Many
"idealists saw the era of industrial capitalism, when public space and urban
infrastructure were created, as a time when rural isolation gave way to a life
in larger human communities."[24] Pessimists thought otherwise. Clearly, technological and architectural changes enabled women, especially, to transform
their living spaces—and thus, their lives—in new and sometimes radical
ways. Observers of the apartment trend had to ask whether the apartment
would transform domesticity beyond all recognition. Would women be contented to consign themselves to the home when the home was surrounded
by and itself resembled the city?[25] Noted one observer in *The Architectural
Record*, "While the apartment hotel is the consummate flower of domestic
co-operation, it is also, unfortunately, the consummate flower of domestic
irresponsibility. It means the sacrifice of everything implied by the word
'home.'"[26]

Moving Walls, Evading History: Charlotte Perkins Gilman's Theories of the Home

Yet even at this critical moment in its development, few observers specified
precisely what the word "home" implied. Charlotte Perkins Gilman was a
notable exception. Gilman most clearly articulated her assessments of the
history and role of the home in two works of nonfiction: *The Home*, published in 1903, explains that environment is constituted through human and
architectural interaction, a theme she first articulated in her widely read
1898 volume, *Women and Economics*. Throughout her career, Gilman linked
the notions of architectural determinism and environmental agency. "Man,"
she wrote in 1916, "not only makes houses, but is in turn made by them, for
good or ill."[27] Whatever the setting, Gilman argued, individuals can act to
shape the architecture that so profoundly shapes them. With this spatial
agency comes the potential for social change.

Like her aunts Catharine Beecher and Harriet Beecher Stowe, Gilman believed that the home was the formative site for human consciousness:
"Whatever else a human being has to meet and bear," she writes, "he has always the home as a governing factor in the formation of character and the
direction of life."[28] This formative influence, importantly, does not stop with

the individual; for Gilman, the notion of home is basic to notions of community. Thus, domestic space becomes the appropriate locus for architectural and social transformation:

> Without this blessed background of all our memories and foreground of all our hopes, life seems empty indeed. In homes we were all born. In homes we all die or hope to die. In homes we all live or want to live. For homes we all labor, in them or out of them. The home is the center and circumference, the start and the finish, of most of our lives. We love it with a love older than the human race. We reverence it with the blind obeisance of those crouching centuries when its cult began. We cling to it with the tenacity of every inmost, oldest instinct of our animal natures, and with the enthusiasm of every latest word in the unbroken chant of adoration which we have sung to it since we first learned to praise.[29]

In terms reminiscent of Charles Darwin and Herbert Spencer, Gilman evokes what might be termed race-memory in arguing for the primacy of the home in human society: It both circumscribes and centers human experience through all of its stages. Instinctive and acquired, reverence for the home is a primal force. Inspiring love, obeisance, and reverence, it fosters the development of personal, familial, and social relations. Though individual homes may vary, the notion of "home" possesses limitless cultural power. Accordingly, Gilman sees in the home the potential for vast social reform.

Establishing the primal quality of our attachment to home is critical to Gilman's critique of domestic space; in her fiction and theory, Gilman argues that women have been crippled by the architecture to which tradition and narrative have confined them. Because detached homes exemplify bygone historical conditions, they enforce outmoded and destructive patterns of thought and action. As Gilman argues in *Women and Economics*, "The life of the female savage is freedom itself, compared with the increasing constriction of custom closing in upon the woman, as civilization advanced, like the iron torture chamber of romance."[30] Restriction to the home has pushed women away from "civilization" and straight into the "iron torture chamber of romance." But, Gilman notes, no romance can veil the impact of constrained domestic spaces: "Her restricted impression, her confinement to the four walls of the home, have done great execution, of course, in limiting her ideas, her information, her thought-processes, and power of judgment."[31] Considered to be women's primary environment, the home threatens to constrain their intellectual and creative capacities, producing horrifying results. "Anywhere in lonely farm houses, the women of to-day, confined absolutely to this strangling cradle of the race, go mad by scores and hundreds. . . . In the cities, where there is less 'home life,' people seem to stand it better."[32] In Gilman's view, isolated homes keep women from participating in a modern culture characterized by the excitement and energy of change, growth, and discovery. If they ignore the modern spatial and technological possibilities for radically remaking the home, Gilman argues, American women will remain tied to an increasingly meaningless space, denying themselves the opportunity to participate in the work of improving the world.

Gilman proposes to solve the problem of women's physical and psychological confinement through a variety of architectural innovations. "Real living," she writes, "perfectly natural, perfectly possible to-day, would build cities more beautiful than the country before them, a comfort and pleasure to every individual, young and old."[33] In the very sites decried by writers like Henry James as particularly destructive of the social order—apartments, apartment hotels, and professionalized boarding houses—Gilman saw potential for social progress. She writes, "From the most primitive caravansary up to the square miles of floor space in our hotels, the public house has met the needs of social evolution as no private house could have done."[34] Because they allow for connective and collective activity among their inhabitants, these buildings radically realign spatial and thus societal relations. Gilman cites the bachelor apartment as a working model for the modern home; she adopts and adapts this model for women and families in the utopian apartment complexes she proposes in her journalism and animates in her fiction.

In hailing apartments as a source of hope for the nation's women, Gilman built upon a tradition of "material solutions [to women's exploitation] involving both economic and spatial change."[35] For Gilman, as for other utopian thinkers, an "infinite array of possible spatial orderings [held] out the prospect of an infinite array of possible social worlds."[36] A generation before Gilman wrote *Herland*, Edward Bellamy's utopian novel *Looking Backward* (1887), which celebrated new forms of urban housing, was widely read and extremely influential.[37] In Bellamy's Boston of the year 2000, apartment dwellers savor meals cooked in communal kitchens, listen to music piped into their apartments, and enjoy a far higher standard of living than their nineteenth-century forbears who were still attached to their detached houses. As it was in Hawthorne's Blithedale and other utopian communities (both fictive and built), communal housing was central to Bellamy's plan. Unlike most nineteenth-century utopian thinkers, Bellamy set his ideal society in urban space; *Looking Backward*'s apartment hotels exemplify and enable a new social order both more just and more sustainable than that which Bellamy himself experienced. As cities grew, these utopian ideas and their architectural manifestations—apartments—drew many adherents, including one writer who, anticipating Le Corbusier, asserted in the staid journal *Technical World* that cities inevitably would become giant apartment buildings, "materializing the sanest idea that man has evolved in centuries."[38] Beautiful, clean, collectively run cities, Gilman claimed, "are not 'Utopian dreams.' They are 'good business.' They are things which would promote human life."[39]

Gilman developed her own plans to improve human life in much of her writing. In *The Forerunner,* the journal she wrote and published from 1909 to 1916, she augmented her social scientific lectures and articles with numerous fictive guides for reinventing domestic spaces and ideologies. Her work in *The Forerunner* makes clear that "Gilman subscribes to a literature that can be called cultural work, can enact social changes, can function as social action, can convey alternative versions or visions of human action— a position of clear self-consciousness regarding literary didacticism."[40] Many of her stories are variations on a common plot: A woman dissatisfied with some aspect of her life—her marriage, her house, her children, her economic prospects, or a combination of these factors—suddenly is able (or is forced) to change her circumstances. Often in the absence of her husband and children, or as a result of a husband's death, work, maturity, or extended foreign travel, the woman reinvents her surroundings. Among other projects, Gilman's heroines sell their homes, take in and eject relatives, design and build new houses for new or reconfigured marriages, develop collective farms, run guest houses, and operate community centers. In short, they bring to fruition a range of architectural projects that result in greater happiness for individuals, families, and communities. Loveless marriages regain their romance. Destitute women become economically successful. Determined artists find creative ways to unite love and career. And in several of these stories, urban space, and apartments in particular, are the sites for social change.

Gilman's didactic stories teach women to see their surroundings as transformable investments that offer personal and social returns. Dubbing them "pragmatopias," Carol Farley Kessler notes, "traditionally these stories might not have been included in bibliographies of utopian fiction. Their mode is realistic. They are 'thought experiments' which extrapolate possibilities from present-day society. They make explicit how Gilman's readers might go about realizing her utopian visions."[41] In story after story, Gilman outlines the potential psychological and economic profits that may accrue to creative women whose vision of home extends beyond its four walls. One of her most appealing stories, "Making a Change" (1911), centers around a family who all share a small apartment in an unnamed city. The harried husband, Frank, suddenly notices that his suicidal wife, testy mother, and cranky infant have been transformed into a model family. What could have caused such a change? The short answer is transformed domestic space. Unbeknownst to Frank, his mother has taken over the adjacent apartment and the building's roof to start a "children's garden," a prototypical daycare center where his son has blossomed. The wife has returned happily to her career as a musician in her child-free time. While Frank initially is taken aback by the women's arrangements, the story ends with his acceptance of the new situation. "'If it makes all of you as happy as that,' he said, 'I guess I can stand it.' And in after years he was heard to remark, 'This being married and bringing up children is as easy as can be—when you learn how!'"[42] Gilman's manipulations of setting always improve lives. But her characters must abandon old notions of domesticity and gender in order to develop and profit from new economic and spatial arrangements.

Many of Gilman's early utopian visions were explicitly architectural, and if she set a story in the city, she usually housed utopia in an apartment hotel featuring roof gardens, child care, beautifully landscaped courtyards, centralized kitchens, and river views. Markedly similar apartment hotels appear in three fictional pieces: the short story "Her Memories," a novella titled "A Woman's Utopia," and a utopian novel, *Moving the Mountain*. Set in a Manhattan of the not-so-distant future, each narrative relates the bliss and fulfillment residents gain from their enlightened mode of living, celebrating the possibilities and addressing common concerns surrounding apartment living. The earliest text, "A Woman's Utopia," is also the most optimistic. The story's narrator, Morgan G. Street, who has given his cousin Hope Cartwright twenty years and twenty million dollars to remake New York City, returns from a sojourn in China to find the city utterly transformed. Tenement districts have been demolished to make room for apartment buildings whose courtyards are filled "with tossing fountains, trees, and climbing vines, shaded cloisters arched and pillared, room for games, for comfortable seats and tiny tables, for ferneries and singing birds and pleasant meeting places; with the walls around [them] rich with mullioned windows, hanging balconies, and fine decoration."[43] Street needs to be convinced, however, that the populace has improved along with the new scenery, which his cousin quickly demonstrates.

Yet the vision Gilman puts forth is not a simple determinism; rather, she claims for women a fairly radical degree of environmental agency. The intrepid Hope explains that once the women of New York understood that "they made the city—*were* the city . . . They rose and rose, a vast, swift, peaceful revolution; town after town was captured by these enthusiastic 'city mothers,' and things began to be done."[44] Social problems are certainly ameliorated in this utopian vision, yet while women have claimed a revolutionary transformative agency, the result seems oddly conservative, as if Gilman has superimposed Catharine Beecher's aesthetic and cultural domestic ideals on a modern skyline.[45] "A Woman's Utopia," like Gilman's other urban utopias, recuperates innovative designs and technologies with conservative, almost sentimental notions of home.

As she does in her theoretical work, in her urban fiction Gilman acknowledges that a profound cultural force creates a powerful emotional tie to home no matter what its design. "Her Memories" opens with a fifty-year-old woman becoming misty eyed at the sight of Home Court, the building on Riverside Drive where she grew up. "I was born there—I was married there—my children were born there—I love every stone of the dear old place, for the whole twelve stories. It's home." While the woman sees nothing odd in her powerful attachment to an apartment building, her companion (the skeptical narrator) looks "up at the bannered towers of the great building high over the Hudson, and wondered at her emotion. Home! An apartment house a 'home'—such as to bring tears to the eyes! That prodigious castle, occupying the four-square block up there near Grant's Tomb; that twelve stories with towers above that—holding some eight hundred persons at least—even with the luxurious room space I knew they enjoyed—that a home!"[46] As he learns about Home Court's amenities, which include a gymnasium, swimming pools, a bowling alley, dining-rooms, dancing-rooms, and clubrooms, along with schoolrooms and playrooms for the youngest residents, he begins to understand the advantages of the arrangement. But his continual comparisons to more commercial spaces: "What kind of a— summer resort hotel is that place anyhow?" "It sounds more like a casino than a home"; "It sounds so like a big hotel"; and "But this appears to be, not only an apartment house, but a—pleasure resort," emphasize how difficult it is to see "home" at work in an unfamiliar guise, regardless of its obvious and manifold attributes.[47] That the narrator never quite comprehends the woman's sentimental attachment to her building reveals that in Gilman's mind a significant obstacle to progress is a cultural inability to decouple powerful spatial and emotional constructions of home.

Tearing down and rebuilding was simple enough, as the ever changing New York landscape that surrounded Gilman at this time demonstrated. But changing people's conceptions about domesticity and architecture proved more daunting. As a character notes in Gilman's 1911 novel *Moving the Mountain*, "Ideas are the real things, sir! Brick and mortar? Bah! We can put brick and mortar in any shape we choose—but we have to choose the shape first!"[48] *Moving the Mountain* shows how outmoded domestic conceptions might be revised within apartment buildings through the tenants' emotional camaraderie. Music animates this possibility. As the narrator stands in the courtyard (which bears more than a passing resemblance to the courts in "A Woman's Utopia"), "from a balcony up there in the moonlight came a delicious burst of melody: a guitar and two voices, and the refrain was taken up from another window, from one corner of the garden, from the roof; all in smooth accord."[49] Here, a connected design is literally harmonious; Gilman's idealized structure defuses the threatening prospect of mingling with one's neighbors. Instead of the shouting and domestic fights we hear through the tenement walls in *Maggie, A Girl of the Streets,* or even the sounds of the hotel that permeate Coverdale's room in *The Blithedale Romance,* in Gilman's vision, dulcet tones waft through the gardened air and bind the resi-

FIGURE 24. On Riverside Drive, N.Y. Library of Congress, Prints and Photographs Division, LC-D4-36555.

dents in harmony. As it does in *Sister Carrie,* music plays a powerful sensory role in dramatizing urban connections' positive force.

Gilman's celebration of the apartment's utopian possibilities was part of a trend that surfaced in surprising places, including the mass-market domestic magazines of the day. Articles in *Ladies' Home Journal, Good Housekeeping,* and *The House Beautiful* charted the trickle-up trend of apartments' acceptance as their technological and economic advantages made them an increasingly desirable housing choice across the class spectrum.[50] *Ladies' Home Journal*'s early articles on apartment living offered tips on how to use living space wisely, advising its readers on topics from constructing furniture out of wooden packing boxes to streamlining and sanitizing baby care in a small apartment.[51]

Magazines offered advice on paint colors (neutral pastels), wallpaper (oatmeal colored), and furniture (wicker), emphasizing that the apartment was, after all, one's *home.* "The successful home does not merely happen," notes one author. "If this is true of the house, far more is it the case with the apartment, which is the concentration, the epitome, the quintessence of the house."[52] As style maven Elsie de Wolfe put it to her readers: "Of course, I do not advise you to spend a lot of money on someone else's property, but why not look the matter squarely in the face? This is to be your home." [Decide] "that you will make a home of this place, and then go ahead and *treat it as a home!*"[53]

Ladies' Home Journal and *House Beautiful* were of course commercial ventures, unlike *The Forerunner,* but all of these publications considered many aspects of apartment living, presenting "conflicting and various material, from which readers could pick and choose."[54] Though many *House Beautiful* contributors wrote with a resigned air: "With all these disadvantages the apartment house has become a fixture of city life," a significant number of articles in *House Beautiful* focus, à la Gilman, on the utopian possibilities of this new domestic arrangement.[55] One article, "The Child in the Apartment," uncannily evokes "Making a Change" as it describes how three families transform the spaces of the apartment building they share. Even though "landlords of apartment houses do not allow much 'making' to be done; indeed, not even a nail may be driven," the parents' creative cooperation, the neighbors' flexibility, and the "community of interest supplied at first by having their children indiscriminately regarded as nuisances, and, presently, by the necessity of improving the condition of things," allow a day nursery, a woodshop, a stair closet, and an outdoor play space to emerge from a building that "architects planned without taking into account the needs of children."[56] Working together, the apartment dwellers make life better for everyone in the building. The same author advances similar pragmatopian plans in a series of articles on topics ranging from urban gardening— "Making the bit of land that belongs to no one person, a pleasant place for all"—to the rear stoop, which she beautifies and renames the "piazza."[57] These optimistic articles show readers that in beautifying their urban surroundings, they render the world a better place. It is worth noting that these articles appear during wartime; they anticipate a certain victory garden patriotism and project a sense of noblesse oblige. Yet it is clear that apartments hold the potential for improving life within and beyond their walls.

However, as Gilman's stories show, apartments always threaten to obliterate traditional domesticity and its attendant values. For every commentator who saw in the apartment a paradise offering "the peace, the quiet, the simplicity, the solid comfort; the benefit to the children; the freedom from interruption during the hours devoted to work; the infinite opportunities for variety in your hours of play," someone else reported that "on all sides one hears complaints from these enforced inhabitants of the long, dismal corridors of apartment hotels."[58] As in Gilman's work, in popular magazines a familiar domestic morality resolves this tension. In a *Ladies' Home Journal* article titled "How an Apartment Burglar Works," an anonymous burglar reveals the tricks of his trade, explaining in detail how he preys on women alone in apartments. He does recollect, however, two cases in which he called off his burgling missions: once when he realized that his intended target was pregnant, and a second time when he noticed his victim tending her baby in the apartment's bedroom. As the article notes, "Sometimes sentiment influences a burglar."[59] Surely *Ladies' Home Journal* readers would be relieved to know that bourgeois domesticity could reform even the most hardened urban criminal! Elsewhere, the cleanliness, thrift, and familial harmony visible in the apartments displayed in *Ladies' Home Journal* defuse the threats posed by its architecture. Even an apartment furnished entirely with packing crates claims an ultradomestic identity and influence. Its mastermind, Louise Brigham, states, "In order to have the work recognized as a power for good my home must be beautiful as well as practical."[60] Brigham stenciled homemaking mottoes around the frieze of her kitchen and opened her home to visitors curious to learn her unusual decorating techniques. But even if a Beecherian domesticity could redeem the apartment as home, imagining the apartment as utopia meant achieving a tricky balance between subverting and recuperating domestic ideology.

Perhaps unsurprisingly, people who lived outside of traditional family settings were early and vocal proponents of apartment life. Apartments allowed unmarried women—bachelor girls in the parlance of the day—to carve out a new and liberating space between their families of origin and the married life that it was assumed they would eventually embrace. Of course, unmarried women could live with relatives who had already emigrated to the city, as Carrie Meeber does when she arrives in Chicago to live with her sister Minnie. At first, Minnie's apartment pleases Carrie because it is visibly and audibly part of the city.

> To Carrie the sound of the little bells upon the horse cars as they tinkled in and out of hearing was as pleasant as it was strange and novel. She gazed into the lighted street when Minnie brought her into the front room and wondered at the sounds, the movement, the, to her new ears, audible murmur of the vast city which stretched for miles and miles in every direction.[61]

The muted sounds, novel and pleasant, represent a connection to the urban life for which Carrie longs. Yet Carrie understands that while the Hanson flat may offer architectural connections to the urban landscape, her position within the family, particularly the economic role that she is expected to play by turning the bulk of her pay over to her sister, will prevent her from exploring the city's possibilities. Through most of the nineteenth century, the boarding house would have been the only respectable step away from the family for unmarried women: recall Ruth in *Ruth Hall* or Zenobia and Priscilla in *The Blithedale Romance*.[62] Olive Chancellor in *The Bostonians* represents the exceptional case of the wealthy single female homeowner; her spinster friends Miss Birdseye and Doctor Prance, who rent rooms in the same boarding house, were far more typical of their day.

By the turn into the twentieth century, the apartment's privacy and autonomy offered unmarried women an appealing alternative to living with family members or renting a "lonely boarding house room with its furniture that never expresses the personality of anyone, not even the landlady. What a warm feeling of hospitality to be able to invite a friend to come and stay with us in a *home of our very own!*"[63] Magazine articles acknowledged and perhaps propelled this move toward apartment living by exploring and celebrating how particular bachelor girls adapted to apartment life: "The daughters' demand for latchkeys a generation ago shook the institution of The Home to its cellar. Yet its walls did not fall. The insurgents possess today not only keys, but whole apartments. Homes have not perished. They have multiplied."[64] These articles make vivid the figure of the apartment-dwelling bachelor girl who "rejoice[s] daily in the privacy which gave her long, quiet hours for study uninterrupted by the gossipy boarder" or "the boarder who borrowed and returned not and was unashamed," who luxuriates in the warm rooms, "clean towels and hot water that were always to be had in abundance."[65] Images of bachelor girls' quarters make clear how little space was cause for rejoicing (see figure 25).

Though many apartment buildings were off-limits to single women, many more were not, and commentators tended to agree that these apartments could bring out the best in the bachelor girl. One of the earliest commentators on apartments argued that "when a wife sees how much trouble and annoyance can be saved by the new way of living, she regards contraction as an advantage to her—a downright luxury, which she never knew of before."[66] An apartment's small size would force her to focus her aesthetic sense as she culled her furniture and other belongings, "retaining only [her] best" to decorate her new home.[67] Observers drew a powerful link between living space and selfhood for bachelor girls: "It is the small inexpensive apartment . . . that has helped to make the bachelor girl the buoyant and contented individual who is such a sign of the times. She is a woman with a business and a home of her very own—a combination that even the most conservative has come to accept."[68] No matter what her relation to familial domesticity, popular periodicals assumed that the bachelor girl would be a lasting figure on the urban scene.

Enter Theodore Dreiser, whose novel *Sister Carrie* would expand the magazines' popular if subversive notion that apartment living would create a new type of womanhood. Before writing *Sister Carrie*, Dreiser joined his peers in the magazine industry in exploring women's experiences in urban domestic space, contributing powerfully to the growth and influence of women's periodicals. From 1907 to 1910, Dreiser edited *The Delineator*, a socially conscious women's magazine published by the Butterick Pattern Company. Dreiser's success at *The Delineator* (under his editorship circulation rose from 400,000 to 1.2 million copies a year) helped to compensate,

FIGURE 25. Charles Dana Gibson, "Rita," from "The Common Law," by Robert W. Chambers, *Cosmopolitan* 51 (September 1911): 436. Library of Congress, Prints and Photographs Division, LC-USZ62-135358.

perhaps, for *Sister Carrie*'s disappointing sales.[69] But his success also built on his 1895–1897 experience at a much smaller publication, *Ev'ry Month*, where his "official capacity was 'editor and arranger,' as noted on the title page, but his small budget also made him the writer for the first issues, reviewer, advertising agent, and designer."[70] Surrounding its centerpiece—sheet music for ballads by Paul Dresser (Dreiser's brother)—*Ev'ry Month*, like many other women's magazines, included stories, art, reviews, and advice columns. Each issue concluded with domestic advice for urban women very similar to that which would appear in more mainstream publications; Amy Kaplan mentions articles on such topics as "how to create a 'cozy corner,' how to turn packing cases into furniture, how to decorate a 'real home,' how to make up an honest bedroom rather than use the folding beds of a makeshift boardinghouse."[71]

In a novel, of course, Dreiser could move beyond the quotidian how-to article to imagine and articulate the broader possibilities that apartment life might offer to unmarried women. *Sister Carrie* opens with Carrie en route to Chicago seeking something undefined; as she occupies apartments and engages in the relationships opened to her by urban architecture, she climbs to unimaginable success. Juxtaposed with Hurstwood's fall, which can be similarly charted in the buildings he occupies, Carrie's rise both aligns the text with Spencerian principles and hints at more radical possibilities for urban women than Gilman ever explores.[72]

Carrie's radical possibilities emerge from Dreiser's representations of urban spaces, which closely resemble the utopian spaces Michel Foucault terms heterotopias. Heterotopias are "effectively enacted utopia[s] in which the real sites, all the other real sites that can be found within the culture"—the home, the street, the railroad car, and the stage, for instance—"are simultaneously represented, contested, and inverted."[73] In *Sister Carrie*, urban spaces echo David Harvey's reading of Foucault's heterotopias, in that the novel

> enables us to look upon the multiple forms of deviant and transgressive behaviors and politics that occur in urban spaces . . . as valid and potentially meaningful reassertions to some kind of right to shape parts of the city in a different image. It forces us to recognize how important it is to have spaces (the jazz club, the dance hall, the communal garden) within which life is experienced differently. . . . It is within these spaces that alternatives can take shape and from these spaces that a critique of existing norms and processes can effectively be mounted.[74]

If Gilman's work on urban homes recasts but ultimately recuperates traditional domestic values, Dreiser's depictions of heterotopic urban spaces such as the apartment, the stage, the restaurant, and Broadway erode the role that traditional domestic and familial relations play in developing a subject who will thrive in urban space. This positive potential is inherent in the notion of heterotopia for, as Adrian Kiernander points out, "The recognition of the heterotopia involves some combination of delight and anxiety. Heterotopias can be distressing, but they can also afford the exhilaration and excitement of the unknown, unsuspected, unthought. They can reveal the world in previously unimagined ways. They are a form of experiment."[75] Through these experimental fictive spaces, Dreiser both critiques normative domesticity and proposes a radical alternative.

What Donald Pizer identifies as Dreiser's "symbolism of the commonplace" is encoded in *Sister Carrie*'s heterotopias, especially the urban domestic space of apartments.[76] Amy Kaplan emphasizes the significance of domestic spaces to urban realism, noting that "The realists are preoccupied with the problem of inhabiting and representing rented space. . . . Rented spaces constitute a world filled with things neither known nor valued through well-worn contact, but cluttered instead with mass-produced furnishings and the unknown lives of strangers and their abandoned possessions, and valued through the measure of time and space as money. The project of the realistic novels is to make these spaces inhabitable and representable. While realistic novels chart the homelessness of their characters, they thereby construct a world in which their readers can feel at home."[77] To Kaplan, apartments are "cluttered," "mass-produced," "unknown," "abandoned." Her pejorative language undercuts the potential for social change that these spaces house. Historically, apartments offered increased mobility and an appealing freedom from the responsibilities of ownership, yet for Dreiser something more significant than market appeal is at stake in making readers feel "at home" in *Sister Carrie*'s urban domestic spaces. Dreiser allows his readers to dwell imaginatively in his novel, enabling them to reorganize their conceptions of environment into ideas that become increasingly flexible, mobile, and amenable to the notion of social change as the novel progresses. The novel's depictions of rented spaces become instrumental in this regard, for they put into practice a variety of relations among people, space, and property that serve to destabilize received ideas that link physical spaces to property ownership. In *Sister Carrie*, apartments offer Carrie the liberty, status, and mobility that appealed to other modern urbanites; simultaneously, they function as narrative spaces where readers can develop more flexible notions of domesticity and environment.

Like Jacob Riis, Dreiser uses several narrative techniques of sentimental literature to engender specific feelings in his readers, yet, like Fanny Fern, he undermines conservative politics by subverting sentimentality's emphasis on marriage and religious morality. As Kaplan notes, "Just as domesticity is relocated in *Sister Carrie* from the stable home to rented spaces, sentimental language is divested of its traditional familial ties and reinvested in market-engendered values and consumer goods."[78] Yet in tracking Carrie's rise,

Dreiser moves far beyond apologizing for or celebrating consumerism. As he explores an array of rented homes, from the squalor of the flophouse to the luxury of the Waldorf Hotel, he reconstitutes domesticity, articulating new modes of desire and positing new manifestations of success. By the end of the novel, thanks largely to connections made and lessons learned through apartment life, Carrie moves beyond market-oriented consumption to enjoy a mode of success that is grounded in perpetual invention.

If Gilman's fiction tends toward the closure of recognizable if unconventional happy endings, Dreiser's work eclipses Gilman's deconstruction of "androcentric" domesticity to question the home's moral impact. Although Carrie experiences a rush of sentimental feelings as she leaves her childhood home for Chicago, it takes only "a gush of tears at her mother's farewell kiss, a touch in the throat when the cars clacked by the flour mill where her father worked by the day, a pathetic sigh as the familiar green environs of the village passed in review, and the threads which bound her so lightly to girlhood and home were broken" (*SC* 3). Carrie's tears and sigh, conventional signs of regret in sentimental texts, signal briefly and powerfully the transience of Carrie's ties to "girlhood and home," to her past and its spatial representation. The effects of Carrie's home upon her may be powerful, but they are temporary. As the site of her upbringing fades into the distance behind the departing train, so does its impact. Carrie becomes a traveler. Doreen Massey notes that "many women have had to leave home precisely in order to forge their own versions of their identities."[79] In cities, Carrie will encounter an array of possibilities unavailable to single women in her small town; she will be shaped by each new environment she encounters. As Carrie enters Chicago, the reader gets prepared for the force Dreiser will ascribe to physical and social environments throughout the text.

Urban life and urban experiences in *Sister Carrie* are structured by forces that both grow from and find expression in the environment. In Chicago, and even in the liminal space of the train, Carrie brings with her not, as Catharine Beecher would have assumed, a set of values instilled by her nuclear family, but a malleable self ready to be remade in her new environment. As Carrie leaves home, the narrator temporarily adopts the moral valuation of "home = good" and "city = bad" that typifies alarmist analyses of urban women. The narrator notes: "When a girl leaves her home at eighteen, she does one of two things. Either she falls into saving hands and becomes better, or she rapidly assumes the cosmopolitan standard of virtue and becomes worse" (*SC*, 3–4). The narrator posits two diametrically opposed options, neither of which ascribe agency to the girl. Whether she becomes better or worse depends not upon her own choices but upon what she encounters in the spaces she inhabits. But these clichés rapidly become inadequate to account for Carrie's trajectory. First, as Alan Trachtenberg and others suggest, Dreiser uses the city as a backdrop for transvaluing commonplace outcomes:

"it is not long (in the following Chicago chapters) before we realize that Carrie may well turn out 'better' in the end for having been 'worse' at the beginning—better, that is, in the transvalued perspective the narrator will meticulously, almost laboriously, construct in the course of the novel."[80] The novel's urban landscapes exert powerful forces upon their inhabitants, yet the city Dreiser constructs is far more complex than the narrator lets on here. Over the course of the novel, Carrie experiences the city not as an either/or proposition but as a setting with the possibility for both/and. By the novel's end, she has exemplified almost the entire spectrum of narrative possibilities for urban women: "Woman is present in cities as temptress, as whore, as fallen woman, as lesbian, but also as virtuous womanhood in danger, as heroic womanhood who triumphs over temptation and tribulation."[81] Carrie does assume the "cosmopolitan standard of virtue," yet as a result of contacts made within urban domestic spaces, particularly the apartments she lives in, she also "falls into" or perhaps constructs for herself the "saving hands" that augur a "better" destiny for her. Most significantly, through the intelligent, compassionate figure of Robert Ames, Carrie learns to see herself as the narrator sees her, as one of, or at least as a channel for, the "forces wholly superhuman" that characterize the urban environment's sway over the individual (SC, 4).

Synechdochizing the City

Sister Carrie's characters inhabit urban environments; Dreiser explores the literal and symbolic meanings of their dwellings. Urban homes may be read as straightforward signs of economic status: Although the particular neighborhoods Dreiser mentions in Chicago and New York change even within the novel's narrative frame, it is always clear which addresses signal prosperity, comfortable middle-class status, or membership in the striving laboring classes. Hurstwood's descent from well-off manager to destitute beggar may be read in his clothes, his jobs, and his body, but Dreiser's spatial calibration of Hurstwood's decline is also numerically clear, first in the dwindling number of rooms that Carrie and Hurstwood rent and then in the descending nightly rate for the boarding houses and flops that Hurstwood eventually occupies. For Carrie, apartments offer something more; they operate as gateways between herself and other urbanites, allowing her to enter into and participate in the sort of urban life she craves.

Carrie's introduction to the interpersonal connections that apartment architecture enables helps her to move from one state of being to another. Although she lives briefly with her older sister Minnie, Carrie's first home outside of her immediate family is in a three-room flat that her lover Charlie Drouet provides. Drouet installs Carrie in Ogden Place, where "by her industry and natural love of order which now developed, the place retained an air pleasing in the extreme" (*SC*, 89). Carrie's domestic development seems to be inspired by the apartment itself. The flat looks out over Union Park, "a little, green-carpeted breathing spot, than which today there is nothing more beautiful in Chicago" (*SC*, 88). Though it offers little more than pleasing surroundings and a lovely view, this otherwise unremarkable urban dwelling allows Carrie her initial access to the emotional greatness that will emerge as her most significant characteristic.

The architecture at Ogden Place is marked by the connection that is characteristic of apartment life; its connectivity enables Carrie to experience and develop new emotional depth. One of her fellow tenants, the daughter of a railroad treasurer, is a music student who practices piano in the building's parlor. Although Carrie occasionally glimpses her neighbor practicing, she also can hear the piano from her own rooms, and her experience of listening is transformative. Carrie is particularly sensitive to music—"her nervous composition responded to certain strains"—and the setting enhances her sensitivity (*SC*, 102). "One short song the woman played in a most soulful and expressive mood. Carrie heard it through the open door of the parlor below. It was at that hour between afternoon and night when for the idle, the wanderers, things are apt to take on a wistful complexion. The mind wanders forth on far journeys and returns with sheaves of withered and departed joys. Carrie sat at her window looking out" (*SC*, 103).

From the relative privacy of her own apartment, Carrie experiences new emotions. Alone, yet connected to the music, Carrie may allow her mind to wander and her spirit to become mobile. Suspending the present and future, she taps into the past and experiences a wistful longing for something that she can no longer have. "Now she sat looking across the park, as wistful and depressed as the nature which craves variety and life can be under such circumstances. As she contemplated her new state, the strain from the parlor stole upward. With it her thoughts became colored and enmeshed. She reverted to the things which were best and saddest within the small limit of her experience. She became for the moment a repentant" (*SC*, 104). Connecting interior and exterior spaces, Carrie becomes a conduit for raw emotion. As Robert Butler notes, "Carrie's window meditations reveal surprising aspects of her own personality which others are often unaware of—she is not a helpless 'waif amid forces' because she is empowered with imagination, intellect, and will, all of which are vividly demonstrated when she transcends the closed space of small rooms by looking out of windows."[82] Initially, this emotional experience does not convert into action; Carrie does not repent, she does not leave Drouet, she does not even insist on marriage. Yet the apartment both inspires unfulfillable desire and gives Carrie the space to lay herself open to this desire, a practice that eventually becomes the cornerstone for her professional career.

Carrie's desire takes many forms; at first the apartment helps to fan the flames of her desire to consume. In addition to initiating Carrie to deep emotion, the treasurer's daughter unconsciously inspires Carrie in the aesthetic realms of fashion and self-display. "This young woman was particularly dressy for her station, and wore a jeweled ring or two which flashed upon her white fingers as she played" (*SC*, 102). The power exuded through her music, her appearance, and her personality "Carrie could not help but feel" (*SC*, 104). Significantly, it is the music permeating the apartment that elevates the otherwise cold, ostentatious, and indifferent neighbor's influence to transformative proportions.

> At night when the tall red-shaded piano lamp stood by the piano, and in its ruddy light the treasurer's daughter played and sang, Carrie saw and felt things which appealed to her imagination. If the melody could, as it once did, arouse thoughts which started the tears, how effectual must have been the impress of the young girl's material state. For Carrie the melody and the light created a halo about nice clothes, showy manners, sparkling rings. It lent an ineffable charm to the world of material display. Accordingly, when Hurstwood called he found a young woman who was much more than the Carrie Drouet [he] had first spoken to. (*SC*, 104–105)

Just as apartment architecture blurs the boundaries around the private home, the light from the lamp dissolves the edges of the room into darkness, creating a space where Carrie can be transformed by mere proximity to the music. In the apartment's common space, sight and sound merge within Carrie and make her something "much more"; she internalizes beauty, developing an aesthetic sense that in turn shines forth from her. Hurstwood, who himself possesses a highly developed aesthetic sense that is demonstrated in his impeccable clothing and beautiful sideboard display, looks "into her pretty face and [feels] the subtle waves of young life radiating therefrom" (*SC*, 105). Her experience in this building prepares her to become a conduit of beauty, life, and youth.

Carrie's other Ogden Place neighbor, Mrs. Hale, is also an aesthetic mentor. While the "passive" Mrs. Hale possesses none of the treasurer's daughter's personality, and concerns herself mainly with "trivialities" and "conventional expressions of morals," she does introduce Carrie to the social life of the city (*SC*, 102). When Carrie accompanies Mrs. Hale on a drive along the lake shore, dusk reveals the interiors of the elegant houses along North Shore Drive. The descending darkness echoes the parlor lamp's dissolving of walls, laying open another world to Carrie's gaze.

> Across the broad lawns, now first freshening into green, she saw lamps faintly glowing upon rich interiors. Now it was but a chair, now a table, now an ornate corner which met her eye, but it appealed to her as almost nothing else

could. Such childish fantasies as she had had of fairy palaces and kingly quarters now came back. She imagined that across these richly carved entranceways where the globed and crystalled lamps shone upon paneled doors, set with stained and designed panels of glass, was neither care nor unsatisfied desire. She was perfectly certain that here was happiness. . . . She gazed and gazed, wondering, delighting, longing, and all the while the siren voice of the unrestful was whispering in her ear. (*SC*, 115–16)

Here are echoes of the emotional processes and effects at work in the apartment. As the walls dissolve, Carrie gains access to beauty; she in turn allows this beauty to evoke powerful emotion. Again, she summons up the past, recalling childhood fantasies linked both to physical space and to the force of desire. Imagining desire satisfied only augments the force of her longing.

Her desire is not something fleeting; rather, Carrie nurtures it, deepening the feeling when she is alone. On the drive, in the context of the happiness she imagines, her unrest only increases as it whispers to her. As with the piano, sound intensifies her feelings. Back in her rooms, with "the roll of cushioned carriages still in her ears," Carrie becomes "too pensive to do aught but rock and sing. Some old tunes crept to her lips and as she sang them her heart sank. She longed and longed and longed" (*SC*, 116). Here, Carrie consciously works to deepen her emotional response, drawing on what she has seen and heard in order to experience a new depth of feeling. "She was sad beyond measure and yet uncertain, wishing and fancying. Finally it seemed as if all her state was one of loneliness and forsakenness and she could scarce refrain from trembling at the lip. She hummed and hummed as the moments went by, sitting in the shadow by the window, and was therein as happy, though she could not perceive it, as ever she would be" (*SC*, 116). In a self-induced trance of sound, movement, and emotion, Carrie develops a working method to induce deep feeling. Eventually, simply rocking will allow her access to this emotional depth. Carrie does not perceive the experience as "happy." Instead, the happiness the narrator ascribes to her clearly develops from the work itself; it derives from the experience of doing what she does best, enveloping herself in her genius.

Paradoxically, the strategy that will allow Carrie to summon and project her emotions initially remains quite private. Even those closest to her do not comprehend Carrie's depth. Hurstwood, for instance, "had not conceived well of her mental ability. That was because he did not understand the nature of emotional greatness. He had never learned that a person might be emotionally instead of intellectually great" (*SC*, 378). Later, on the stage, her emotional greatness, which Donald Pizer defines as "her ability to sense the emotional realities of life and communicate them to others through her art," will attain its highest expression.[83] Before her acting career begins, Carrie's apartment offers her a liminal space similar to the stage, protected yet public, where she can work on deepening the feelings of longing that will enable her, as an actress, to embody her viewers' desires. Indeed, Carrie's powerful emotion, developed and nurtured in urban spatial arrangements, motivates her to seek out the stage as a professional venue for success in the city. Pizer points out that Carrie's "fate is not determined by her surroundings, but her surroundings nevertheless can be said to play a powerful role in her life in that the deep response of her nature to the specifics of her immediate world prompts the direction of her life."[84] The direction, of course, is to the theater, where Carrie can profit by projecting publicly the emotional greatness she has developed in her urban home.

At home in her rocking chair, Carrie consciously heightens her own emotional responses to her environment. Fittingly, her first dramatic role is in an urban domestic drama; as Laura in *Under the Gaslight*, Carrie projects all of the pathos of a good woman fighting the evil circumstances thrust upon her by the vagaries of chance and fate at work in the city. Like Carrie, Laura inhabits a variety of domestic arrangements, but whereas Laura's pure true womanhood prevails despite the city's force, Carrie's more flexible essence allows her to adapt to changing circumstances and embody the city.

Initially, the stage is figured in *Sister Carrie* as a house, a dwelling far more open and welcoming than the houses on North Shore Drive. "Since her arrival in the city, many things had influenced her but always in a far-removed manner. This new atmosphere was more friendly. It was wholly unlike the great, brilliant mansions which waved her coolly away, permitting her only awe and distant wonder. This took her by the hand kindly, as one who says, 'My dear, come in.' It opened for her as if for its own" (*SC*, 177). This domestic image of the stage, complete with the welcoming, almost maternal figure of the hostess, seems significant in at least two ways. The stage's kind welcome is in direct contrast to the very limited and unappealing familial domesticity we glimpse in the novel. It is difficult to imagine either Carrie's sister or Hurstwood's family offering anyone the kind of warm embrace that envelops Carrie when she ventures into "the world behind the curtain" (*SC*, 176). The theater's easy hospitality much more closely resembles the welcome Carrie will receive later in the novel when, as a successful actress, she is invited to occupy a suite at a New York hotel, gratis, on the strength of the publicity her name will provide. In addition, because the stage at this time generally was constructed as an antidomestic space, we can read the door that opens here as evoking a type of domesticity that subverts the contained home, replacing it with something flexible, transformable, and urban.[85]

Thanks to her experiences in Chicago, Carrie has become highly attuned to the power of connections. While she abandons nineteenth-century morality by moving in (unmarried) with Drouet and then taking up with the married Hurstwood, the interpersonal connections she makes do improve her according to urban standards. They make her day-to-day life easier and fit her for the city by demonstrating to her the modes of technological and architectural connection that make urban life enjoyable and desirable. When she arrives there with Hurstwood, New York seems to magnify Chicago's patterns and possibilities. It is fitting that Carrie and Hurstwood's first New York apartment reactivates Carrie's urban experience of transformative desire.

Initially, New York's architecture confuses and disorients Carrie; she does not yet know how to read the landscape:

> "Where is the residence part?" asked Carrie, who did not take the tall five-story walls on either hand to be the abode of families.
>
> "Everywhere," said Hurstwood, who knew the city fairly well. "There are no lawns in New York. All these are houses."
>
> "Well, then I don't like it," said Carrie, who was beginning to have a few opinions of her own. (*SC*, 304)

Carrie may not like New York's domestic architecture at first, but she rapidly adapts to it, and it in turn serves her well. First, the apartment woos Carrie with its attractive technologies: "The stationary range, bath with hot and cold water, dumb-waiter, speaking tubes and call bell for the janitor pleased her very much" (*SC*, 307). While the height of the buildings initially repels Carrie, their third-floor vantage point allows her a perspective on her new environment that is far more appealing than that attainable from the street. Like Carrie's Chicago flat, the New York apartment occupies a kind of middle ground between the urban and the natural worlds. "It was possible to see east to the green tops of the trees in Central Park and west to the broad waters of the Hudson" (*SC*, 307). And as the apartment in Chicago did, the new flat quickly leaves its imprint upon Carrie's identity. After they move in, Hurstwood has "a little plate bearing the name 'G. W. Wheeler' made, which he placed on his letter box in the hall. It sounded exceedingly odd to Carrie to be called 'Mrs. Wheeler' by the janitor, but in time she became used to it, and looked upon the name as her own" (*SC*, 307). Just as living in Drouet's apartment turned her into Carrie Drouet, in New York Carrie is flexible enough to take on a new identity as the building and its practices bestow it on her. The novel thus presents a view of "identity as variable, flexible, infinitely achievable . . . identity as something chosen."[86] Thanks in part to this building, Carrie rises to her environment's standards and becomes a model urbanite.

As she did in Chicago, Carrie initially uses the New York apartment to launch a foray into domesticity, perfecting her biscuit recipe and arranging an attractive table for Hurstwood. Like Drouet before him, Hurstwood appears "to value Carrie less for a risqué liaison than for a cozy domesticity."[87] But while Hurstwood begins "to imagine that she was of the thoroughly domestic type of mind," Carrie's infatuation with homemaking does not last, perhaps because traditional domesticity is not the practice best suited to apartment life (SC, 316). Though some observers enthused about the cunning ways one could play house in the city by concealing cooking devices and screening off sinks, apartments at this time were designed specifically to discourage cooking. Cooking was illegal in many apartment buildings, although tenants often set up small gas rings to heat incidental dishes like the canned oyster stews that were Carrie's specialty in Chicago. Carrie, of course, believes that she and Hurstwood are married, which could explain why her early efforts at homemaking are so ambitious. But the apartment quickly reveals to Carrie alternate models of marriage and of womanhood that will transform her anew.

Carrie's apartments operate as microcosms of the city. They are potent yet safe venues that allow her to practice urban modes of connection. Carrie's friendship with her new neighbor Mrs. Vance demonstrates how the building's design aligns with Carrie's desire to transcend social boundaries. Mrs. Vance transforms Carrie's urban experience and identity, introducing her to New York theater, dining, and fashion, and most importantly, to Robert Ames. Mrs. Vance's musical ability initially sparks Carrie's interest; as she could in Chicago, in New York Carrie can hear her neighbor "play through the thin walls which divided the front rooms of the flat and [is] pleased by the merry selection of pieces and the brilliance of their rendition" (SC, 319). From Mrs. Vance's ability and choice of tunes, Carrie intuits that her neighbor is "in a measure refined and in comfortable circumstances. So Carrie [is] ready for any extension of the friendship which might follow" (SC, 319). And just as the Chicago apartment's common room allowed Carrie to meet her first musical neighbor, the New York apartment building's design allows for meaningful personal connections.[88]

The technological features that initially endear the building to Carrie hasten her attraction to and cement her friendship with Mrs. Vance. The women's relationship reverberates both in its presence and its absence throughout the New York portion of the novel, yet its origins are quite mundane; it is "brought about solely by the arrangement of the flats, which were united in one place, as it were, by the dumbwaiter. This useful elevator, by which fuel, groceries, and the like were sent up from the basement, and garbage, waste, and the like sent down, was used by both residents of one floor—that is, a small door opened into it from each flat" (SC, 317). A popular apartment feature, the dumbwaiter was designed to minimize contact between the resident and the janitor, and to minimize labor for both. But in the novel, the dumbwaiter brings Carrie and Mrs. Vance face to face when they both answer the janitor's whistle at the same time. Their connection is furthered through the technology of the electric doorbell; when Mrs. Vance is locked out, she rings Carrie's bell and Carrie's servant automatically buzzes Mrs. Vance into the building, precipitating a meeting and conversation between the two women that leads to friendship.

Mrs. Vance represents a highly developed urban subjectivity. She is well suited to and revels in her environment. Married to an older, wealthy man, Mrs. Vance enjoys the city as fantasyland. A champion shopper, she monitors fashion trends for Carrie and introduces the younger woman to the display parade of Broadway. Janet Wolff argues that "the modern consciousness consists in the parade of impressions, the particular beauty appropriate to the modern age," and appropriately, Mrs. Vance introduces Carrie to modern consciousness by building on Charlie Drouet's sidewalk lessons in fashion and comportment that transformed Carrie in Chicago.[89] The Vances are highly mobile; they move from one apartment to another as New York's sensitive social and architectural barometers shift. Thus they typify *Architectural Review*'s 1903 assessment of apartment dwellers: "Such people have generally lived in boarding-houses and family hotels. They are numerous in all American cities. [They are] constantly moving, and have no desire for a residence that is permanent and hampers such freedom of movement."[90] In this sense, they personify mobility, one of the most powerful forces by which urban space is produced. As David Harvey notes, "The production of space means more than merely the ability to circulate in a pre-ordained spatially-structured world. It also means the right to reconstruct spatial relations . . . in ways that turn space from an absolute framework of action into a more malleable and relational aspect of social life."[91] The Vances are hardly revolutionaries in this regard, though Carrie might be—and the novel itself tries to be. Yet, in experiencing all of the pleasures the city offers, the Vances welcome and develop new contacts, deepening Carrie's relational view of urban space. They reach out generously to Carrie, inviting her to the theater and to expensive restaurants that are increasingly off limits to the constrained Hurstwood. On one of these evenings, the Vances introduce Carrie to Robert Ames, the inventor who becomes Carrie's mentor in matching her genius to her age. According to Kevin McNamara, Ames "preaches not the minimizing of desire but the careful channeling of desire and capital in directions likely to benefit both the individual self and the larger social 'organism.'"[92] Personally and professionally, it is the single most profitable connection that Carrie makes in New York.

Although their initial meeting is brief, it opens new possibilities to Carrie. Suitably, what pass between the emotional Carrie and Ames the electrical engineer are currents of feeling and sympathy. Carrie has been open to these urban currents since her arrival in Chicago. "She senses even from the train the energy of the city, feels its flow embodied in the crowds she watches from Hanson's doorstep, as well as in the public spaces (avenues, parks, restaurants, hotels) that immediately catch her attention."[93] The energy that flows

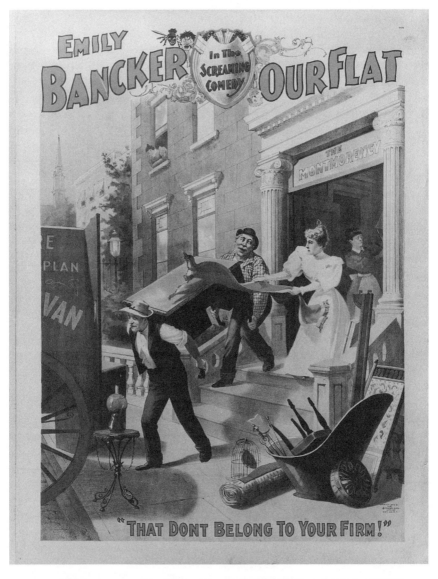

FIGURE 26. Theater poster, 1895. Library of Congress, Prints and Photographs Division, LC-USZ6-412.

between Carrie and Ames, however, has a different valance. Like Carrie, Ames' "sympathies for . . . people were quick and warm" (*SC*, 335). On a larger scale, Ames is working out his sympathies by inventing products that will serve peoples' desires and improve their lives, and he instills in Carrie the desire to use her own sympathetic qualities for a similar purpose.

He mentioned things in the play she most approved of—things which swayed her deeply.

"Don't you think it's rather fine to be an actor?" she asked once.

"Yes—I do" he said. "To be a good one. I think the theater's a great thing."

Just this little approval sent Carrie's heart bounding. Ah, if she could only be an actress—a good one. This man was wise—he knew—and he approved of it. (*SC*, 336)

Though Carrie cannot analyze this feeling, she senses the import of Ames's largely tacit approbation. His approval unleashes a new, empowering desire.

Significantly, Carrie's meeting with Ames, like both of their geniuses, stems from connection. Carrie's ability to open herself to interpersonal connections and distill their emotional content allows her to grasp the import of the ineffable current that flows between herself and Ames. As the couples chat through their elaborate dinner at Sherry's, "the atmosphere that went with the youth impressed itself upon Carrie without words" (*SC*, 336). And afterward, "the ideal brought into her life by Ames remained. He had gone, but here was his word that riches were not everything, that there was a great deal more in the world than she knew, that the stage was good and the literature she read poor" (*SC*, 346). Later, Ames's words will come to mean more.

At the end of the novel, through the magic of urban connection as personified by Mrs. Vance, Carrie and Ames are reunited in a meeting that emphasizes their similarities and reveals that their particular (and related) geniuses are both products of and productive of their age. When they meet for the second time, they have something new in common—their talents have made them famous. As they reencounter one another, Ames remarks,

"I needn't ask how you've been. I've been reading about you."

"Oh, have you?" said Carrie. "Well, I know what you've been doing. I read it all while I was in London."

"Yes, I know," said Ames. "I didn't want that published. It wasn't—"

"There you go again, Bob," put in Mrs. Vance. "Oh dear, these celebrities!" (*SC*, 480)

Though they perform on different stages, Carrie and Ames have both become stars whose activities are broadcast to a wide audience. They each benefit from the attention: Ames builds his own laboratory, while Carrie negotiates a successful stage career.

Perhaps because of their shared attunement to and use of a variety of urban networks, the nonverbal current of sympathy Ames and Carrie initially felt is amped up, as it were, in their second meeting. "Now Carrie seemed the most pleasing character present. She extended to him that sympathy and attention which he needed to show his mind at its best. At its best it was speculative and idealistic—far above anything which she had as yet conceived, and yet, curiously, he could talk to her. She made him feel as if she understood, and he unconsciously strove to make himself plain. Thus the bond between them was drawn closer than they knew" (*SC*, 481). Carrie's emotional greatness, the cornerstone of her acting career, here finds an interpersonal outlet that, the narrator intimates, will open to her new levels of conception. Carrie remains a conduit; her value is what she elicits from Ames. And like alternating current, Ames responds with reciprocal force. "He was thinking to start her off on a course of reading which would improve her. Anyone so susceptible to improvement should be aided. Her mind seemed free and quick enough to grasp most anything. 'Read all of Balzac's. They will do you good'" (*SC*, 482). Part of Ames's genius lies in his ability to recognize problems and to imagine innovative solutions, like suggesting that Carrie read Balzac, perhaps a surprising choice for the young inventor but perfectly apt for Carrie, since to Balzac the city is, among other things, "a world . . . of infinite beauty and delight as long as the heart and the spirit have the strength and the desire to seek."[94] His remarks upon her free, quick mind, emphasize that Ames sees Carrie differently from anyone else in the novel, perhaps even the narrator.

He sees, perhaps, a kindred spirit. The emotional conduit runs both ways, profiting both people. Ames is an inventor, and in *Sister Carrie* his inventions are seen as social contributions, as means to improve society. And when Ames lectures to Carrie on her possibilities, he draws an implied parallel between his work and hers. He clearly sees himself and Carrie in the same light: "You and I are both mediums, through which something is expressing itself. Now, our duty is to make ourselves ready mediums" (*SC*, 485). In urban novels, mediums are a typical urban persona, but whereas Priscilla in *The Blithedale Romance* and Verena in *The Bostonians* are freakish, Bob and Carrie's skill as mediums perfectly fits them for their age. As Donald Pizer argues: "Dreiser's point, one that runs counter to expectations inherent in a naturalist ideology, is that the right kind of temperament can capitalize on the possibilities for personal gain in an otherwise threatening environment and thus advance rather than be crushed."[95] Through the city's ever-growing networks, the nation as a whole is catching up to the urban environment that demands and nurtures the qualities of the medium. As the city becomes constituted more forcefully as home for Americans, the characteristics evoked by the urban home—here, apartments—become increasingly characteristic of and less threatening to the culture writ large. Both embodying and developing channels for emotion and power, Ames and Carrie represent the zenith of what the urban environment can produce.

Their ability does not just bring them fame and fortune; it offers them the chance to act for social good. Ames, of course, positions himself beyond the claims of consumption by rejecting the values of greed and display at work in Sherry's. Paradoxically, his rejection of capitalism's endgame has brought him great profit, and he suggests to Carrie that she may profit in a similar way. Highly attuned to her genius and its risks, he tells Carrie: "You can't become self-interested, selfish, and luxurious, without having these sympathies and longings disappear, and then you will sit there and wonder what has become of them. You can't remain tender and sympathetic, and desire to serve the world, without having it show in your face and in your art. If you want to do most, do good. Serve the many. Be kind and humanitarian. Then you can't help but be great" (*SC,* 486). And though Carrie has played the urban temptress, whore, and fallen woman, she can still serve, even in the eyes of the upright Ames, as a force for social good. Perhaps at this point, Carrie, like Ames, has moved beyond needing to grasp at things. Apartment life has allowed her to experience and finally transcend a desire that is largely consumptive in nature. As Alan Trachtenberg points out, Carrie, "far from suffering remorse or moral blame for enjoying sex outside of marriage and inside of adultery, actually grows in self-awareness and independence, . . . unmarried, unattached, successful in her career at the close of the narrative, [she] seems poised to make something more and better of herself, 'redeeming' in a trans-valued sense of the word those very experiences unacceptable, sordid and 'unreal' in the eyes of gentility (including Howells) and becoming—we are led to believe it possible—a serious artist and serious person."[96] Donald Pizer sees that Carrie's spirit rises to "a higher calling, one in which the pursuit of beauty becomes primarily an attempt to aid others rather than herself."[97] Through her environment, Carrie comes to represent, and her narrative to promote, a sense for the possibilities available to urban women that echoes and transcends Gilman's analysis.

Generally, Dreiser's novels do not embrace the sort of unfettered optimism that propels (and many would say weakens) Gilman's work. Polly Wynn Allen notes that Gilman was a true progressive who adhered, perhaps blindly, to the notion that society was on an upward trend and that change would necessarily be for the better.[98] As Hurstwood's descent and most of Dreiser's other novels make clear, Dreiser understood that progress would always leave casualties in its wake; his romantic belief in possibility was tempered by the fact that failure was as least as much a possibility as success for any individual.[99] Yet at the same time, Dresier's utopian vista seems broader than Gilman's. In *Sister Carrie,* the possibility for intellectual, spiritual, and economic growth is open to Carrie, a person whose social position, especially as determined by her class, gender, and sexual practices, would have closed doors to her in most of Gilman's bourgeois utopias. Along with the racism that many readers have found at work in Gilman's texts is an impulse toward a moral and biological cleansing that certainly would touch a woman like Carrie if she were to enter into the world of *Moving a Mountain,* where "'hopeless degenerates' and idiots have been 'mercifully' done away with, that is to say, killed. In addition, a policy of forced sterilization is applied to certain types of 'defectives and degenerates . . . criminals and perverts.'"[100] While the possibly degenerate Carrie never has children, she does reproduce herself via the stage and the print media, extending the influence that she and her story may have.

In moving beyond outmoded spaces, Dreiser also moves beyond an outmoded morality and extends the city's possibilities to a new group of urbanites. Kaplan claims that "the characters in *Sister Carrie* continually pursue an image of themselves as they might be—not as they are."[101] While in Kaplan's reading this focus dooms them to disappointment, I feel that it also contains a certain optimism. At its best, Dreiser's city and the apartments that synecdochize urban space in *Sister Carrie* offer the room that David Harvey endorses in his heterotopias, space "for the private and personal—a space in which doubt, anger, anxiety and despair as well as certitude, altruism, hope and elation may flourish."[102] When Carrie's mobility and malleability are aligned with a desire for transformative beauty, she begins to embody the hope and possibilities that are lodged in the city itself. She becomes a figure, then, for urban utopianism. Carrie becomes a conduit through which Trachtenberg's moral "transvaluation" is projected into the urban landscape; simultaneously, Dreiser's transfigured notions of domestic morality are projected through the novel into his readers. From her experiences in apartments, from Bob Ames, and from the city itself, Carrie, like her fellow bachelor girls, learns to look forward—to perceive opportunities in the interstices of urban life. Her desire, perhaps, will never be fulfilled, yet embedded in that desire is the possibility for positive change. As Dreiser reminds us, in Carrie the "magic of passion, which will yet dissolve the world, [is] here at work" (*SC*, 185).

Chapter 5

From Artifact to Investment

*Hotel Homes, the Economics of Luxury,
and* The Custom of the Country

*. . . what Popple called society was really just like the houses it lived in: a
muddle of misapplied ornament over a thin shell of utility.*
—Edith Wharton[1]

Considering Carrie Meeber's meteoric rise in *Sister Carrie,* Amy Kaplan notes,
"the greatest measure of her success in the novel occurs when her name and
image are employed as an advertisement. She is asked to live at a new residential hotel [an apartment hotel, to be precise] for a nominal fee because
her 'name is worth something.' . . . Carrie exchanges her name for the realization of her fantasies, the reconstitution of domesticity in a rented space."[2]
In fact, Carrie moves even further than this; her rocking chair is last seen
stationed at the window of the Waldorf Hotel, a name that is still recognizable as one of New York's great luxury hotels. A form of urban housing
that was just coming into vogue at the turn into the twentieth century,
the luxury hotel constituted urban domesticity anew, its technologies and
living arrangements positioning it even farther from the contained home
than urban apartments.

In American cities, as urban housing choices developed, each new form
was met with a mixture of celebration and skepticism. Perhaps no living
arrangement got a bigger reaction than the luxury hotels that became American cities' landmark buildings in the early twentieth century. Bigger, brasher,
and more opulent than most boarding houses, row houses, or apartment
buildings, luxury hotels provoked a strong and divided response from their
observers. Quasi-public spaces, they drew crowds of diners, dancers, and
hangers-on to their restaurants and rooftops. Beautiful, expensive, and fascinating, luxury hotels were also sources of anxiety for many onlookers. As
sociologist Norman Hayner noted, "Hotel life seems to facilitate family dis-
organization. . . . In fact, the relative number of hotel rooms and divorces

increases as one moves westward from the Atlantic through the Central to the Western states. The hotel environment no doubt accentuates those tensions that are the real causes of domestic discord. It also provides a refuge for the divorced."[3] What better setting could Edith Wharton have chosen to open her 1913 "divorce novel," *The Custom of the Country?*

The Custom of the Country is, of course, about divorce, but while marriages are indeed made and dissolved at a dizzying speed according to the country's custom, Wharton's concerns about dissolution run far beyond the precarious institution of marriage.[4] Beyond the novel's many literal divorces, Wharton displays an even more disturbing prospect, the growing American tendency to divorce space from history. As I noted in the introduction, Wharton's friend Henry James voiced similar concerns in *The American Scene.* James saw modern New York as a landscape of flux and change, where only his memory and his fiction might offer permanence. James's memory of a past located in a particular space, he feared, would recede as a way of life he termed the "hotel-spirit" came to dominate New York. Edith Wharton embodies this hotel spirit in Undine Spragg, *The Custom of the Country*'s protagonist. Undine's narrative limns the fate of a culture shaped by structures that have been constructed on the rubble of history; in the novel, it is not simply exterior space that, in James's phrase, "runs to the skyscraper" or apartment or hotel, but interior space—subjectivity itself. As Debra Ann MacComb notes, "James reads in the obliteration of familiar settings and structures an emblem of the new social dislocation—a divorce between present and past selves," while for Wharton, "the logic of consumption and disposal extends most insidiously into the home, where familial relations that transmit identity, continuity, and tradition are similarly at risk of being unmade."[5] Historically and architecturally, Undine's association with the hotel perfectly fits a character who divorces space from history.

Most commonly read as a narrative of the detestable protagonist's social rise through serial marriage, *Custom* explores intersections among space, time, and economics at a moment of societal change. The novel develops a logic of investment that is most clearly visible in the character of Elmer Moffatt, the Wall Street *wunderkind* who is also Undine's first (and fourth) husband. Moffatt understands the world in terms of potential. Scheming and patient, he sails through temporary setbacks including financial ruin, personal ridicule, political scandals, and even an early divorce from Undine, buoyed by his belief in the future and his willingness to ignore, remake, or trade on the past as the situation warrants. Elmer's investment success is paralleled in Undine's rise from Kansas nobody to international socialite. But unlike Moffatt, who can mark his rise in terms of cash flow, precious objects (including Undine), and eventually, the power to control the values of commodities themselves, Undine's success must be measured in spatial terms.

As a woman, Undine is barred from trading on Wall Street. She can, however, trade in settings and manipulate environments in order to produce and project the self she wishes to convey. Undine's self-reinvention reflects her larger setting; in this era, Manhattan's landscape was transformed incessantly by new construction that the landmark structures of luxury hotels exemplified. Such hotels offered women of Undine's economic class unparalleled social opportunities, for they allowed rich people to purchase access to elite domesticity. Through the narrator's critical lens, Undine's gleeful manipulations of real estate come to represent a profound and lamentable cultural shift, a divorce between place and past. Beyond evoking nostalgia for what has been and will be lost, the novel claims that the modern subject essentially becomes a person without a past of her own, even as she profits from other peoples' pasts. *The Custom of the Country* depicts tradition's losing battle with progress as a struggle between historic and economic values that is played out in urban domestic space.

The Rise of the Luxury Hotel

Her particular sensitivity to interiors makes domestic space critical to Wharton's conceptions of subjectivity and culture, both past and present.[6] In her autobiography, *A Backward Glance*, for instance, Wharton charts her own history by detailing the settings of origin that are central to her family's identity. She writes, "My photographic memory of rooms and houses—even those seen briefly, or at long intervals—was from my earliest days a source of inarticulate misery."[7] Remembering the details of housekeeping is painful to Wharton for two reasons: first, because each object she recalls evokes memories of departed days and people, and secondly because few of the homes she recalls ever lived up to her fastidious standards for beauty and taste. In some ways, Wharton recapitulates Gilman's claim that "The home is an incarnate past to us. It is our very oldest thing, and holds the heart more deeply than all others."[8] Her first book, *The Decoration of Houses*, aimed to ease or prevent the pain of bad decoration by articulating classical principles of design. Many of Wharton's actual and fictional homes are sites where the past is stored and displayed, and where the objects that constitute individual and family histories are housed. The idea that a home might be transformed from a site where history—especially family or class history—is preserved, into merely another site for conspicuous display both fascinates and repulses Wharton.[9]

While in her own life Wharton had the resources to buy property and extensively renovate her surroundings, in her fiction she explores the limits of this ability. Perhaps this is why Edmund Wilson called Wharton "the poet of

interior decoration."[10] Her best known characters, including Lily Bart, Newland Archer, and Ellen Olenska, are all highly attuned to their surroundings,
yet are not always capable of creating the environments they desire. In Wharton's novels, the balance between architectural agency and determinism shifts,
but her characters usually are marked by and identified with their settings,
whether they actively construct these surroundings or are merely shaped by
them. When characters can personalize their living spaces, as Ellen Olenska
does in *The Age of Innocence* when she transforms an unremarkable apartment into a setting that (figuratively) transports Newland Archer from New
York to Samarkand, they can define themselves and retain a measure of control over the self they present.

Overtly commercial dwellings like hotels posed a special problem—and
opportunity—for Wharton. Given that a hotel's furnishings and decorations
generally were selected by the hotel and not the guest, what effect would
hotel life have upon its inhabitants? Wharton would have had good reason
to wonder, for at the time, wealthy New Yorkers and their counterparts in
other cities increasingly were choosing to make their homes in luxury hotels
that offered all of the modern advantages of apartment life, and then some.

Like apartment buildings, hotels transformed spatial conceptions of the
urban home and changed the cultural meaning of urban domesticity.[11] Though
luxury apartments and hotels often alluded to the past through their names
or designs, they stood as architectural symbols of the new. They were the
first buildings to install new technologies, such as plumbing, electricity, and
elevators. Always on the cutting edge of architecture and technology, the
luxury hotels of Wharton's day represented a break with the past. A 1902
observer noted nostalgically, "The old New York hotel was a spacious home
where people returned year after year, where they knew the proprietor, clerk
and the office boy. There was something personal and *gemüthlich* about it.
All that is now changed. The modern hotel is a great institution. Its keynote
is impersonality."[12] In new hotels, a modern model of technologically networked domesticity replaced a homelike sense of the personal, reframing the
way in which the home was understood. In Manhattan, limited space and
new building technologies led to an unprecedented real estate boom; the late
1800s saw New York's richest property owners developing apartments and
hotels (or selling out to developers) in order to capitalize on the incredible
rise in property values. In New York, all trends pointed to a new way for the
bourgeois and upper classes to inhabit urban space, and the luxury hotel
came to exemplify this new mode of living. Hotels emphasized that home in
the city was no longer a repository of history; instead it was a real estate investment, an impersonal institution.

Although they may have seemed impersonal, hotels and apartment hotels
did serve as homes for many urban dwellers. But could hotels be considered
permanent homes? This was a difficult question to answer; hotels muddied

many of the analytical categories that have applied to homes—even homes in apartments. Commentators of the day, in attempting to understand how the ideal of home would play out in hotels, argued that permanence was a primary quality of the home. But even permanence was quite transitory. Geographer Paul Groth notes that living for one month or more in a hotel or apartment qualifies one as a permanent resident; he dates this requirement to the Civil War era.[13] Accordingly, a 1930 United States *Census of Hotels* attempted to label hotels as "Mainly transient" and "Mainly permanent," but the majority of hotels in the census fell into the category of "Mixed transient and permanent."[14] Although "the hotel developed naturally as an abode for transients," one architect noted in 1929, "the modern hotel frequently serves as a place of permanent residence for many of its guests."[15] Occupying a liminal zone between permanence and transience, luxury hotels make visible a cultural concern about the meaning of home that threatens definitions of property and ownership. Just as the hotel can rebuild itself in a more profitable location, a person like Undine Spragg can buy in, temporarily or permanently, to the setting that best suits her needs, and extract herself when she finds a more profitable setting.

The desire to figure out who is permanent and who is transient marks an anxiety over seeing the home as temporary, even if transience has always been part of the American practice of inhabiting space. In the United States, especially in the middle classes, people buy and sell their homes—they generally don't inherit. As was true of boarding houses in the nineteenth century and of apartments today, hotels could offer members of the American middle class a first independent home en route to eventual property ownership. Anthony Trollope observed of young married hotel dwellers in 1861, "Young men and women marry without any means collected on which to commence their life. They are content to look forward and to hope that such means will come. . . . But [the young man] must live on the fruits of that employment, and can only pay his way from week to week and day to day."[16] Eventually, we assume, such couples would move out of their hotels. But they might always rent, especially in a dense and expensive city like New York. Anxieties about transience and a desire to think of the hotels as permanent (by building landmark structures or publishing cutaway views identifying permanent residents) show how people tried to maintain ideas of home as permanent when it was quickly becoming simple property.

If hotel and boarding house life made economic sense for city dwellers of all classes in the mid–nineteenth century, by the turn into the twentieth century, luxury hotels also offered social returns on a financial investment. Groth notes that "multiple architectural advantages favored public hotels over private houses as social incubators. . . . With at least one hundred rooms, imposing architectural style, luxurious service and food, and often a famous manager, first class hotels became an urban social center for the elite."[17] Appropriately, Undine's social entrée happens in one of New York's first-class hotels, where connections are a part of the package.

Newspapers, guidebooks, and word of mouth cemented a hotel's reputation as a social center; published guides would even advise tourists on how to experience some of the reflected gilt of the high-end lodgings. In 1890, for instance, *Appletons' Dictionary of New York* lists a number of first-class hotels with their addresses, noting that "no signs are displayed on the fronts of the new hotels of the better class except in an inconspicuous place over the main entrance."[18] Clearly, one had to be in the know (or have Appletons' guidebook) in order to gain access to these particular structures. Groth notes that because hotels were private property, undesirable visitors could be screened out and presumably never reach the interior.[19] This had been true in the United States at least since the Tremont Hotel opened in Boston in 1829. Yet in other cases, hotels did allow and even encourage the public to use their interior spaces, at least those who might enhance the hotel's image. This pattern is exemplified in *Sister Carrie*; Hurstwood initially resists the temptation, but eventually he uses New York hotel lobbies as pleasant extensions of his living room. Although he recognizes his fellow chair-warmers as parasites of a sort, as long as he can still dress the part of the bourgeois manager, he reads his daily newspaper in the hotel lobby unmolested. Necessary to Hurstwood, this practice alarmed other observers: "Gilbert K. Chesterton, the brilliant English essayist, was impressed by the public nature of American hotel lobbies. 'It is not merely the Babylonian size and scale of the hotels,' he remarked, 'but the way that they are used that struck me. They are used almost as public streets, or rather as public squares. People drift in and out again, while, as a matter of fact, they have no more to do with the hotel than I have with Buckingham Palace.'"[20]

As they offered a comforting domestic space to the Hurstwoods of the world, hotels also represented an aspect of uniquely urban life that no tourist should miss, whether he or she could afford the luxury or not. In hotels "of international reputation," Henry Collins Brown pointed out in 1917, life "is as much a source of amusement as any other attraction in New York, and to those to whom it is unfamiliar the indulgence is well worth the cost."[21] But in a passage addressed to "Women Who Travel Alone," Brown offers a less expensive alternative: stay in a decent room, eat at a reasonable restaurant, "and then walk through the big hotels afterwards. You can even go to the writing room and send a letter home on the richly crested stationery if you wish, and no one will object."[22] Clearly, even for the independent, budget-conscious woman, hotels offered the attraction of opulent surroundings; further, they were prepared to confer their status even on "guests" who entered the building with no intention of paying for whatever amenities they might receive. The "richly crested stationery" conferred some sort of cachet, or at least, Brown imagined, the act of writing the card from the hotel would

FIGURE 27. Astor Hotel, Public Rooms, 1907. Museum of the City of New York, The Byron Collection, 93.1.1.5592.

offer an evening's pleasure to the woman who wrote the card and sent it to a friend or relative outside of New York. At the same time, the hotel's name, supported by the quality of the stationery, went out into the world, an emissary proclaiming the hotel's free hand with its riches.

Not surprisingly, their promotional materials confirm that first-class hotels positioned themselves and were regarded as the primary places where increasingly cosmopolitan urbanites could see and be seen in a beautiful, luxurious setting. An 1870s drawing of the Park Avenue Hotel Court, for instance, while clearly an interior space, reads as a small urban park, albeit with palm trees and tropical flowers. Couples stroll on paths around a fountain, women engage in conversation, and men in beaver hats exchange greetings, all to the accompaniment of a small orchestra. A 1907 promotional brochure for the Hotel Astor reproduced numerous watercolor paintings of fashionably dressed guests thronging the hotel's street-level public areas: the ballroom, the restaurants, the conservatory, the lobby, even the roof garden (figure 27). These images celebrate the luxury hotel as a site where the privileged gather.

A cutaway drawing or cross-section of the Hotel Astor from 1915, however, reveals a second important tension that marked the hotel-as-home; like the balance between permanence and transience, the pull between privacy and publicity was spatially on display and at play in the luxury hotel (figure 28). The cutaway view represents many of the same rooms pictured in the Hotel Astor watercolors, but in miniature. We see the same rooms thronged

FIGURE 28. Hotel Astor, Times Square, New York, 1915. Museum of the City of New York, The Byron Collection, 93.1.1.5403.

with the fashionable people who fill the larger paintings. We even gain access to the working part of the hotel, where we see figures busily engaged in running the machinery, both physical and social, that keeps the hotel running but generally is invisible to its patrons. We see coal being shoveled, carpenters hard at work, engines being maintained, and, several floors up, the telephone switchboard operators at their posts. Yet in this drawing, the bulk of the Hotel Astor is empty. The furnishings of guest bedrooms, parlors, and bathrooms are clearly visible, yet these spaces are devoid of any human presence. The emptiness of the guests' space, especially when contrasted to the busyness of the public spaces, emphasizes the degree to which privacy matters in the world of the luxury hotel. No one will ever know, or even begin to represent what goes on within these rooms, the image tells us. Only the hotel guest him or herself can access the human experience of staying (or living) in the hotel. Interestingly, this privacy extends to two upper-story rooms, the Belvedere and the North Ball Room; one imagines that these rooms are rented to private parties. They clearly are closed to public entry and to the public gaze, even when that public is carefully screened.

But that closure might not matter to most hotel goers; *The Custom of the Country* seems to confirm that simply entering the luxury hotel can help to launch visitors into new social realms. Initially, the Spraggs seem to be "stranded in lonely splendour in a sumptuous West Side hotel," the Stentorian, "with a father compelled to seek a semblance of social life at the hotel bar, and a mother deprived of even this contact with her kind, and reduced to illness by boredom and inactivity" (*CC*, 27). However, the novel's plot is set rapidly in motion by the hotel. Undine encounters Ralph Marvell at a dance held in the Spraggs' hotel; later, she will meet her next husband, Raymond de Chelles, in the busy dining room of the Hotel Nouveau Luxe in Paris, which reads as a transplanted first-class New York hotel. To Undine, the Nouveau Luxe resembles the Stentorian, "in which the opening scenes of her own history had been enacted," and as Chelles himself somewhat ironically puts it as he surveys the scene, "it's charming and sympathetic and original—we owe America a debt of gratitude for inventing it (*CC*, 301, 243). What America has invented, it seems, is a space in which a select group of people can mingle in a commercial setting that replicates but encloses public space. On the most basic level, these quasi-public spaces allow Undine to encounter the men she will marry; luxury hotels launch her from "public" to private relations that will allow her to participate, if only through her husbands, in the sort of private ownership of property that hotels spatially obscure.

Undine Spragg: The Hotel Spirit

Even as they efface their commercial nature by appropriating qualities of private space, luxury hotels emphasize the eradication of the past from space, which is especially alarming if the hotel is considered a home. Shades of this alarm are visible in Wharton's horror at Norma Hatch's home in the Emporium Hotel in *The House of Mirth*. The hotel, a home without a history, emerges in *The Custom of the Country* as a distinctly American invention indicating that every aspect of the culture may be bought and sold.[23] At the same time, the mobility and rootlessness associated with a modern commercialization of the notion of home is linked consistently with the hotel. "It was natural that the Americans, who had no homes, who were born and died in hotels, should have contracted nomadic habits," Wharton's French characters think (*CC*, 441). Mobility here is figured as a disease "contracted" from American hotel architecture. Clearly, the modes of living that accompany certain architectural practices have, at least in the eyes of outsiders, the potential to shape a culture that reflects the structures it builds. This deterministic perspective was voiced by writers from Henry James to journalists in the popular press. As a writer in *The Cosmopolitan* noted, "The children of hotel residents become precocious, wayward, and self-assertive, and learn from strangers many things the knowledge of which should be kept from children."[24] Whether they inhabit tenements, apartments, or cottage homes, children consistently are portrayed in urban literature as highly influenced by their surroundings. The notion that children might be imbued with the "hotel-spirit"—that in a single generation a conception of the past could be wiped out—is alarming not just on an individual basis but because of what such a development augurs for an American culture that is exerting an increasingly global force (figure 29).[25]

Thus, hotel culture comes to represent a uniquely and detestably American quality: a lack of concern for the past exemplified in and enforced by the ever-changing, always temporary American architecture. The hotel-ness of American life is precisely what is at issue in the scene that marks the disintegration of Undine Spragg's second official marriage. Raymond de Chelles, whom Undine marries after Ralph Marvell's death, is a French aristocrat whose title and wealth retain nuances of the past and of history that are entirely foreign to Undine. After Undine suggests selling the Chelles family château, Saint Désert, the shocked Chelles responds:

> You [Americans] come among us from a country we don't know, and can't imagine, a country you care for so little that before you've been a day in ours you've forgotten the very house you were born in—if it wasn't torn down before you knew it! . . . you come from hotels as big as towns, and from towns as flimsy as paper, where the streets haven't had time to be named, and the buildings are demolished before they're dry, and the people are as proud of changing as we are of holding to what we have. (CC, 468)

Here, Chelles links an American pride in mutability to the flimsy scrim that passes for permanence in the United States. The "house you were born in" represents a past that is obliterated continually before it has even had the chance to imprint itself on a child's psyche. It is a far cry from Ralph Marvell's youth. The only home that, Chelles imagines, could produce Undine is a hotel that transforms a house into a town, a flimsy, unnamed structure that exudes only the new and will fade as soon as something newer appears. And of course, he is almost exactly right—Undine's hotel-influenced subjectivity represents the future of the urban nation.

According to Chelles, history is eviscerated from the modern American home as the nation becomes a setting dominated by investment. The American hotel-home that Chelles deplores, ironically, is the very setting that the young Undine Spragg has always hoped to inhabit. As Elaine Showalter notes, Undine's "natural milieu is a hotel, whether the Nouveau Luxe in

FIGURE 29. Surprise Party, the Hotel Ansonia to Its Children Guests, February 22, 1910. Museum of the City of New York, The Byron Collection, 93.1.1.5369.

Paris or the Engadine Palace in Saint Moritz."[26] Undine's modern status depends on her relationships to ever-changing surroundings, and her ceaseless quest to inhabit the perfect setting reveals qualities of mobility, desire, and adaptability that she inherits from modern characters in earlier texts like *The Bostonians* and *Sister Carrie*. Cynthia Griffin Wolff argues that at Undine's core is "a terrible spirit of desire" whose "essence is energy."[27] It is an energy that is sublimated but refuses to be confined to the domestic concerns that are her "appropriate" sphere. "Possessing the energy needed to conquer life (possessing it even as her counterpart Elmer Moffatt does), she has been debarred from victory by reasons of sex."[28] Certainly, Undine pursues conquest through marriage, but her marriages represent neither emotional nor purely economic decisions (we can see this when Undine is prevented from participating in the financial aspects of her marriages). They are spatial transactions.

Undine channels her energy into seeking out new environments, developing her talent for adapting to them, and inhabiting them while always remaining alert to other opportunities, thus aligning her desire for "everything" with the means to which her gender confines her. Like other modern fictional urbanites such as Ruth Hall and Verena Tarrant, Undine Spragg taps the particular logic of her day, in this case, a logic of investment, and aligns it with the possibilities inherent in the city's domestic spaces in order to achieve her goals. Summoning up the spatial capital she has accrued in one environment, Undine cashes in and reinvests in order to transform the imaginary into the actual. Even as she adapts to each new environment, Undine shapes her settings to better reflect her new self, and thus develops the reality she desires. In other words, in order to transform herself, Undine must both absorb and create suitable settings.

Undine continually seeks "the appropriate setting to a pretty woman" (*CC*, 471). Like Lily Bart in *The House of Mirth*, Undine is highly attuned to her environment, but in contrast to Lily, whose most appropriate setting is the immobilizing *tableau vivante*, Undine's favorite settings are dynamic. Undine moves from one place to another on the assumption not only that her settings should be appropriate to her, but that the appropriate surroundings will in some way transform her even as she transforms them. In *The Custom of the Country*, as in Gilman's work, the ability to manipulate environment emerges as the greatest societal power a woman can possess. As we have seen, in the American tradition this idea harks back at least as far as notions of Republican motherhood and Catharine Beecher. But the way in which Undine mobilizes this tenet of femininity becomes an impulse far removed from Beecher's formulations. For instead of desiring settings appropriate to raising model families or developing "Christian neighborhoods," Undine wants only to inhabit settings that will elevate her social and economic standing. And from the time of Undine's youth, hotels have epitomized settings laden with transformative potential.

Like her notions of class status, Undine's ideas about what constitutes a desirable setting are shaped in large part by newspaper articles. As an inhabitant of Apex, Kansas, she was introduced to New York society by the Sunday papers. Indeed, the very media representations that prove to be Ralph Marvell's eventual undoing have initiated Undine to Fifth Avenue. Syndication has made available the "lively anecdotes of the Van Degens, the Driscolls, the Chauncy Ellings and other social potentates whose least doings Mrs. Spragg and Undine had followed from afar in the Apex papers" (*CC*, 27). In this era, hotels were a city's architectural landmarks, unmistakable from the street, visible in the news. As New York grew, and fashionable districts moved uptown, new hotels were built and old hotels relocated. As one New York newspaper pointed out, "Fifty Million Dollars' Worth of Hotels," including the new Plaza and the Astor had been built in a five year span.[29] Not just the hotel architecture but the inhabitants were newsworthy when a new landmark hotel was in the works; before the new Plaza opened in 1902, a cutaway view of the building showed its distinctive exterior but emphasized the imagined interior. The exterior walls of the most desirable suites had been pulled aside to expose the dwellings that would comprise "the largest millionaire colony in the city, or, as a matter of fact, the entire world."[30] The apartments were labeled, and images of the millionaire women provided so that readers could imaginatively fill the otherwise private spaces of the hotel (this is an interesting contrast to the starkly empty rooms of the Astor's cut-away, figure 28). Syndicated nationally, articles like these would have helped to shape Undine's sense that "all the fashionable people she knew either boarded or lived in hotels" (*CC*, 30).

Once she has arrived in New York, Undine's initiation into the workings of wealth develops in conversations with Mrs. Heeney, a "'society' manicure and masseuse" who tracks her clients' activities from her voluminous bag of newspaper clippings (*CC*, 22). Undine's comprehension of the societal world she wishes to enter becomes a collage of published words and images. As Paul Groth points out, "Every famous and influential hotel resident attracted a dozen other people like the Spraggs, people who needed to know and be seen with the dominant social group of the city and the nation."[31]

The novel's narrator constructs Undine's desire to live in hotels as an outgrowth of her urge to escape the detached home, the "yellow 'frame' cottage" in a "squalid suburb" where she was born (*CC*, 60–61). To supplement her time spent away at boarding school, Undine and her parents enjoy

> the comparative gentility of summer vacations at the Mealey House. . . . The tessellated floors, the plush parlours and organ-like radiators of the Mealey House had, aside from their intrinsic elegance, the immense advantage of . . . making it possible for Undine, when she met Indiana in the street or at school, to chill her advances by a careless allusion to the splendours of hotel life. (*CC*, 61)

The narrator's condescension emphasizes that the Mealey House lacks any real status. However, the plush interior that the narrator disparages is a mark of class distinction for the young Undine, who sees the hotel's significance in the social standing that it confers upon her. Undine's temporary occupation of the hotel's networked spaces signals both a desire and an opportunity to transform herself, to find settings that are desirable according to her readings of national print culture. By participating in hotel life, even on the level of the Mealey House, Undine enters the national culture of wealth and consumption heralded in the papers she reads.

Undine's experiences in American hotels trace the historical development of the luxury hotel; this trajectory emphasizes both Undine's awareness of housing trends and her desire to follow them. The Mealey house is the Spraggs' first stop on a hotel itinerary that includes summer stays in resort hotels including "a staring hotel on a glaring lake," a Virginia resort featuring "an atmosphere of Christmas-chromo sentimentality that tempered her hard edges a little," and, in Skog Harbor, Maine, a "bare weather-beaten inn, all shingles without and blueberry pies within . . . exclusive, parochial [and] Bostonian" (*CC*, 62–64). The social possibilities for the large resort hotel are made clear in *Ruth Hall,* where Ruth and her family make meaningful interpersonal connections even in a space that seems to Ruth "an artificial atmosphere" with "room for everything but—thought."[32] Decades later, Undine's experience reveals that resort hotels provide neither the social connections nor the context that will allow her to achieve the status she craves. Undine's "pioneer blood" leads her from setting to setting, and in each place she endures a "terrible initiation" that reveals to her that there is "something still better beyond, then—more luxurious, more exciting, more worthy of her" (CC, 62). For better or worse, this always unfulfilled desire becomes a hallmark of Undine's personality, a characteristic that aligns her with both her father (who "cast[s] a slow pioneering glance about [the Stentorian's] gilded void" (CC, 30)) and Elmer Moffatt. It is reminiscent, too, of Carrie Meeber's eternal desire in Sister Carrie. Just as Carrie's desire increases in apartment buildings, Undine's desire is heightened by the hotels she inhabits.

Like Carrie, Undine makes connections with other hotel guests that stoke her unquenchable desire for fashion, luxury, and novelty. When she befriends a woman from Richmond at a midwestern hotel, for instance, "the southern visitor's dismay, her repugnancies, her recoil from the faces, the food, the amusements, the general bareness and stridency of the scene" convince Undine that only an Eastern hotel will do for the following summer's vacation (CC, 61). But in the midst of Undine's enjoyment of Virginia, "again everything was spoiled by a peep through another door" (CC, 62). This "peep" is made possible by the proximity among guests facilitated by the hotel architecture; Undine can pick up "scraps of Miss Wincher's conversation . . . [by] straining her ears behind a column of the long veranda, [and obtain] a new glimpse into the unimagined" (CC, 63). Undine's eavesdropping is one aspect of the promiscuity Wharton associates with Undine; according to Mary Ellis Gibson, Undine represents "the new order [that] is contaminating because it has no respect for the old boundaries. . . . The parvenus operate in the interstices of the old order, and this is their danger."[33] In allowing apparently private exchanges to enter into publicly accessible space, the hotel facilitates much the same kind of connection that the newspapers do. Blending public and private, the hotel's spatial arrangements offer Undine a glimpse of the world beyond.

Undine's peeping is reminiscent of Coverdale's spying in The Blithedale Romance, but Undine is not alarmed by the urban connections that shake Coverdale; rather, she sees the networked setting as a desirable backdrop for her performance of self. This difference is highlighted by the accessibility of the settings Undine admires. While in Blithedale, Zenobia's boarding house and Coverdale's hotel were indeed for rent and thus purchasable, at least temporarily, Hawthorne does not present them primarily as consumable products. In Custom, however, Undine's assumption that her surroundings are temporary, attainable, and always changeable emphasizes her faith in consumerism's ability to fulfill desires and to provide ever-new settings. Indeed, increasingly desirable settings are always available to Undine—for a price. Significantly, though, they are not simply products. They are investments.

Like the hotel investors who factored location and design into their calculations of profitability, reinventing older hotels in new locations in order to maintain interest and excitement, Undine manipulates settings and aesthetics when she speculates. The cost of a new setting is exacted—from Undine herself at times—but more frequently she extracts capital from one man or another in order to gain access to the setting she most desires at a particular moment. Sometimes, these settings are highly public, such as the opera box she extorts from her father in order to display herself to Ralph Marvell. In the investment logic of the novel, Undine is speculating with space, a different sort of resource from the eponymous hairwavers upon which her father builds his financial success. Like Elmer Moffatt with his railroads, political deals on public utilities, and speculative real estate ventures, Undine invests in a resource whose value is part physical and part cultural. She must endure the market's vicissitudes in order to achieve material gain. And so Undine moves from setting to setting, gleaning from each a new set of resources and connections to help her contemplate, and eventually to make, new investments.

If Undine cannot buy her way into Fifth Avenue in the way that hotel investors could, she can use some of their other methods to gain access to that exclusive world. At times, Undine is attracted to settings that will mirror her—or at least reflect the version of herself she wishes to display. In that sense, the Spraggs' first New York hotel residence, the Stentorian, is an ideal setting for Undine:

> Celeste, before leaving, had drawn down the blinds and turned on the electric light, and the white and gold room, with its blazing wall-brackets, formed a sufficiently brilliant background to carry out the illusion. So untempered a glare would have been destructive to all half-tones and subtleties of modelling, but Undine's beauty was almost as vivid, and almost as crude, as the brightness suffusing it. Her black brows, her reddish-tawny hair, and the pure red and white of her complexion defied the searching decomposing radiance: she might have been some fabled creature whose home was in a beam of light. (CC, 36)

This setting mirrors and amplifies the crudity and vividness that Undine displays at the novel's opening. The modern backdrop with its electrified glare is appropriate for Undine's harsh radiance; the "destructive" and "decomposing" effects of the modern electric brightness cannot be sustained by anything less resilient than Undine's impenetrable yet pliable beauty.

Yet ironically, while Undine's beauty is amplified by the electric glow, in fashion's fickle eye, vivid and crude are on their way out; "half-tones and subtleties" are coming in. Undine recognizes that if she stays in the setting of the Stentorian, she risks amplifying her harsh and crude features to the extent personified by her friend Mabel Lipscomb. A veritable doyenne of the hotel world, Mabel moves easily among "the lofty hotels moored like a fleet of battle-ships along the upper reaches of the West Side: the Olympian, the Incandescent, the Ormolu . . ." (CC, 40). Mabel has come to embody these settings; as Undine sits with her friend in the coveted opera box, she sees "Mabel, monumental and moulded while the fashionable were flexible and diaphanous, Mabel strident and explicit while they were subdued and allu-sive" (CC, 71). "Flexible and diaphanous," the wealthy New Yorkers Un-dine observes from her opera box exude an aspect that she wants to emulate precisely because of who demonstrates it. Of course, if the fashionable people were strident and explicit, Undine would want to be too; she is eager, and able, to imitate the qualities prized by those in possession of money and social power.

Conveniently, Undine's desire to embody whatever qualities exemplify the height of fashion dovetails nicely with her long-held fascination with dress-ing up, creating scenes, and assuming different identities. But Undine does not wish simply to be like the elite, she wants to join the elite group while retaining her distinctiveness. As with the vaudeville mimics popular in Un-dine's day, for Undine "to imitate [is] not simply to copy, it [is] also to cre-ate something new."[34] The mutable, flexible identity she wishes to construct both appropriates and transforms the flexibility and diaphanousness she no-tices in the members of the social elite. Because personality is on display, it is available for the mimic's pleasure and profit. Like the vaudeville mimic, Undine as hotel-spirit makes personality public—and in becoming public, her personality becomes movable property.

The mimic's mutability both arises from and is sustained by variety in set-ting. For Undine, role playing comes naturally; it is the one unchanging ele-ment in her mobile personality. As a child, she "had cared little for dolls or skipping ropes. . . . Already Undine's chief delight was to 'dress up' in her mother's Sunday skirt and 'play lady' before the wardrobe mirror. This prac-tise had outlasted childhood" (CC, 36). Indeed, Undine becomes a woman whose desire to play roles has evolved into a sometimes debilitating habit: "Undine was fiercely independent and yet passionately imitative. She wanted to surprise everyone with her dash and originality, but she could not help modeling herself on the last person she met" (CC, 34). Undine's desire for originality is predicated upon imitation; she constructs a series of appear-ances that resemble those presented to her as desirable. Significantly, the hotel culture she embraces allows her to do just that.

What, then, can distinguish the imitation from the real? Clearly, this is one of the novel's central concerns. A society that exemplifies "human na-ture's passion for the factitious, its incorrigible habit of imitating the imita-tion" becomes a "slavish imitation," demanding "a prompt and reverent faith in the reality of the sham they had created" (CC, 243). The nouveau riche society is disparaged within the novel by observer Charles Bowen as "a phantom 'society,' with all the rules, smirks, gestures of its model, but evoked out of promiscuity and incoherence while the other had been the product of continuity and choice" (*CC*, 243). Bowen's observations show that the issue of mimicry is not consigned simply to vaudevillians or performers. Indeed, the process of entering the "new class of world-compellers" becomes a test of a person's imitative powers and ability to believe in imitations. This concern with imitating the imitation makes problematic both passing convincingly and believing in the "sham" the imitations have produced.

The cultural capital that class mimicry confers adds an interesting dimension to the recurring problem in Wharton's fiction of the blurring of class lines and bloodlines. The parallel marriages of the "subtle" Ralph Marvell to the "explicit" Undine, and of Ralph's subdued cousin Clare Dagonet to the very explicit Peter Van Degen epitomize this dynamic in *The Custom of the Country*. Undine's desire to imitate, combined with the sense of setting she has gained from the papers, has made New York the first stage she encounters that will allow her to play the nebulous but compelling role of wealthy and privileged woman. At the same time, the hotel culture of New York changes her, emphasizing and rewarding her most urban qualities. She comes to resemble the cutaway image of the Astor Hotel, her public self forever displaying the interactions of the wealthy and fashionable, her interior blank and empty. Her habitation of space, then, is a part of the dialectic that helps to constitute her as particularly modern.

Wharton's descriptions emphasize that Undine embodies the urban. If not completely "a creature without a soul," as Cynthia Griffin Wolff claims, Undine psychologically mirrors and physically suits the city's spaces of consumption, display, mobility, and desire.[35] Her drive to consume is not marked simply by the men she seems to devour. In fact, it is founded on a more material desire. In Paris, for example, "Her senses luxuriated in all its material details: the thronging motors, the brilliant shops, the novelty and daring of the women's dresses, the piled-up colours of the ambulant flower carts, the appetizing expanse of the fruiterers' windows, even the chromatic effects of the petit fours behind the plate glass of the pastry-cooks: all the surface-sparkle and variety of the inexhaustible streets of Paris" (*CC*, 250). The sensual appeal of her Paris experience emphasizes Undine's responsiveness to metropolitan surroundings. She is intoxicated by the physical sense of luxury in the colors, the fabrics, and the foods. But Undine is not simply consumed with consuming; she is equally preoccupied with the act of displaying herself.

The self-display in which Undine engages throughout the novel, whether in the New York Opera or the Parisian Grand Luxe Hotel, takes its cues from the exclusive yet public spaces of the luxury hotel. In her relationships, Ralph Marvell observes, "She wanted to enjoy herself, and her conception of enjoyment was publicity, promiscuity—the band, the banners, the crowd, the close contact of covetous impulses, and the sense of walking among them in cool security. Any personal entanglement might mean 'bother,' and bother was the thing she most abhorred" (*CC*, 202). "Publicity, promiscuity," and "close contact," all experiences of the urban landscape, are the dynamics Undine desires. The combination of proximity, security, and promiscuity without bother marketed by the luxury hotel extracts the threat from the urban experience and transforms it into an enjoyable publicity. Imagined and experienced as a hotel, the city allows Undine to construct a personality that is public and consumable, to her a mark of class distinction. After all, she has been raised on newspaper accounts of the rich and famous; from Undine's perspective, publicity does not threaten but helps to solidify one's status. In urban spaces, the projection of self brings with it a cool anonymity that protects whatever interior Undine might possess.

Along with her facility for consumption and display, Undine expresses a modern fascination with mobility; she also reflects her era in her wide-ranging, international movement. To Undine "the noise, the crowd, the promiscuity beneath her eyes symbolized the glare and movement of her life" (*CC*, 250). In what Wharton calls her "abundant present," Undine is surrounded by and caught up in movement. Her penchant for mobility both makes her a perfect hotel dweller and ensures that no one place will ever satisfy. Her drive to move necessitates multiple dwelling places, long wedding journeys, and commutes between city and country in all of her marriages. And eventually, it draws her back to Elmer Moffatt, the charismatic itinerant speculator turned "Railroad King" with whom she first eloped (by train) as a teenager. Although that first marriage was quickly annulled, Undine and Elmer each combine a drive to move with a passion for settings, a combination that marks them as modern cosmopolitans and destines them eventually to reunite.

Transforming the Setting

Wharton's novels always come back to questions of space. Her dialectic model of relations between subject and setting furthers the pattern I have traced in earlier urban fiction. That is, as Undine transforms her environment, her modern mutability allows her to adapt herself to it. Her business then becomes designing environments that will allow her to develop the kinds of qualities she wishes to project.

This spatial dialectic links many of Wharton's works to one another. *The Age of Innocence*, for example, charts the transformation of a class through the decisions they make about domestic spaces. Ellen Olenska's decision to inhabit a bohemian neighborhood uncharted to the Fifth Avenue "tribe" prefigures her ostracism from that tribal world; Catherine Mingott's move to the wilderness near the nascent Central Park marks her as a maverick and Ellen's lone ally; May and Newland Archer's new house, which replicates and reinforces the spatial arrangements and relations of their own childhood homes, cements their family and class status. Similarly, in *The House of Mirth*, Lily's ability to adapt to the settings she inhabits is her salient feature. Like Undine, Lily knows which settings will suit her and she blends in accordingly. "There were moments when she longed for anything different, anything strange, remote and untried; but the utmost realm of her imagination did not go beyond picturing her usual life in a new setting. She could not figure herself as anywhere but in a drawing room, diffusing elegance as a flower sheds perfume."[36] As *House of Mirth* makes clear, Lily Bart can inhabit spaces but can neither imagine nor manipulate them with Undine's energy.

Lily does move among many different settings, but always at the invitation of others. In fascinating contrast to Undine, Lily's hotel experience brings her to a social precipice; it is her last stop before she moves out of society's reaches and into New York's working-class neighborhoods. When Lawrence Selden visits Lily in Norma Hatch's suite at the luxurious Emporium Hotel, he tries to extract her from its disturbing surroundings. Lily eventually removes herself, but it is worth noting that Selden does not see Lily in her "own" surroundings, the boarding house that is her last stop, until after she is dead. For a man like Selden, who "carries his own artistic-moral complications into the relationship," the Emporium represents the hotel at its most threatening. In harboring the divorced Mrs. Hatch and her shockingly well-born paramours, the Emporium seems "virtually untouched by the social contracts and tacit supervision of life found in a family house."[37] Selden's horror at seeing Lily in the modern hotel is buttressed by an ethos passed down from his mother, who represents the genteel morality of another generation. Although she leaves Mrs. Hatch soon after this conversation, Lily does point out to Selden that she has little choice but to accept a job, and a home, with Mrs. Hatch. She does not exert agency in regard to her settings except to inhabit the surroundings she is offered. In contrast to Lily, Undine can always think beyond her current circumstances. Undine manipulates the settings she inhabits precisely because she sees settings not simply as static backgrounds, but as mutable environments that can in turn change her.

Just as Undine's mutability allows her to adapt to the settings she enters, her insatiable desire leads her to seek out ever more fashionable milieux within which to move. She both reflects and is shaped by her consumable, transformable environments. Having joined the smart expatriate set in Paris, Undine stands out to "sociologist" Charles Bowen as strikingly adaptable: he notices that Undine "isolated herself in a kind of soft abstraction; and he admired the adaptability which enabled her to draw from such surroundings the contrasting graces of reserve" (CC, 247). Ever changing, Undine has used her skills as a mimic and her facility for selecting and adapting to environments to embody the "flexible and diaphanous" members of the upper class she once admired from her New York opera box and then make her imitation a compelling contrast to a different setting. Throughout the text, Wharton emphasizes that this environmental dialectic of selection and adaptation cannot be separated from the economic relations of investment it structures and mirrors.

As she reflects the environments she enters, Undine transforms them. In some cases, the changes that Undine effects are mild, even benign, as shown by her habit of transforming her temporary lodgings in hotels and rented houses into appropriate backdrops for her current role. This transformation of the hotel into a home is evident in the 1902 image of Mrs. L. C. Simpson's suite in the Lorraine, which is decorated with her own floral arrangements, pictures, and statues, along with personal effects such as photographs and piano music (figure 30). Similarly, when the Marvell family rents a country house in upstate New York, Undine creates a setting that emphasizes the qualities she wishes to project. In this case, she wishes to embody "wife" and "mother":

> In the low-ceilinged drawing-room . . . Undine had adapted her usual background of cushions, bric-a-brac and flowers—since one must make one's setting "home-like," however little one's habits happened to correspond with that particular effect. Undine was conscious of the intimate charm of her *mise-en-scène,* and of the recovered freshness and bloom which put her in harmony with it. (CC, 207)

Undine's home is a set, a *mise-en-scène* that is not a home but that appears homelike. Undine needs this kind of setting in order to capitalize on another investment—a flirtation with Peter Van Degen that is accompanied by a flurry of checks and gifts. Projecting "wife" protects her from crossing the line between sycophant and mistress. The logic of setting as investment, though, is not lost on Van Degen, who exclaims, "Look here—the installment plan's all right, but ain't you a bit behind even on that? . . . Anyhow, I think I'd rather let the interest accumulate for a while" (CC, 207). Van Degen refers here to his affair with Undine, a relationship in which he invests "installments" of jewelry, dresses, and money toward the ultimate payoff of her personal and sexual favors. The world of the novel is a world of investments and returns, and Undine knows that her own success can come only through entering, inhabiting, and transforming her various settings so that she can profit from them. Undine develops a practice of inhabiting space that imitates hotel architecture; she uses public spaces in order to gain control of private ones. By this logic, she does not need an invitation, only the right appearance, or money, to launch herself into society. Initially, of course, she needs to be invited into the private homes that represent the amassed re-

FIGURE 30. Mrs. L. C. Simpson, Hotel Lorraine, 1902 or 1903. Museum of the City of New York, The Byron Collection, 93.1.1.10458.

sources and ancestry that constitute the status she desires. But in this novel, spaces imbued with the past are destined for destruction.

Marriage: Domesticity, Alliance, Merger?

Undine comes from Apex, Kansas, to New York with her parents, hoping to trade her unusual beauty and some of her father's wealth for a marriage into New York's elite class. But as the requirements for membership in the elite shift from family associations to simple wealth, Undine divorces and re-marries accordingly. Undine's marriages simultaneously track the era's changing economic paradigm and its shifting sense of the home. Initially a site of living history, the home becomes a consumable commodity. Undine's husbands, Ralph Marvell, Raymond de Chelles, and Elmer Moffatt, in their various relations to home and space, embody these conflicting notions of urban domesticity. Each of Undine's husbands are highly attuned to the spaces they inhabit; each man embraces particular physical spaces both for their aesthetic value and for the version of self they reflect and construct. In other words, they "mark points along a continuum of relationships between per-

sons and their property or personal attributes."[38] The critical difference between Elmer Moffatt and Undine's other husbands is Moffatt's ability to see
space as a commodity—to understand and inhabit urban space as a mobile,
shifting interplay between economic and cultural values.

   Ralph Marvell, Undine's "first" husband, offers the clearest parallel to
Henry James's persona in *The American Scene*. Like James, Marvell's sense
of self revolves around a notion of history that has been constructed in large
part by his childhood home. Marvell's relationship to his family home also
mirrors Wharton's personal construction of home as repository for history,
a space where physical and spiritual pasts merge with—and produce—the
present. Before he marries Undine, Ralph lives in the family home in Washington Square, a site that embodies a personal and communal past. "Ralph
Marvell, mounting his grandfather's door-step, looked up at the symmetri-
cal old red house-front, with its frugal marble ornament, as he might have
looked at a familiar human face" (CC, 76–77). Just as the house becomes
almost human to Marvell, the people who live there have merged with the
house itself. "'They' were his mother and old Mr. Urban Dagonet, both,
from Ralph's earliest memories, so closely identified with the old house in
Washington Square that they might have passed for its inner consciousness
as it might have stood for their outward form" (CC, 77). The physical
identification between Ralph's home and his soul emphasizes his rootedness
and connection to the past. In this space that blends past and present, Ralph
lives among the "dim portraits of 'Signers' and their females" that dominate
the spaces of his old New York home, in the process developing a subjectivity that is itself outmoded (CC, 91). Christopher Gair points out that
"Wharton explicitly links the disappearance of the 'old' families with the
earlier passing of other American cultures," and Ralph Marvell is a vestige
of just such a disappearing past.[39] The deep interplay between structure and
subjectivity in the Marvell home makes it a living relic.

   Unlike his mutable contemporaries, Undine and Elmer, Ralph has an inner
essence, a fixed interior that links him to a type of subjectivity no longer advantageous in the modern city:

> [T]here was a world of wonders within him. As a boy at the seaside, Ralph,
> between tides, had once come on a cave—a secret inaccessible place with glau-
> cous lights, mysterious murmurs, and a single shaft of communication with the
> sky. . . . And so with his inner world. Though so coloured by outside impres-
> sions, it wove a secret curtain about him, and he came and went in it with the
> same joy of furtive possession. (CC, 80)

Like Henry James in *The American Scene,* Ralph's interior is at odds with
the moving, changing, networked city that surrounds him. His sense of
detachment from the haze of the outside world ultimately is untenable if
Ralph is to enter into relationships with the modern women who people his
world. Undine, of course, is indifferent to this kind of detachment. Even

Clare Van Degen, the cousin whose "light foot had reached the threshold" of Ralph's interior, is entwined in the same networks of economics and consumption that Undine more obviously represents. Maintaining his "world of wonder" in the modern city can only lead to isolation and destruction for Ralph Marvell.

A vestige of an earlier type of subjectivity, one defined in part by this conception of intact interior space, Ralph cannot acquire the penetrability and transformability necessary to thrive in the modern networked city. When his friend Charles Bowen recognizes this, he feels "the pang of the sociologist over the individual havoc wrought by every social readjustment: it had so long been clear to him that Ralph was a survival, and destined, as such, to go down in any conflict with the rising forces" (CC, 249). The rising forces to which Bowen alludes are of course consumption and mobility, the very forces that Wharton believes will eliminate history—and a unified subjectivity—from the American home.

Ralph's destruction is prefigured by his interior decorating. If the Washington Square house has served as a psychic sanctuary for Ralph, his "old brown room" operates as the inner sanctum. And yet, this protected space comes to be dominated by Undine, or, at least, by her image. "The walls and tables were covered with photographs of Undine, effigies of all shapes and sizes, expressing every possible sentiment dear to the photographic tradition" (CC, 297). The photograph, that modern, reproducible form of portraiture, has replaced for Ralph the family portraits that dominate the rest of the house. History has been usurped by the multiple images that represent the collage of modernity. Mechanically produced modernity now dominates Ralph's former haven, signaling that his fiercely protected interior is no longer defensible against the modern "rising forces" embodied in the hotel-spirit.

Although Undine will desert him and demand a divorce, Ralph Marvell's eventual decline into suicide seems to be hastened less by her actions than by the penetration of his interior by the publicity networks so central to his wife's perceptions of the world.

> As he sat in the Subway on his way down-town, his eye was caught by his own name on the front page of the heavily headlined paper which the unshaved occupant of the next seat held between grimy fists. The blood rushed to Ralph's forehead as he looked over the man's arm and read: "Society Leader Gets Decree," and beneath it the subordinate clause: "Says Husband Too Absorbed In Business To Make Home Happy." . . . For the first time in his life the coarse fingering of public curiosity had touched the secret places of his soul, and nothing that had come before seemed as humiliating as this trivial comment on his tragedy. (CC, 300)

Here, the penetration of the "secret places of his soul" by the media signals Ralph's sense of repulsion and violation. The griminess of his unshaved neighbor, the proximity and mingling forced by the subway, and the proclivity of media and transportation networks to erode the boundaries that otherwise would separate Marvell from his fellow passengers all coalesce in Wharton's description of being read as physical molestation, a "coarse fingering" that is "humiliating." Mixed with this sense of violation is a potent sign of another equally alarming shift—the transformation of the home from ideal to commodity. The "Happy Home" that Ralph apparently has destroyed becomes a headline that sells his story. Here, "home" is a come-on that makes its way into readers' letters, editorials, pulpits, and finally the *"Family Weekly,* as one of the 'Heart problems' propounded to subscribers, with a Gramophone, a Straight-front Corset, and a Vanity-box among the prizes offered for its solution" (*CC,* 300). Ralph's personal history thus becomes fodder for syndication, his dissolving marriage merely one weekly "Heart problem" among countless others. And the dissemination and standardization of Ralph's narrative goes hand in glove with the dissolution of the notion of home so central to Ralph's old-fashioned subjectivity. Home has been incorporated fully into the networks of the media, revealed as a desirable commodity along the lines of the Corset and Vanity-box the magazine promises to readers who can make the Home Happy again.

The Heart problems so troubling to Ralph and the readers of the *Family Weekly* have little effect on Undine, who continually moves on, adopting the luxury hotel's strategy of decamping and building anew when she feels that new surroundings might be more profitable. When she marries the French nobleman Raymond de Chelles, Undine moves into a house farther from the American urban core, and indeed, deeper into history. With Chelles, Undine inhabits domestic spaces that enforce far more regimented gender and family roles than those with which she is familiar. Though the clippings-obsessed Mrs. Heeney confuses the Hôtel de Chelles with an American hotel: "oh, they call their houses hotels, do they? That's funny: I suppose it's because they let out part of 'em,'" of course the French ancestral home is the American hotel's opposite (*CC,* 420). It is steeped in history, structured by tradition, and imbricated in economic relationships that approach the feudal. At least at first.

In both Saint Désert and their Paris hôtel, the Chelles's family honor and responsibilities structure domestic space in ways that are foreign to Undine. For instance, Undine believes that as the wife of the oldest Chelles son she should wield a powerful influence in determining the uses of the family property. And yet, decisions about who should occupy which apartments of the hôtel become transactions in which "she did not weigh a feather" (*CC,* 436). Even so, into this space dedicated to "the huge voracious fetish they called The Family," Undine finds a way to introduce the hotel-spirit (*CC,* 442).

The problem with Saint Désert is that its value as a repository for history— and in particular, family history—does not register on Undine's internal ledger. She must convert the home into a consumable product in order to comprehend and thus exert power over it. Undine is practiced at such transactions. While married to Ralph Marvell, after all, she has the jewels from a pair of family rings reset. Undine gives the ancient stones a more modern appearance, wrests them from the incalculable valuation system of family and history, and returns them to the market logic that organizes her perceptions of the world. In the case of the Marvell jewels, Undine also removes the stones from the bodily, human connection they once signified. Outside of the physical settings that gave the rings a familial meaning, the stones become pure commodity. A similar evisceration of history occurs with the Chelles tapestries.

Before Undine arrives, the tapestries that decorate Saint Désert's long grey hallways are imbued with three sets of value: familial, historic, and aesthetic. Though the most famous tapestries were gifts from Louis XV, the majority have been produced by the generations of women who have inhabited the chateau: "The innumerable rooms of Saint Désert were furnished with the embroidered hangings and tapestry chairs produced by generations of diligent châtelaines, and the untiring needles of the old Marquise, her daughters and dependents were still steadily increasing the provision" (*CC*, 442). This familial tradition inscribes a history that goes beyond nation, and, it is implied, almost beyond memory. "Dynasties have fallen, institutions changed, manners and morals, alas, deplorably declined; but as far back as memory went, the ladies of the line of Chelles had always sat at their needle-work on the terrace of Saint Désert" (*CC*, 443). Through their intensely physical connection with the women of Chelles, as well as their centuries-old presence within the château, the tapestries function as living relics of the family's past, shaping the current inhabitants' perceptions of the present and future, and reinforcing the home's function as a site defined by its continuous—and continuing—history. Family heirlooms become metonyms for an enduring connection to the family home. Together, home and heirloom become history. As Sara Quay points out, "the narrative with which heirlooms are attributed includes the story that the family tells about itself through its possession of the inherited thing."[40]

But even though they are imbued with complex value within and outside of the family, by Undine's logic the tapestries are worthless until they are converted to the monetary value they represent. As art, the "splendid" tapestries are without peer (*CC*, 423). Containing "the fabulous pinks and blues of the Boucher series," they are the kind of rare work that reduces even a practiced dealer to a series of "Ah—"s (*CC*, 455). Unsold, the tapestries are merely trophies signifying a coveted social status—the appropriate scenery for a French ancestral home. From the moment when Undine first sees them, they become the distinguishing feature of a desirable setting. After her first visit to the château, she reports to a friend: "Chelles said he wanted me to see just how they lived at home, and I did; I saw everything: the tapestries that Louis Quinze gave them, and the family portraits, and the chapel, where their own priest says mass, and they sit by themselves in a balcony with crowns all over it" (CC, 256). Clearly, the tapestries, portraits, and chapel are the most important constitutive elements of the family's existence. History, lineage, and religion are central to their identity. But in her report to her friend, Undine transforms the château into a stage set, describing it as a "real castle, with towers, and water all round it, and a funny kind of bridge they pull up" (CC, 256). The tapestries, the portraits, and even the priest become nothing more than set decorations—properties. As with everything in Undine's universe, eventually the value of her choice must come down to its value on the open market. Because the tapestries form a part of the setting that she considers to be desirable and appropriate, Undine assumes that they must be worth millions. As she points out to Raymond, "There's a fortune in this one room: you could get anything you chose for those tapestries" (CC, 453). As MacComb suggests, by "removing the jewels—or the ancient Saint-Desert tapestries—from their associative settings, Undine inflicts a very personal 'wound' (CC, 214) upon family tradition and community. She then carries these objects, as objects, into each new marital setting as emblems of the new social dislocation, the 'divorce' of the present from the past."[41] The setting Undine initially considers so appropriate to her beauty quickly slips from the mesh of the multiple meanings that construct it and becomes a potential site for profiteering.

Undine's modern move to eviscerate history from the home at last succeeds when she reconnects with Elmer Moffatt, the once and future husband she has concealed from everyone except for her parents. Undine's kindred spirit, Moffatt embodies a mutability similar to her own. When Undine sees him, she notes that "something in his look seemed to promise the capacity to develop into any character he might care to assume; though it did not seem probable that, for the present, that of a gentleman would be among them" (CC, 107). Like Undine, Elmer can reinvent himself in order to profit from new opportunities. He is also highly mobile; his gender and lack of personal history allow him to move from place to place far more rapidly than Undine can. When together, the couple never stays in one place for very long. Both of their weddings are preceded by rapid train rides to new states where marriage is famously temporary. But even more significant than this shared mobility is their common fascination with settings. Significantly, Elmer's relationship to urban space reveals that Wharton does not particularly gender the ability to remake settings for economic reasons. Both Undine and Elmer are practiced decorators. For Wharton, the transformation of a setting's function from historical truth-telling to consumable advertisement emphasizes that skill in manipulating setting is a quality, however objectionable, of modern subjectivity.

To Undine, Elmer represents settings. "While he talked of building up railways she was building up palaces, and picturing all the multiple lives he would lead in them" (*CC*, 461). Highly modern, her vision of success departs completely from the unifying ideals of family and history and lights instead on the multiplicity that plenty of money can buy. Indeed, Moffatt's ability to construct settings becomes a large part of his appeal for Undine.

> She liked to see such things about her—without any real sense of their meaning she felt them to be the appropriate setting of a pretty woman, to embody something of the rareness and distinction she had always considered she possessed; and she reflected that if she had still been Moffatt's wife he would have given her just such a setting, and the power to live in it as became her. (*CC*, 471)

As she sits in Saint Désert, the setting she has chosen as particularly appropriate for herself, Undine reflects that there is something lacking in her marriage to Raymond de Chelles. She seeks a power that only someone like Moffatt can bestow; only sheer wealth will allow her actively to remake and then inhabit settings as she chooses. To live among the château's artifacts is one thing, to "live in [a place] as became her" quite another. Undine wants the opportunity to adapt herself to the beauty and monetary worth of her surroundings even as she transforms them.

Like Undine, Moffatt is particularly conscious of environment, but because we do not see him at home until the end of the novel, his rise in the world of Wall Street is best read in his offices. In the early days of his success, Moffatt can only imitate the settings of wealth, power, and prestige to which he aspires. But as he makes money, he redecorates:

> Moffatt's office had been transformed since Ralph's last visit. Paint, varnish, and brass railings gave an air of opulence to the outer precincts, and the inner room, with its mahogany bookcases containing morocco-bound "sets" and its wide blue leather arm-chairs, lacked only a palm or two to resemble the lounge of a fashionable hotel. Moffatt himself, as he came forward, gave Ralph the impression of having been done over by the same hand. (*CC*, 389)

Just as Undine attempts to manipulate her settings to create a desirable reality, Elmer must give the impression of material success if he is to achieve it. Wharton's emphasis that these "sets" are copies signals both the presence of wealth and Moffatt's pretensions; his office is nothing more than a "fashionable hotel."[42] By the novel's end, the super-rich Moffatt has moved up to Paris's Hotel Luxe, where he fills his office with unique objects such as "a lapis bowl in a renaissance mounting of enamel . . . a vase of Phenician glass that was like a bit of rainbow caught in cobwebs . . . [and] a little Greek marble." Only the "false colours and crude contours of the hotel furniture" and the "old numbers of *Town Talk* and the *New York Radiator*" remain to mark Moffatt's origins and date his recent acquisition of wealth (*CC*, 487). Here, the hotel furniture has a double significance; it represents something temporary, a shoddy contrast to the unique objets d'art that juxtapose it. At the same time, the furniture, possibly bought at auction when a hotel closed or (even more likely in this era) relocated to a more fashionable locale, it also represents a past—if only a collapsed sense of what the past means. Further, all of Moffatt's acquisitions are removed from history. As the country's "greatest" collector, Elmer Moffatt continuously enacts the deracination of objects from their pasts. Every object he collects shares that fate, especially the Saint Désert tapestries, which he wants to remove from their centuries-old resting place and assign to perpetual transit through Europe in his private railroad car.

As a collector, Moffatt transforms historic value into something purely monetary. He has the power not simply to purchase objects but to set their value, creating a new matrix of worth to replace historical, familial, and aesthetic measures. Mrs. Heeney's clipping bag attests to Moffatt's power: "It is reported in London that the price paid by Mr. Elmer Moffatt for the celebrated Grey Boy is the largest sum ever given for a Vandyck. Since Mr. Moffatt began to buy extensively it is estimated in art circles that values have gone up at least seventy-five per cent" (CC, 500). "The necklace, which was formerly the property of an Austrian Archduchess, is composed of five hundred perfectly matched pearls that took thirty years to collect. It is estimated among dealers in precious stones that since Mr. Moffatt began to buy the price of pearls has gone up over fifty per cent" (CC, 501). In creating settings for himself and eventually for Undine, Moffatt revalues the objects he chooses. The Railroad King uses a fortune gained through mobility in order to make valuable objects portable. "By collecting rare items, Moffatt commodifies them—treating them as fungible and reducing their value to its cash equivalent."[43] No longer historicized, they are thoroughly commodified.

This erasure of historical contexts is particularly noticeable and painful to Paul Marvell, Ralph and Undine's young son. Paul, like his father, has grown up in homes that embody history and family. He has been surrounded by familial artifacts throughout his life. In Washington Square, of course, there were the family portraits that mirrored not only the house's ancient inhabitants, but Paul himself. When he moves to Saint Désert to live with Undine and Chelles, Paul enters "a drawing-room hung with portraits of high-nosed personages in perukes and orders," and meets "a circle of ladies and gentlemen, looking not unlike every-day versions of the official figures above their heads" (CC, 413). Attuned to these resemblances, Paul is clearly struck by the differences between these settings and the one Moffatt has constructed. After his mother remarries Elmer Moffatt, Paul wanders through Moffatt's new Paris hôtel, "wondering whether the wigged and corseleted heroes on the walls represented Mr. Moffatt's ancestors, and why, if they did, he looked so little like them" (CC, 497). The portraits, like the tapestries and objets d'art in Moffatt's office, have all been converted from a familial meaning to an economic one. The reconfiguration of the family that accompanies the reconstruction of the urban home is highlighted in these objects. Elmer and Undine display ancient portraits, but of course they are not ancestral; they are trophies that announce the victory of economics over history. The evisceration of history from the home leaves a wound, an absence marked here by Paul's desire.

The portraits that give Paul Marvell pause powerfully signal Elmer Moffatt's particular skill as a modern businessman: his ability to bring space, time, and economics into a profitable balance. Although Undine sees him as someone without a past, Moffatt is at least as attuned to the power of the past as Ralph Marvell or Raymond de Chelles. But he uses it differently. For Moffatt, the past is at least as much a commodity as the art, property, collectibles—or even the woman—he eventually pursues. All of his best business deals, including his relationship with Undine, revolve around his knowledge of the past, his patience (in other words, his ability to use time differently than those around him), and a knack for timing that allows him to trade on the past precisely when it will be most valuable to him. Moffatt both treasures and trades on the past. And as his art purchases and his final interaction with Undine show, he is never forgetful of history's power in determining market value.

The association of home with the past depends on maintaining a class and family structure antithetical both to physical and class mobility and to the eternal desire that is associated with urban modernity. While the hotel offers Undine a setting in which she may indulge her passions for consumption, display and mobility, it also instills in her a desire that is always unfulfilled. She is composed, in part, of "deep-seated wants for which her acquired vocabulary had no terms" (CC, 460). And this lack of fulfillment is a permanent condition. Like Carrie Meeber in *Sister Carrie*, Undine is condemned to eternal desire, as the last line of *The Custom of the Country* emphasizes: "She could never become an Ambassador's wife; and as she advanced to welcome her first guests she said to herself that it was the one part she was really made for" (CC, 509). Elmer, of course, has just reminded her that her divorces bar her from the post of Ambassadress. Her past takes her off the market; she too has been collected. Undine "is doomed to pursue the phantom of 'everything' until her dream explodes"[44] when she learns that "there was something she could never get, something that neither beauty, nor influence, nor millions could ever buy for her" (CC, 509). Although Undine can choose and manipulate her settings to get what she wants at a given moment, her modern surroundings produce a self that is rooted only in commodified desire.

Over the course of *The Custom of the Country*, Undine Spragg moves from her "Looey" suite at New York's Stentorian Hotel to a custom-built copy of the Pitti Palace in Paris. Broadened by each space she inhabits, Undine's expansive trajectory grows throughout the novel, encompassing and transforming ever greater territory, until the Stentorian comes to seem a relatively stable space, a relic of an older time. Through Undine's history, Wharton presciently charts the increasingly nodal function of the American city as national networks began to reach overseas, giving rise to an interconnected world where commodities, property, and objects once thought to be ancestral—and immobile—change hands and begin to move with astonishing speed. Adept at acquiring spaces and property, Undine and her final husband, Elmer Moffatt, can also skillfully borrow other peoples' pasts when their own histories become undesirable. The Moffatts' acquisition of a gallery of ancestral portraits—along with the Chelles tapestries—visibly shows that the past has become mobile. And while Undine can't completely escape her past, with Elmer's help she eventually manages to extract history from space. Through the narrative, Wharton engages analytically and suggestively with the temporal and spatial concerns raised by the shifting, growing American city of the 1910s that Elmer and Undine Moffatt represent.

Despite their Middle American beginnings, Elmer and Undine are not typical American urbanites. Their ambitions, social connections, and eventual wealth allow them to construct an urban experience marked by a privileged mobility that would have been out of reach for most Americans (and especially American women) at the time. Yet the paradigm of cosmopolitan, international mobility that Undine and Elmer represent would become more and more central to urban life as the cities that preoccupied novelists increasingly were scrutinized by urban sociologists in the 1910s and 1920s.

In *The Custom of the Country*, Wharton theorizes urban operations (in this case, the divorce between place and history effected by the hotel-spirit) through the novel's familiar narrative mode, but she nods toward an emerging paradigm for understanding Undine as urban phenomenon in her character Charles Bowen, a sociologist. It is clear from the sociology and fiction of the 1920s, a decade that saw both the wane of the industrial city and the rise of the automotive metropolis in the United States, that novels still provided a potent frame for representing the complexity of the urban landscape. However, as the field of sociology evolved in the early twentieth century, academic sociologists attempted to distance their work from novels by positioning their discipline as an objective, scientific approach to understanding cities. Sociology, its practitioners argued, offered a potent new means for analyzing modern urban realities, especially the relationships between subject and environment with which novelists had experimented for decades. By the mid-1920s, urban sociology was emerging as a newly theoretical discipline, thanks largely to the work of Robert Park.

Chapter 6

The Paradox of Intimacy

Mobility, Sociology, and the Function of Home in Quicksand

> *... in the city all the secret ambitions and all the suppressed desires find*
> *somewhere an expression. The city magnifies, spreads out, and advertises*
> *human nature in all its various manifestations. It is this that makes the city*
> *interesting, even fascinating. It is this, however, that makes it of all places*
> *the one in which to discover the secrets of human hearts.*
>
> —Robert Park[1]

> *It was so easy and so pleasant to think about freedom and cities.*
> —Nella Larsen[2]

In the introduction to his seminal 1915 essay, "The City: Suggestions for the
Investigation of Human Behavior in the Urban Environment," Robert Park, a
new lecturer in the nationally renowned sociology department at the University of Chicago, claimed that "we are mainly indebted to our writers of fiction
for our more intimate knowledge of contemporary urban life."[3] Arguing that
the novel's subjective understanding of urban life no longer offered an adequate framework for analyzing the city's complexity, he wrote, "The life of
our cities demands a more searching and disinterested study than even Emile
Zola has given us in his 'experimental novels'" (CS, 15). Thus Park called for
a new mode of inquiry into urban life—the academic discipline of sociology.

To differentiate his approach to the urban from that taken by novelists,
Park grounded his scientific, "searching and disinterested" approach to cities
in a series of questions on urban topics including the neighborhood, voca-
tions, the mob, the courts, the family, and commercialized vice, asking:

> What is the relation of mobility to suggestion, imitation, etc.? What are the
> practical devices by which suggestibility and mobility are increased in a com-
> munity or an individual? Are there pathological conditions in communities
> corresponding to hysteria in individuals? If so, how are they produced and
> how controlled? (CS, 19–20)

Questions like these structured Robert Park's self-consciously theoretical conception of the urban and largely would determine the trajectory of modern sociology. Park imagined that modern sociology would make scientific the narrative project that urban novelists had begun. Indeed, his questions bear witness to concerns about environment and subject long at work in American urban novels. Echoed here are Nathaniel Hawthorne's and Henry James's concerns about urban pathologies; Steven Crane's link between urban surroundings and personal characteristics; Edith Wharton's concerns with fashion and imitation.

Because novels reveal that the complex relationships among urban people and the spaces they inhabit cannot be reduced to "objective" statistics, Park's decision to adopt the disinterested stance of social science left novelists a wide arena in which to challenge and complicate his formulations of urban subjectivity. Significantly and perhaps not surprisingly, the novel's "intimate knowledge" troubles Park's social scientific approach to the city and its inhabitants. Park's disinterested theoretical formulations stumble when they confront the specters of the body, of gender, of race, and of sexuality, elemental in urban novels. Seen in the context of the urban novels written in his own era, Park's work emerges as a vexed negotiation between the competing demands of scientific objectivity and narrative intimacy.

Shot through with the very dynamics that trouble Park's work, numerous texts of the Harlem Renaissance, particularly Nella Larsen's 1928 novel *Quicksand,* explore how intimacy undermines theoretical assessments of urban life, particularly formulations of mobility and marginality like those Park published in his essay of the same year, "Human Migration and the Marginal Man." The figure of the Mulatto, who for Park embodied the "personality type" of marginality, is a familiar figure in modernist novels; in *Quicksand,* Larsen embodies marginality not in a mulatto man but in a female character, the complex half-Danish, half-Negro character Helga Crane. Helga both enacts and subverts Park's conception of a mobile identity. Through this biracial figure, *Quicksand* animates the theories Park played out through the marginal man. In many ways, Helga might seem to be, as Mary Esteve argues, "destined to carry out Park's 'fascinating but dangerous manner of living' in a self-divided manner."[4] But beyond simply carrying out Park's theories, Helga actively challenges them. As a female protagonist, Helga calls attention to the power of sentimental and affective bonds in the urban landscape, confounding Park's assertion that the city makes such bonds obsolete. Through Helga's powerful and competing desires for home and for mobility in the urban landscapes she inhabits, *Quicksand* asserts that "home" and the ideas about gender roles and intimacy that are spatialized there— what Michel Foucault terms "the little tactics of the habitat"—must remain central to theoretical and practical discussions of urban subjectivity in the twentieth century.[5]

Like the narratives that precede them, Park's and Larsen's explorations of intimacy and mobility in the urban landscape examine the status, risks, and rewards associated with new degrees of urban mobility and marginality. At the same time, they bring race and gender to the fore. Urban spaces in Park's and Larsen's texts reveal how twentieth-century concepts of mobility, home, the city, marginality, and perhaps even space itself are produced in relation to race and gender. As literary critics begin to analyze textual operations of space in social practice (in a move similar to the shift in the geographic imagination Edward Soja charts in *Postmodern Geographies*), modernist urban texts like *Quicksand* can help show that even as social scientists rejected the novel as a form of inquiry into urban operations, novelists persistently and provocatively analyzed and theorized the operations of race and gender in urban space.[6]

Mobility, Marginality, and the Harlem Renaissance

As Park and his protégés worked on their "searching and disinterested study" of the urban in the 1920s, novelists who we identify with the Harlem Renaissance registered and theorized emergent sociological concerns about mobility and marginality. And while each of these movements rightly is associated with a particular city, both the Chicago School and the Harlem Renaissance drew on local dynamics to redefine the meaning of "city" more broadly. The Harlem Renaissance, by its very name, was grounded in 1920s Manhattan above 125th Street, yet it registered broad cultural forces and spoke to a wide audience, raising concerns both specific to Harlem and common to urban areas throughout the United States and beyond. Emerging as the "Negro capital of the world" at a moment of internationalism, as well as intranational movement and migration, Harlem came to matter not as a novelty or an aberration but as a representation of a new type of urban space, a place that augured new sorts of spatial relations.[7] Similarly, although Park's work drew him to Chicago and affiliated him with that city, both the theoretical nature of his work and the mobile lifestyle that preceded his academic career led Park to develop a universalized vision of the city as a mobile space of interracial and international connection. Harlem and its novels magnified, broadcast, and undermined the Chicago School's early concerns.

At the end of the industrial city's heyday, the possibilities and stakes of mobility crystallized for both black and white Americans.[8] In Harlem, urban ownership and tenancy became possible for black Americans on an unprecedented scale. As James Weldon Johnson explains,

> With thousands of Negroes pouring into Harlem month by month, two things happened: first, a sheer pressure for room was set up that was irresistible; second, old residents and new-comers got work as fast as they could take it, at

wages never dreamed of, so there was now plenty of money for renting or buying. And the Negro in Harlem did, contrary to all the burlesque notions about
what Negroes do when they get hold of money, take advantage of the low
prices of property and begin to buy.[9]

Harlem's development as "the most exciting urban community in Afro-
America—or anywhere else for that matter" brought black Americans new
opportunities for property ownership.[10] African Americans who historically
had been barred from owning property (and who continued to be barred
elsewhere), even those who could only afford to pay rent, could look to
ownership as a possibility—in Harlem. "With the memory still fresh of the
race riots of the late 1910s . . . in which blacks were associated, both as victims and perpetrators, with brutal savagery, images of respectable collective
behavior such as buying property advertised African Americans' capacity to
participate in and enjoy normative American pursuits of happiness."[11] In
part, this possibility allowed black Americans to develop a relationship to
urban space that, while unique to Harlem, more closely resembles the white
and immigrant experiences of urban spaces that I have traced in earlier novels. That is, the city, and not the suburbs or countryside, was the first place
where large numbers of black Americans owned property.

As black Americans gained control over urban space, they also carved out
space in the literary landscape. Significantly, as Ann Douglas points out, during the Harlem Renaissance, "for the first time in American history, many
blacks and some whites viewed the black tradition in the arts not as a slight
and inferior tributary to white culture but as a dominant influence on it."[12]
Just as black Harlemites took advantage of a propitious moment to gain
control over the physical landscape, black authors seized the opportunity to
assert themselves artistically, bringing new assessments of and questions
about modern urban life to the center of American discourse.

Unsurprisingly, in many of the novels that emerged in the late 1920s, issues of environment are at stake. In these novels, the questions of how home
might be defined and where it might be found, especially poignant and pressing concerns for a largely disempowered population, are resolved in the assertion that Harlem, an unquestionably urban space, was home. At the end
of the industrial era, we see a culmination of sorts: ideas about mobility and
marginality central to discussions of the urban home reach their apogee in
the Harlem Renaissance. The characteristics that Chicago School sociologists would identify as central to urban society—mobility and marginality—
take on new forms, offer new meanings, and bring urbanites into increasingly international cities. Simultaneously, these new theoretical formulations
of mobility and marginality bring into sharp relief the formulations of race
in the urban landscape that had been obscured by questions of class and gender in earlier urban fiction.

Robert Park: Theorizing Mobility

The conceptions of urban mobility and marginality articulated in the novels of the Harlem Renaissance emerged contemporaneously with Robert Park's work on the subject. Park's thinking, of course, had a significant history. Reflecting on his career, Park traced his interest in sociology, as well as his fascination with the urban, to his experience as a city reporter at the turn into the twentieth century:

> The Sunday paper was willing to publish all sorts of things as long as it concerned the local community and was interesting. I wrote about all sorts of things and became in this way intimately acquainted with many different aspects of city life. I expect that I have actually covered more ground, tramping about in cities in different parts of the world, than any other living man. Out of this I gained, among other things, a conception of the city, the community, and the region, not as a geographical phenomenon merely but as a kind of social organism.[13]

Like Selah Tarrant in *The Bostonians*, Park's urban wanderings are linked to the newspaper. But instead of becoming the subject of human interest journalism, Park writes the text. His physical mobility—tramping—allows him an intimate acquaintance with the city and inspires intellectual mobility. Through movement and writing, Park claims, he came to see the city broadly, theoretically—to conceive of the city as an "organism," a notion that would structure much of his later work. Echoing the perspective of the nineteenth-century flâneur, Park's experience led him to argue that mobility itself engenders intellectual freedom.[14] His travels gave Park a broad, universalizing conception of the city; yet by the time his best-known work was published, this mode of knowing cities was increasingly passé.[15]

After a peripatetic career that included stints in academics, journalism, and several years as a traveling companion to Booker T. Washington, Robert Park joined the faculty of the University of Chicago in 1919. He was fifty-five.[16] When he arrived, the university was nurturing the developing field of sociology. Park's colleagues included Albion Small, who founded and edited the *American Journal of Sociology;* William I. Thomas, whose 1918 text *The Polish Peasant in Europe and America* set a new standard for statistical methods in social science; and Ernest Burgess, Park's co-author on *Introduction to the Science of Society* (1921), which served as sociology's main introductory textbook until the 1940s. A coeducational university, Chicago attracted women faculty and students who played powerful roles in the nascent field. Dean of Women Sophonisba Breckinridge and her student Edith Abbott, author of the "classic statement on women's role in the marketplace, *Women in Industry,*" through their work on "education, housing, urban

childhood, labor, and working women," defined the purview of social policy study at Chicago.[17] By 1920, however, the group had split along gender
lines, with the women identifying themselves as social workers and the men as
sociologists.[18] This split divided practice from theory, as Eugene Rochberg-
Halton explains:

> Park and the academic Chicago sociologists . . . generalized from the unique
> and rapidly industrializing Chicago ("the city without a past") to claim a uni-
> versal scientific sociology of urban life. Their fear of history and fervor for posi-
> tive science were symptoms of scientism, of an ideology of science which was
> itself the product of modern materialism.[19]

Emphasizing sociology's theoretical aspects, Park and his protégés distanced
themselves and the discipline from the efforts of the social reformers who
worked directly to ameliorate living conditions in early twentieth-century
Chicago. In order to do so, he had to purge sociology of several of its central early concerns, particularly the family and the home.[20]

In attempting to move beyond reformers' and novelists' constructions of
the relationships among people and physical structures in the city, Park drew
on a variety of social scientific approaches, including ecology, anthropology,
and geography. He hoped to use the quantitative and qualitative tools of
these disciplines in order to "discover how these physical vessels [the built
environments of the city] shape the emotional, human experience of city
men."[21] A social scientific approach could lay bare the workings of architectural determinism as well as the possibilities for human agency in the urban
environment. Park writes, "We may, if we choose, think of the city, that is
to say, the place and the people, with all the machinery and administrative
devices that go with them, as organically related; a kind of psychophysical
mechanism" (CS, 2). From ecology, Park derived the notion of environment
as a system: Structures and people together construct one another and the
wider environment. As Park notes, "The city possesses a moral as well as a
physical organization, and these two mutually interact in characteristic ways
to mold and modify one another" (CS, 4). This ecological notion of environment is structured by a dialectic between self and space similar to that
which animates urban novels. Yet from the nineteenth century on, American
urban novels show this dialectic to be unpredictable and often messy, a far
cry from the clear-cut science Park is trying to develop. In attempting to
align his groundbreaking sociological work with fiction's long tradition of
exploring the city's "moral and physical organization" while simultaneously
rejecting the novel's methods, Park ironically reveals that scientific objectivity is inadequate to account for the complexities of urban space.

Park's attention to the city's affective qualities, its "moral organization,"
which was manifested in his desire to explore the city's spontaneity, contin-
gency, and unmappability, distinguished his work from that of his peers in

the discipline. Throughout his career, he emphasized that although people act upon the urban environment, they cannot always understand either the ramifications of their individual actions or the ways in which their actions will interact with the activities of others. In contrast to contemporaries like E. A. Ross, who believed that "deliberative, autonomous selfhood is a requisite for spontaneous, innovative action, which in turn is requisite for the progress of civilization," Park's analysis of the city as organism imparts an almost accidental quality to human action in urban spaces.[22]

Yet the urban organism is productive; for Park the city is humankind's ultimate, if fortuitous, creation. In "The City as a Social Laboratory," he notes that

> it is in the urban environment—in a world that man himself has made—that mankind first achieved an intellectual life and acquired those characteristics which most distinguish him from the lower animals and from primitive man. For the city and the urban environment represent man's most consistent and, on the whole, his most successful attempt to remake the world he lives in more to his heart's desire. But if the city is the world which man created, it is the world in which he is henceforth condemned to live. Thus, indirectly, and without any clear sense of the nature of his task, in making the city man has remade himself.[23]

Here, Park describes a mutuality between space and subject. The city offers humanity its best shot at fulfilling its collective ideals. While the city has made (or at least remade) the civilized, intellectual man, it is also clearly the product of individual action. The city is a "world that man himself has made," a physical manifestation of his "heart's desire." The affective component of Park's thinking is visible here; clearly man's relationship to this environment is powerfully emotional. It is both exhilarating and horrifying. For while he has risen above the lower, primitive orders, Park's urbanite has condemned himself to inhabit the world that he has created without fully understanding what he has done. Man remakes himself as he makes the city, but the city's unwitting spatial and social architects cannot begin to imagine the consequences of their actions.

People have made a city that is both a "state of mind" and a "physical construction," and the complexity of this construct is marked by the plethora of terms that Park summons to describe it (CS, 1). Arguing that the physical spaces and human inhabitants of the city become a "psychophysical mechanism" that is "both artifact and utility," Park claims that the city is a "living entity," not an "artificial construction" (CS, 4, 3). Urban institutions change quickly: "They grow under our very eyes."[24] As this entity moves beyond the control of its creators, it makes demands upon its inhabitants and theorists that are difficult to meet.

Mobility, Park argues, both allows people to adapt to urban spaces and erodes individual ties to geographic or psychic homes. Park writes, "The easy means of communication and of transportation, which enable individuals to distribute their attention and live at the same time in several different worlds, tend to destroy the permanency and intimacy of the neighborhood"(*CS*, 9). *The Blithedale Romance, Sister Carrie,* and *The Custom of the Country* all bolster Park's argument that physical mobility can "enable individuals . . . to live at the same time in several different worlds," enacting a particularly urban simultaneity (*CS*, 9).

For Park, the state of mind that is the city resembles:

> a mosaic of little worlds which touch but do not interpenetrate. This makes it possible for individuals to pass quickly and easily from one moral milieu to another, and encourages the fascinating but dangerous experiment of living at the same time in contiguous, but otherwise widely separated, worlds. (*CS*, 40–41)

Because the city is many different things simultaneously, Park's urbanites are defined not by their presence in one world, but, like Helga Crane in *Quicksand* or Angela Murray/Angèle Mory in Jessie Fauset's *Plum Bun,* by their "fascinating but dangerous" habit of moving among different milieux. The networks of the modern city liberate urbanites from the constraints of their particular pasts, and may liberate them from the past in general. Mobility leads to freedom; Park animates this liberatory mobile identity through the figure he calls the "marginal man."

Considering Marginality

While Park was consciously attempting to move the field of sociology toward a disinterested scientific approach, he remained fascinated by ideas central to the work of his predecessors, particularly marginality. Marginality, in concept if not in name, had been the focus of much early Chicago scholarship, including studies on immigrants (W. I. Thomas, George Mead), deviance (Henderson, Burgess), and race (Thomas, Park). Concerns about gender were also central to the work of early Chicago reformers and theorists, especially to Thomas's work on young female juvenile delinquents.[25] Yet while Park identified Thomas as his primary academic mentor at Chicago, his own work on marginality virtually eliminates gender as a consideration, an elision that privileges a masculinized mobility while pushing the notion of intimacy to the borders of Park's work.

In his 1928 essay "Human Migration and the Marginal Man," Park develops the notion that increased mobility may emancipate urban dwellers from the constraints of the past; he genders the concepts of mobility and marginality as he makes his argument. Here, Park personifies the city's liberatory potential in an urban subject who is "migrational" and therefore "marginal"; he is "freed for new enterprises and associations" while "striving to live in . . . diverse cultural groups."[26] Park notes: "The effect is to produce an unstable character. . . . This is the 'marginal man.' It is in the mind of the marginal man that the process of civilization is visibly going on, and it is in the mind of the marginal man that the process of civilization may best be studied" (*HM*, 131). Significantly, the "process of civilization" to which Park refers involves liberation from domesticity. "Migration," he writes, "is not to be identified with mere movement. It involves, at the very least, change of residence and the breaking of home ties" (*HM*, 136).

In order to explain the unique freedoms that cities offer, Park contrasts urban liberty to domestic stability:

> A very large part of the populations of great cities, including those who make their homes in tenements and apartment houses, live much as people do in some great hotel, meeting but not knowing one another. The effect of this is to substitute fortuitous and casual relationships for the more intimate and permanent associations of the smaller community. (*CS*, 40)

By Park's logic, if the city is essentially a "great hotel," not a home, then hotels, apartments, tenements—all of the city dwellings that elicit the powerful dual fantasies of containment and dissolution in urban novels—are not homes. The luck and randomness of the "great hotel" overpower any claim urban domestic spaces might make to intimacy or permanence. Park will argue that this development is a good thing for the marginal man. For the marginal woman, as we will see in *Quicksand*, the dynamic is a little more complicated.

Elsewhere in Park's work, the tension between desires for mobility and stasis is even more clearly gendered. In "The City: Suggestions for the Investigation of Human Behavior in the Urban Environment," Park describes a conflict between the feminized "sentiment" inspired by the home and the "interests" one may pursue in the city. In contrast to the home, where sentiment overcomes rationality, the city is a place where "communities of interest" operate as means to rational ends (*CS*, 9–10). Here, sentiment is an unexamined emotion. It is irrational, perhaps even primitive. Sentiment seems to be a relic of the cave, an outmoded bond to the home, an instinctual desire for a fixed place with which to associate. Park had introduced these terms in his 1923 article "The Mind of the Rover."

> It is still true that the human creature is a good deal of a vegetable. This is evident in the invincible attachment of mankind to localities and places; in man's and particularly in woman's, inveterate and irrational ambition to have a home—some cave or hut or tenement—in which to live and vegetate; some secure hole or corner from which to come forth in the morning and return to at night.

As long as man is thus attached to the earth and to places on the earth, as long as nostalgia and plain homesickness hold him and draw him inevitably back to the haunts and places he knows best, he will never fully realize that other characteristic of mankind, namely, to move freely and untrammeled over the surface of mundane things and to live, like pure spirit, in his mind and in his imagination alone.[27]

Here, the gendering of the difference between stasis and mobility, between nostalgia and freedom, between vegetation and spirituality is pronounced. Sentiment—here conceived as women's "inveterate and irrational ambition to have a home"—is antithetical to the Emersonian imagination, freedom, and movement that Park associates with urban spaces. In the urban environment, a higher plane of "interests" draws people together and allows them to add to the development of urban civilization.

For Park, becoming marginal requires suspending relations to any one place and substituting the liberating possibilities of the rapidly changing urban landscape for the confining status quo of the home. Race and nation break down in Park's conception of the city, which becomes a global space populated by and exemplified in the "city man, the man who ranges widely, lives preferably in a hotel, in short, a cosmopolite" (*HM*, 141). The hotel is both an attractive setting for and a salient force in constructing the city man. It is no longer scandalous, as it was in *The House of Mirth*, but worldly. To Park, the city offers freedom; it is where "the emancipated individual invariably becomes . . . a cosmopolitan. He learns to look upon the world in which he was born and bred with something of the detachment of the stranger" (*HM*, 137). Though the estranged cosmopolitan is often a vaguely threatening figure in fiction (think of Westervelt in *Blithedale* or Simon Rosedale in *The House of Mirth*), for Park, detachment augurs emancipation and cultural progress.[28] Clearly, the cosmopolite is the twentieth-century representative of a long line of American flâneurs, beginning in this study with Miles Coverdale in *The Blithedale Romance*. As Richard Sennett notes, "Park saw the city as the medium for the emergence of free men, whose personal development could transcend general societal standards, whose innovations could provide the basis for historical change in urban society itself."[29] Mobility leads to marginality; it is therefore the source of innovation, emancipation, and societal transformation.

In "Human Migration," the dichotomies between stasis and mobility, home and city, structure individuals' relationships to the larger community. "Unsettled" people and their "hotel culture" enjoy a relation to the community that Park describes as "symbiotic rather than social" (*HM*, 136). The wanderer is the "freer man" because he is detached from social ties. Perpetually unsettled, Park's marginal man occupies a position "between worlds" that engenders a more or less permanently "divided self"—the marginal

man is an always unassimilated immigrant characterized by "spiritual instability, intensified self-consciousness, restlessness and *malaise*" (*HM*, 142). If
he can never assimilate, he remains in the symbiotic relation Park describes—
and it is precisely this experience of instability that drives modern culture.
Noting that "it is in the mind of the marginal man that the process of civilization is visibly going on, and it is in the mind of the marginal man that the
process of civilization may best be studied," Park situates marginality at the
center of urban civilization (*HM*, 131). Significantly, Park specifies that "ordinarily the marginal man is a mixed blood, like the mulatto in the United
States" (*HM*, 142).

As Park was publishing this work, the questions about marginality, mobility, home, and race that concerned him were also resonating in one of the
forms that Park's version of sociology aimed to displace: the novel. They
were particularly at stake in the novels that emerged from the Harlem Renaissance. As it does in Park's work, the figure of the mulatto occupies a central position in the literary productions of the era.

While, as Ann Douglas notes, Harlem Renaissance literature did not
achieve nearly the popularity or influence that it may have merited, black
writers "were getting more exposure and backing than they ever had before;
political advancement might be curtailed, but cultural success looked possible."[30] *Quicksand* was one of a number of urban novels that emerged in
this moment of possibility, including Claude McKay's *Home to Harlem*
(1928), Wallace Thurman's *The Blacker the Berry* (1929), Fauset's *Plum
Bun* (1929), and James Weldon Johnson's *Autobiography of an Ex-Colored
Man* (printed anonymously 1912, reissued 1927). In different ways, each of
these novels emphasizes mobility within and beyond national borders, questions the constructedness and constraints of racialized identities, and presents Harlem (and therefore urban space) as home. In these novels, neither
physical mobility nor racial identity is always voluntarily chosen, yet the
urban space of Harlem consistently offers characters new possibilities for
exerting control over movement and identity. As a group, the texts clarify
that black urban culture—and urban identity considered more broadly—is
increasingly mobile. Yet as the city became home, new concerns emerged.
How, these novels ask, will the interpersonal and extrafamilial ties that enabled black Americans to survive before the Great Migration shift? How,
they ask, will intimacy survive in urban space?

Gendering Marginality: Sentiment and Mobility in Quicksand

His own intimacy with urban spaces provided Park with his insights into the
city, yet Park's theoretical work downplays the significance of intimacy with
people or places to marginality, an effacement that urban novels question.

As they are in other Harlem Renaissance texts, marginality, intimacy, and sentiment are at the center of Nella Larsen's *Quicksand*. Through protagonist Helga Crane, *Quicksand* asks what constitutes marginality, asserts gender's theoretical significance in questions of modern identity, questions Park's privileging of disinterestedness, and explores the force of intimacy and finally biology in social relations.

The novel traces Helga's journey from a desirable teaching position at a school called Naxos to her paralyzing marriage to a poor Alabama preacher, with stops in the urbane and sophisticated cities of 1920s Harlem and Copenhagen along the way. For much of the novel, Helga avoids entangling herself too deeply in interpersonal relationships, preferring to remain mobile as she searches for an elusive feeling of belonging. In many ways, Helga embraces the freedom from stasis that Park claims as a hallmark of marginality, yet for her, unlike for the marginal man, symbiotic and social relations are inseparable—they are entwined both in her mulatta identity and in her relationships with other people.[31] Helga does not separate the symbiotic from the social, or her interests from her sentiments. Rather, sentimental bonds are instrumental for Helga: they allow her to explore the tensions between mobility and stasis, distance and intimacy, modernity and home that emerge as her perpetual crises. Played out in urban space, these conflicts ultimately cannot be resolved.

Through Helga's desire for and resistance to the notion of home, Larsen explores the ramifications of urban life for a subject who—except for her gender—embodies Park's notion of marginality. Like Park, Larsen links mobility and marginality to modernity; she too depicts the modern subject as living between worlds. But while Larsen presents Helga as a fragmented character, one who moves among different settings, classes, and occupations but for whom any single role is unbearably restrictive, Helga's overwhelming and eventually self-destructive desire to belong somewhere, to ally herself with "her people" without "naturalizing," ultimately undermines her ability to play with the many roles that a fragmentary urban setting offers her (*Q*, 7). For both Park and Larsen, the city operates as a space beyond nation; *Quicksand* explores the psychological effects of this racialized expatriate identity by linking Helga's experiences in Chicago, Harlem, and Copenhagen.[32] Like Park's work, Larsen's narrative resonates with the concerns about the destabilized self, the permeable, the mobile, the public, and the modern so critical to earlier urban novels in the United States. And like these prior texts, *Quicksand*'s constructions of urban subjectivity are animated through the spatial operations of the urban home. Torn between a need for home and an impulse for change, Helga moves from place to place, initially charmed by the possibilities of the new and inevitably repulsed by the routines of the familiar. While she fantasizes about finding a place where she belongs, Helga prefers to remain, in Park's terms, "at large, and in transition" to "becom[ing] incorporated into the permanent economic and social order around" her.[33] Larsen renders Helga's conflicting desires at once sympathetic and alien by alternately sentimentalizing and pathologizing Helga's simultaneous needs to stay and go. Further, through the motif of spatial "borrowing," Larsen offers a theoretically possible, if ultimately untenable way for Helga to resolve her competing desires.

The orphaned daughter of a Danish mother and an African-American father, Helga Crane both embodies and revises Park's marginal figure. Like the marginal man, Helga is hungry for change and for the new. Yet Helga is not seeking to disrupt the political or social status quo. Instead of attempting to revise cultural ideas of permanence, stability, or home as the marginal man does, Helga's quest is itself a dialectic; she seeks permanence at her most mobile moments, mobility when she feels at home. For instance, when she contemplates a voyage to Denmark, Helga starts "to make plans and to dream delightful dreams of change, of life somewhere else. Some place where at last she would be permanently satisfied. Her anticipatory thoughts waltzed and eddied about to the sweet silent music of change" (*Q*, 56–57). Here, a succession of contrasts reveals the depth of the tension Helga experiences between her desire for change and her desire to be "permanently satisfied." The silent music allows her thoughts to waltz and eddy—to swirl in motion and to swirl in stillness. Her fantasy is not to transcend stability, as Park's marginal man does, but to attain both mobility and safety at once. Thus, as Mary Esteve notes, "For all of her flightiness, perhaps because of her flightiness, Helga embodies the principal qualities of quicksand, inert materiality and immaterial motility."[34] These qualities are most visible in Helga's spatial relations.

Larsen explores the tension between the symbiotic and the social through Helga's simultaneous and unresolvable desires for mobility and home. Throughout the novel, Helga articulates a need for home, a need that helps to make sense of her otherwise surprising decision to marry a conservative evangelical minister and move with him from New York to his rural Alabama community. If the fantasy of home is undermined by the final reality of rural Alabama, the fantasy of mobility sustains Helga throughout the novel, especially when she feels that she is becoming attached to any one place. As she thinks about returning to Denmark to live with her aunt and uncle, she idealizes the sense of home a previous stay had instilled in her: "Aunt Katrina had begged for her to be allowed to remain. Why, she wondered, hadn't her mother consented? To Helga it seemed that it would have been the solution to all their problems" (*Q*, 55). As she matures, her sense of home remains just as powerful, but it begins to be associated with race rather than family: She thinks, "I'm homesick, not for America, but for Negroes" (*Q*, 92). Helga's yearnings make clear that home has shifting meanings. Ironically, however, the stability she seeks is associated with a very volatile conception of home.

Helga's simultaneous desire for home and for mobility is so pronounced that she begins to equate home with mobility. Logically, the idea that home might not mean stasis first occurs to Helga when she enters urban space. In Chicago, for instance, "as she stepped out into the moving, multicolored crowd, there came to her a queer feeling of enthusiasm, as if she were tasting some agreeable, exotic food—sweetbreads, smothered with truffles and mushrooms—perhaps. And, oddly enough, she felt, too, that she had come home. She, Helga Crane, who had no home" (Q, 30). And in Harlem, "again she had had that strange transforming experience, this time not so fleetingly, that magic sense of having come home" (Q, 43). As Park notes, the city facilitates and perhaps even demands a certain mobility from its inhabitants; this motion feels like home to Helga. The crowd is moving, multicolored, agreeable, and exotic. Both familiar and excitingly new, the motion of the city seems to offer Helga the home she seeks. Helga's sense of home in transit asserts itself again when she travels to Denmark. On board the ship, Helga "revel[s] like a released bird in her returned feeling of happiness and freedom, that blessed sense of belonging to herself alone and not to a race. Again, she had put the past behind her with an ease that astonished even herself" (Q, 64). This conflation of home with mobility "invokes . . . the condition historically made available by urban modernity of becoming anonymous, of being-becoming matter in motion."[35] Yet Helga is not simply shedding an identity imposed upon her by others; she claims her own identity, one that belongs "to herself alone." Helga's modern identification of the city as home allows her temporarily to suspend her conflicted desires and reach for a mobile identity—a freedom—that echoes the liberation that Park's marginal man enjoys.

While in "Human Migration" Park defines mobility as the ultimate form of liberation from an oppressive status quo, a way to defer assimilation into any one of the "little worlds" that comprise the mosaic of urban space, elsewhere in his work, Park explores a tension between desires for stasis and motion similar to the conflict Helga Crane experiences in Quicksand. In Park's work, as in Larsen's, it is unclear whether or how a mobile identity might be sustained. In a sense, intellect arises from mobility: Urban space allows man "to move freely and untrammeled over the surface of mundane things and to live, like pure spirit, in his mind and in his imagination alone."[36] Yet this untrammeled motion eventually ends in the stasis of home. Park notes in "Local Communities in the Metropolis" (1929) that the

> young and adventurous people, who come into the city to seek their fortune . . . will find their places somewhere in the broad cadre of occupations which the great city offers them. In this way they will become incorporated into the permanent economic and social order about them. In the meantime they are at large, and in transition.[37]

Here, Park argues that the city tends toward a permanent order, and that incorporation into this order is simply a matter of time. Marginal status comes to seem temporary in that it can be erased through class mobility. *Quicksand* seems to support Park's notion that markers of class status, such as taste, manners, and speech, may be developed. Yet unlike *Sister Carrie*, *Quicksand* shows us a character who cannot adopt these markers without a sense for what she risks in the process.

Certainly Helga's innate affinities and tastes tend to affiliate her with a class to which she does not belong. Meredith Goldsmith notes that "Larsen's fiction suggests that class is performed and policed just as rigorously as are gender, race, and sexuality," and certainly Helga is never incorporated permanently into the social class to which she is drawn.[38] But markers of Helga's race and gender are less easily effaced than those that mark her class position; their persistent presence in *Quicksand* begs the question of whether a marginal figure can be assimilated into urban culture as easily as Park assumes.

Certainly Helga is never "incorporated" into the city. Her blackness makes it impossible for race not to be an issue; her unwillingness to adopt the notions of race at work in Harlem (or Naxos, or Copenhagen, or Alabama) similarly prevents her incorporation into any of those worlds. That Helga is unwilling to adopt other people's conceptions of racial identity is clear from her refusals to marry either James Vance, who offers incorporation into a high-status black family, or the white painter Axel Olsen, who sees Helga as an exotic other. Similarly, in Jessie Fauset's novel *Plum Bun*, Angela's decision to pass for white initially is undermined when it becomes clear that a marriage to white Roger Fielding, which would seal her assumed white identity, is impossible for class reasons.[39]

Eventually, Angela stops passing when she publicly identifies herself as black to the fellowship committee that would have helped to assure her professional success as an artist. If Angela initially "incorporates," a latent sense of justice, a desire to align herself with her family (in this case her visibly black sister Virginia), and her decision to marry the ambiguously raced (and gendered) Anthony Cross/Cruz leaves her between racial worlds. In other Harlem Renaissance novels, the apparently white characters who do assimilate into white families are wracked permanently by the fear of discovery, especially the fear that they will have children who are visibly black. We see this dynamic at work in Johnson's *Autobiography of an Ex-Colored Man* and Larsen's *Passing*.[40] In a mosaic-like world more racially fractured than Park might admit, "incorporation" into any one tile is a vexed prospect at best.

Marginal characters in these novels, even those who incorporate more successfully than Helga, retain the sense of existing between worlds; Larsen makes clear in *Quicksand* that heavy psychological consequences belie the freedom Park attaches to marginality. Larsen complicates Park's idealized construction of modern subjectivity by figuring Helga's desires as phobias. As Helga vacillates between home and mobility, she becomes alternately claustrophobic and agoraphobic. She has, for instance, "a sudden attack of nerves at the prospect of traversing [a] great outer room which was the workplace of some twenty odd people. This was a disease from which Helga had suffered at intervals all her life . . ." (*Q*, 17). Here, Helga seems to suffer from a fear of public places: the twenty-odd people transform the room into a fearful place. Helga's affliction, agoraphobia, extends to the very city streets that at other times thrill her with a sense of homecoming: "As the days became hotter and the streets more swarming, a kind of repulsion came upon her. She recoiled in aversion from the sight of the grinning faces and the sound of the easy laughter of all these people who strolled, aimlessly now, it seemed, up and down the avenues" (*Q*, 48). This feeling develops at times into "an excruciating agony" that colors her experiences of vibrant, crowded urban spaces (*Q*, 53). "Even the great buildings, the flying cabs, and the swirling crowds seemed manifestations of purposed malevolence" (*Q*, 40). If these attacks usefully may be seen as examples of what William James defines as "pure experience," a way of living in the present moment, "which precedes the categorical casting of experience into subject or object," it is less clear that they culminate in "thoughtless movement at the peak of thought, without purpose or object."[41] Helga's attacks of agoraphobia lead her consciously to seek, not avoid, further mobility.

While Helga fears open spaces at times, at other moments she fears being trapped or confined. Larsen was not alone in connecting agora- and claustrophobia; in this era, most authors who discussed these topics linked the two. In psychology journals and the popular press in the 1920s, Freud's connection between childhood experiences, particularly those related to sexuality, and phobic behavior was at the center of discussions of phobias. Significantly, many articles in the popular press about phobias stress the power of fear. Describing fear as "our mortal foe," authors compare the sensation of fear to dynamite, call it a "poisonous dose," explain that it is "a paralyzing, inhibiting, intensely disagreeable emotion."[42] Yet the pleasure associated with fear also fascinates these authors. "Almost or quite the greatest human happiness possible to the human mind follows the sudden casting-off of fear or the discovery of the possession of courage. It may literally and actually rejuvenate—change the very physical form."[43] As Larsen does in *Quicksand*, writers associated a pleasurable fear with the allure of the city, particularly New York: "New York is full of the realization of this kind of pleasure."[44]

As it vacillates between pleasure and pain, Helga's disease shifts to become a claustrophobia that is as debilitating as her agoraphobia. "She felt shut in, trapped. 'Perhaps I'm tired, need a tonic, or something,' she reflected. . . . Helga tried this, but it was no good. All the interest had gone out of living. Nothing seemed any good" (*Q*, 47). Like her agoraphobia, Helga's claustrophobia seems to strike in a variety of places, and is linked to the prospect of coming to terms with her racial identity. After her white uncle sends her money in order to ensure that Helga will never communicate with his family again, for instance, "she demanded in fierce rebellion, [why] should she be yoked to these despised black folk? Back in the privacy of her own cubicle . . . Panic seized her. She'd have to get out. She terribly needed to. Snatching hat and purse, she hurried to the narrow door" (Q, 55). And in one of the novel's most strongly racialized scenes, panic at enclosure strikes as "wild music from the heart of the jungle" washes over Helga in a cabaret. "She saw only two figures, closely clinging. She felt her heart throbbing. She felt the room receding. She went out the door. She climbed endless stairs. At last, panting, confused, thankful to have escaped, she found herself again out in the dark night alone" (Q, 62). Here, thoughts of race and sexuality combine to produce powerful feelings of entrapment for Helga.

Unlike her agoraphobia, Helga's claustrophobia has merited a good deal of critical attention. Labeling Helga's claustrophobic moments "images of suffocation," Anne E. Hostetler notes that these moments "occur in the novel when Helga sees herself through a confining construction of race and gender." Critics see these attacks as "projections of Negro self-hatred," representations of "the dual price—marriage and pregnancy—that women must pay for sexual expression," or simply as manifestations that Helga is "extremely neurotic."[45] Yet these representations shift as the novel progresses. By the end of the novel, Helga's claustrophobic moments become less explicitly racialized; they begin to emphasize "gender constructed as a biological prison."[46] The changes in Helga's feelings of suffocation suggest that these moments do not merely reveal personal neuroses but reference cultural anxieties about space and identity. The complexity of Helga's spatial identity is made clear when, in the scene before the novel's orgiastic revival meeting, Helga recalls her sexual desire for Dr. Anderson and experiences a similar "attack of nerves: "'I can't stay in this place any longer. I must get out or I'll choke' . . . Distracted, agitated, incapable of containing herself, she tore open drawers and closets trying desperately to take some interest in the selection of her apparel" (Q, 110). Here, Helga's claustrophobia is linked explicitly to her spatial identity. She fears being contained but cannot contain herself. Through these images, Larsen pathologizes Helga's spatial desires for freedom and stasis, underlining the difficulty of bringing a stable sense of place to bear upon an inherently unstable, marginal, yet untrammeled urban subjectivity.

Helga imagines that she might resolve the tension she feels between her desires for home and for mobility by leading multiple lives simultaneously, a tactic we have seen at work in a variety of urban novels. As she occupies multiple social, economic, and racialized identities, she imagines her way into multiple consciousnesses.

> She understood and sympathized with Mrs. Nilssen's point of view, as she had
> always been able to understand her mother's, her stepfather's, and his chil-
> dren's point of view. She saw herself for an obscene sore in all their lives, at all
> costs to be hidden. She understood, even while she resented. It would have
> been easier if she had not. (*Q,* 29)

All of the family members with whom Helga sympathizes here are white, a
fact that is never far from Helga's consciousness but which her appearance
belies to others. Here, Helga's ability to sympathize with her white relatives
forces her to internalize their racialized perceptions. Visibly black, she understands that she is "obscene" and embarrassing to them.

Later, however, she embraces this different perspective and extends her
powerful sympathy to her black father.

> For the first time Helga felt sympathy rather than hatred and contempt for
> that father. . . . She understood his yearning, his intolerable need for the in-
> exhaustible humor and the incessant hope of his own kind, his need for those
> things, not material, indigenous to all Negro environments. She understood
> and could sympathize with his facile surrender to the irresistible ties of race,
> now that they dragged on her own heart. (*Q,* 92)

As the intimacy of identification moves her from one racialized perspective
to another, Helga experiences a variety of painful desires and powerful feelings. Echoing W. E. B. DuBois's notion of double consciousness, she has the
"sense of always looking at one's self through the eyes of others, of measuring one's soul by the tape of a world that looks on in amused contempt and
pity."[47] The pain that Helga feels seems to be linked to an intense experience
of a restrictive subject position that forces her to abandon her usually mobile sense of self.

In some ways, Helga's desire and ability to adopt new identities echoes a
type of mobile identity that we have seen in other urban novels' female characters, such as Priscilla in *The Blithedale Romance,* Verena in *The Bostonians,* Carrie in *Sister Carrie,* and Undine in *The Custom of the Country.* But
unlike these characters, whose mobility is associated most significantly with
changes in class status, Helga's biracial background and brown skin make
an untrammeled mobility impossible. Helga's racial history, unlike a particularly classed past, can never be erased. Thus, the relationship between appearance and identity registers very differently in *Quicksand* than it does in
Custom or *Carrie.* Once they learn how to use them, Undine's beauty and
Carrie's appeal become indispensable tools in their professional and social
ascents. Helga does possess a striking appearance; like Carrie she learns how
to play up her looks. Yet for Helga, an attractive appearance is always associated with a demeaning sexual objectification that Larsen persistently
links to race. Even as Helga attempts to adopt the serial mode of identity

that is available to Carrie and Undine, her racial background makes this impossible.

The sense that a serial self might offer Helga relief from the stress of leading multiple lives is spatialized in her belief that happiness might be best found in transit. Geographic motion offers her—at least temporarily—a peace that she cannot otherwise attain. On board her ship for Denmark, Helga revels "like a released bird in her returned feeling of happiness and freedom, that blessed sense of belonging to herself alone and not to a race" (Q, 64). On her return to New York, she more thoroughly considers her drive for motion.

> She couldn't stay. Nor, she saw now, could she remain away. Leaving, she would have to come back. This knowledge, this certainty of the division of her life into two parts in two lands, into physical freedom in Europe and spiritual freedom in America was unfortunate, inconvenient, expensive. It was, too . . . a trifle ridiculous, and mentally she caricatured herself moving shuttle-like from continent to continent. (Q, 96)

These fleeting moments of freedom and peace make clear that mobility itself is critical to Helga's happiness, yet the fact that (unlike Undine and Elmer Spragg) she does not have the means to shuttle perpetually between continents emphasizes that mobility is a privilege, a luxury not always available to those on the economic margins.

Because the "divided self" that Park so hopefully links with modernity, progress, and civilization requires a certain level of economic independence, it eventually becomes as unsustainable for Helga as it is problematic for Park. Yet, the intimacy that structures her novel allows Larsen to outline a psychological and spatial strategy for coping with the tension between psychological/geographic stasis and mobility. Repeatedly, yet always temporarily, Helga attains a tenable equilibrium between motion and stasis by enacting a relation to space for which Park's theoretical detachment from intimacy cannot allow.

Borrowing Space, Mobilizing Intimacy

Through most of *Quicksand,* Helga's spatial strategy is to borrow the spaces she wishes to inhabit, postponing the stasis and economic demands of ownership. She cultivates affective bonds with her Danish relatives and her friend Anne Grey in order to inhabit the spaces they have constructed. Through borrowing, she develops a relationship to space that allows her to suspend ownership, assume prefabricated identities, and operate outside the realms of both production and consumption. If Helga's shifting consciousness seems to be linked to her racial identity, her strategy for coping with the pain

inflicted by a set subject position is linked to her gender. She utilizes sentimental strategies in order to gain access to the spaces she desires. And, as
long as she remains unmarried and postpones reducing herself to the biological determinism of motherhood, Helga can enjoy the luxury of settings
she cannot otherwise afford. An interesting parallel to Helga's strategy is
visible in James Weldon Johnson's *Autobiography of an Ex-Colored Man*
(1912). Before his marriage, the ex-colored man assumes the somewhat
emasculated position of companion to his wealthy patron, a decision that allows him to travel to Europe. In this way, he borrows a luxury he cannot access alone. When he marries, however, he must abandon this flexibility and
identify himself as a white heterosexual man in order to maintain the degree
of privilege that he has come to enjoy with his patron. Like the ex-colored
man, Helga cultivates a detachment from heterosexual relationships, especially marriage, in order to maintain her physical mobility and psychological freedom.

From the beginning of the novel, Helga defers the tension between her desire for home and her need for mobility by borrowing other peoples' spaces.
The homes Helga constructs are emphatically not her own; she is both
housed and homeless, safe and mobile. Spatial borrowing is at work from
the novel's first scene, which introduces Helga by describing the setting she
has created for herself in the dormitory room that she occupies as a teacher
at Naxos, a fictional all-black school that combines elements of the Tuskegee
Institute and Fisk University.[48] Helga's room is a place for "intentional isolation," a refuge from the restrictive "educational community of which she
[is] an insignificant part at Naxos" (Q, 1). She has taken great care to select
items for her surroundings that will make her room a beautiful haven. "Furnished with rare and personal taste," the room contains vibrant decorations:
a blue Chinese carpet, brightly covered books, a brass bowl "crowded with
many-colored nasturtiums," and a stool covered in "oriental silk" (Q, 1).
Within Naxos's confining institutional structure, Helga has constructed a
temporary home, a space that defines and protects her in part because the
elements that make it hers are eminently portable. The room itself belongs
to Naxos; Helga's stay there, as we quickly learn, is brief. The home she has
constructed can be tossed in a suitcase or abandoned, as it is when Helga
leaves Naxos for Chicago and then New York.

Like Park's marginal man, Helga maintains her freedom to borrow by
resisting the stasis of home. For Helga, this means avoiding intimacy, marriage, sex, and especially motherhood. She embodies Park's notion of cultural adaptation; he claims that as individuals move through different communities, they "learn to accommodate themselves more or less completely to
the conditions and the code of the area into which they move" even if they
are not "able to adapt . . . fundamentally and biologically to [a] new environment."[49] The distinction between biology and culture is significant here.

Park seems to think that the two can be separated, and that the biological somehow can be subsumed to the cultural; in Helga's case this is impossible. Biology, both racialized and sexualized, continually asserts itself in the novel, threatening to contain Helga and impinge upon her freedom.

At Naxos, the problem of biology is emphasized through discussions of Helga's parentage. When she considers marrying James Vayle, her Naxos suitor, Helga's inability to "naturalize" at the school stands in sharp contrast to her would-be husband's smooth acculturation there. While Helga blames this difference on her lack of prestigious family ties, she also notes her own unwillingness to give up her own ties: "She hadn't really wanted to be made over" (Q, 7). Later, she asserts first the place and then the biology of her birth when she explains to the school's principal her decision to leave. Although the class-conscious Dr. Anderson reassures Helga that her birth in the slums of Chicago "can't destroy tendencies inherited from good stock," her reply emphasizes the racial, ethnic, and cultural irregularities of her parents: "The joke is on you, Dr. Anderson. My father was a gambler who deserted my mother, a white immigrant. It is even uncertain they were married" (Q, 21). When the biological "truth" about Helga's identity emerges, she must move on.

Larsen situates Helga's borrowing in a larger cultural moment by drawing a parallel between Helga's activity and the relationship between Harlemites and New York. "While the continuously gorgeous panorama of Harlem fascinated her, thrilled her, the sober mad rush of New York failed entirely to stir her. Like thousands of other Harlem dwellers she patronized its shops, its theaters, its art galleries and its restaurants, and read its papers without considering herself a part of the monster" (Q, 45). Here, Helga can participate in the culture of a place without joining it. In an urban symbiosis, Helga can buy goods and entertainment; she can eat, read, and appreciate art without committing herself to the experience. She is not stirred. She cannot elude or deny the meaning of place, but borrowing allows her to defer it. This image also explicitly links Helga's mobility to her urban identity, and back to Park's construction of mobility and marginality. Here, her status as a Harlem resident (read, her race) allows her to suspend her relation to New York. It does not threaten to consume her; there is no danger that she will become "part of the monster." Importantly, in this borrowed place, Helga is free of her competing spatial desires.

Helga's pattern of borrowing develops as she moves from place to place, assuming the identities that other people construct for her as she temporarily inhabits their homes. The nature of Helga's transitory existence is prefigured by her choice to purchase a berth in a Pullman car instead of sharing a seat with another passenger on the train from Alabama to Chicago. Here, she is deciding what kind(s) of proximity she can tolerate. Although she can hardly afford it, Helga opts for the Pullman berth, which offers personal space in the midst of activity and connection as well as freedom from the overwhelming sensory experiences of the train. The Pullman car echoes the spatial function of the dormitory even as it casts privacy as a commodity that Helga can barely manage to buy.

While Park's marginal man maintains his mobile identity by resisting the intimate bonds of home, Helga maintains her mobility by animating narratives of affect and sentiment. If she cannot buy her own space, Helga can negotiate identities that will allow her to use desirable spaces without paying for the privilege. After hearing Helga's life story, her first post-Naxos employer, the lecturer Mrs. Hayes-Rore, fabricates a background for Helga that will allow her social and spatial entrée into Harlem's upper class. Advising Helga not to reveal that her mother was white, Mrs. Hayes-Rore muses, "I'll just tell Anne that you're a friend of mine whose mother's dead. That'll place you well enough and it's all true. I never tell lies. She can fill in the gaps well enough to suit herself and anyone who asks" (Q, 41). The affective impact of an orphan girl, the sentimental novel's stock in trade, works remarkably well upon Anne Grey. After Mrs. Hayes-Rore's introduction, Helga feels "her hand grasped in quick sympathy, and [hears] Anne Grey's pleasant voice, with its note of wistfulness, saying, I'm so sorry, and I'm glad Aunt Jeanette brought you here" (Q, 42). By gaining Anne's sympathy, Helga gains access to her home.

In New York, then, Helga animates a stock identity in order to attain the luxury of personal space within the urban landscape; she uses the housing she occupies to create the sense of stillness in motion that she craves. When Anne offers to share her home with Helga, "Helga didn't, of course, require to think it over, because lodgement in Anne's home was in complete accord with what she designated as her 'aesthetic sense'" (Q, 44). As Goldsmith notes, "Anne has achieved that harmonious interplay between her body and physical space that Helga craves."[50] Anne's beautiful home is filled with furniture, art, and artifacts that Helga appreciates but could never afford: "brass-bound Chinese tea-chests, luxurious deep chairs and davenports, tiny tables of gay color, a lacquered jade-green settee with gleaming black satin cushions, lustrous Eastern rugs, ancient copper, Japanese prints, some fine etchings, a profusion of precious bric-a-brac, and endless shelves filled with books" (Q, 44). Living as Anne's guest allows Helga to enjoy proximity to Anne's beautiful possessions while remaining unfettered. At first, borrowing seems to be the one experience Helga has that is not preferable as fantasy but becomes better as it continues. "Gradually in the charm of this new and delightful pattern of her life she lost that tantalizing oppression which always, it seemed, had been a part of her existence" (Q, 45). Yet the charm eventually erodes, and a liberating inheritance, combined with the threat of a binding sexual desire for Dr. Anderson, who has moved to New York, pushes Helga to seek a new equilibrium through motion—and a new home in Denmark.

Finding a new space to occupy requires Helga to take on a new identity. If the innocuous orphan girl inspires affective bonds of sympathy, Helga's Copenhagen role as an exoticized, "savage" black woman alludes to a different story of intimacy, a story of desire for the hyper-racialized other. Helga understands that this exotic identity is her Danish aunt and uncle's—and perhaps Europe's—construction; she assumes it as she puts on the revealing clothing, rich fabrics, and conspicuous jewelry that her relatives choose and buy for her. By consciously inhabiting a racialized and sexualized "jungle creature" identity, Helga can enjoy the beauty, luxury, and relative privacy of her surroundings. In the Dahls' house, she experiences the "sensation of lavish contentment and well-being enjoyed by impecunious sybarites waking in the houses of the rich. But there was something more than mere contentment and well-being. . . . Always she had wanted, not money, but the things which money could give, leisure, attention, beautiful surroundings" (*Q*, 67). Like Undine Spragg, Helga sees this luxury as "her proper setting," but unlike Undine, Helga makes no particular commitment to it. She does not attempt to change it to suit her changing desires. Though she assumes this home and the aesthetic experiences it offers, Helga retains her mobility by discarding rather than remaking it when it no longer suits her needs. Marriage, which offers Undine economic and spatial mobility (and which for Undine, after all, is only temporary), to Helga represents the threat of stasis and the impossibility of psychological or geographic change. As long as she rejects the social bond of marriage and the biological bind of motherhood, Helga can remain free. But this neat formulation, like many a theoretical framework, breaks down in the face of lived experience; Helga's theory doesn't account for her powerfully disruptive desire.

Along with her desires for home and motion, which are present throughout the novel, Helga's sexual desire develops as the novel progresses. Primarily, Helga is dogged by her attraction to Dr. Anderson. This attraction, which becomes inconvenient when Anderson marries Helga's friend and former host, Anne Grey, is made manifest in a furtive yet passionate kiss at a cocktail party. Though Helga initially fights

> against him with all her might. . . strangely, all power seemed to ebb away, and a long-hidden, half-understood desire swelled up in her with the suddenness of a dream. Helga Crane's own arms went up about the man's neck. When she drew away, consciously confused and embarrassed, everything seemed to have changed in a space of time which she knew to have been only seconds. (*Q*, 104)

This fabulous kiss unleashes an "irrepressible longing," throwing her into a "mental quagmire" (*Q*, 106). Ultimately, the kiss leads her, in the face of convention and her own "feeling of fear from possible exposure," to make an appointment for an assignation with Anderson (*Q*, 107). But this is a major miscalculation on Helga's part.

Helga's decision to consummate her desire for Anderson works differently from her decisions to choose home or mobility. For when Anderson rejects her, instead of veering immediately toward an exaggerated chastity (in the way she decides to travel when she begins to feel confined), Helga experiences an obliteration of self that makes her earlier troubles seem minor. Helga is devastated. "She felt alone, isolated from all other human beings, separated from even her own anterior existence by the disaster of yesterday" (Q, 109). The experience of exposing her desire and having it rejected disconnects Helga from others and from her self, from her past—from her identity. "Over and over she repeated: 'There's nothing left but to go now.' Her anguish seemed unbearable" (Q, 109). Leaving, which always has seemed so attractive to Helga, now becomes not empowering but isolating. It is anguish even to think about. Yet she refuses to extinguish herself. Death, which she briefly contemplates, "would reduce her, Helga Crane, to unimportance, to nothingness. Even in her unhappy present state, that did not appeal to her" (Q, 109). As she returns to her senses, she turns to the solution that she has always relied on.

Helga, of course, does go out. And when she does, she is incorporated into her environment in a way she never has been before. Helga is "walking rapidly, aimlessly," when the city becomes active. Rain and wind soak her clothes. "The streets become swirling rivers." And then a "whirl of wind lashed her, and, scornful of her strength, tossed her into the swollen gutter" (Q, 110). Suddenly, she merges with her environment. In one way, she achieves the "incorporation" that Park sees as inevitable in the urban landscape. But Larsen presents this incorporation as ugly, violent, and distinctly unappealing to the fastidious Helga. If Helga has opened herself to this incorporation by acknowledging her desire, Larsen quickly reveals the dangers of Helga's ambivalent position. A part of the city, she reacts to its force by exerting agency of her own. But her effort only lands her in the evangelical church where she will meet her future husband, beginning a spiral of desire and stasis that becomes Helga's quicksand.

In the storefront church where Helga takes refuge, Park's notion of incorporation takes a different turn, becoming a merging of the self into the bodies that make up the church. Three motifs in this section show how Helga's incorporation experience in the church is both like and unlike the urban incorporation that Park imagines. Most obviously, the parishioners sing a hymn whose refrains progress from "All of self and none of Thee" to "Some of self and some of Thee" and finally, to "less of self and more of Thee" (Q, 112). Although the hymn ostensibly emphasizes oneness with God, it is easy to read the lyrics as advocating an abnegation of self altogether. The second motif is the rain that continues falling and can be heard even over the voices of the choir. The rain merges the church with the city outside; as Helga connects with the parishioners she "weeps unrestrainedly" in an echo of the downpour outside (Q, 112).

Although the narrator remarks that Helga is "well entertained," not taken in by the performance, she is sucked quickly into the orgiastic service, "foul, vile, and terrible, with its mixture of breaths, its contact of bodies, its concerted convulsions, all in wild appeal for a single soul. Her soul" (*Q*, 113). This orgy image is described more graphically than the earlier "jungle" dance club scene. Like the dance club, and like the city itself, the church becomes a place of contact among bodies; but in the church, the contact has an aim. And it works: Helga cries "torrents of tears" and merges with the crowd (she refuses to do this in the dance club), becoming one with the city and with the church that echoes it. Hours later, after she sleeps with the Reverend Pleasant Green, she decides to marry him and choose a life of sex and stasis over mobility. Marriage to Green represents "a chance at stability, at permanent happiness" (*Q*, 117). Unfortunately for Helga, permanence is calamitous.

Helga's last journey is to the premodern world of the rural South, where her strategy of borrowing proves unsustainable. When Helga returns to Alabama having married Reverend Green, she attempts at first to situate herself as an outsider who can provide a progressive dose of uplift to the rural community by introducing modern practices and aesthetics. "Her young joy and zest for the uplifting of her fellow men came back to her. She meant to subdue the cleanly scrubbed ugliness of her surroundings to soft inoffensive beauty, and to help the other women to do likewise" (*Q*, 119). Perhaps Helga here is attempting to borrow yet another identity, that of the female reformer "lifting as we rise" in the manner of Frances E. W. Harper's title character Iola Leroy.[51] Yet Helga's effort to maintain her outsider status— to borrow the rural South in order to fulfill yet another idealized version of her identity—quickly breaks down. In a rural world, where home is static, she no longer can adopt new identities and discard old ones.

When she arrives in Alabama to begin her married life, it is clear what role sentimental fantasies have played in constructing Helga's visions of rural life, marriage and motherhood.

> To Helga this was a new experience. She was charmed by it. To be mistress in one's own house, to have a garden and chickens, and a pig; to have a husband— and to be "right with God"—what pleasure did that other world which she had left contain that could surpass these? Here, she had found, she was sure, the intangible thing for which, indefinitely, always she had craved. It had received embodiment. (*Q*, 120)

In an otherwise unsentimental novel, Helga's desire for home is overtly and overly romanticized; it is clearly the stuff of fantasy, a fantasy shared, Dana Brand notes, by a "distressingly large proportion of well-educated Americans [who] have given credence to the idea that peace of mind can only be attained in the modern world by fleeing the city."[52] The fact that Helga considers the house her own reinforces the economic position that she has gained as a result of her marriage, yet it emphasizes that she has left her borderland beyond the economics of possession.

As a cultural fantasy, Helga's rural house initially takes on the valence of the idealized cottages in nineteenth-century literature. As it did for Ruth Hall, by effacing its ties to modernity, "home" comes to exist for Helga outside of and in opposition to "that other world" of the city; it fulfills the cravings Park genders as irrational—the desire for "some cave or hut or tenement—in which to live and vegetate."[53] Physical reality, biology, and gendered imperatives seem more powerful than the ephemeral pleasures of the urban.

Yet, echoing *Ruth Hall*'s critique of the sentimentalized cottage, in *Quicksand* the realities of marriage and motherhood in poverty render the rural home confining, not sustaining. When the stasis of home "receives embodiment" in Helga's pregnancies, her sentimental notions quickly evaporate. After giving birth to twin boys and a daughter in "the short space of twenty months," Helga can only summon a "sick disgust at the disorder around her, the permanent assembly of partly emptied medicine bottles on the clockshelf, the perpetual array of drying baby-clothes on the chair-backs, the constant debris of broken toys on the floor, [and] the unceasing litter of half-dead flowers on the table" (Q, 124). As the physical manifestations of home are destabilized and displaced, Helga's home begins to resemble Park's cave, while the people become vegetables.

In the rural setting, biology curtails Helga's strategy of spatial borrowing. Through a continuous (and continuing) stream of pregnancy and childbirth, Helga's own body becomes borrowed space. No longer borrower but borrowed, she is immobilized, captive to the stasis of home, shut out from the modern world. The only remaining vestiges of her modern mobility are found in books; yet because she is too weak to read, her books must be read to her by people who do not understand their meanings. As she recuperates, Helga's imagination carries her to the freedom of urban space. "It was so easy and so pleasant to think about freedom and cities, about clothes and books, about the sweet mingled smell of Houbigant and cigarettes in softly-lighted rooms filled with inconsequential chatter and laughter and sophisticated tuneless music. It was so hard to think out a feasible way of retrieving all these agreeable, desired things" (Q, 135).

Ironically, in her complete immobility Helga transcends the vegetative state Park attributes mainly to women; she finally comes to "realize that other characteristic of mankind, namely, to move freely and untrammeled over the surface of mundane things and to live, like pure spirit, in [her] mind and in [her] imagination alone."[54] The fact that her travels are imaginary perhaps allows her more freedom than she might enjoy in an actual city; at the same time, this passage highlights the importance of translating theory into practice. Imagining the city, if easy and pleasant, does not replicate the experience—actually experiencing urban life simply is not feasible.

Helga, of course, has chosen this path: "With [Green] she willingly, even eagerly, left the sins and temptations of New York behind her to, as he put it, 'labor in the vineyard of the Lord' in the tiny Alabama town where he was pastor to a scattered and primitive flock" (*Q*, 118). Helga's desire to find something authentic in rural life shows how powerfully the pastoral mode, so significant in the urban novels of Hawthorne and Fern, still asserts itself in the 1920s. As I noted in chapter 1, the complex pastoral's protagonist travels from city to country and returns; once the traveler returns to the city, he or she becomes the author. But unlike Ruth Hall or Coverdale, who retain their mobility and gain the creative power of authorship, Helga becomes stuck when she reaches Alabama.

Helga may see marriage as the fitting ending to her story, but as we have seen time and time again, the linear narrative ending happily ever after in marriage rarely structures urban texts. Urban novels present the city as a place of creative generation, especially for women—of literature (*Ruth Hall*), of political theory (*The Bostonians*), of theater (*Sister Carrie*), and of wealth (*The Custom of the Country*). Taking various trips from country to city, these texts both rely on and revise the complex pastoral. Significantly, in all of these texts, the city is the place where ideas and stories are created; creating children, as Helga does in *Quicksand*, prevents her from returning to urban space as she has done so many times before in the novel. Of the other protagonists in this study, only Undine Spragg and Ruth Hall have children, managing to combine mobility and maternity. At the end of the novel, Helga attempts to return to the city imaginatively, through literature. But her relationship to literature is distant and mediated. She lacks the strength even to read the books she craves, let alone write her own narrative. Though children are created, the pastoral cycle—and Helga's creative life—are aborted.

Helga's inability to return to the city shows, perhaps, that the pastoral fantasy cannot resonate when the body is allowed to assert itself. The pastoral connects city and country through the assumption that people can always go back and forth, an assumption that Park extends in his argument linking marginality and mobility to liberation. But *Quicksand* reminds us that that mobility is a privilege: a class privilege, a race privilege, a gender privilege. And it is a privilege disrupted by sexuality and biology. For Helga, sexual desire is a powerful force that brings the brain and body together—that, in Park's terms, combines the biological and the spiritual, the mundane and the imagination. But, as Claudia Tate notes, "by repeatedly reducing desire to sexual desire, Helga condemns herself to the consequences of female biology—too frequent pregnancies."[55] First her body, and forever her soul will be occupied by the presence of other people. For Helga, ethereal desire has very concrete consequences. The results of her actions cannot be suspended; they are not theoretical.

Thus Helga's borrowing reaches its limit. As Hostetler notes, "Helga finds that one cannot escape from the cultural constructs of race and gender in a life of the body—for this is where these constructs are the most imprisoning. And when she abandons her restless search for identity, she finds that the search is the only self she knows."[56] The body similarly troubles Park's theory. Only by ignoring gender, race, and intimate bonds can he construct a workable theory of marginality. Urban novels like *Quicksand* reveal that the body's particularity—and individuals' particular experiences within these bodies—are never effaced, especially for "marginal" urban subjects. As novels emphasize, urban spaces are only successfully constructed when they make concrete the connections between motion and stasis, anonymity and intimacy, freedom and safety.

The tension between interest and sentiment is not resolved easily; novels clearly show that intimacy, the home, and the family always make part of the urban landscape, and this disrupts Park's neat oppositions. George Hutchinson argues that "the desire of the text in *Quicksand* is for a world in which races would not exist and women's bodies would not be mortgaged to them."[57] Park theorizes a world where this is so—and though the novel may indeed desire these things, it will not allow us to believe that this desire can be achieved. Helga's gender and sexuality complicate Park's notions of marginality, asserting not only that gender is centrally significant to discussions of marginality but that intimacy itself must register in these discussions as well. Park notes that "in the long run, however, people and races who live together, sharing in the same economy, inevitably interbreed, and in this way if in no other, the relations which were merely cooperative and economic become social and cultural" (*HM*, 140). For Park, then, the mulatto/mulatta, subject embodies the tension and transition between the "symbiotic" and the "social." Freed from social bonds by his or her mobility, the mulatto/mulatta urbanite also operates as the identifiable sign of intimacy and affective bonds that in effect stabilize—by bringing "home"—the movement of the city.

If marginal class status may be erased or obscured in the urban mosaic, racial and gender characteristics are not effaced as easily, and this is problematic for Park's formulations. Park's concern with race both as inheritance and as appearance is emphasized when he cites a 1914 essay on "Racial Assimilation in Secondary Groups" declaring that individuals who bear a "distinctive racial hallmark . . . cannot become a mere individual indistinguishable in the cosmopolitan mass of the population." "The Negro," the essay continues, "is condemned to remain among us an abstraction, a symbol" of difference (*HM*, 150). Race's role in an urban identity cannot be resolved in Park's terms, for those like Helga who are marked racially as "other" can never be incorporated into the urban mosaic.

Mixing race guarantees that the social can never be replaced by the symbiotic and that sentiment cannot be displaced by interests. Park's utopian notion that the marginal man is the emancipated man thus has problems in its own right, for the mulatto, unless he does not carry a "distinctive racial hallmark"—unless, in other words, he can pass for white, "cannot become a mere individual indistinguishable in the cosmopolitan mass of the population." These problems are compounded by gender: The mulatta's presence indicates not simply a biological but a familial connection that for Park implies the presence—or at least the trace—of intimacy and sentiment. Even in Park's clearest statements on marginality, from which he attempts to exclude considerations of gender and intimacy, a person of mixed race cannot be seen as thoroughly marginal and therefore freed from bonds of sentiment, even if the person inhabits a space that emphasizes his or her mobility. The mulatta body, then, visibly signifies the highest degree of unresolved tension between mobility and home in the urban landscape.

Quicksand's conclusion describes Helga surfing a wave of pregnancies that continues past the book's last lines: "And hardly had she left her bed and become able to walk again without pain, hardly had the children returned from the homes of the neighbors, when she began to have her fifth child" (*Q*, 135). The forces of gender, sexuality, and the body virtually to imprison Helga are clear to contemporary critics, most of whom read the novel's ending as signaling Helga's death. Evoking the novel's title, most readers agree that Helga finally succumbs to cultural and physical forces that conspire to entrap her. "The dinginess of her physical surroundings (poverty), the lack of intellectual stimulation, the petty hostility of the preacher's congregation, and the continual strain of childbearing finally succeed in suffocating her, drawing her into the quicksand from which she had been trying to escape all her life."[58] Noting that "the structure of the novel is a vertical line downward," Deborah McDowell asserts that "Helga goes to the deep South where she is buried alive. Perhaps this resolution was as unsatisfying for Larsen as it has remained for her readers."[59]

If the last lines of *Quicksand* emphasize that Helga is entrapped by her biology, they do not state unequivocally that her imprisonment is permanent. Indeed, the ambiguity of the novel's ending can imply a dramatically different ending: "there is no telling that Helga will remain submerged in the quagmire of a Southern rural life and childbearing. Her fate is both *of* quicksand and *as* quicksand; and, as bodily motion is the 'essence of life,' she may indeed resurface."[60] The suspended quality of the novel's ending might lead us to imagine a future for Helga; perhaps it is more useful, however, to emphasize that even in her physical stasis, Helga retains a desire and ability to move mentally, if not physically. Mobility stands alongside gender and sexuality as the last vestige of modernity that clings to Helga when all of the other trappings of the modern are stripped away.

Sentiment and Social Science

Larsen's depictions of Helga's relations to urban space and to the home in Harlem, Copenhagen, and Alabama must be seen as more than a series of contradictory yet coexistent images. Not simply a pastiche echoing Park's construction of the city as "a mosaic of little worlds," *Quicksand* positions the novel as the vehicle that can best carry out Park's mission of understanding subjective relations to space in the city (*CS*, 40). As I have noted, whether by coincidence or intent, Park's work helped to shift sociology's focus away from social reform (where women played a strong role) and toward social theory (an exclusively male domain). Aiming to bring a scientific vigor to sociology, Park demanded of (or inspired in) his protégés a commitment to developing the questions, methods, and theories that would further an "objective" understanding of the city. As he argued in 1929, "Natural science came into existence in an effort of man to obtain control over external and physical nature. Social science is now seeking, by the same methods of disinterested observation and research, to give man control over himself."[61] Mary Jo Deegan notes that "Park employed the rhetoric of 'objectivity' and 'science' . . . to strip away the linkages between theory and application."[62] In privileging scientific methods and "disinterested" observation and research, Park distanced himself and his work from the more practical efforts of his activist colleagues at the University of Chicago.

Park aimed to move social science from a practical to a theoretical realm, yet modeling sociological methods on the natural sciences meant rejecting the intimacy practiced by reformers like Jane Addams and her Hull House colleagues. At the same time, the intimate knowledge of cities that Park gained in his reportorial wandering, along with his fascination with cities' human elements, leads the question of intimacy to surface in—and disrupt—even his most highly theoretical works. In "The City as a Social Laboratory," an essay originally published in *Chicago: An Experiment in Social Science Research,* Park ends his discussion of the field (divided neatly into sections with headings such as "Human Nature and the City" and "The Urban Community") with an almost Hawthornean sentiment:

> in the city all the secret ambitions and all the suppressed desires find somewhere an expression. The city magnifies, spreads out, and advertises human nature in all its various manifestations. It is this that makes the city interesting, even fascinating. It is this, however, that makes it of all places the one in which to discover the secrets of human hearts.[63]

Here, the intimacy with the city that Park derives from personal experience seems to be the very thing he yearns for, here wistfully, in the midst of an academic text devoted to objective social science. Intimacy enables knowledge while emphasizing the transient quality of that knowledge. Park finds the city's secrets and "suppressed desires . . . interesting, even fascinating." But it remains unclear both whether these secrets and desires could be mapped, numbered, or analyzed statistically, and how truths about these affective qualities of urban life would emerge from disinterested social scientific study. Even as he tries to eliminate subjective concerns from his theoretical approach, "the secrets of human hearts" continue to penetrate, trouble, and perhaps ultimately drive Park's theoretical formulations of urban space.

I began this chapter by referencing Park's connections between fiction and sociology; I end by suggesting that even as Park was developing his methods for understanding relationships between place and identity, novels would continue to represent urban spatial identities—in the case of *Quicksand,* the possibilities for a mobile identity forced to grapple with realities of race and gender—in ways that sociology could not. The novel form narrates the bodily experience of a theoretical "what if?" as it imagines how characters' subjectivities develop in relation to the spaces they inhabit. In constructing a novel whose structure animates Park's mosaic, Larsen can represent, through fiction, the complexity and turbulence of the state of mind Park ascribes to the modern subject. Thus, even as social science turned away from considering the affective impact of the city's spatial operations, urban novels kept these questions in play by continually asking and constructing what it means to be at home in the city.

Epilogue

As we collectively produce our cities, so we collectively produce ourselves. Projects concerning what we want our cities to be are, therefore, projects concerning human possibilities, who we want or, perhaps more pertinently, who we do not want to become. Every single one of us has something to think, say, and do about that.   —David Harvey[1]

In this study, I have explored fictional and historical characters' complicated interactions with and interventions into two competing views of the American urban landscape. One, the deterministic view articulated most clearly in the naturalism of Stephen Crane and the utopianism of Charlotte Perkins Gilman, sees the urban environment as an irresistibly shaping force that insinuates itself into the very beings of the people who live there. In these narratives, only a superhuman effort, combined with luck, money, and political support, can allow people to take control of their lives in urban space. Most urban novels, however, ascribe more complexity to the relationships among characters and settings. Many urban characters clearly seize opportunities for control over their settings, from the individual bachelor girl's apartment to the grand scale of Undine Spragg's Fifth Avenue Pitti Palace.

These competing views of the city rarely operate in such a tidy manner, and their force has not been balanced. In novels, in literary history, in historical narratives, and in real life, the deterministic narrative has tended to be privileged over the agency narrative in the development of American cities. Even Jane Addams, whose work in the Hull House settlement was geared toward giving some of Chicago's poorest and least powerful residents the opportunities and support they needed to thrive as they adjusted to modern urban life, recently has been recast as a meddling bourgeois spinster whose central project was to force her captive audience to erase their ethnic identities as they subscribed to her middle-class ideals. For urban activists, it is hardly a heartening trend.

Yet I believe that one of the enduring appeals of urban life is precisely that agency successfully combats such cultural determinism, often in small but significant ways. Urban observers such as Jane Jacobs, Michel de Certeau, and David Harvey have pointed out that despite its monolithic façade, the city is a place of myriad opportunities. As I noted in chapter 1, de Certeau reminds us that "beneath the discourses that idealogize the city, the uses and combinations of powers that have no readable identity proliferate."[2] Whether they express their conceptions of the city through novels or landscape architecture, photography or sociology, most of the urbanists in this study allow for this possibility of resistance, of agency, to percolate through their work.

Throughout this book, I have argued that the stories told about the spaces that we inhabit constitute the most fundamental way in which we understand who we are in relation to where we live. Stories help us to understand ourselves as urban dwellers and help define our relationships to the urban spaces we share with others. In novels, this dynamic is played out in symbolic connections between setting and character, as well as in narrative relationships among setting, character, and plot. As an academic exercise, exploring these relationships in novels and historical documents is interesting, but the bigger question of how stories operate in the consciousnesses of real people is harder to answer. Novels, photographs, and architectural plans all register traces of thinking, ideas, and experience about urban subjectivity. I believe, however, that novels offer something unique to students of relationships between environment and humanity: Through narrative, novels vivify imagined landscapes and allow the reader to enter into, to inhabit, to share these settings. Many novels, of course, allow readers the opportunity to experience, imaginatively, places that are inaccessible through other means. Twenty-first-century readers gain access to cultures, societies, times, and places that only exist in story; for many readers this access is one of the novel's chief attractions. In urban novels, this is especially important because the experience of sharing space with characters and inhabiting someone else's narrative is so similar to the experience of inhabiting urban space.

In my first chapter, I argued that the story offers one powerful way to enact agency in urban space. According to de Certeau, "stories diversify, rumors totalize . . . stories [become] private and sink into the secluded places in neighborhoods, families and individuals."[3] As this book has revealed, the stories that urban dwellers construct about the spaces they inhabit, though perhaps initially private, may be summoned out of seclusion and into public space to become some of the most powerful tools to effect change—or to resist the seemingly totalizing forces at work in the urban landscape, even today. Recently, I had occasion to put this insight to use.

When I began this project, I lived in a small single-family house in Seattle, Washington, a city very unlike the urban landscapes I have sketched in this book. My neighborhood was filled with the 1920s version of Andrew Jackson Downing's cottages—the small bungalows on small lots that are characteristic of many American cities in the Midwest and West. And even though, when we put the house on the market, our real estate agent marketed it as "in the heart of an urban village," the closest we got to inhabiting shared space with our neighbors was building a gate between our tiny backyards—and sharing a lawnmower for the even tinier strips of grass between our sidewalk and the street.

When I was halfway through writing this study, my family left Seattle and moved to Somerville, Massachusetts, exchanging the leave-it-to-Beaver atmosphere of our blocks of bungalows for a side-by-side duplex defined on our title as a "tenement dwelling." My new neighborhood, like many city neighborhoods around Boston, is in transition. The end of rent control in neighboring Cambridge, the forces of gentrification, low interest rates, and the profitability of converting apartments to condominiums all have led to major development pressure and an influx of new residents into what was once a streetcar suburb.[4] In a city like Somerville, where a person is considered "new" if he or she moved into a particular ward (from another area of the city) fewer than twenty years ago, there is certainly tension between the old timers and new arrivals like my family and me.

Living in this changing landscape has led me to think about my scholarship in new ways. I still call attention to the moments in novels when sounds and smells permeate shared spaces, but now that my own experience includes hearing my neighbor's vacuum through our shared wall and closing my windows so I don't have to smell her tenant's cigarettes, I have a new perspective on the dynamics at work in the novels I study. Most of the time, my neighborhood only vaguely echoes the earlier spaces I have discussed in this book. The houses outwardly have not changed much since they were built a century ago, but patterns of work and family life in the city have shifted, leaving the block with fewer extended families, fewer children, more professionals, and a less vibrant shared culture than the neighborhood had, according to some of my neighbors, even thirty years ago. Yet we are still connected to one another.

Beyond sounds and smells, the most powerful element connecting me to my new neighbors is our shared open space. Somerville is one of the densest cities in the country, and open space is rare. From the front, my tightly packed street of duplex houses is very typical of the Somerville landscape. But behind our houses, things look very different. Five yards in a row are separated by low fences, but are connected by a canopy of green in a series of gardens. At one end of the block, an ivy-covered brick building, formerly a winemaking factory but today a major architecture firm, shields us from the noise of the nearby arterial road. On a hot summer day, the temperature is at least ten degrees lower in the back than it is in the front by the street, and in the cool of the evening, all of the neighbors are out in their gardens or on their patios and decks, enjoying the oasis we have built in our corner of town.

But this part of the city, like the rest of Somerville, is under incredible development pressure. On our block alone, we have seen three major housing construction projects in the last two years. Although they have all added to the density of housing in the area, most of the projects that have been built in our neighborhood have developed moribund sites—a set of derelict garages became row-house condominiums; a house destroyed by fire is being replaced by three large single-family structures; a long-vacant lot eventually will hold a massive apartment building. Each of these projects, of course, had to be approved by the city's zoning and planning boards, and in every case a neighborhood meeting allowed residents to give their input on the projects. And we did, even if, in many cases, our concerns seemed to go by the wayside as construction progressed.

Although they may not see it this way, the urban developers in our neighborhood operate under the assumption—often correct—that a largely transient population will mount little or no opposition to particular projects. This assumption both relies upon and extends the narrative of architectural determinism that I have outlined in this study. It is both an abstraction that accounts for a particular relationship between people and the built environment, and more importantly it is a force with significant power to transform actual landscapes. If the inhabitants of an area are assumed to be without agency, they simply are not worth considering when it comes time to build.

Recently, a real estate developer bought one of the houses on our street. He proposed building a house behind the original structure that would fill the entire backyard—a yard that sits in the middle of the contiguous lots that afford us our green space. Apparently, he expected little opposition to his plans. The deterministic narrative—and the corollary that urban dwellers will not tend to fight development—was at work. Even though he had himself lived in one of the houses around the corner from the proposed project, he obviously saw urban property as an investment rather than as home.

As the house sat vacant, and the grass in the backyard grew longer and longer, the future of the property became a source for great neighborhood gossip. First, much to my daughter's delight, we heard that a family with young children had bought the house. Then we saw surveyors out measuring the property. My neighbor Ed heard from Rocco, the retired man who walks his arthritic dog around the block, that "something big" was going to happen back there. When the house had been vacant for about six months, we received a notice from the city's Zoning Board of Appeals, notifying us that the owners intended to seek a special permit to build a second single-family house on the lot.

When the notice came out, the neighborhood came to life. The neighbor who owns the other side of my duplex cornered first me and then my husband to tell us how incredibly upset she was, dissolving into tears at the thought of a new house encroaching on her backyard. My husband called a friend who previously had worked as a city planner to find out what the Zoning Board was likely to do. That evening, more neighbors, this time a couple I had spoken to only in passing, dropped by (a common occurrence in Seattle; virtually unheard of in Boston) to strategize and make a plan. The threat we perceived moved all of us to act—to claim the agency that city dwellers always have exerted over their spaces—in order to protect the shared space we all considered vital to our life in the city.

What did we do? We looked at the plans, wrote letters to the Planning Board, circulated a petition, and called our aldermen. Once our alderman got wind of how upset we were, she told the developers that they needed to call a neighborhood meeting. We packed the room, expressed our opposition to the plans at the meeting, and two days later, the house was back on the market.

In claiming the agency to determine the future of our property and neighborhood, what we did was probably typical of what most people do when they feel their homes are threatened. What is more remarkable, though I didn't think about it in these terms at the time, is how much our tactics echoed the strategies and arguments I advance in this book. We went to the Planning Office, copied the plans, studied them, and circulated them among our neighbors. I read the zoning laws with the kind of attention I usually reserve for novels, looking for details that would allow us to speak the Zoning Board's language. When the city planner who was working on this case mentioned that the ZBA might listen to arguments about green space, I drew on all of the Olmstedian language I could muster in order to make claims about links between trees and urban health. Like Jacob Riis, we took photographs of the neighborhood and property from porches, skylights, and a neighbor's roof.

But most importantly, we told stories. The planner told us that we could do three things to fight the permit: attend the Planning and Zoning Board meetings, circulate a petition, and write letters. He didn't tell us what to write in our letters, but when we started to receive copies of the letters that people wrote, it became clear why letters were so effective. The arguments our neighbors made about the importance of the space were bolstered most powerfully by the stories we told. We are a diverse group of people. We have different backgrounds, are different ages, speak different languages. But we all were willing to fight to protect "our" green space. And we all felt that stories were our best hope.

Two neighbors who represent two different faces of the city told especially powerful stories about the space. Elaine Murphy, sixty, is a lifelong Somerville resident. The daughter of Portuguese immigrants, Elaine lived with different members of her extended family both in her childhood and after a brief marriage left her a single mother in the late 1960s. After she re-married, she and her husband bought the other half of our house, where Elaine has lived since 1979. A passionate gardener and devout Catholic, Elaine has a strong commitment to the community and to her land. This commitment is shared by Kate Wheeler, a relative newcomer who has lived on my street for ten years.

Kate begins her letter with perhaps the most familiar narrative opening in the English language. "Once upon a time," she writes, "we had an idyllic neighborhood here. Our lots were unusually large, there was little traffic, and we felt this counteracted the crowded, treeless, aluminum-sided atmo-sphere that has led many people to call our city 'Slummerville.' We had only a few trees on the sidewalks but several large trees in the backyards com-pensated, especially the large white pine trees at _____. I still look at them from my kitchen every morning. In the past few years my husband and I have listened sadly as saws ripped down two large street trees to accommo-date more parking on our street. Now there is only one street tree left."[5] Here Kate evokes a sort of urban pastoral. She calls the neighborhood idyl-lic and emphasizes the natural landscape. Here are echoes of Frederick Law Olmsted, who wrote: "We want, especially, the greatest possible contrast with the restraining and confining conditions of the town, those conditions which compel us to walk circumspectly, watchfully, jealously, which compel us to look closely upon others without sympathy."[6] As Olmsted did, Kate makes the trees an integral part of the urban scene; for both, the town and the trees only make sense in combination.

Kate evokes pastoral elements at other points in her letter, each time hark-ing back to a past that has been destroyed even in the relatively short time she has lived on the street. "Meanwhile there's heavy construction of a large condo building . . . where crabapples and wild catalpas once grew. It wasn't a park, it was a vacant lot, but it was at least open space. Soon our street will be gated by two big brick towers."[7] Clearly, the vacant lot that Kate de-scribes is not some kind of rural retreat. Yet she emphasizes that it was a space that allowed native plants to grow, that provided a contrast to the brick towers, and that is now irrevocably gone. It is important to notice how this stance ironizes the "Once upon a time" of Kate's beginning. Clearly, this is not a fairy tale set in the mythic past. The story is happening now; and she is calling on the city government to intervene and give the story a happy ending.

Elaine's letter begins as another conventional narrative: the memoir. She writes:

> I've lived in Somerville just about all my life. My family lived for five years at my grandmother's two-family house around the corner from my property with grapevines in the back yard, family gatherings, wonderful times. My grand-mother would point out from her kitchen window—since she was unable to

climb stairs—a speck of paper that might have fallen from a barrel put out on trash day for me to pick up. Respect for property, land, neighbors, that's what I learned very young.

My parents went on their own and I grew up in a three-decker with a backyard that was not kept up by the landlord—with tall weeds and an old jalopy in the backyard, a gigantic plot of unused land—but there was a patch of soil next to the house. I got a bag of morning glory seeds and beautified that part of our yard—next to the in-the-ground garbage pails. It didn't matter; beauty was near it all day.[8]

Like Kate, Elaine evokes an idyllic past. But Elaine refers here to a past marked by connections—among neighbors, within families, and between individuals and the landscape in which they live. Elaine's opening recalls an older Somerville that is increasingly less familiar except in the parts of the city that remain populated by recent immigrants: a city of multi-unit dwellings often shared by family members. When Elaine's parents "went out on their own," they did not go far but remained several blocks away; Elaine now lives "around the corner" from her grandmother's old house. Notably, Elaine emphasizes the responsibility to the landscape she "learned very young": the grandmother directing her to the paper littering the sidewalk, her decision to plant flowers near the garbage pails on a property that clearly was neglected by the landlord. This story is a different version of Kate's urban pastoral. It is not a landscape where neighbors stand by and listen sadly while trees are cut down; rather, it is a setting where a young girl has the power—and the duty—to improve the place where she lives.

The second feature these stories share is an emphasis on the connected backyards as common space. Kate, maintaining her Olmstedian belief in the power of greenery, shifts gears in her letter to construct the series of backyards as one piece of property held in common by the neighbors. She writes, "The gardens behind this side of _____ are a precious, breathing spot of green that enlivens the whole block. All homeowners—around the corner and all the way to _____ Street—enjoy the green that still remains behind our houses. It is like a park held in common."[9] The word "common," defined in the *Oxford English Dictionary* as "of general, public, or non-private nature," is significant here.[10] Rhetorically, referring to the land as "a park held in common" allows Kate to distance her argument from the not-in-my-backyard resistance that homeowners often mount against deleterious projects (which, of course, often results in those projects simply moving to places where residents lack the means or wherewithal to oppose them). In fact, these backyards are fenced private property. But they are connected visually, and we might see Kate putting forward a new definition of "common" that relies on vision and makes the city dweller king of all he or she surveys. Constructing the space as public space—as a common—has extra resonance in the Boston area, where many communities have maintained as parks the town commons that developed as shared pastureland when the cities had a more rural character. These commons are also communal property: "the common land or estate; the undivided land belonging to the members of a local community as a whole. Hence, often the patch of unenclosed or 'waste' land which remains to represent that."[11] Somerville, unlike neighboring Cambridge and Boston, does not have a common, and in fact has very little park space. Kate thus obliquely raises the claim that if the city can't be a steward for the land, the residents can.

Shared stewardship is a prominent theme in Elaine's letter as well. Like Kate, Elaine stresses the natural landscape and the sense of responsibility that it instills in its inhabitants. She writes that throughout the twenty-five years that she has lived in her house, the neighbors next door all tended to the plot of land where the new house would stand:

> The last property owner . . . and previous renters all took pride and received pleasure from the property in the rear of the house—pleasure in nature with the three majestic pine trees that line up in the back of the property, roses, green grass. A wedding took place there, numerous activities, musical groups, cookouts all took place in that backyard property; even an award from the Somerville Garden Club was presented to one of the *renters* for his gardening and beautification attempts in that backyard. Vegetable gardens in some yards, flowers in others enjoyed by all (emphasis in original).[12]

Again, in contrast to Kate's emphasis on urban nature, Elaine's narrative accentuates the variety of positive relationships that people have had to the particular property in question. All of us, of course, can see each other's backyards; everyone would have heard the bands, smelled the cookouts, and witnessed the wedding. This is a story of shared space linking people together, allowing them to participate, if passively, in the landmarks, celebrations, and rituals that give our lives meaning.

The idea that inhabitants exert agency in the landscape runs throughout Elaine's letter; here she extends her narrative from the land to the built structures. "I chose to buy a house already in existence—my neighbors chose to buy already existing homes also—replacing and fixing what we financially could [to] have the convenience of city living while enjoying our piece of heaven in our own and our neighbors' already existing plots of back yards."[13] The message of this story is clear. Our commitment to our homes and our community allow us to enjoy a communal heaven on earth.

If Nathaniel Hawthorne was correct when he argued in his *American Notebooks* for "the greater picturesqueness and reality of back-yards, and everything appertaining to the rear of a house; as compared with the front," what can we learn from the ways in which these residents understand the function of the backyards?[14] The arguments we see in these letters suggest a conception of communal property and shared responsibility that is the natural outgrowth of Elaine's early lessons about who may exert control over a landscape—namely, the people who inhabit it. I have suggested throughout this book that the shared spaces of the urban landscape can help build a dispersal of self over property that can take on utopian tones, as it does in *Ruth Hall*, *Sister Carrie*, and much of Charlotte Perkins Gilman's fiction set in cities. This belief clearly structures the stories my neighbors tell about the landscape as they redefine private space as public, shared space. In a landscape where children are taught to be stewards, protecting this heavenly space emerges as a natural, almost sacred duty.

In keeping with the notion that we are trying to halt the proposed development out of a sense of duty, all of the neighbors tend to end the narratives with a jeremiad (again perhaps appropriate to the New England landscape!). Kate asks, "Who will want to live here when there's nothing left but fumes and huge packed-in boxes of housing jammed side by side and one behind the other, covering every inch of ground?"[15] Other neighbors echo the concern that the proposed changes are permanent. Everyone reminds city officials about their responsibility to the city and warns them not to set bad precedents.

Perhaps unsurprisingly, as the longest-term resident (and as the person with the most to lose), Elaine's sermon has the fieriest tone:

> Is this the direction Somerville is heading—*No open spaces for anyone—who cares!! I care, the other property owners on my street care, I'm sad to say I know the developers don't care, the only green that is appreciated is the green earned in their own pockets not the green in our yards, and the size of their open spaces that they have in their yards—in what ever city they may live in. Do the members of the Planning Board and Zoning Board care?*
>
> I've lived here in the city once called "Slummerville" and laughed when THIS city received the "All American City" award. It has become a very popular city to live in *now*. But again times change—people move, jobs change—I'll still be here at my property but so will the congestion of property next to me with the building of this misplaced housing (emphasis in original).[16]

As it turned out, unlike so many jeremiads about the urban environment, this one seemed to resonate. All of the abutters came to the hastily called neighborhood meeting. It was a diverse group that included a one-year-old baby and a neighbor in his eighties. Our neighbor Rosa came to speak on behalf of her father, who speaks only Portuguese. Elaine's tenant felt a strong connection to the project and was there as well. We packed the room and gave written and oral testimony opposing the project. The day after the meeting, the fence between the driveway and backyard was removed, revealing the backyard to the street. The next day, we saw a photographer taking pictures for a real estate listing that obviously would emphasize the backyard, and the day after that, a For Sale sign went up in front of the house.

Was it our presence that worked? Our photographs or phone calls? We believed that the stories we told would matter—that narrative could best articulate the powerful relationship we all felt to the small plots of land behind our houses. And because we felt that we all shared the space, all of us—renters, owners, newcomers, and long-term residents—worked together to protect the resource. Perhaps as property owners we were more committed stakeholders in the process than renters might have been. But we could not have been nearly so effective a force if we had not had a flexible notion of property; we all felt that the backyard of the house in question "belonged" to us in some way. As Elaine put it, "When I go out onto my back porch at _____ or in my yard, the feeling of openness, serenity, and pleasure at the surrounding from *all of the properties in my neighborhood as well as my own,* homeowners, neighbors, friends that I am sure do not have my background but they also have a respect for the land and love of beauty of the surroundings" (emphasis in original).[17]

For all of us, the space is an important part of who we are. The space itself, combined with the action we all took to protect it, reinforced and helped to develop the vision we have for our community. And even though of course things are different now, I can't help but think that our feelings of community, of belonging, of the desire and the wherewithal to resist the totalizing narrative a developer took for granted had to have been felt by city dwellers of an earlier day.

Above all, the letters bring me full circle to *Ruth Hall* and the multiplicity of voices that structure that novel. As I have noted, Fern uses multiple voices in her novel to resist a totalizing and oppressive narrative. Susan Harris calls this pattern "skaz" and notes that "the play of many voices, then, is Fern's primary tool for first rendering the verbal-political structure of gender relationships in mid-nineteenth century American culture and then casting the values associated with it into doubt."[18] The question is: Why is this strategy so powerful? When thinking about the novel in gendered terms, critics have seen Fern's strategy as a façade or a "cover." They argue that the presence of sentimental language and codes disguises the novel's radical content; more fundamentally, it allows Fern, a woman, to write at all.[19]

But beyond operating as a disguise, Fern's narrative strategy is pitched directly at odds with one strand of urban narrative: the deterministic narrative that, in denying urban voices a hearing denies city dwellers the power to use urban freedom to shape a new vision of life. In addition to first constructing and then dismantling "the verbal-political structure of gender relationships," *Ruth Hall*'s pastiche undermines gendered and political expectations about spatial relationships in the city. The voices of the novel are Ruth's material and Fern's construction, yet within the constraints of the print medium, Fern allows the voices to speak for themselves, and together they allow Ruth to develop a powerful, creative, independent, and successful subjectivity that is decidedly urban.

Ruth Hall's structure reminds us of two things: first, that many voices comprise the urban experience; and second, that together these voices can reconstruct urban space. The city, then, is like the novel, for in it many people speak, often in contradictory ways. As in any novel, some voices are powerful, and others are not. *Ruth Hall*'s radicalism lies, I think, in the way in which the standard voices of power are undermined and the regular people's are brought to the fore. The novel—the stories—allows the normative relationships of power, gender, space, and subjectivity to be broken down, rearranged, and brought into new configurations in which the least powerful have the last word.

I'm not sure that my neighbors and I have had the last word on what will or won't happen in that infamous backyard. In fact, the reason I kept the letters initially was in case another speculator bought the property and we had another fight on our hands. What I do know is that Fanny Fern's construction of urban space as a place where many conflicting stories are told and have the power to overturn readers' expectations proved to be surprisingly prescient. It was our voices, our stories, that stemmed the tide of development. Perhaps more importantly, it was our stories that allowed us as neighbors to make political one another and to make political the powerful, if previously tacit, sense that we were a community.

My last chapter shows the novel continuing to hold its own alongside sociology as a mode for understanding the city. Whether or not the novel still has compelling force in arguments about urban space and development and reform except on the most theoretical level, my experience shows me that the story still matters, that it can have political force, that it can make a difference. And that perhaps as we continue to grapple with who we are and what relationship(s) we have to the landscapes we inhabit, the urban novel can matter as a form through which our questions, and possibly some answers, have already been theorized. These texts can help those of us who embrace urban life—and perhaps others who choose to reject it—to understand our motivations, to acknowledge what is at stake in our choices, and to understand the power we have to shape the place: the city, our home.

Notes

Introduction (pages 1–15)

1. Charles Baudelaire, "The Painter of Modern Life," in *The Painter of Modern Life and Other Essays*, trans. and ed. Jonathan Mayne (London: Phaidon Publishers, 1964), 9.

2. Henry James, *The American Scene* (1907; reprint, New York: Penguin Books, 1994), 125.

3. Ibid., 70–71.

4. Ibid., 71.

5. My use of the term "industrial city" to describe American cities between the mid-nineteenth century and 1920 derives from Dolores Hayden. See *The Grand Domestic Revolution* (Cambridge: The MIT Press, 1981), 10.

6. Sharon Marcus, *Apartment Stories: City and Home in Nineteenth-Century Paris and London* (Berkeley: University of California Press, 1999), 9.

7. My discussion of these relationships is informed by the arguments laid out in: Howard Horwitz, *By the Law of Nature: Form and Value in Nineteenth-Century America* (New York: Oxford University Press, 1991); Myra Jehlen, *American Incarnation: The Individual, the Nation, and the Continent* (Cambridge, Mass.: Harvard University Press, 1986); Annette Kolodny, *The Lay of the Land: Metaphor as Experience and History in American Life and Letters* (Chapel Hill: University of North Carolina Press, 1975); Angela Miller, *The Empire of the Eye: Landscape Representation and American Cultural Politics, 1825–1875* (Ithaca: Cornell University Press, 1993); Roderick Nash, *Wilderness and the American Mind,* 3rd ed. (New Haven, Conn.: Yale University Press, 1982); Richard Slotkin, *Regeneration through Violence: The Mythology of the American Frontier, 1600–1860* (Middletown, Conn.: Wesleyan University Press, 1973); Henry Nash Smith, *Virgin Land: The American West as Symbol and Myth* (1950; reprint, New York: Vintage Books, 1957); and Gwendolyn Wright, *Building the Dream: A Social History of Housing in America* (New York: Pantheon, 1981).

8. Catharine Beecher, *A Treatise on Domestic Economy* (1841; reprint, New York: Schocken Books, 1977), 268. Adam Sweeting points out the salient difference between Beecher and Downing: Beecher's designs stressed practicality while Downing's emphasized style. For an extensive analysis of Downing's work in its cultural context, see Sweeting's *Reading Houses and Building Books: Andrew Jackson Downing and the Architecture of Popular Antebellum Literature, 1835–1855* (Hanover, N.H.: University Press of New England, 1996), 45.

9. Lora Romero, *Home Fronts: Domesticity and Its Critics in the Antebellum United States* (Durham: Duke University Press, 1997), 25.

10. See Christine Stansell, *City of Women* (New York: Alfred A. Knopf, 1986) for a cogent discussion of the association between city and vice from the late 1700s on.

11. Janet Wolff, "The Invisible *Flâneuse:* Women and the Literature of Modernity," *Theory, Culture and Society* 2, no. 3 (1985): 38. See also Dana Brand's discussion of the American flâneur in *The Spectator and the City in Nineteenth-Century American Literature* (Cambridge: Cambridge University Press, 1991).

12. Mona Domosh, *Invented Cities* (New Haven: Yale University Press, 1996), 8.

13. *Oxford English Dictionary,* Online Edition, Accessed December 1, 2004. I am grateful to Gwendolyn Wright for alluding to the etymology of the word "home" in her lecture "Desires and Domesticities," delivered at the Radcliffe Institute on November 30, 2004.

14. And sometimes not even by family members. In their analyses of Downing's cottage plans, Wright and Sweeting show how spaces inside middle-class homes, such as the library or parlor, were designed to be the exclusive domain of one sex or the other.

15. Marcus, *Apartment Stories,* 11–12. Emphasis in original.

16. Michel Foucault, trans. Jay Miskowiec, "Of Other Spaces," *Diacritics* 16, no. 1 (1986): 22.

17. Ibid., 23.

18. On separate spheres in literary scholarship, see Cathy N. Davidson, "Preface: No More Separate Spheres!" *American Literature* 70, no. 3 (1998): 443–63. See also Cathy N. Davidson and Jessamyn Hatcher, eds., *No More Separate Spheres! A Next Wave American Studies Reader* (Durham: Duke University Press, 2002); and Monika M. Elbert, ed., *Separate Spheres No More: Gender Convergence in American Literature, 1830–1930* (Tuscaloosa: University of Alabama Press, 2000). For an historiographic study of the notion of separate spheres, see Linda K. Kerber, "Separate Spheres, Female Worlds, Woman's Place: The Rhetoric of Women's History," *Journal of American History* (June 1988): 9–39.

19. Davidson, "Preface," 444.

20. Janet Wolff, "The Invisible *Flâneuse,*" 44.

21. Marcus, *Apartment Stories,* 2–3.

22. Kerber, "Separate Spheres," 22.

23. Marcus, *Apartment Stories,* 3.

24. Henri Lefebvre, *Right to the City,* in *Writings on Cities,* trans. and ed. Eleonore Kofman and Elizabeth LeBas (Oxford: Blackwell Publishers, 1996), 103.

25. Kerber, "Separate Spheres," 31.

26. The phrase comes from the title of Christopher Lasch's book, *Haven in a Heartless World: The Family Besieged* (New York: Basic Books, 1977).

27. Doreen Massey, *Space, Place and Gender* (Minneapolis: University of Minnesota Press, 1994), 2–3.

28. Ibid.

29. David Harvey, *Justice, Nature, and the Geography of Difference* (Oxford: Blackwell Publishers, 1996), 42.

30. Foucault, "Other Spaces," 24.

31. James, *American Scene,* 125.

32. Ibid.

33. Ibid.

34. Ibid. Emphasis in original.

1. Architectural Determinism and the Industrial City in The Blithedale Romance and Ruth Hall *(pages 16–50)*

1. Nathaniel Hawthorne, *American Notebooks* (entry dated May 6, 1850) in *Hawthorne's Works,* volume 9 (Boston: Houghton, Mifflin and Company, 1883), 377.

2. Herman Melville, "Bartleby the Scrivener," in *Bartleby and Benito Cereno,* reprint, (1853; New York: Dover Publications, 1990), 9.

3. Ibid., 17.

4. Herman Melville, *Pierre, or The Ambiguities* (1852; reprint, New York: Signet Classic, 1964), 23.

5. For more on Melville and the city, see Wyn Kelley, *Melville's City: Literary and Urban Form in Nineteenth-Century New York* (Cambridge: Cambridge University Press, 1996).

6. As Nina Baym notes regarding Hawthorne and domesticity, "The example of his own *The House of the Seven Gables,* which he persisted in calling his best and favorite novel, makes absolutely clear that he had a considerable stake in domestic ideology himself." (Baym, "Again and Again, the Scribbling Women," in *Hawthorne and Women,* ed. John L. Idol, Jr., and Melinda M. Ponder (Amherst: University of Massachusetts Press, 1999), 25–26. See also Gillian Brown's *Domestic Individualism: Imagining Self in Nineteenth-Century America* (Berkeley: University of California Press, 1990).

7. See Cathy N. Davidson, "Preface: No More Separate Spheres!" *American Literature* 70, no. 3 (1998): 443–63. See also Cathy N. Davidson and Jessamyn Hatcher, eds., *No More Separate Spheres! A Next Wave American Studies Reader* (Durham: Duke University Press, 2002); Monika M. Elbert, ed., *Separate Spheres No More: Gender Convergence in American Literature, 1830–1930* (Tuscaloosa: University of Alabama Press, 2000); and Linda K. Kerber, "Separate Spheres, Female Worlds, Women's Place: The Rhetoric of Women's History," *Journal of American History* (June 1988): 9–39.

8. Amy Kaplan, "Manifest Domesticity," *American Literature* 70, no. 3 (October 1998): 600.

9. See Barbara Foley, "From Wall Street to Astor Place: Historicizing Melville's 'Bartleby,'" *American Literature* 72, no. 1 (March 2000): 87–116.

10. See Joyce W. Warren, "Performativity and the Repositioning of American Literature," in *Challenging Boundaries: Gender and Periodization,* ed. Joyce W. Warren and Margaret Dickie (Athens: University of Georgia Press, 2000), 3–25.

11. Gillian Brown, *Domestic Individualism,* 121.

12. Judy Schaaf Anhorn, "'Gifted Simplicity of Vision': Pastoral Expectations in *The Blithedale Romance,*" *ESQ* 28 (1982): 136.

13. Leo Marx, *The Machine in the Garden* (Oxford: Oxford University Press, 1964), 25.

14. Anhorn, "Gifted Simplicity," 138.

15. On plans for cottages, see chapter 5 of Gwendolyn Wright, *Building the Dream: A Social History of Housing in America* (New York: Pantheon, 1981).

16. Dolores Hayden, *Seven American Utopias: The Architecture of Communitarian Socialism, 1790–1975* (Cambridge: MIT Press, 1976), 15.

17. Dana Brand, *The Spectator and the City in Nineteenth-Century American Literature* (Cambridge: Cambridge University Press, 1991), 139.

18. I refer here to Ralph Waldo Emerson's line in his 1836 essay "Nature": "Nature is thoroughly mediate." Reprinted in *Selected Essays* (New York: Penguin Books, 1985), 57.

19. Nathaniel Hawthorne, *The Blithedale Romance* (1851; reprint, New York and London: W.W. Norton, 1978), 21. Subsequent parenthetical notations cited with *BR*, refer to this edition.

20. On nineteenth-century anxieties over appearance, disguise, and identity, see Karen Halttunen's *Confidence Men and Painted Women: A Study of Middle-Class Culture in America, 1830–1870* (New Haven: Yale University Press, 1982).

21. Marx, *Machine in the Garden*, 19.

22. Leo B. Levy, "*The Blithedale Romance:* Hawthorne's Voyage through Chaos," *Studies in Romanticism* 8 (1968): 1–15. Cited in, Hawthorne, *The Blithedale Romance*, 316.

23. Marx, *Machine in the Garden*, 22.

24. See Brand, *The Spectator and the City*, for an extended discussion of Coverdale as flâneur.

25. Fanny Fern, *Ruth Hall* (1854) in *Ruth Hall and Other Writings*, edited and with an introduction by Joyce W. Warren (New Brunswick: Rutgers University Press, 1986), 28. Subsequent parenthetical notations cited with *RH*, refer to this edition.

26. Henri Lefebvre, *Right to the City*, in *Writings on Cities*, trans. and ed. Eleonore Kofman and Elizabeth LeBas (Oxford: Blackwell Publishers, 1996), 78.

27. Mastering housekeeping skills emerges as an important motif in domestic literature. Many of the most popular American novels of the nineteenth century, including Harriet Beecher Stowe's *Uncle Tom's Cabin* (1852; reprint, New York: Penguin Classics, 1986), Maria Susanna Cummins's *The Lamplighter* (1854; reprint, New Brunswick: Rutgers University Press, 1988), Louisa May Alcott's *Little Women* (1869; reprint, New York: Modern Library, 1983), and Susan Warner's *The Wide, Wide World* (1850; reprint, New York: The Feminist Press, 1987) emphasize homemaking as a reflection of the self-control so prized in a sentimental heroine.

28. Andrew Jackson Downing, *The Architecture of Country Houses* (1850; reprint, New York: Dover, 1969), 1.

29. Wright, *Building the Dream*, 80.

30. Ibid., 81.

31. Andrew Jackson Downing, *Victorian Cottage Residences* (1842; reprint, New York: Dover, 1981), 9.

32. Wright, *Building the Dream*, 86.

33. See Maria C. Sanchez, "Re-Possessing Individualism in Fanny Fern's *Ruth Hall*," *Arizona Quarterly* 56, no. 4 (Winter 2000): 25–56, for an excellent discussion of Ruth's parlor.

34. Susan K. Harris, *19th-Century American Women's Novels: Interpretive Strategies* (Cambridge: Cambridge University Press, 1990), 113.

35. Gale Temple, "A Purchase on Goodness: Fanny Fern, *Ruth Hall*, and Fraught Individualism," *Studies in American Fiction* 31, no. 2 (Autumn 2003): 140.

36. Catharine Beecher's *A Treatise on Domestic Economy* (1841; reprint, New York: Schochen Books, 1977) is perhaps the best-known, but numerous other advice manuals for homebuilders and homemakers were published in the mid-nineteenth century.

37. Gillian Brown, *Domestic Individualism*, 3.

38. Adam Sweeting, *Reading Houses and Building Books: Andrew Jackson Downing and the Architecture of Popular Antebellum Literature, 1835–1855* (Hanover, N.H.: University Press of New England, 1996), 56.

39. See Brook Thomas, "The Construction of Privacy In and Around *The Bostonians*," *American Literature* 64, no. 4 (December 1992): 721.

40. Paul Groth notes that, "By 1850 a young couple living in a boarding house or hotel were thought 'to occupy a position just as respectable as if they resided in a house of their own.'" Groth, "Forbidden Housing: The Evolution and Exclusion of Hotels, Boarding Houses, Rooming Houses and Lodging Houses in American Cities, 1880–1930" (Ph.D. diss., University of California, Berkeley, 1983), 141. Groth's quotation is from Richard A. Van Orman, *A Room for the Night: Hotels of the Old West* (Bloomington: Indiana University Press, 1966).

41. Anthony Trollope, *North America* (1862; reprint, New York: Knopf, 1951), 484; Groth, *Living Downtown: The History of Residential Hotels in the United States* (Berkeley: University of California Press, 1994), 57.

42. John Modell and Tamara K. Hareven, "Urbanization and the Malleable Household: An Examination of Boarding and Lodging in American Families," in *Family and Kin in Urban Communities, 1700–1930*, ed. Tamara K. Hareven (New York: New Viewpoints, 1977), 165; Hareven, "Introduction" to *Family and Kin*, 9.

43. Groth notes that though no legal definitions exist for either the boarding house or the hotel, one difference between the two is that by tradition stemming from English law, hotels had to accept any guest who was able to pay and "fit to be received," while lodging-house managers could choose their guests and enter into individual agreements with different guests for their room and board. Groth, "Forbidden Housing," 29.

44. Wright, *Building the Dream*, 38. As Paul Groth notes, however, "by the 1830s, boardinghouse life had become rather prevalent among well-to-do men and women in American cities." Groth, "Forbidden Housing," 37.

45. See, for example, Maria Georgina Milward, "Mrs. Sad's Private Boarding House," *Southern Literary Messenger* 12 (1846): 691.

46. I treat the idea of urban contagion more fully in chapter 3.

47. Examples of disease and death occurring at home under the care of the family abound in sentimental literature. In *Little Women*, Beth dies clinging "to the hands that had led her all her life, as father and mother guided her tenderly through the valley of the shadow, and gave her up to God" (Alcott, 514). Similarly, Alice's death in *The Wide, Wide World* occurs in the presence of her brother John and their charge, Ellen. Little Eva's death in *Uncle Tom's Cabin* is another tableau that evokes the transformative power of family and death.

48. Milward, "Mrs. Sad's Private Boarding House," 691.

49. Norman S. Hayner, *Hotel Life* (Chapel Hill: University of North Carolina Press, 1936), 98–99.

50. Thomas Butler Gunn, *The Physiology of New York Boarding Houses* (New York: Mason Brothers, 1857), 135, 138.

51. Gwendolyn Wright notes: "The homes of the elite—whether mansions, row-houses, or fashionable boardinghouses—were grouped together." Wright, *Building the Dream*, 39.

52. Groth, "Forbidden Housing," 38–39.

53. Groth, *Living Downtown,* 127.

54. Leslie Dorsey and Janice Devine, *Fare Thee Well: A Backward Look at Two Centuries of Historic American Hostelries, Fashionable Spas, and Seaside Resorts* (New York: Crown Publishers, 1964), 188.

55. Costard Sly, *Sayings and Doings at the Tremont House in the Year 1832,* volume 2 (Boston: Allen and Ticknor, 1833), 103. Emphasis in original.

56. Ibid., 105.

57. See Brand, *The Spectator and the City,* 133 for another discussion of this important passage.

58. Lefebvre, *Right to the City,* 89.

59. Michel de Certeau, *The Practice of Everyday Life,* trans. Steven Rendall (Berkeley: University of California Press, 1984), 92.

60. Ibid., 97.

61. Nathaniel Hawthorne, *American Notebooks,* quoted in *The Blithedale Romance,* 249 fn 7.

62. Henri Lefebvre, *The Production of Space* (Oxford: Blackwell Publishers, 1991), 143.

63. Wright, *Building the Dream,* 25.

64. Brand, *The Spectator and the City,* 134.

65. Later, Robert Park would call this persona the "marginal man," a concept I explore more fully in chapter 6. See Park, "Human Migration and the Marginal Man," in *Classic Essays on the Culture of Cities,* ed. Richard Sennett (1928; reprint, Englewood Cliffs: N.J.: Prentice Hall, 1969), 131–42.

66. Here couched in a bad joke at the expense of the Irish, the phenomenon of many unrelated people sharing a single room was fairly common in U.S. cities in the eighteenth and nineteenth centuries. See Groth, "Forbidden Housing," chapter 2.

67. See Sharon Marcus *Apartment Stories: City and Home in Nineteenth-Century Paris and London* (Berkeley: University of California Press, 1999), on the presence of ghosts in British and French fiction about apartments.

68. Gunn, *Physiology of New York Boarding Houses,* 32–33.

69. David Harvey, *The Urban Experience* (Baltimore and London: Johns Hopkins University Press, 1989), 83.

70. Ibid.

71. Ibid., 230.

72. de Certeau, *Practice of Everyday Life,* 109.

73. Gillian Brown, *Domestic Individualism,* 123–24.

74. Richard Brodhead, "Veiled Ladies: Toward a History of Antebellum Entertainment," *ALH* 1, no. 2 (Summer 1989): 274.

75. Ibid.

76. See, for instance, Barbara F. Lefcovicz and Allan B. Lefcovicz, "Some Rents in the Veil: New Light on Priscilla and Zenobia," *Nineteenth-Century Fiction,* 21 (1966): 263–75.

77. Nina Baym, "*The Blithedale Romance:* A Radical Reading," *Journal of English and Germanic Philology* 67 (1968): 560.

78. Groth, *Living Downtown,* 126.

79. Gale Temple extends Habermas's argument to claim that "Ruth's tiny family

of herself and two daughters" constitutes itself "in opposition to a hostile and alien-ating public realm" ("Purchase on Goodness," 134).

80. "Samuel Simpleton," Letter to the Editor, *Rambler's Magazine* 1 (1809): 85; E.B.C., "Mr. Clarence Gower: or, a Peep Into a 'Genteel' Boarding House," *Knicker-bocker* 4 (1834): 49.

81. Wright, *Building the Dream*, 39.

82. Charles E. Norton, "Model Lodging-Houses in Boston," *Atlantic Monthly* 5 (1860): 680.

83. E. B. C., "Mr. Clarence Gower," 49.

84. Milward, "Mrs. Sad's Private Boarding House," 691.

85. "Prayer Meetings in Boarding-Houses," *Christian Herald* 8 (1822): 732; Norton, "Model Lodging Houses," 680.

86. Groth, *Living Downtown*, 127.

87. Karen Waldron, "No Separations in the City: The Public-Private Novel and Private-Public Authorship," in Elbert, *Separate Spheres*, 98.

88. Lefebvre, *Right to the City*, 105.

89. de Certeau, *Practice of Everyday Life*, 95.

90. Ibid., 108.

91. Review of *Ruth Hall*, Crescent City (New Orleans), January 1885. Cited in Joyce W. Warren, Introduction to *Ruth Hall*, xvii. The "she" in this quotation could have referred to either Ruth Hall or her creator, for the novel was highly auto-biographical and several of Fern's portraits of Ruth's relatives were easily recogniza-ble as members of Fern's family.

92. Cited in Linda Grasso, "Anger in the House: Fanny Fern's *Ruth Hall* and the Redrawing of Emotional Boundaries in Mid-Nineteenth-Century America," *Studies in the American Renaissance* (1995): 252.

93. Sanchez, "Re-Possessing Individualism," 28.

94. David M. Henkin, *City Reading: Written Words and Public Spaces in Ante-bellum New York* (New York: Columbia University Press, 1998), 12.

95. Ibid.

96. See Waldron, "No Separations."

97. Brodhead, "Veiled Ladies," 288.

98. Henkin, *City Reading*, 11.

99. Lefebvre, *Right to the City*, 109.

100. See Harris, *19th-Century Women's Novels*, 116.

101. Brand, *The Spectator and the City*, 155.

102. See Jane Jacobs, *The Death and Life of Great American Cities* (New York: Vintage Books, 1992), for a very positive look at neighborly surveillance.

103. de Certeau, *Practice of Everyday Life*, 92.

104. Denis Cosgrove, "Spectacle and Society: Landscape as Theater in Premodern and Postmodern Cities," in *Understanding Ordinary Landscapes*, ed. Paul Groth and Todd W. Bressi (New Haven: Yale University Press, 1997), 101.

105. Anhorn, "Gifted Simplicity," 141.

106. de Certeau, *Practice of Everyday Life*, 92.

107. Ibid., 93. The city Hawthorne presents is never planned and readable—it can only appear so in the eyes of the very unreliable narrator.

2. The City's Drawing-Room (pages 51–89)

1. Henry James, *The American Scene* (1907; reprint, New York: Penguin Books, 1994), 133.

2. Roy Rosenzweig and Elizabeth Blackmar, *The Park and the People: A History of Central Park* (1992; reprint, New York: Henry Holt and Company, 1994), 28; Granville Ganter, "N. P. Willis," *The Encyclopedia of American Literature* (New York: Continuum Press, 1999), 1244–45.

3. Willis's publicity, however, was not always positive. He was "satirized as a scandal-mongering dilettante" by many observers, including William Makepeace Thackeray. Ganter, "N. P. Willis," 1244–45.

4. Calvert Vaux, *Villas and Cottages* (1857; reprint, New York: Da Capo Press, 1968), 248.

5. Rosenzweig and Blackmar, *The Park and the People*, 217.

6. Henry James's anxieties over modernity stood in marked contrast to his brother William's more optimistic pragmatism about the prospects for the cosmopolitan city in American culture. See Ann Douglas, *Terrible Honesty* (New York: Farrar, Straus and Giroux, 1995); and Ross Posnock, *The Trial of Curiosity* (New York: Oxford University Press, 1991).

7. Anthony Scott, "Basil, Olive, and Verena: *The Bostonians* and the Problem of Politics," *Arizona Quarterly* 49, no. 1 (Spring 1993): 50.

8. Mona Domosh argues that "Boston's wealth was most evidently displayed in its domestic landscape (parks and residential architecture)." *Invented Cities* (New Haven: Yale University Press, 1996), 4.

9. Several articles on *The Bostonians* draw connections between the novel and modern material culture, including: Ian F. A. Bell, "Language, Setting and Self in *The Bostonians*," *MLQ* 49, no. 3 (1988): 211–38, and "The Personal, the Private, and the Public in *The Bostonians*," *Texas Studies in Literature and Language* 32, no. 2 (Summer 1990): 240–56; Janet Wolf Bowen, "Architectural Envy: 'A Figure Is Nothing without a Setting,'" *New England Quarterly* 65, no. 1 (1992): 3–23; Wai Chee Dimock, "Gender, the Market, and the Non-trivial in James," *The Henry James Review* 15 (1994): 24–30; Philip Fisher, "Appearing and Disappearing in Public: Social Space in Late-Nineteenth-Century Literature and Culture," in *Reconstructing American Literary History*, ed. Sacvan Berkovitch (Cambridge, Mass.: Harvard University Press, 1986), 155–88; Brook Thomas, "The Construction of Privacy In and Around *The Bostonians*," *American Literature* 64, no. 4 (December 1992): 719–47; Chris Walsh, "Stardom Is Born: The Religion and Economy of Publicity in Henry James' *The Bostonians*," *American Literary Realism* 29, no. 3 (1997): 15–25; and Lynn Wardley, "Woman's Voice, Democracy's Body, and *The Bostonians*," *ELH* 56, no. 3 (Fall 1989): 639–65. Ross Posnock's "Henry James, Veblen and Adorno: The Crisis of the Modern Self," *Journal of American Studies* 21 (1987): 32–53, is also very helpful in situating James's take on modernity within economic critiques.

10. Doreen Massey, *Space, Place and Gender* (Minneapolis: University of Minnesota Press, 1994), 170.

11. Ibid., 7.

12. Dolores Hayden, *Redesigning the American Dream* (New York: W.W. Norton, 1984), 28.

13. Edmund Burke, *A Philosophical Enquiry into the Origin of Our Ideas of the Sublime and Beautiful* (Notre Dame: University of Notre Dame Press, 1968), 137.

14. Vaux, *Villas*, 51.

15. Angela Miller, *The Empire of the Eye: Landscape Representation and American Cultural Politics, 1825–1875* (Ithaca: Cornell University Press, 1993), 13.

16. Frederick Law Olmsted, "Public Parks and the Enlargement of Towns," in *Civilizing American Cities: A Selection of Frederick Law Olmsted's Writings on City Landscapes*, ed. S. B. Sutton (Cambridge: The MIT Press, 1971), 77.

17. Ibid., 82.

18. Miller, *Empire of the Eye*, 13.

19. Olmsted, "Public Parks," 96.

20. Karen Halttunen, "From Parlor to Living Room: Domestic Space, Interior Decoration and the Cult of Personality," in *Consuming Visions*, ed. Simon J. Bronner (New York: W.W. Norton and Company, 1989), 159.

21. Rosenzweig and Blackmar, *The Park and the People*, 185.

22. Olmsted, "Public Parks," 70.

23. Ibid., 72.

24. Miller, *Empire of the Eye*, 11.

25. Olmsted, "Public Parks," 77.

26. Rosenzweig and Blackmar, *The Park and the People*, 185.

27. See Tamara K. Hareven, "The Home and the Family in Historical Perspective," in *Home: A Place in the World*, ed. Arien Mack (New York: New York University Press, 1993), 227–59, for a lucid discussion of the transition from the home defined as a space of sociability to the home as private space.

28. Vaux, *Villas*, 43.

29. Ibid., 44.

30. Ibid.

31. William Alex, *Calvert Vaux, Architect and Planner* (New York: Ink, Inc., 1994), 92.

32. Ibid., 91.

33. Calvert Vaux, "Parisian Buildings for the City's Residents," *Harper's Weekly*, December 19, 1857, 809.

34. Ibid., 810.

35. Vaux, *Villas*, 55.

36. Vaux, "Parisian Buildings," 810.

37. Edith Wharton, *The House of Mirth* (1905; reprint, New York: W. W. Norton, 1990), 32.

38. This was a commitment to which Vaux adhered throughout his professional career; many of his later architectural commissions were for social service buildings in New York such as hospitals, museums, numerous lodging houses for boys and girls, and, as I will discuss in the next chapter, model tenements for the Improved Dwellings Association. See Alex, *Calvert Vaux*.

39. Olmsted, "Public Parks," 65–66.

40. Ibid., 70, 73.

41. Ibid., 81.

42. Ibid., 70, 73.
43. Ibid., 80.
44. James, *American Scene*, 132.
45. Olmsted, "Public Parks," 93.
46. Rosenzweig and Blackmar, *The Park and the People*, 211.
47. Olmsted, "Public Parks," 52.
48. Ibid., 53.
49. Ibid., 56.
50. Ibid., 54.
51. Rosenzweig and Blackmar, *The Park and the People*, 307.
52. Ibid., 222.
53. Ibid., 221.
54. Ibid., 308.
55. *New York Herald*, May 31, 1877. Quoted in Ibid., 320.
56. Abraham Cahan's *Yekl*, in *Yekl and the Imported Bridegroom* (1896; reprint, New York: Dover Publications, 1970); and Charles Chesnutt's "The Wife of His Youth" in *The Wife of His Youth and Other Stories of the Color Line* (Ann Arbor: University of Michigan Press, 1972), provide two fictional accounts of the conflicts between modern "American" and earlier marriages. See Werner Sollors, *Beyond Ethnicity* (New York: Oxford University Press, 1986).
57. Rosenzweig and Blackmar, *The Park and the People*, 225.
58. Ibid., 308.
59. James, *American Scene*, 131–32.
60. Ibid., 132.
61. For an extended discussion of the figure of the actress in literature at the turn of the century, see my article, "A Taste for Center Stage," in *Exploring Lost Borders: Critical Essays on Mary Austin*, ed. Melody Graulich and Elizabeth Klimasmith (Reno: University of Nevada Press, 1999), 129–49.
62. James, *American Scene*, 133.
63. Ibid., 137.
64. Ibid.
65. Henry James, *The Bostonians* (1886; reprint, New York: Penguin Classics, 1986), 320. Subsequent parenthetical notations marked *TB*, refer to this edition of the novel.
66. Bowen, "Architectural Envy," 6.
67. Ibid., 4.
68. Halttunen, "From Parlor to Living Room," 171.
69. Vaux, *Villas*, 95–97.
70. Quoted in Halttunen, "From Parlor to Living Room," 187.
71. Domosh notes that "Boston's elite espoused an ideology of commitment to the community and to the welfare of its citizens" (*Inverted Cities*, 10).
72. Janet Wolf Bowen notes that Olive's "house, as is evident from its location on Charles Street and from James's descriptions, is a Boston row house, that stalwart monument to mythic American claims to equality, simplicity and order" ("Architechtural Envy," 9).
73. Domosh, *Invented Cities*, 33.

74. Caroline Field Levander, *Voices of the Nation: Women and Public Speech in Nineteenth-Century American Literature and Culture* (Cambridge: Cambridge University Press, 1998), 31.

75. Theodore Dreiser, *Sister Carrie* (1907; reprint, New York: Bantam Books, 1992), 353.

76. Wardley, "Woman's Voice," 643.

77. Walsh, "Stardom," 16.

78. See Ann Douglas, *The Feminization of American Culture* for an extended discussion of feminizing influence in nineteenth-century American culture (New York: Knopf, 1977).

79. Jane Tompkins, *Sensational Designs: The Cultural Work of American Fiction, 1790–1860* (New York: Oxford University Press, 1985), xi.

80. Catharine E. Beecher and Harriet Beecher Stowe, *The American Woman's Home* (1869; reprint, New York: Arno Press, 1971), 459.

81. Gillian Brown, *Domestic Individualism,* 21.

82. Tompkins, *Sensational Designs,* 171.

83. Wardley, "Woman's Voice," 640.

84. Walsh, "Stardom," 16.

85. Wardley, "Woman's Voice," 643.

86. For an extended discussion of James's stance on these characters and on journalism more generally, see David Kramer, "Masculine Rivalry in *The Bostonians:* Henry James and the Rhetoric of Newspaper Making," *Henry James Review* 19 (1998): 139–47.

87. See David M. Henkin's chapter on newspapers in *City Reading: Written Words and Public Spaces in Antebellum New York* (New York: Columbia University Press, 1998).

88. See Posnock, "Henry James." Posnock refers to *The American Scene,* but the dialectic he imagines for James, which "sees a positive moment in commodity fetishism and conspicuous consumption as inevitably entangled with human expressiveness, creativity, and happiness" is clearly present in *The Bostonians* (34).

89. Kramer, "Masculine Rivalry," 143.

90. Scott, "Basil, Olive, and Verena," 50.

91. Samuel Warren and Louis Brandeis, "The Right to Privacy," *Harvard Law Review* 4 (1908): 196; quoted in Brook Thomas, "The Construction of Privacy In and Around *The Bostonians,*" *American Literature* 64, no. 4 (December 1992), 721.

92. In the language of landscape architects, desire lines are the paths that develop over time as pedestrians inscribe their own chosen routes onto the green spaces of a park.

93. Wardley, "Woman's Voice," 658.

94. By this I mean that entry into modern communication and transportation networks, especially through the presence of a train station (where telegraphs could be sent and received) could effectively move a rural southern community from the feudal to the modern era. Suzanne Lebsock argues that, therefore, different time periods existed in close proximity in the nineteenth-century American South. (Lebsock, unpublished lecture, University of Washington, 1996).

95. Ransom's impulse to confine Verena's performances to his home has been the

object of much critical scrutiny, with critics like Philip Fisher and Alan Tractenberg arguing that Verena's escape from the mechanisms of modern performance will allow a restoration of a "private self" (Fisher, "Appearing and Disappearing," 189). Wardley and Brook Thomas counter that, in fact, "we may only imagine an escape, for when Basil promises Verena that 'the dining-table itself shall be our platform, and you shall mount on top of that,' (*TB,* 379) we see that she will never not be performing" (Wardley, "Woman's Voice," 660). My argument that Verena's modern subjectivity is essentially a performance governed by the influence of her setting aligns me with Wardley and Thomas.

96. Bowen, "Architectural Envy," 13.

97. Chromolithographs, more commonly known as "chromos," were inexpensive reproductions of paintings popular in the nineteenth century. See Michael Clapper, "The Chromo and the Art Museum: Popular and Elite Art Institutions in Late Nineteenth-Century America," in *Not At Home: The Suppression of Domesticity in Modern Art and Architecture,* ed. Christopher Reed (London: Thames and Hudson, 1996), 33–47.

98. Bell, "Language, Setting and Self," 214.

99. Walsh, "Stardom," 15.

100. Brook Thomas, "Construction of Privacy," 733.

101. See Posnock, "Henry James."

102. Wardley, "Woman's Voice," 646.

103. Elsie de Wolfe, *The House in Good Taste* (New York: The Century Co., 1914), 159.

104. Domosh, *Invented Cities,* 63.

105. Joyce A. Rowe, "'Murder, what a lovely voice': Sex, Speech, and the Public/ Private Problem in *The Bostonians,*" *Texas Studies in Literature and Language* 40, no. 2 (Summer 1998): 162, 171.

106. Nancy Cott, *The Grounding of Modern Feminism* (New Haven: Yale University Press, 1987), 174.

107. In the Merchant-Ivory film version of *The Bostonians,* we see the beginnings of Olive's performance. James Ivory, dir. (1984; VHS reproduction Los Angeles: Rhino Home Video, 1993).

108. Massey, *Space, Place and Gender,* 7.

109. This is particularly true of Bowen's article, which situates Olive's house in the Back Bay.

110. Karl Haglund, *Inventing the Charles River* (Cambridge: MIT University Press, 2003), 101.

111. Charles E. Beveridge and Carolyn F. Hoffman, eds., *Papers of Frederick Law Olmsted, Supplementary Series Volume 1* (Writings on Public Parks, Parkways, and Park Systems) (Baltimore: Johns Hopkins University Press, 1997), 50. Though his concern with ameliorating the physical experience of tenement dwellers through a combination of aesthetic and scientific means was perhaps new for Olmsted, it was increasingly typical of reformers as the Progressive Era, with its settlement houses, urban housekeeping, and public health campaigns, unfolded. Playgrounds and parks would play a significant role in these reforms.

112. Haglund, *Inventing the Charles River,* 101.

113. Massey, *Space, Place and Gender,* 5. Emphasis in original.

3. The Tenement Home (pages 90–127)

1. Jacob Riis, *The Peril and Preservation of the Home* (Philadelphia: George W. Jacobs and Company, 1903), 79.

2. Edward W. Townsend, *A Daughter of the Tenements* (New York: Lovell, Coryell and Company, 1895), 70.

3. Jacob Riis, *How the Other Half Lives* (1890; reprint, New York: Dover Publications, 1971), 1. All further references to this volume will be noted parenthetically in the text with *OH*.

4. Cindy Weinstein, "How Many Others Are There in the Other Half? Jacob Riis and the Tenement Population," *Nineteenth-Century Contexts* 24, no. 2 (2002): 201.

5. Doreen Massey, "A place called home?" in *Space, Place and Gender* (Minneapolis: University of Minnesota Press, 1994), 169.

6. Riis was not alone in this belief; see Gwendolyn Wright, *Building the Dream: A Social History of Housing in America* (New York: Pantheon, 1981), 125–128, for an overview of the impact of the separation ideal on plans for urban housing.

7. Peter B. Hales, *Silver Cities: The Photography of American Urbanization, 1839–1915* (Philadelphia: Temple University Press, 1984), 194.

8. Luc Sante, *Low Life: Lures and Snares of Old New York* (New York: Farrar, Strauss and Giroux, 1991), 29.

9. Peter Hall, *Cities of Tomorrow: An Intellectual History of Urban Planning and Design in the Twentieth Century* (London: Blackwell Publishers, 1996), 36.

10. William Dean Howells, *A Hazard of New Fortunes* (1890; reprint, New York: Bantam Books, 1960), 61.

11. David Harvey, *The Urban Experience* (Baltimore and London: Johns Hopkins University Press, 1989), 238.

12. Keith Gandal, *The Virtues of the Vicious: Jacob Riis, Stephen Crane and the Spectacle of the Slum* (New York: Oxford University Press, 1997), 77. For Riis's relationship to Theodore Dreiser's work, see chapter 3 of Carol Shloss, *In Visible Light: Photography and the American Writer 1840–1940* (New York: Oxford University Press, 1987).

13. The line between the bedroom and the rest of the house was critical to the conception of "home"; thus, apartments in which the bedroom was visible were considered to be quite shocking, at least through the turn of the century. As Charles Loring Brace puts it: "The privacy of a home is undoubtedly one of the most favorable conditions to virtue, especially in a girl. . . . Living, sleeping, and doing her work in the same apartment with men and boys of various ages, it is well-nigh impossible for her to retain any feminine reserve, and she passes almost unconsciously the line of purity at a very early age." *The Dangerous Classes of New York* (New York: Wynkoop and Hallenbeck, 1880), 55. Later, the iconoclastic Granny Mingott's visible first-floor bedroom would shock her respectable relatives in Edith Wharton's *The Age of Innocence*. Catharine Beecher was the notable exception who advocated multiple uses for the bedroom in both suburban and urban homes. See Catharine E. Beecher and Harriet Beecher Stowe, *The American Woman's Home* (1869; reprint, New York: Arno Press, 1971).

14. Weinstein, "How Many Others," 205.

15. Jane Jacobs, *The Death and Life of Great American Cities* (New York: Vintage Books, 1992), 83.

16. Jacob Riis, *The Children of the Poor* (New York: Charles Scribner's Sons, 1902), 64.

17. Ibid., 71. Keith Gandal points out that in practical terms the desire for excitement and entertainment helped Riis as well; tenement dwellers flocked to magic lantern slide shows like those Riis produced. Gandal, *Virtues,* 82.

18. Stephen Crane, *Maggie, A Girl of the Streets,* in *The Portable Stephen Crane,* ed. Joseph Katz (1893; reprint, New York: Penguin Books, 1979), 7. Subsequent references to this text will be cited parenthetically with *MG.*)

19. Edgar Fawcett, *The Evil That Men Do* (New York: Belford Co., 1889).

20. Abraham Cahan, *Yekl,* in *Yekl and the Imported Bridegroom* (1896; reprint, New York: Dover Publications, 1970), 14.

21. Ibid., 15.

22. David M. Fine, "Abraham Cahan, Stephen Crane, and the Romantic Tenement Tale of the Nineties," *American Studies* 14 (1973): 104.

23. In fact, the Bend was razed to create a park. A subplot in *A Daughter of the Tenements* involves a Mulberry Bend resident who welcomes the change and takes the opportunity to purchase his own farm on Long Island, which he names Mulberry Court! This was not a typical fate for residents of Mulberry Bend.

24. Wright, *Building the Dream,* 118.

25. See Jacobs, *Death and Life,* 119. Keith Gandal offers an extensive analysis of Riis's tenement tourism in *Virtues;* the topic is also treated in Fine, "Abraham Cahan," 102.

26. Gandal, *Virtues,* 82.

27. The practice of listening and attempting to identify a building's sounds echoes Coverdale's hotel reveries in *The Blithedale Romance.*

28. Crane, *George's Mother,* in *The Portable Stephen Crane* (1896; reprint, New York, Penguin Books, 1979), 130.

29. Mona Domosh, *Invented Cities* (New Haven: Yale University Press, 1996), 42.

30. See Massey, *Space, Place and Gender,* 197–99.

31. Mary Sherman, National Consumers' League, "Manufacturing of Foods in the Tenements," *Charities and the Commons* 15 (1906): 670.

32. Ibid., 671.

33. Ibid., 669.

34. Ibid., 673.

35. Ibid., 669.

36. Ibid., 671.

37. Ibid., 672.

38. Ibid., 672.

39. Annie S. Daniel, "The Wreck of the Home: How Wearing Apparel is Manufactured in the Tenements," *Charities and the Commons* 14, no. 1 (1 April 1905): 624.

40. Ibid.

41. Ibid.

42. Mary Van Kleeck, "Child Labor in New York City Tenements," *Charities and the Commons* 18 (18 January 1908): 1410.

43. Amy Kaplan, "Manifest Domesticity," *American Literature* 70, no. 3 (October 1998): 582.

44. Hales, *Silver Cities,* 195.

45. The "nurseries of crime" are mentioned again on page 69 of *How the Other Half Lives,* but this time the language is attributed to Inspector Byrnes, the "chief of the Secret Police."

46. See Weinstein, "How Many Others," 200, for a discussion of Riis and mapping.

47. Robert Ezra Park, "The City as a Social Laboratory," in *Human Communities: The City and Human Ecology* (1929; reprint, Glencoe, Ill.: The Free Press, 1952), 75.

48. The map is even coded to represent apartments in which different families fill different categories. This variation necessitated the use of color, which militated against the book being reprinted, a fact that irked Addams.

49. Agnes Sinclair Holbrook, "Map Notes and Comments," in *Hull-House Maps and Papers,* by residents of Hull House (New York: Thomas Y. Crowell and Co., 1895), 9.

50. Ibid., 12.

51. Hales, *Silver Cities,* 29.

52. Ibid., 73.

53. See William Alex, *Calvert Vaux, Architect and Planner* (New York: Ink, Inc., 1994), for an extensive analysis of Vaux's reform architecture.

54. Wright, *Building the Dream,* 123.

55. Frederick Law Olmsted, "Public Parks and the Enlargement of Towns," in *Civilizing American Cities: A Selection of Frederick Law Olmstead's Writings on City Landscapes,* ed. S. B. Sutton (Cambridge, Mass: The MIT Press, 1971), 77.

56. Fine, "Abraham Cahan," 101. Note that here Fine assumes that the home is not operating as a sphere of influence in the tenement.

57. Riis further links environment to national identity in his autobiography, in which he apparently becomes American simply through his experiences in the United States. Because nothing except his long tenure in American surroundings actively transforms Riis, his autobiography offers anecdotal evidence to support Riis's environmental determinism. *The Making of an American* (1901; reprint, New York: MacMillan Company, 1924).

58. Kaplan, "Manifest Domesticity," 582.

59. Riis, *Making of a American,* 287.

60. Ibid., 288.

61. Ibid., 287, 441.

62. Ibid., 287.

63. Interestingly, Downing's distaste for multiple uses was not shared by Beecher, who often advocated the use of a rolling screen to allow a bedroom to serve as a sitting room, dining room, or parlor. Both her designs for model homes and model tenements feature these screens and emphasize the versatility of such transformable spaces.

64. Daniel, "Wreck of the Home," 624. Emphasis mine.

65. Tamara K. Hareven, "Introduction" to *Family and Kin in Urban Communities, 1700–1930* (New York: New Viewpoints, 1977), 8–9.

66. John Modell and Tamara K. Hareven, "Urbanization and the Malleable

Household: An Examination of Boarding and Lodging in American Families," in *Family and Kin in Urban Communities, 1700–1930,* ed. Tamara K. Hareven (New York: New Viewpoints, 1977), 167.

67. Elizabeth C. Watson, "Home Work in the Tenements," *Survey* 25 (4 February 1911): 777.

68. Modell and Hareven, "Urbanization," 164.

69. Jane Tompkins and Claudia Tate offer thorough examinations of the personal and public ramifications of such a feeling. See Tompkins, *Sensational Designs: The Cultural Work of American Fiction 1790–1860* (New York: Oxford University Press, 1985); and Tate, *Domestic Allegories of Political Desire: The Black Heroine's Text at the Turn of the Century* (Durham: Duke University Press, 1995). On the blend of sentimentalism and another shocking genre, the Gothic, see Betsy Klimasmith, "Slave, Master, Mistress, Slave: Genre and Interracial Desire in Louisa May Alcott's Fiction," *ATQ* 11, no. 2 (June 1997): 115–35.

70. Wright, *Building the Dream,* 131.

71. Fawcett, *The Evil That Men Do,* 19. Mass-produced chromos, a staple of middle-class decorating in the late nineteenth century, fell out of favor as "art." Michael Clapper notes that "by the early twentieth century museums had gained the power to define "high" art, and art in the home was consigned to other classifications—decoration, crafts, entertainment, kitsch, etc.—and accorded much lower status." "The Chromo and the Art Museum: Popular and Elite Art Institutions in Late Nineteenth-Century America," in *Not at Home: The Suppression of Domesticity in Modern Art and Architecture,* ed. Christopher Reed (London: Thames and Hudson, 1996), 33.

72. Crane, *George's Mother,* 95.

73. See chapter 11 of Beecher and Stowe, *American Woman's Home.* Chapter 37, "Homeless, Helpless, and Vicious," features images of tenement rooms filled with decorations.

74. Hales, *Silver Cities,* 194.

75. Wright, *Building the Dream,* 131–32.

76. For more on the transition from Beecher's aesthetic to the modern domestic aesthetic, see my "A Taste for Center Stage: Consumption and Feminism in *A Woman of Genius,*" in *Exploring Lost Borders: Critical Essays on Mary Austin,* ed. Melody Graulich and Elizabeth Klimasmith (Reno: University of Nevada Press, 1999): 129–149.

77. "Are Apartments Necessary," *Survey Midmonthly* 44 (19 June 1920): 412.

78. Mabel Kittredge, "Home-making in a Model Flat," *Charities and the Commons* 15 (4 November 1905): 176.

79. Ibid., 181.

4. The Apartment as Utopia (pages 128–60)

1. Elsie de Wolfe, *The House in Good Taste* (New York: The Century Co., 1914), 237.

2. Abraham Cahan, *Yekl,* in *Yekl and the Imported Bridegroom* (1896; reprint, New York: Dover Publications, 1970), 88.

3. Ibid.

4. On *Sister Carrie* as a naturalist text, see Philip Fisher, *Hard Facts: Setting and Form in the American Novel* (New York: Oxford University Press, 1987); June Howard, *Form and History in American Literary Naturalism* (Chapel Hill: University of North Carolina Press, 1985); Walter Benn Michaels, *The Gold Standard and the Logic of Naturalism* (Berkeley: University of California Press, 1987); Donald Pizer, "The Problem of American Literary Naturalism and Theodore Dreiser's *Sister Carrie*," *American Literary Realism* 32 (Fall 1999): 1–11.

5. Carol Farley Kessler, *Charlotte Perkins Gilman: Her Progress Toward Utopia with Selected Writings* (Syracuse: Syracuse University Press, 1995), 8.

6. Amy Kaplan, *The Social Construction of American Realism* (Chicago: University of Chicago Press, 1986), 12.

7. See Dolores Hayden, *Seven American Utopias: The Architecture of Communitarian Socialism, 1790–1975* (Cambridge, Mass.: MIT Press, 1976).

8. Charlotte Perkins Gilman, *The Man-Made World, or Our Androcentric Culture* (New York: Charlton, 1911), 21.

9. Donald Pizer, *The Novels of Theodore Dreiser* (Minneapolis: University of Minnesota Press, 1976), 21.

10. Alan Trachtenberg, "Who Narrates? Dreiser's Presence in *Sister Carrie*," in *New Essays on Sister Carrie,* ed. Donald Pizer (Cambridge: Cambridge University Press, 1991), 115.

11. David Harvey, *Spaces of Hope* (Berkeley: University of California Press, 2000), 157.

12. Pizer, *Novels of Theodore Dreiser,* 36, 53.

13. The term "apartment hotel" describes an apartment building that provided meals and other hotel amenities (telephones, laundry and janitorial services, etc.) to its tenants. The suites in apartment hotels did not have kitchens. Eventually, the categories, always overlapping, merged. Here, I refer to both apartments and apartment hotels as apartments. For a further discussion of the categories of apartments, apartment hotels, and hotels, see Paul Groth, *Living Downtown: The History of Residential Hotels in the United States* (Berkeley: University of California Press, 1994).

14. "Apartment Houses Practically Considered," *Putnam's Monthly Magazine* 6 (September 1870): 307.

15. This first apartment was the Stuyvesant Apartments designed by prominent nineteenth-century architect Richard Morris Hunt. See Elizabeth Collins Cromley, *Alone Together: A History of New York's Early Apartments* (Ithaca: Cornell University Press, 1990); and Elizabeth Hawes, *New York, New York* (New York: Alfred A. Knopf, 1993), for histories of early apartments in New York City.

16. Sharon Marcus, *Apartment Stories: City and Home in Nineteenth-Century Paris and London* (Berkeley: University of California Press, 1999), 2.

17. Charles H. Israels, "New York Apartment Houses," *Architectural Record* 11 (1901): 477.

18. This isn't really true. Luc Sante and Paul Groth point out that tenement dwellers were charged exorbitant rates for even the most undesirable lodgings. See Sante, *Low Life: Lures and Snares of Old New York* (New York: Farrar, Straus and Giroux, 1991); and Groth, *Living Downtown.*

19. Everett N. Blanke, "The Cliff-Dwellers of New York," *The Cosmopolitan* 15 (July 1893): 355.

20. Steven Ruttenbaum, *Mansions in the Clouds: The Skyscraper Palazzi of Emery Roth* (New York: Balsam Press, 1986), 42.

21. Albert Bigleow Paine, "The Flat-Dwellers of a Great City," *World's Work* 5 (April 1903): 3288–89.

22. William Dean Howells, *A Hazard of New Fortunes* (1890; reprint, New York: Bantam Books, 1960), 40.

23. Israels, "New York Apartment Houses," 499–500.

24. Delores Hayden, *The Grand Domestic Revolution* (Cambridge, Mass.: MIT Press, 1981), 11.

25. For a gender-inflected discussion of apartments, see Cromley, *Alone Together.*

26. "Over the Draughting Board: Apartment Hotels in New York City," *Architectural Record* 13 (1903): 89.

27. Charlotte Perkins Gilman, "The Best for the Poorest," *Forerunner* 7 (1916): 260.

28. Charlotte Perkins Gilman, *The Home* (1903; reprint, Urbana: University of Illinois Press, 1972), 4.

29. Charlotte Perkins Gilman, *Women and Economics* (1898; reprint, Berkeley: University of California Press, 1998), 204.

30. Ibid., 65.

31. Ibid., 65–6.

32. Ibid., 267.

33. Charlotte Perkins Gilman, "Growth and Combat," *Forerunner* 7 (1916): 332.

34. Gilman, *Women and Economics,* 265.

35. Polly Wynn Allen, *Building Domestic Liberty* (Amherst: University of Massachusetts Press, 1988), 20.

36. Harvey, *Spaces of Hope,* 161.

37. Bellamy's novel had both intellectual and political appeal; it influenced thinkers such as Gilman, John Dewey, and Thorstein Veblen as well as the platform of the Populist Party. Erich Fromm, foreword to Edward Bellamy, *Looking Backward* (1888; reprint, New York: Signet Classic, 1960), v–vi.

38. Felix Koch, "Future City One Great Apartment House," *Technical World* 28 (February 1914): 849.

39. Gilman, "Growth and Combat," 332.

40. Kessler, *Charlotte Perkins Gilman,* 6.

41. Carol Farley Kessler, "Consider Her Ways: The Cultural Work of Charlotte Perkins Gilman's Pragmatopian Stories: 1908–1913," in *Charlotte Perkins Gilman: A Study of the Short Fiction,* ed. Denise D. Knight (New York: Twayne Publishers, 1997), 212.

42. Charlotte Perkins Gilman, "Making a Change," in *Herland and Selected Stories by Charlotte Perkins Gilman,* ed. Barbara H. Solomon (1911; reprint, New York: Signet Classics, 1992), 275.

43. Charlotte Perkins Gilman, "A Woman's Utopia," in *Daring to Dream: Utopian Fiction by United States Women before 1950,* 2nd ed., ed. Carol Farley Kessler (1907; reprint, Syracuse: Syracuse University Press, 1995), 153.

44. Ibid., 157.

45. See chapters 1 and 3 for discussions of Beecher's aesthetic at work in rural and urban homes.

46. Charlotte Perkins Gilman, "Her Memories" (1912), in Kessler, *Charlotte Perkins Gilman,* 174–75.

47. Ibid., 179–180.

48. Charlotte Perkins Gilman, *Moving the Mountain* (New York: Charlton Co., 1911), 130.

49. Ibid., 97.

50. Just as they do today, women's magazines at the turn into the twentieth century aimed at different niche audiences. In 1912, *Ladies' Home Journal,* which targeted the middle-class housewife, had the largest circulation of the women's magazines (1,538,360); *Good Housekeeping* aimed at a more progressive, scientifically minded woman and had a circulation of about 300,000. *The House Beautiful* aimed at a far more up-scale, aesthetically minded audience, and enjoyed a circulation of 25,000. N. W. Ayer, and Son, *American Newspaper Annual.* (Philadelphia: N. W. Ayer and Son, 1912).

51. Louise Brigham, "How I Furnished My Entire Flat from Boxes," *Ladies' Home Journal* 27 (1 December 1910); 68; Betty Allen, "A Baby in a Three-Room Flat," *Ladies' Home Journal* 31 (10 March 1914); 43; Ethel Davis Seal, "Furnishing the Small Apartment," *Ladies' Home Journal* 36 (November 1919); 175.

52. Edward Stratton Holloway, "Apartments and How to Live in Them," *The House Beautiful* 42 (November 1917): 341.

53. de Wolfe, *House in Good Taste,* 242–43

54. Mary Ellen Zuckerman, *A History of Popular Women's Magazines in the United States: 1792–1995* (Westport, Conn.: Greenwood Press, 1998), xv.

55. Florence Finch Kelly, "Hunting an Apartment," *The House Beautiful* 34 (November 1913): xxii supp.

56. Elizabeth McCracken, "The Child in the Apartment," *The House Beautiful* 40 (July 1916): 101.

57. Elizabeth McCracken, "The Apartment House Garden," *The House Beautiful* 42 (July 1917): 96–97; McCracken, "Redeeming the Back Piazza of the Apartment," *The House Beautiful* 42 (August 1917): 168.

58. Jesse Lynch Williams, "Back to the Town," *Scribners* 58 (November 1915): 536; Margaret Withington, "An Unusual Duplex Apartnment," *The House Beautiful* 44 (November 1918): 301.

59. "How an Apartment Burglar Works," *Ladies' Home Journal* 24 (January 1907): 16.

60. Brigham, "How I Furnished," 74.

61. Theodore Dreiser, *Sister Carrie* (1900; reprint, New York: Penguin Books, 1994). Unless otherwise noted, I quote here from the 1900 edition of *Sister Carrie,* which was largely suppressed when it first appeared. Initially republished in 1981 by the University of Pennsylvania Press, it is now available in the paperback edition I cite here. Subsequent refrences to this edition will be indicated with *SC.*

62. See chapter 1 for an extended discussion of gender and boarding house life in the nineteenth century.

63. Clara Savage, "How the Bachelor Girl Lives in New York," *The House Beautiful* 40 (November 1916): 370. Emphasis mine.

64. Mary Alden Hopkins, "Homes without Husbands," *The House Beautiful* 44 (November 1918): 315.

65. Savage, "Bachelor Girl," 315; Ella Louise Taylor, "Rose and Elisebeth in a Flat," *The House Beautiful* 11 (February 1902): 163.

66. "Apartment Houses Practically Considered," 307.

67. Eulalie Andreas, "Apartments for Bachelor Girls," *The House Beautiful* 32 (November 1912): 169.

68. Savage, "Bachelor Girl," 335. The particular woman in question here lives in an unheated New York apartment, but clearly is glad to trade heat for autonomy.

69. See Zuckerman, *History of Popular Woman's Magazines,* 46–49 for a sketch of Dreiser's successful term as editor of *The Delineator.*

70. Kaplan, *Social Construction,* 117.

71. Ibid., 125.

72. See Christopher G. Katope, "*Sister Carrie* and Spencer's *First Principles,*" *American Literature* 41 (March 1969): 64–75.

73. Michel Foucault, "Of Other Spaces," trans. Jay Miskowiec, *Diacritics* 16 (1986): 24.

74. Harvey, *Spaces of Hope,* 184.

75. Adrian Kiernander, *Staging Heterotopia: The Theater of Other Spaces* (Armidale, New South Wales: University of New England Press, 1997): 4–5.

76. Pizer, *Novels of Theodore Dreiser,* 92.

77. Kaplan, *Social Construction,* 12.

78. Ibid., 144.

79. Doreen Massey, *Space, Place and Gender* (Minneapolis: University of Minnesota Press, 1994), 11.

80. Trachtenberg, "Who Narrates?" 93.

81. Elizabeth Wilson, *The Sphinx in the City* (Berkeley: University of California Press, 1991), 6.

82. Robert Butler, "Urban Frontiers, Neighborhoods and Traps: The City in Dreiser's *Sister Carrie,* Farrell's *Studs Lonigan,* and Wright's *Native Son,*" in *Theodore Dreiser and American Culture: New Readings,* ed. Yoshinobu Hakutani (Newark: University of Delaware Press, 2000): 281.

83. Pizer, *Novels of Theodore Dreiser,* 71.

84. Pizer, "Problem of American Literary Naturalism," 8.

85. See Elizabeth Klimasmith, "A Taste For Center Stage: Consumption and Feminism in A Woman of Genius," in *Exploring Lost Borders: Critical Essays on Mary Austin,* ed. Melody Granlich and Elizabeth Klimasmith (Reno: University of Nevada Press, 1999).

86. Karl F. Zender, "Walking Away from the Impossible Thing: Identity and Denial in *Sister Carrie,*" *Studies in the Novel* 30, no. 1 (Spring 1998): 65.

87. Kaplan, *Social Construction,* 144.

88. Donald Pizer notes that Dreiser cut another helpful New York neighbor, a Mrs. Wilson who helps Carrie get an acting job, from the manuscript version of the novel. Pizer, *Novels of Theodore Dreiser,* 48.

89. Janet Wolff, "The Invisible *Flâneuse:* Women and the Literature of Modernity," *Theory, Culture and Society* 2, no. 3 (1985): 40.

90. "Over the Draughting Board," 88.

91. Harvey, *Spaces of Hope*, 251.
92. Kevin McNamara, "The Ames of the Good Society: *Sister Carrie* and Social Engineering," *Criticism* 34, no. 2 (Spring 1992): 220.
93. Richard Lehan, "*Sister Carrie:* The City, the Self, and the Modes of Narrative Discourse," in *New Essays on Sister Carrie,* ed. Donald Pizer, 71.
94. Pizer, *Novels of Theodore Dreiser,* 19.
95. Pizer, "Problem of American Literary Naturalism," 5.
96. Trachtenberg, "Who Narrates," 107.
97. Pizer, *Novels of Theodore Dreiser,* 65.
98. Polly Wynn Allen, *Building Domestic Liberty,* 77.
99. This sense is magnified in Dreiser's later novels, which rarely feature characters who enjoy Carrie and Ames's success.
100. Polly Wynn Allen, *Building Domestic Liberty,* 101–102.
101. Kaplan, *Social Construction,* 149.
102. Harvey, *Spaces of Hope,* 235.

5. From Artifact to Investment (pages 161–90)

1. Edith Wharton, *The Custom of the Country* (1913; reprint, New York: Scribner Paperback Fiction, 1997), 77. All subsequent references to this text are cited parenthetically with *CC.*
2. Amy Kaplan, *The Social Construction of American Realism* (Chicago: University of Chicago Press, 1986), 157.
3. Norman S. Hayner, *Hotel Life* (Chapel Hill: University of North Carolina Press, 1936), 110.
4. For a full treatment of Wharton, divorce, and the economics of marriage and divorce, see Debra Ann MacComb, "New Wives for Old: Divorce and the Leisure-Class Marriage Market in Edith Wharton's *The Custom of the Country,*" *American Literature* 68, no. 4 (1996): 765–97.
5. Ibid., 771.
6. For a full treatment of Wharton's psychological attachments to physical space, see Ticien Marie Sassoubre, "Property and Identity in *The Custom of the Country,*" *Modern Fiction Studies* 49, no. 4 (Winter 2003): 687–713.
7. Edith Wharton, *A Backward Glance* (1934; reprint, New York: Charles Scribner's Sons, 1964), 28.
8. Charlotte Perkins Gilman, *The Home* (1903; reprint, Urbana: University of Illinois Press, 1972), 29.
9. After all, Wharton was adept at acquiring and constructing new settings for herself throughout her life. See R. W. B. Lewis, *Edith Wharton: A Biography* (New York: Harper, 1975).
10. Edmund Wilson, "Justice to Edith Wharton," in *The Wound and the Bow* (New York: Oxford University Press, 1947), 163.
11. "Apartment hotel" was the term used to describe an apartment building that provided meals and other hotel amenities (telephones, laundry services) to its tenants. Rooms in luxury hotels and apartment hotels were arranged en suite.

12. William Hutchins, "New York Hotels," *The Architectural Record* 12 (1902): 621.

13. Paul Groth, *Living Downtown: The History of Residential Hotels in the United States* (Berkeley: University of California Press, 1994), 6.

14. U.S. Bureau of the Census, *Fifteenth Census of the United States: Census of Hotels, 1930* (Washington, D.C.: United States Government Printing Office, 1931), 5, 6.

15. R. W. Sexton, *American Apartment Houses, Hotels and Apartment Hotels of Today* (New York: Architectural Book Publishing Company, 1929), 5.

16. Anthony Trollope, *North America* (1862; reprint, New York: Alfred A. Knopf, 1951), 484.

17. Groth, *Living Downtown*, 39.

18. *Appletons' Dictionary of New York* (New York: D. Appleton and Co., 1890), 111. The practice of listing hotels as tourist sights extended to apartments as well. In 1890, apartment buildings were new enough to merit descriptions in *Appletons'* as "really magnificent," "striking," "imposing," "conspicuous," and "remarkable" (4–5).

19. Groth, *Living Downtown*, 53.

20. Hayner, *Hotel Life*, 145.

21. Henry Collins Brown, *New York of To-Day* (New York: The Old Colony Press, 1917), 271.

22. Ibid., 271.

23. Wharton did, of course, write about European hotels in quite a different way in her poem "Terminus" and her 1912 novel *The Reef*. In these works, the seedy railway station hotel is a trysting site for passionate lovers, including Wharton herself in "Terminus." For more on Wharton's treatment of European hotels, see Susan Koprince, "Edith Wharton's Hotels," *Massachusetts Studies in English* 10, no. 1 (Spring 1985): 12–23.

24. Everett N. Blanke, "The Cliff-Dwellers of New York," *The Cosmopolitan* 15 (July 1893): 356.

25. Later, Chicago School sociologist Robert Park would refer to the Jew as the "city man, the man who ranges widely, lives preferably in a hotel, in short, a cosmopolite." See chapter 6.

26. Elaine Showalter, "Spragg: The Art of the Deal," in *The Cambridge Companion to Edith Wharton*, ed. Millicent Bell (Cambridge: Cambridge University Press, 1995): 87.

27. Cynthia Griffin Wolff, *A Feast of Words: The Triumph of Edith Wharton*, 2nd ed. (Reading, Mass.: Addison-Wesley, 1995), 234.

28. Ibid., 237.

29. Leslie Dorsey and Janice Devine, *Fare Thee Well: A Backward Look at Two Centuries of Historic American Hostelries, Fashionable Spas and Seaside Resorts* (New York: Crown Publishers, 1964), 148. This reference is unattributed in *Fare Thee Well*, but the new Plaza opened in 1902.

30. Ibid., 139.

31. Groth, *Living Downtown*, 34.

32. Fanny Fern, *Ruth Hall* (1854), reprinted in *Ruth Hall and Other Writings*, ed. and with an introduction by Joyce W. Warren (New Brunswick: Rutgers University Press, 1986), 50.

33. Mary Ellis Gibson, "Edith Wharton and the Ethnography of Old New York," *Studies in American Fiction* 13, no. 1 (1985): 63–64.

34. Susan Glenn, "'Give an Imitation of Me': Vaudeville Mimics and the Play of the Self," *American Quarterly* 50 (March 1998): 69.
35. Cynthia Griffin Wolff, *Feast of Words,* 225.
36. Edith Wharton, *The House of Mirth* (1905; reprint New York: W. W. Norton, 1990), 79.
37. Groth, *Living Downtown,* 7.
38. Sassoubre, "Property and Identity," 691.
39. Christopher Gair, "The Crumbling Structure of 'Appearances': Representation and Authenticity in *The House of Mirth* and *The Custom of the Country,*" *Modern Fiction Studies* 43, no. 2 (1997): 354.
40. Sara Quay, "Edith Wharton's Narrative of Inheritance," *American Literary Realism* 29, no. 3 (1997): 28.
41. MacComb, "New Wives for Old," 787.
42. See Quay, "Edith Wharton's Narrative."
43. Sassoubre, "Property and Identity," 697.
44. Cynthia Griffin Wolff, *Feast of Words,* 238.

6. The Paradox of Intimacy (pages 191–221)

1. Robert Ezra Park, "The City as a Social Laboratory" (1929), reprinted in *Human Communities: The City and Human Ecology* (Glencoe, Ill.: The Free Press, 1952), 87.
2. Nella Larsen, *Quicksand* (1928), reprinted in *Quicksand and Passing,* ed. Deborah McDowell (New Brunswick: Rutgers University Press, 1993), 135. All subsequent references to this novel will be cited parenthetically in the text and designated with *Q*.
3. Robert Ezra Park, "The City: Suggestions for the Investigation of Human Behavior in the Urban Environment," in *The City,* ed. Robert E. Park, Ernest W. Burgess, and Roderick D. McKenzie (Chicago: University of Chicago Press, 1925), 15. All subsequent references to this essay will be cited parenthetically in the text and designated with *CS*.
4. Mary Esteve, *The Aesthetics and Politics of the Crowd in American Literature* (Cambridge: Cambridge University Press, 2003), 159.
5. Michel Foucault, "The Eye of Power," in *Power/Knowledge* (London: Harvester Wheatsheaf, 1980), 149.
6. Edward W. Soja, *Postmodern Geographies: The Reassertion of Space in Critical Social Theory* (London: Verso Press, 1989), 10–11.
7. David Levering Lewis, *When Harlem Was in Vogue* (New York: Oxford University Press, 1981), 27.
8. See Ann Douglas, *Terrible Honesty* (New York: Farrar, Straus and Giroux, 1995), for a full treatment of the interconnections between black and white moderns in America in the 1920s. See also David Levering Lewis, *When Harlem Was in Vogue;* and Matthew Pratt Guterl, *The Color of Race in America, 1900–1940* (Cambridge: Harvard University Press, 2001).
9. James Weldon Johnson, *Black Manhattan* (1930; reprint, New York: Da Capo, 1991), 153.

10. David Levering Lewis, *When Harlem Was in Vogue,* 27.

11. Esteve, *Aesthetics and Politics,* 152–3.

12. Douglas, *Terrible Honesty,* 303.

13. Robert Park, "An Autobiographical Note," in *Race and Culture* (New York: The Free Press, 1950), viii. Interestingly, Park was working as a reporter at almost the same time that Riis, Crane, and Dreiser were.

14. See Dana Brand, *The Spectator and the City in Nineteenth-Century American Literature* (Cambridge: Cambridge University Press, 1991), for a discussion of the nineteenth-century American flâneur and his European roots.

15. See Frederick Lewis Allen, *Only Yesterday: An Informal History of the Nineteen-Twenties* (New York: Blue Ribbon Books, 1931).

16. Park had begun teaching part-time at Chicago in 1913, according to Mary Jo Deegan in *Jane Addams and the Men of the Chicago School* (New Brunswick: Transaction Books, 1988), 23.

17. Ibid., 44.

18. Ibid., 45.

19. Eugene Rochberg-Halton, "Life, Literature and Sociology in Turn-of-the-Century Chicago," in *Consuming Visions,* ed. Simon J. Bronner (New York: W. W. Norton and Company, 1989), 329.

20. See Deegan, *Jane Addams,* especially 152–60.

21. Richard Sennett, "Introduction," *Classic Essays on the Culture of Cities* (Englewood Cliffs, N.J.: Prentice Hall, 1969), 13.

22. Mary Esteve, "Nella Larsen's 'Moving Mosaic': Harlem, Crowds, and Anonymity," *ALH* 9, no. 2 (Summer 1997): 270.

23. Park, "The City as a Social Laboratory," 73.

24. Ibid., 86.

25. See W. I. Thomas, *The Unadjusted Girl: With Cases and Standpoints for Behavior Analysis* (1923; reprint, Boston: Little Brown and Company, 1925).

26. Robert Ezra Park, "Human Migration and the Marginal Man" (1928), reprinted in *Classic Essays on the Culture of Cities,* ed. Richard Sennet (Englewood Cliffs, N.J.: Prentice Hall, 1969), 131. All subsequent references to this essay will be cited parenthetically in the text and designated with *HM.*

27. Robert Ezra Park, "The Mind of the Rover" (1923), reprinted as "The Mind of the Hobo: Reflections upon the Relation between Mentality and Locomotion," in *Human Communities: The City and Human Ecology* (Glencoe, Ill.: The Free Press, 1952), 91.

28. In interesting ways, the cosmopolitan figure of Simon Rosedale in *The House of Mirth* (or his later, marriageable counterpart, Elmer Moffatt in *The Custom of the Country*) animates Park's positive definition of marginality. Both exert considerable power and gain immense profit from their position on the margins. And as Wharton shows, in both cases they force New York society to shift enough to assimilate them.

29. Sennett, "Introduction," 16.

30. Douglas, *Terrible Honesty,* 90.

31. Because "Larsen's novel does not fit any of the critical stereotypes of 'tragic mulatto' tales," George Hutchinson identifies Helga as "biracial" rather than "mulatto." Hutchinson, "Subject to Disappearance: Interracial Identity in Nella Larsen's *Quicksand,"* in *Temples for Tomorrow: Looking Back at the Harlem Renaissance,*

Geneviève Fabre and Michel Feith, eds. (Bloomington: Indiana University Press, 2001), 178. I use the term mulatta to connect Helga to the marginal man: The term "biracial" came into circulation in 1922, but Larsen does not use the term in *Quicksand*. Oxford English Dictionary, 2nd ed., vol. 3 (Oxford: Clarendon Press, 1989), 212.

32. This internationalism is present in many Harlem Renaissance novels including *Home to Harlem, Plum Bun,* and *Autobiography of an Ex-Colored Man.*

33. Robert Ezra Park, "Local Communities in the Metropolis" (1929), reprinted in *Human Communities,* 89.

34. Esteve, "Nella Larsen's 'Moving Mosaic,'" 276. Karen M. Chandler links Helga's "anxious" mobility to the formal concerns of melodrama. See "Nella Larsen's Fatal Polarities: Melodrama and Its Limits in *Quicksand,*" *CLA Journal* 42, no. 1 (September 1998): 24–47.

35. Esteve, "Nella Larsen's 'Moving Mosaic,'" 279.

36. Park, "The Mind of the Rover," 91.

37. Park, "Local Communities in the Metropolis," 89.

38. Meredith Goldsmith, "Shopping to Pass, Passing to Shop: Consumer Self-Fashioning in the Fiction of Nella Larsen," in *Middlebrow Moderns: Popular American Women Writers of the 1920s,* ed. Lisa Botshon and Meredith Goldsmith (Boston: Northeastern University Press, 2003), 264.

39. Jessie Fauset, *Plum Bun* (1928; reprint, Boston: Beacon Press, 1990).

40. The fear of racial identification through one's children is at work in earlier fiction such as Charles Chesnutt's *The House Behind the Cedars* (1900) and Kate Chopin's "Desirée's Baby" (1892), as well as in contemporary novels including Philip Roth's *The Human Stain* (2000).

41. Esteve, "Nella Larsen's 'Moving Mosaic,'" 272, 275.

42. Sir W. Beach Thomas, "Our Mortal Foe," *Atlantic Monthly* 137 (1926): 783–89; Frank Howard Richardson, "Abnormal Fears," *Hygeia* (May 1927): 243–44;

43. W. Beach Thomas, "Our Mortal Foe," 787.

44. Frederick S. Hoppin, "The Pleasures of Fear," *Forum* 79 (1928): 834.

45. Robert Bone, *The Negro Novel in America* (New Haven: Yale University Press, 1959), 103; Deborah E. McDowell, "Introduction," to *Quicksand and Passing* (New Brunswick: Rutgers University Press, 1986), xxi; Barbara Christian, *Black Women Novelists: The Development of a Tradition, 1892–1976* (Westport, Conn.: Greenwood Press, 1980), 51.

46. Anne E. Hostetler, "The Aesthetics of Race and Gender in Nella Larsen's *Quicksand,*" *PMLA* 105 (1990): 40.

47. W. E. B. DuBois, *The Souls of Black Folk,* 3. Like many of the other authors in this study, DuBois turned to novels as his career progressed. His novel *Dark Princess* (New York: Harcourt, Brace and Company, 1928) features some interesting Whitmanesque tableaus of urban workers.

48. See Deborah McDowell's "Introduction" to *Quicksand and Passing,* note 23.

49. Park, "The City as a Social Laboratory," 80, 74.

50. Goldsmith, "Shopping to Pass," 271.

51. Frances Ellen Walker Harper, *Iola Leroy* (1892; reprint, New York: AMS Press, 1971).

52. Brand, *The Spectator and the City,* 193.

53. Park, "The Mind of the Rover," 91.

54. Ibid.

55. Claudia Tate, "Desire and Death in *Quicksand,* by Nella Larsen," *American Literary History* 7, no. 2 (Summer 1995): 252.

56. Hostetler, "Aesthetics of Race," 44.

57. Hutchinson, "Subject to Disappearance," 178.

58. Christian, *Black Women Novelists,* 53.

59. McDowell, "Introduction" xxii. Ann DuCille, Claudia Tate, and Hazel Carby also read the ending as implying that Helga will die as a result of her next pregnancy.

60. Esteve, "Nella Larson's 'Moving Mosaic,'" 282.

61. Park, "The City as a Social Laboratory," 75.

62. Deegan, *Jane Addams,* 153.

63. Park, "The City as a Social Laboratory," 87.

Epilogue (pages 223–33)

1. Harvey, *Spaces of Hope,* 159.

2. Michel de Certeau, *The Practice of Everyday Life,* trans. Steven Rendall (Berkeley: University of California Press, 1984), 95.

3. Ibid., 108.

4. Sam Bass Warner, *Streetcar Suburbs: The Process of Growth in Boston* (Cambridge: Harvard University Press, 1978).

5. Kate Wheeler to Scott Walker, September 16, 2004, in the author's possession. Typographical errors in letters have been corrected silently.

6. Frederick Law Olmsted, "Public Parks and the Enlargement of Towns," in *Civilizing American Cities: A Selection of Frederick Law Olmstead's Writings on City Landscapes,* ed. S. B. Sutton (Cambridge, Mass.: MIT Press, 1971), 80.

7. Wheeler to Walker.

8. Elaine Leary to Zoning Board of Appeals, undated, in the author's possession.

9. Wheeler to Walker.

10. *Oxford English Dictionary,* 2nd ed., vol. 3 (Oxford: Clarendon Press, 1989), 565.

11. Ibid., 567.

12. Leary to ZBA.

13. Ibid.

14. Nathaniel Hawthorne, *American Notebooks,* quoted in *The Blithedale Romance* (1851; reprint, New York and London: W. W. Norton, 1978), 249 fn 7.

15. Wheeler to Walker.

16. Leary to ZBA.

17. Ibid.

18. Susan K. Harris, *19th-Century American Women's Novels: Interpretive Strategies* (Cambridge: Cambridge University Press, 1990), 116.

19. Ibid., 112. Harris cites Nina Baym's *Woman's Fiction,* Mary Kelley's *Private Woman, Public Stage,* Joyce Warren's introduction to the Rutgers University Press edition of *Ruth Hall,* and Ann Douglas Wood's "The 'Scribbling Women' and Fanny Fern: Why Women Wrote."

Bibliography

Alcott, Louisa May. *Little Women.* 1869. Reprint, New York: Modern Library, 1983.

Alex, William. *Calvert Vaux, Architect and Planner.* New York: Ink, Inc., 1994.

Allen, Betty. "A Baby in a Three-Room Flat." *Ladies' Home Journal* 31 (10 March 1914): 43.

Allen, Frederick Lewis. *Only Yesterday: An Informal History of the Nineteen-Twenties.* New York: Blue Ribbon Books, 1931.

Allen, Polly Wynn. *Building Domestic Liberty.* Amherst: University of Massachusetts Press, 1988.

Anderson, Benedict. *Imagined Communities.* London: Verso, 1983.

Andreas, Eulalie. "Apartments for Bachelor Girls." *The House Beautiful* 32 (November 1912): 168–70.

Anhorn, Judy Schaaf. "'Gifted Simplicity of Vision': Pastoral Expectations in *The Blithedale Romance.*" *ESQ* 28 (1982): 135–53.

"Apartment Houses Practically Considered." *Putnam's Monthly Magazine* 6 (September 1870): 306–13.

Appletons' Dictionary of New York. New York: D. Appleton and Co., 1890.

"Are Apartments Necessary." *Survey Midmonthly* 44 (19 June 1920): 412.

Ayer, N. W. and Son. *American Newspaper Annual.* Philadelphia: N. W. Ayer and Son, 1912.

"The Baby Carriage Case." *New York Times,* 30 July 1878.

Barth, Gunther. *City People: The Rise of Modern City Culture in Nineteenth-Century America.* Oxford: Oxford University Press, 1980.

Baudelaire, Charles. "The Painter of Modern Life." In *The Painter of Modern Life and Other Essays.* Translated and edited by Jonathan Mayne. London: Phaidon Publishers, 1964.

Baym, Nina. "Again and Again, the Scribbling Women." In *Hawthorne and Women,* edited by John L. Idol, Jr., and Melinda M. Ponder. Amherst: University of Massachusetts Press, 1999.

———. "*The Blithedale Romance:* A Radical Reading." *Journal of English and Germanic Philology* 67 (1968): 545–69.

———. *Woman's Fiction: A Guide to Novels by and about Women in America, 1820–1870.* Ithaca: Cornell University Press, 1978.

Beecher, Catharine. *A Treatise on Domestic Economy.* 1841. Reprint, New York: Schocken Books, 1977.

Beecher, Catharine E., and Harriet Beecher Stowe. *The American Woman's Home.* 1869. Reprint, New York: Arno Press, 1971.

Bell, Ian F. A. "Language, Setting and Self in *The Bostonians.*" *MLQ* 49 (1988): 211–38.

———. "The Personal, the Private, and the Public in *The Bostonians.*" *Texas Studies in Literature and Language* 32, no. 2 (Summer 1990): 240–56.

Beveridge, Charles E., and Carolyn F. Hoffman, eds. *Papers of Frederick Law Olmsted, Supplementary Series.* Vol. 1. Baltimore: Johns Hopkins University Press, 1997.

Blanke, Everett N. "The Cliff-Dwellers of New York." *The Cosmopolitan* 15 (July 1893): 354–62.

Bone, Robert. *The Negro Novel in America.* New Haven: Yale University Press, 1959.

Bowen, Janet Wolf. "Architectural Envy: 'A Figure Is Nothing without a Setting.'" *New England Quarterly* 65, no. 1 (1992): 3–23.

Brace, Charles Loring. *The Dangerous Classes of New York.* New York: Wynkoop and Hallenbeck, 1880.

Brand, Dana. *The Spectator and the City in Nineteenth-Century American Literature.* Cambridge: Cambridge University Press, 1991.

Brigham, Louise. "How I Furnished My Entire Flat from Boxes." *Ladies' Home Journal* 27 (1 December 1910): 68–69.

Brodhead, Richard. "Veiled Ladies: Toward a History of Antebellum Entertainment," *ALH* 1, no. 2 (Summer 1989): 273–94.

Brown, Gillian. *Domestic Individualism: Imagining Self in Nineteenth-Century America.* Berkeley: University of California Press, 1990.

Brown, Henry Collins. *New York of To-Day.* New York: The Old Colony Press, 1917.

Burke, Edmund. *A Philosophical Enquiry into the Origin of Our Ideas of the Sublime and Beautiful.* Notre Dame: University of Notre Dame Press, 1968.

Butler, Robert. "Urban Frontiers, Neighborhoods and Traps: The City in Dreiser's *Sister Carrie,* Farell's *Studs Lonigan,* and Wright's *Native Son.*" In *Theodore Dreiser and American Culture: New Readings,* edited by Yoshinobu Hakutani. Newark: University of Delaware Press, 2000.

Cahan, Abraham. *Yekl.* 1896. Reprinted in *Yekl and the Imported Bridegroom.* New York: Dover Publications, 1970.

Carby, Hazel V. *Reconstructing Womanhood: The Emergence of the Afro-American Woman Novelist.* New York: Oxford University Press, 1987.

Chandler, Karen M. "Nella Larsen's Fatal Polarities: Melodrama and Its Limits in *Quicksand.*" *CLA Journal* 42, no. 1 (September 1998): 24–47.

Chandler, Marilyn R. *Dwelling in the Text.* Berkeley: University of California Press, 1991.

Chesnutt, Charles. *The House Behind the Cedars.* 1900. Reprint, Athens: University of Georgia Press, 1988.

———. "The Wife of His Youth." In *The Wife of His Youth and Other Stories of the Color Line.* Ann Arbor: University of Michigan Press, 1972.

Chopin, Kate. "Desirée's Baby." 1892. Reprinted in *Heath Anthology of American Literature.* 2d ed. Vol. 2. Lexington: D. C. Heath and Company, 1994.

Christian, Barbara. *Black Women Novelists: The Development of a Tradition, 1892–1976.* Westport, Conn.: Greenwood Press, 1980.

Clapper, Michael. "The Chromo and the Art Museum: Popular and Elite Art Institutions in Late Nineteenth-Century America." In *Not at Home: The Suppression of Domesticity in Modern Art and Architecture,* edited by Christopher Reed. London: Thames and Hudson, 1996.

Clarke, Graham, ed. *The American City: Literary and Cultural Perspectives.* New York: St. Martin's Press, 1988.

Cosgrove, Denis. "Spectacle and Society: Landscape as Theater in Premodern and Postmodern Cities." In *Understanding Ordinary Landscapes,* edited by Paul Groth and Todd W. Bressi. New Haven: Yale University Press, 1997.

Cott, Nancy. *The Grounding of Modern Feminism.* New Haven: Yale University Press, 1987.

Crane, Stephen. *George's Mother.* 1896. Reprinted in *The Portable Stephen Crane,* edited by Joseph Katz. New York: Penguin Books, 1979.

———. *Maggie, A Girl of the Streets.* 1893. Reprinted in *The Portable Stephen Crane,* edited by Joseph Katz. New York: Penguin Books, 1979.

Cromley, Elizabeth Collins. *Alone Together: A History of New York's Early Apartments.* Ithaca: Cornell University Press, 1990.

Cronon, Willam. *Nature's Metropolis.* New York: W. W. Norton, 1991.

Cummins, Maria Susanna. *The Lamplighter.* 1854. Reprint, New Brunswick: Rutgers University Press, 1988.

Daniel, Annie S. "The Wreck of the Home: How Wearing Apparel is Manufactured in the Tenements." *Charities and the Commons* 14, no. 1 (1 April 1905): 624–29.

Davidson, Cathy N. "Preface: No More Separate Spheres!" *American Literature* 70, no. 3 (1998): 443–63.

Davidson, Cathy N., and Jessamyn Hatcher, eds. *No More Separate Spheres! A Next Wave American Studies Reader.* Durham: Duke University Press, 2002.

de Certeau, Michel. *The Practice of Everyday Life.* Translated by Steven Rendall. Berkeley: University of California Press, 1984.

de Wolfe, Elsie. *The House in Good Taste.* New York: The Century Co., 1914.

Deegan, Mary Jo. *Jane Addams and the Men of the Chicago School.* New Brunswick: Transaction Books, 1988.

Dimock, Wai Chee. "Gender, the Market, and the Non-trivial in James." *The Henry James Review* 15 (1994): 24–30.

Domosh, Mona. *Invented Cities.* New Haven: Yale University Press, 1996.

Dorsey, Leslie, and Janice Devine. *Fare Thee Well: A Backward Look at Two Centuries of Historic American Hostelries, Fashionable Spas and Seaside Resorts.* New York: Crown Publishers, 1964.

Douglas, Ann. *The Feminization of American Culture.* New York: Knopf, 1977.

———. *Terrible Honesty.* New York: Farrar, Straus and Giroux, 1995.

Downing, Andrew Jackson. *The Architecture of Country Houses.* 1850. Reprint, New York: Dover Publications, 1969.

———. *Victorian Cottage Residences.* 1842. Reprint, New York: Dover Publications, 1981.

Dreiser, Theodore. *Sister Carrie.* 1907. Reprint, New York: Bantam Books, 1992.

DuBois, W. E. B. *Dark Princess.* New York: Harcourt, Brace and Company, 1928.

———. *The Souls of Black Folk.* Chicago: A. C. McClurg and Co., 1903.

DuCille, Ann. *The Coupling Convention: Sex, Text, and Tradition in Black Women's Fiction.* New York: Oxford University Press, 1993.

Dunbar, Paul Laurence. *The Sport of the Gods.* 1902. Reprint, Miami: Mnemosyne Publishing, 1969.

E. B. C. "Mr. Clarence Gower: or, a Peep Into a 'Genteel' Boarding House." *Knickerbocker* 4 (1834): 49.

Elbert, Monika M., ed. *Separate Spheres No More: Gender Convergence in American Literature, 1830–1930.* Tuscaloosa: University of Alabama Press, 2000.

Eliot, W. H. *A Description of the Tremont House*. Boston: Gray and Bowen, 1830.

Emerson, Ralph Waldo. "Nature." 1836. Reprinted in *Selected Essays*. New York: Penguin Books, 1985.

Esteve, Mary. *The Aesthetics and Politics of the Crowd in American Literature*. Cambridge: Cambridge University Press, 2003.

———. "Nella Larsen's 'Moving Mosaic': Harlem, Crowds, and Anonymity." *ALH* 9, no. 2 (Summer 1997): 268–86.

Fauset, Jessie. *Plum Bun*. 1928. Reprint, Boston: Beacon Press, 1990.

Fawcett, Edgar. *The Evil That Men Do*. New York: Belford Co., 1889.

Fern, Fanny. *Ruth Hall*. 1854. Reprinted in *Ruth Hall and Other Writings*, edited and with an introduction by Joyce W. Warren. New Brunswick: Rutgers University Press, 1986.

Fine, David M. "Abraham Cahan, Stephen Crane, and the Romantic Tenement Tale of the Nineties." *American Studies* 14 (1973): 95–107.

Fisher, Philip. "Appearing and Disappearing in Public: Social Space in Late-Nineteenth-Century Literature and Culture." In *Reconstructing American Literary History*, edited by Sacvan Berkovitch. Cambridge: Harvard University Press, 1986.

———. *Hard Facts: Setting and Form in the American Novel*. New York: Oxford University Press, 1987.

Fitzgerald, F. Scott. *The Great Gatsby*. 1925. Reprint, New York: Scribner, 1995.

Foley, Barbara. "From Wall Street to Astor Place: Historicizing Melville's 'Bartleby.'" *American Literature* 72, no. 1 (March 2000): 87–116.

Foucault, Michel. "The Eye of Power." In *Power/Knowledge*. London: Harvester Wheatsheaf, 1980.

———. "Of Other Spaces." Translated by Jay Miskowiec. *Diacritics* 16, no. 1 (1986): 22–27.

Fried, Lewis F. *Makers of the City*. Amherst: University of Massachusetts Press, 1990.

Fromm, Erich. "Foreword" to *Looking Backward*, by Edward Bellamy. 1888. Reprint, New York: Signet Classic, 1960.

Gair, Christopher. "The Crumbling Structure of 'Appearances': Representation and Authenticity in *The House of Mirth* and *The Custom of the Country*." *Modern Fiction Studies* 43, no. 2 (1997): 349–73.

Gandal, Keith. *The Virtues of the Vicious: Jacob Riis, Stephen Crane and the Spectacle of the Slum*. New York: Oxford University Press, 1997.

Ganter, Granville. "N. P. Willis." *The Encyclopedia of American Literature*, 1244–45. New York: Continuum Press, 1999.

Gelfant, Blanche Housman. *The American City Novel*. Norman: University of Oklahoma Press, 1954.

Gibson, Mary Ellis. "Edith Wharton and the Ethnography of Old New York." *Studies in American Fiction* 13, no. 1 (1985): 57–69.

Gilman, Charlotte Perkins. "The Best for the Poorest." *Forerunner* 7 (1916): 260–62.

———. "Growth and Combat," *Forerunner* 7 (1916): 328–34.

———. *Herland and Selected Stories by Charlotte Perkins Gilman*, edited by Barbara H. Solomon. New York: Signet Classics, 1992.

———. "Her Memories." 1912. Reprinted in *Charlotte Perkins Gilman: Her Progress Toward Utopia*, edited by Carol Farley Kessler. Syracuse: Syracuse University Press, 1995.

———. *The Home.* 1903. Reprint, Urbana: University of Illinois Press, 1972.

———. "Making a Change." 1911. Reprinted in *Herland and Selected Stories by Charlotte Perkins Gilman,* edited by Barbara H. Solomon. New York: Signet Classics, 1992.

———. *The Man-Made World, or Our Androcentric Culture.* New York: Charlton, 1911.

———. *Moving the Mountain.* New York: Charlton Co., 1911.

———. "A Woman's Utopia." 1907. Reprinted in *Daring to Dream: Utopian Fiction by United States Women before 1950,* edited by Carol Farley Kessler. Syracuse: Syracuse University Press, 1995.

———. *Women and Economics.* 1898. Reprint, Berkeley: University of California Press, 1998.

———. "The Yellow Wallpaper." 1899. Reprint, New York: The Feminist Press, 1973.

Glenn, Susan. *Daughters of the Shtetl.* Ithaca: Cornell University Press, 1990.

———. "'Give an Imitation of Me': Vaudeville Mimics and the Play of the Self." *American Quarterly* 50 (March 1998): 47–76.

Goldsmith, Meredith. "Shopping to Pass, Passing to Shop: Consumer Self-Fashioning in the Fiction of Nella Larsen." In *Middlebrow Moderns: Popular American Women Writers of the 1920s,* edited by Lisa Botshon and Meredith Goldsmith. Boston: Northeastern University Press, 2003.

Grasso, Linda. "Anger in the House: Fanny Fern's *Ruth Hall* and the Redrawing of Emotional Boundaries in Mid-Nineteenth-Century America." *Studies in the American Renaissance* (1995): 251–61.

Groth, Paul. "Forbidden Housing: The Evolution and Exclusion of Hotels, Boarding Houses, Rooming Houses and Lodging Houses in American Cities, 1880–1930." Ph.D. diss., University of California, Berkeley, 1983.

———. *Living Downtown: The History of Residential Hotels in the United States.* Berkeley: University of California Press, 1994.

Gunn, Thomas Butler. *The Physiology of New York Boarding Houses.* New York: Mason Brothers, 1857.

Guterl, Matthew Pratt. *The Color of Race in America, 1900–1940.* Cambridge: Harvard University Press, 2001.

Haglund, Karl. *Inventing the Charles River.* Cambridge: MIT Press, 2003.

Hales, Peter B. *Silver Cities: The Photography of American Urbanization, 1839–1915.* Philadelphia: Temple University Press, 1984.

Hall, Peter. *Cities of Tomorrow: An Intellectual History of Urban Planning and Design in the Twentieth Century.* London: Blackwell Publishers, 1996.

Halttunen, Karen. *Confidence Men and Painted Women: A Study of Middle-Class Culture in America, 1830–1870.* New Haven: Yale University Press, 1982.

———. "From Parlor to Living Room: Domestic Space, Interior Decoration and the Cult of Personality." In *Consuming Visions,* edited by Simon J. Bronner. New York: W. W. Norton and Company, 1989.

Hareven, Tamara K. "The Home and the Family in Historical Perspective." In *Home: A Place in the World,* edited by Arien Mack. New York: New York University Press, 1993.

———. "Introduction" to *Family and Kin in Urban Communities, 1700–1930,* edited by Tamara Hareven. New York: New Viewpoints, 1977.

Harper, Frances Ellen Walker. *Iola Leroy.* 1892. Reprint, New York: AMS Press, 1971.

Harris, Susan K. *19th-Century American Women's Novels: Interpretive Strategies.* Cambridge: Cambridge University Press, 1990.

Harvey, David. *Justice, Nature, and The Geography of Difference Justice.* Oxford: Blackwell Publishers, 1996.

———. *Spaces of Hope.* Berkeley: University of California Press, 2000.

———. *The Urban Experience.* Baltimore: Johns Hopkins University Press, 1989.

Hawes, Elizabeth. *New York, New York.* New York: Alfred A. Knopf, 1993.

Hawthorne, Nathaniel. *American Notebooks,* volume 9 of *Hawthorne's Works.* Boston: Houghton, Mifflin, 1883.

———. *The Blithedale Romance.* 1851. Reprint, New York: W. W. Norton, 1978.

Hayden, Dolores. *The Grand Domestic Revolution.* Cambridge: MIT Press, 1981.

———. *Redesigning the American Dream.* New York: W. W. Norton, 1984.

———. *Seven American Utopias: The Architecture of Communitarian Socialism, 1790–1975.* Cambridge: MIT Press, 1976.

Hayner, Norman S. *Hotel Life.* Chapel Hill: University of North Carolina Press, 1936.

Henkin, David M. *City Reading: Written Words and Public Spaces in Antebellum New York.* New York: Columbia University Press, 1998.

Holbrook, Agnes Sinclair. "Map Notes and Comments." In *Hull House Maps and Papers,* by Residents of Hull House. New York: Thomas Y. Crowell and Co., 1895.

Holloway, Edward Stratton. "Apartments and How to Live in Them." *The House Beautiful* 42 (November 1917): 337–41.

Hopkins, Mary Alden. "Homes without Husbands." *The House Beautiful* 44 (November 1918): 315–16.

Hoppin, Frederick S. "The Pleasures of Fear." *Forum* 79 (1928): 832–36.

Horwitz, Howard. *By the Law of Nature: Form and Value in Nineteenth-Century America.* New York: Oxford University Press, 1991.

Hostetler, Anne E. "The Aesthetics of Race and Gender in Nella Larsen's *Quicksand.*" *PMLA* 105 (1990): 35–46.

"How an Apartment Burglar Works." *Ladies' Home Journal* 24 (January 1907): 16.

Howard, June. *Form and History in American Literary Naturalism.* Chapel Hill: University of North Carolina Press, 1985.

Howells, William Dean. *A Hazard of New Fortunes.* 1890. Reprint, New York: Bantam Books, 1960.

Huf, Linda. *A Portrait of the Artist as a Young Woman: The Writer as Heroine in American Literature.* New York: Frederick Ungar Publishing Co., 1983.

Hunter, John Michael. *Land into Landscape.* London: George Goodwin, 1985.

Hutchins, William. "New York Hotels." *The Architectural Record* 12 (1902): 459–71; 620–35.

Hutchinson, George. "Subject to Disappearance: Interracial Identity in Nella Larsen's *Quicksand.*" In *Temples for Tomorrow: Looking Back at the Harlem Renaissance,* edited by Geneviève Fabre and Michel Feith. Bloomington: Indiana University Press, 2001.

Israels, Charles H. "New York Apartment Houses." *Architectural Record* 11 (1901): 476–508.

Ivory, James, dir. *The Bostonians.* VHS. 1984; Los Angeles: Rhino Home Video, 1993.

Jacobs, Jane. *The Death and Life of Great American Cities.* New York: Vintage Books, 1992.

James, Henry. *The American Scene.* 1907. Reprint, New York: Penguin Books, 1994.

———. *The Bostonians.* 1886. Reprint, New York: Penguin Classics, 1986.

Jehlen, Myra. *American Incarnation: The Individual, the Nation, and the Continent.* Cambridge: Harvard University Press, 1986.

Johnson, James Weldon. *Autobiography of an Ex-Colored Man.* Boston: Sherman, French and Company, 1912.

———. *Black Manhattan.* 1930. Reprint, New York: Da Capo, 1991.

Jones, Elizabeth Fitzpatrick. "Hotel Design in the Work of Isaiah Rogers and Henry Whitestone." In *Victorian Resorts and Hotels: Essays from a Victorian Society Autumn Symposium,* edited by Richard Guy Wilson. Philadelphia: The Victorian Society in America, 1982.

Kaplan, Amy. "Manifest Domesticity." *American Literature* 70, no. 3 (October 1998): 581–606.

———. *The Social Construction of American Realism.* Chicago: University of Chicago Press, 1986.

Katope, Christopher G. "*Sister Carrie* and Spencer's First Principles." *American Literature* 41 (March 1969): 64–75.

Kelley, Mary. *Private Woman, Public Stage.* Chapel Hill: University of North Carolina Press, 2002.

Kelley, Wyn. *Melville's City: Literary and Urban Form in Nineteenth-Century New York.* Cambridge: Cambridge University Press, 1996.

Kelly, Florence Finch. "Hunting an Apartment." *The House Beautiful* 34 (November 1913): p. supp. xxii, xxiv, xxx.

Kerber, Linda K. "Separate Spheres, Female Worlds, Woman's Place: The Rhetoric of Women's History." *Journal of American History* (June 1988): 9–39.

Kessler, Carol Farley. *Charlotte Perkins Gilman: Her Progress Toward Utopia with Selected Writings.* Syracuse: Syracuse University Press, 1995.

———. "Consider Her Ways: The Cultural Work of Charlotte Perkins Gilman's Pragmatopian Stories: 1908–1913." In *Charlotte Perkins Gilman: A Study of the Short Fiction,* edited by Denise D. Knight. New York: Twayne Publishers, 1997.

Kiernander, Adrian. *Staging Heterotopia: The Theater of Other Spaces.* Armidale, New South Wales: University of New England Press, 1997.

Kittredge, Mabel. "Home-making in a Model Flat." *Charities and the Commons* 15 (4 November 1905): 176–81.

Klimasmith, Elizabeth M. "Slave, Master, Mistress, Slave: Genre and Interracial Desire in Louisa May Alcott's Fiction." *ATQ* 11, no. 2 (June 1997): 115–35.

———. "A Taste for Center Stage: Consumption and Feminism in *A Woman of Genius.*" In *Exploring Lost Borders: Critical Essays on Mary Austin,* edited by Melody Graulich and Elizabeth M. Klimasmith. Reno: University of Nevada Press, 1999.

Koch, Felix. "Future City One Great Apartment House." *Technical World* 28 (February 1914): 849–51.

Kolodny, Annette. *The Lay of the Land: Metaphor as Experience and History in American Life and Letters.* Chapel Hill: University of North Carolina Press, 1975.

Koprince, Susan. "Edith Wharton's Hotels." *Massachusetts Studies in English* 10, no. 1 (Spring 1985): 12–23.

Kramer, David. "Masculine Rivalry in *The Bostonians:* Henry James and the Rhetoric of Newspaper Making." *Henry James Review* 19 (1998): 139–47.

Larsen, Nella. *Quicksand.* 1928. Reprinted in *Quicksand and Passing,* edited by Deborah McDowell. New Brunswick: Rutgers University Press, 1986.

Lasch, Christopher. *Haven in a Heartless World: The Family Beseiged.* New York: Basic Books, 1977.

Leary, Elaine. Letter to City of Somerville Zoning Board of Appeals, related to case #2004–54. Copy in the author's possession, September 2004.

Lefcovicz, Barbara F. and Allan B. Lefcovicz. "Some Rents in the Veil: New Light on Priscilla and Zenobia." *Nineteenth-Century Fiction* 21 (1966): 263–75.

Lefebvre, Henri. *The Production of Space.* Oxford: Blackwell Publishers, 1991.

———. *Right to the City.* In *Writings on Cities,* translated and edited by Eleonore Kofman and Elizabeth LeBas. Oxford: Blackwell Publishers, 1996.

Lehan, Richard. "*Sister Carrie:* The City, the Self, and the Modes of Narrative Discourse." In *New Essays on Sister Carrie,* edited by Donald Pizer. Cambridge: Cambridge University Press, 1991.

Levander, Caroline Field. *Voices of the Nation: Women and Public Speech in Nineteenth-Century American Literature and Culture.* Cambridge: Cambridge University Press, 1998.

Levy, Leo B. "*The Blithedale Romance:* Hawthorne's Voyage through Chaos." *Studies in Romanticism* 8 (1968): 1–15.

Lewis, David Levering. *When Harlem Was in Vogue.* New York: Oxford University Press, 1981.

Lewis, R. W. B. *Edith Wharton: A Biography.* New York: Harper, 1975.

Lockwood, Charles. *Bricks and Brownstone: The New York Row House, 1783–1929.* New York: McGraw-Hill, 1972.

MacComb, Debra Ann. "New Wives for Old: Divorce and the Leisure-Class Marriage Market in Edith Wharton's *The Custom of the Country.*" *American Literature* 68, no. 4 (1996): 765–97.

Marcus, Sharon. *Apartment Stories: City and Home in Nineteenth-Century Paris and London.* Berkeley: University of California Press, 1999.

Marx, Leo. *The Machine in the Garden.* Oxford: Oxford University Press, 1964.

Massey, Doreen. *Space, Place and Gender.* Minneapolis: University of Minnesota Press, 1994.

McCracken, Elizabeth. "The Apartment House Garden." *The House Beautiful* 42 (July 1917): 96–97.

———. "The Child in the Apartment." *The House Beautiful* 40 (July 1916): 100–101.

———. "Redeeming the Back Piazza of the Apartment." *The House Beautiful* 42 (August 1917): 168.

McDowell, Deborah E. "Introduction" to *Quicksand and Passing.* New Brunswick: Rutgers University Press, 1986.

McKay, Claude. *Home to Harlem.* 1928. Reprint, Boston: Northeastern University Press, 1987.

McNamara, Kevin. "The Ames of the Good Society: *Sister Carrie* and Social Engineering." *Criticism* 34, no. 2 (Spring 1992): 217–35.

Melville, Herman. "Bartleby the Scrivener." *Bartleby and Benito Cereno*. 1853. Reprint, New York: Dover Publications, 1990.

———. *Pierre, or The Ambiguities*. 1852. Reprint, New York: Signet Classic, 1964.

Michaels, Walter Benn. *The Gold Standard and the Logic of Naturalism*. Berkeley: University of California Press, 1987.

———. *Our America*. Durham: Duke University Press, 1995.

Miller, Angela. *The Empire of the Eye: Landscape Representation and American Cultural Politics, 1825–1875*. Ithaca: Cornell University Press, 1993.

Milward, Maria Georgina. "Mrs. Sad's Private Boarding House." *Southern Literary Messenger* 12 (1846): 690–96.

Modell, John, and Tamara K. Hareven. "Urbanization and the Malleable Household: An Examination of Boarding and Lodging in American Families," in *Family and Kin in Urban Communities, 1700–1930*, edited by Tamara K. Hareven. New York: New Viewpoints, 1977.

Nash, Roderick. *Wilderness and the American Mind*. 3rd edition. New Haven: Yale University Press, 1982.

Norton, Charles E. "Model Lodging-Houses in Boston. " *Atlantic Monthly* 5 (1860): 673–80.

Olmsted, Frederick Law. "Public Parks and the Enlargement of Towns." In *Civilizing American Cities: A Selection of Frederick Law Olmsted's Writings on City Landscapes*, edited by S. B. Sutton. Cambridge: MIT Press, 1971.

"Over the Draughting Board: Apartment Hotels in New York City." *Architectural Record* 13 (1903): 85–91.

Oxford English Dictionary. 2d ed. Vol. 3. Oxford: Clarendon Press, 1989.

Oxford English Dictionary. Online edition, Accessed December 1, 2004.

Paine, Albert Bigleow. "The Flat-Dwellers of a Great City." *World's Work* 5 (April 1903): 3281–94.

Park, Robert Ezra. "An Autobiographical Note." In *Race and Culture*. New York: The Free Press, 1950.

———. "The City as a Social Laboratory." 1929. Reprinted in *Human Communities: The City and Human Ecology*. Glencoe, Ill.: The Free Press, 1952.

———. "The City: Suggestions for the Investigation of Human Behavior in the Urban Environment." 1916. Reprinted in *The City*, ed. Robert E. Park, Ernest W. Burgess, and Roderick D. McKenzie. Chicago: University of Chicago Press, 1925.

———. "Human Migration and the Marginal Man." 1928. Reprinted in *Classic Essays on the Culture of Cities*, edited by Richard Sennett. Englewood Cliffs, N.J.: Prentice Hall, 1969.

———. "Local Communities in the Metropolis." 1929. Reprinted in *Human Communities: The City and Human Ecology*. Glencoe, Ill.: The Free Press, 1952.

———. "The Mind of the Rover." 1923. Reprinted as "The Mind of the Hobo: Reflections upon the Relation between Mentality and Locomotion" in *Human Communities: The City and Human Ecology*. Glencoe, Ill.: The Free Press, 1952.

Pattee, Fred. *The Feminine Fifties*. New York: Appleton-Century, 1940.

Peiss, Kathy. *Cheap Amusements*. Philadelphia: Temple University Press, 1986.

Pizer, Donald. *The Novels of Theodore Dreiser*. Minneapolis: University of Minnesota Press, 1976.

———. "The Problem of American Literary Naturalism and Theodore Dreiser's *Sister Carrie*." *American Literary Realism* 32 (Fall 1999): 1–11.

Posnock, Ross. "Henry James, Veblen and Adorno: The Crisis of the Modern Self." *Journal of American Studies* 21 (1987): 32–53.

———. *The Trial of Curiosity*. New York: Oxford University Press, 1991.

"Prayer Meetings in Boarding-Houses." *Christian Herald* 8 (1822): 732.

Quay, Sara. "Edith Wharton's Narrative of Inheritance." *American Literary Realism* 29, no. 3 (1997): 26–48.

Richardson, Frank Howard. "Abnormal Fears." *Hygeia* (May 1927): 243–44.

Riis, Jacob. *The Children of the Poor*. New York: Charles Scribner's Sons, 1902.

———. *How the Other Half Lives*. 1890. Reprint, New York: Dover Publications, 1971.

———. *The Making of an American*. 1901. Reprint, New York: MacMillan, 1924.

———. *The Peril and Preservation of the Home*. Philadelphia: George W. Jacobs and Company, 1903.

Rochberg-Halton, Eugene. "Life, Literature and Sociology in Turn-of-the-Century Chicago." In *Consuming Visions,* edited by Simon J. Bronner. New York: W. W. Norton and Company, 1989.

Romero, Lora. *Home Fronts: Domesticity and Its Critics in the Antebellum United States*. Durham: Duke University Press, 1997.

Rosenzweig, Roy, and Elizabeth Blackmar. *The Park and the People: A History of Central Park*. 1992. Reprint, New York: Henry Holt and Company, 1994.

Rowe, Joyce A. "'Murder, what a lovely voice': Sex, Speech, and the Public/Private Problem in *The Bostonians*." *Texas Studies in Literature and Language* 40, no. 2 (Summer 1998): 158–83.

Ruttenbaum, Steven. *Mansions in the Clouds: The Skyscraper Palazzi of Emery Roth*. New York: Balsam Press, 1986.

"Samuel Simpleton." Letter to the Editor. *Rambler's Magazine* 1 (1809): 85.

Sanchez, Maria C. "Re-Possessing Individualism in Fanny Fern's *Ruth Hall*." *Arizona Quarterly* 56, no. 4 (Winter 2000): 25–56.

Sante, Luc. *Low Life: Lures and Snares of Old New York*. New York: Farrar, Strauss and Giroux, 1991.

Sassoubre, Ticien Marie. "Property and Identity in *The Custom of the Country*." *Modern Fiction Studies* 49, no. 4 (Winter 2003): 687–713.

Savage, Clara. "How the Bachelor Girl Lives in New York." *The House Beautiful* 40 (November 1916): 334–70.

Scott, Anthony. "Basil, Olive, and Verena: *The Bostonians* and the Problem of Politics." *Arizona Quarterly* 49, no. 1 (Spring 1993): 49–72.

Seal, Ethel Davis. "Furnishing the Small Apartment." *Ladies' Home Journal* 36 (November 1919): 175.

Sennett, Richard. *The Fall of Public Man*. New York: W. W. Norton, 1982.

———. *Flesh and Stone*. New York: W. W. Norton, 1994.

———. "Introduction" to *Classic Essays on the Culture of Cities*. Englewood Cliffs, N.J.: Prentice Hall, 1969.

Sexton, R. W. *American Apartment Houses, Hotels and Apartment Hotels of Today*. New York: Architectural Book Publishing Company, 1929.

Sherman, Mary, for the National Consumer's League. "Manufacturing of Foods in the Tenements." *Charities and the Commons* 15 (1906): 669–73.

Shloss, Carol. *In Visible Light: Photography and the American Writer: 1840–1940.* New York: Oxford University Press, 1987.

Showalter, Elaine. "Spragg: The Art of the Deal," in *The Cambridge Companion to Edith Wharton*, edited by Millicent Bell. Cambridge: Cambridge University Press, 1995.

Slotkin, Richard. *Regeneration through Violence: The Mythology of the American Frontier, 1600–1860.* Middletown, Conn.: Wesleyan University Press, 1973.

Sly, Costard. *Sayings and Doings at the Tremont House in the Year 1832.* Vol. 2. Boston: Allen and Ticknor, 1833.

Smith, Henry Nash. *Virgin Land: The American West as Symbol and Myth.* 1950. Reprint, New York: Vintage Books, 1957.

Smith-Rosenberg, Carroll. *Disorderly Conduct.* New York: A. A. Knopf, 1985.

Soja, Edward W. *Postmodern Geographies: The Reassertion of Space in Critical Social Theory.* London: Verso Press, 1989.

Sollors, Werner. *Beyond Ethnicity.* New York: Oxford University Press, 1986.

Stansell, Christine. *City of Women.* New York: Alfred A. Knopf, 1986.

Stowe, Harriet Beecher. *Uncle Tom's Cabin.* 1852. Reprint, New York: Penguin Classics, 1986.

Sweeting, Adam. *Reading Houses and Building Books: Andrew Jackson Downing and the Architecture of Popular Antebellum Literature, 1835–1855.* Hanover, N.H.: University Press of New England, 1996.

Tate, Claudia. "Desire and Death in *Quicksand*, by Nella Larsen." *American Literary History* 7, no. 2 (Summer 1995): 234–60.

———. *Domestic Allegories of Political Desire: The Black Heroine's Text at the Turn of the Century.* Durham: Duke University Press, 1995.

Taylor, Ella Louise. "Rose and Elisebeth in a Flat," *The House Beautiful* 11 (February 1902): 163–64.

Temple, Gale. "A Purchase on Goodness: Fanny Fern, *Ruth Hall*, and Fraught Individualism." *Studies in American Fiction* 31, no. 2 (Autumn 2003): 131–63.

Thomas, Brook. "The Construction of Privacy In and Around *The Bostonians*." *American Literature* 64, no. 4 (December 1992): 719–47.

Thomas, Sir W. Beach. "Our Mortal Foe." *Atlantic Monthly* 137 (1926): 783–89.

Thomas, W. I. *The Unadjusted Girl: With Cases and Standpoints for Behavior Analysis.* 1923. Reprint, Boston: Little Brown and Company, 1925.

Tompkins, Jane. *Sensational Designs: The Cultural Work of American Fiction 1790–1860*. New York: Oxford University Press, 1985.

Townsend, Edward W. *A Daughter of the Tenements.* New York: Lovell, Coryell and Company, 1895.

Trachtenberg, Alan. "Who Narrates? Dreiser's Presence in *Sister Carrie.*" In *New Essays on Sister Carrie*, edited by Donald Pizer. Cambridge: Cambridge University Press, 1991.

Trollope, Anthony. *North America.* 1862. Reprint, New York: Alfred A. Knopf, 1951.

U.S. Bureau of the Census. *Fifteenth Census of the United States: Census of Hotels, 1930.* Washington, D.C.: U.S. Bureau of the Census, 1931.

Van Kleeck, Mary. "Child Labor in New York City Tenements." *Charities and the Commons* 18 (18 January 1908): 1405–20.

Van Orman, Richard A. *A Room for the Night: Hotels of the Old West.* Bloomington: Indiana University Press, 1966.

Vaux, Calvert. "Parisian Buildings for the City's Residents." *Harper's Weekly*, December 19, 1857, 809–10.

———. *Villas and Cottages.* 1857. Reprint, New York: Da Capo Press, 1968.

Vernon, John. *Money and Fiction.* Ithaca: Cornell University Press, 1984.

Waldron, Karen. "No Separations in the City: The Public-Private Novel and Private-Public Authorship." In *Separate Spheres No More: Gender Convergence in American Literature: 1830–1930,* edited by Monika M. Elbert. Tuscaloosa: University of Alabama Press, 2000.

Walsh, Chris. "Stardom Is Born: The Religion and Economy of Publicity in Henry James' *The Bostonians.*" *American Literary Realism* 29, no. 3 (1997): 15–25.

Wardley, Lynn. "Woman's Voice, Democracy's Body, and *The Bostonians.*" *ELH* 56, no. 3 (Fall 1989): 639–65.

Warner, Sam Bass. *Streetcar Suburbs: The Process of Growth in Boston.* Cambridge: Harvard University Press, 1978.

Warner, Susan. *The Wide, Wide World.* 1850. Reprint, New York: The Feminist Press, 1987.

Warren, Joyce W. "Introduction" to *Ruth Hall,* Fanny Fern. New Brunswick: Rutgers University Press, 1986.

———. "Performativity and the Repositioning of American Literature." In *Challenging Boundaries: Gender and Periodization,* edited by Joyce W. Warren and Margaret Dickie. Athens: University of Georgia Press, 2000.

Warren, Samuel, and Louis Brandeis. "The Right to Privacy." *Harvard Law Review* 4 (1908): 196. Quoted in Brook Thomas, "The Construction of Privacy In and Around *The Bostonians.*" *American Literature* 64, no. 4 (December 1992): 719–47.

Watson, Elizabeth C. "Home Work in the Tenements." *Survey* 25 (4 February 1911): 772–81.

Weinstein, Cindy. "How Many Others Are There in the Other Half? Jacob Riis and the Tenement Population." *Nineteenth-Century Contexts* 24, no. 2 (2002): 195–216.

Welter, Barbara. *Dimity Convictions.* Athens: Ohio University Press, 1976.

Wharton, Edith. *The Age of Innocence: A Norton Critical Edition,* edited by Candace Waid. New York: W. W. Norton and Company, 2002.

———. *A Backward Glance.* 1934. Reprint, New York: Charles Scribner's Sons, 1964.

———. *The Custom of the Country.* 1913. Reprint, New York: Scribner Paperback Fiction, 1997.

———. *The House of Mirth.* 1905. Reprint, New York: W. W. Norton, 1990.

———. *The Reef.* 1912. Reprint, New York: Charles Scribner's Sons, 1996.

Wharton, Edith, and Ogden Codman. *The Decoration of Houses.* 1902. Reprint, New York: W. W. Norton and Company, 1978.

Wheeler, Kate. Letter to Scott Walker, Somerville City Planner, related to case #2004–54. Copy in the author's possession, September 16, 2004.

Williams, Jesse Lynch. "Back to the Town." *Scribners* 58 (November 1915): 534–44.

Wilson, Edmund. "Justice to Edith Wharton." In *The Wound and the Bow.* New York: Oxford University Press, 1947.

Wilson, Elizabeth. *The Sphinx in the City.* Berkeley: University of California Press, 1991.

Wirth, Louis. "Urbanism as a Way of Life." 1938. Reprinted in *Classic Essays on the Culture of Cities,* edited by Richard Sennett. Englewood Cliffs, N.J.: Prentice Hall, 1969.

Withington, Margaret. "An Unusual Duplex Apartment." *The House Beautiful* 44 (November 1918): 301–303.

Wolff, Cynthia Griffin. *A Feast of Words: The Triumph of Edith Wharton.* 2nd ed. Reading, Mass.: Addison-Wesley, 1995.

Wolff, Janet. "The Invisible *Flâneuse:* Women and the Literature of Modernity." *Theory, Culture and Society* 2, no. 3 (1985): 37–46.

Wood, Ann Douglas. "The 'Scribbling Women' and Fanny Fern: Why Women Wrote." *American Quarterly* 23 (1971): 3–24.

Wright, Gwendolyn. *Building the Dream: A Social History of Housing in America.* New York: Pantheon, 1981.

Yezierska, Anzia. *Bread Givers.* 1925. Reprint, New York: Persea Press, 1975.

Zender, Karl F. "Walking Away from the Impossible Thing: Identity and Denial in *Sister Carrie.*" *Studies in the Novel* 30, no. 1 (Spring 1998): 63–76.

Zitkala-Sa. *American Indian Stories.* Lincoln: University of Nebraska Press, 1985.

Zuckerman, Mary Ellen. *A History of Popular Women's Magazines in the United States: 1792–1995.* Westport, Conn.: Greenwood Press, 1998.

Index

Page numbers in italics indicate illustrations.

communication: American city transformed by, 52, 61; middle-class home
enmeshed in networks of, 93; modern
urban subject shaped by, 18, 19; Park
on, 198; postal system, 46, 63, 83;
telegraph, 63, 77, 245n.94; tenements
enmeshed in networks of, 93–94; time
periods affected by networks of,
245n.94; urban homes integrated into
networks of, 8. *See also* media; publicity
community: in apartment buildings, 137;
in boarding houses, 30; Gilman on
home and, 135; in tenements, 102,
103; urban home as new type of, 47;
in urban novels, 5, 6; in utopian projects, 20
connections: in apartment buildings, 136,
148–49, 154–55; in boarding houses,
28, 30; in Central Park, 61–66; the
city as place of, 6, 18, 42, 152–53,
156, 157; in Fern's *Ruth Hall*, 30,
46–47; hallways providing, 5, 100;
hotels as places of, 28, 30, 174; Olmsted on rural-urban, 61–63; Progressive Era reformers pathologizing, 92,
94; Riis's *How the Other Half Lives*
condemning physical, 94–100; shared
open space as, 225–26; streets and alleys symbolizing, 94; tenements as sites
of, 91, 92, 115, 125–27; urban homes
as connective and connecting, 8, 10; in
urban texts, 2; Vaux on excessive, 58.
See also communication; media;
networks; transportation
consumerism, 84, 147, 174–75
consumption: conspicuous, 105; in
Crane's *Maggie, A Girl of the Streets*,
121; drawing-room as place for, 70; in
Dreiser's *Sister Carrie*, 147, 150, 158;
glorification of, 86; in Hawthorne's
The Blithedale Romance, 82; home as
commodity, 181, 184–86; middle-class
home becoming enmeshed in, 93; production separated from, 104; urban
homes integrated in network of, 8;
Wharton on logic of, 162; in Wharton's *The Custom of the Country*, 177,
178, 183, 189

contagion, 90–91, 92, 94, 100–101,
104–8, 127
cooking, 154
Cosgrove, Denis, 48
Cosmopolitan, The (periodical), 170
Cott, Nancy, 86
cottages: Central Park incorporating references to, 55–58; Downing's Gothic
cottage, 23, 24, 25–26, 224–25; in
Fern's *Ruth Hall*, 17, 19, 22–26, 216;
in Hawthorne's *The Blithedale Romance*, 17, 19; in Larsen's *Quicksand*,
216; mass-produced suburban, 20; in
Melville's *Pierre*, 17; moving of, 112;
redemptive power attributed to, 18;
urge to escape, 173; Vaux on spatial
arrangements in, 57–58; Vaux's *Villas
and Cottages*, 52, 54, 57, 59
Crane, Stephen: architectural determinism
of, 223; *George's Mother*, 101, 104,
121–22; *Maggie, A Girl of the Streets*,
11, 92, 97, 101–4, 121, 125, 139;
Park compared with, 192
crime: Riis on cities as nurseries of,
91–92; tenements seen as nurseries of,
108, 117
"Crossing Brooklyn Ferry" (Whitman), 3
cultural adaptation, 210–11
Cummins, Maria Susanna, 17, 74,
238n.27
Custom of the Country, The (Wharton),
161–90; ancestral portraits in, 188–89,
190; Central Park in, 64; cities as
places of creative generation in, 217;
consumption in, 177, 178, 183, 189;
cosmopolitan in, 258n.28; on disappearance of "old" families, 182;
display in, 175, 176, 177–78, 189;
on distinguishing imitation from
real, 176–77; as divorce novel, 162;
on divorce of space from history, 12,
162, 169–78, 181, 186, 188–89, 190;
expansive trajectory in, 189–90;
family heirlooms in, 185–86;
Hawthorne's *The Blithedale Romance*
compared with, 82; Larsen's *Quicksand* compared with, 208, 213; last
line of, 189; logic of investment in,
162–63, 171–72, 175, 180;